Dog's Best Friend

A portrait of an unbreakable bond

Giuseppe Santamaria

Dog's Best Friend

A portrait of an unbreakable bond

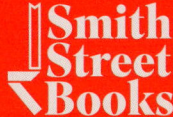

Smith
Street
Books

Dedicated to Josh and his best friends, past and present,
Benny, Buddy, Baxter and Sebastian.

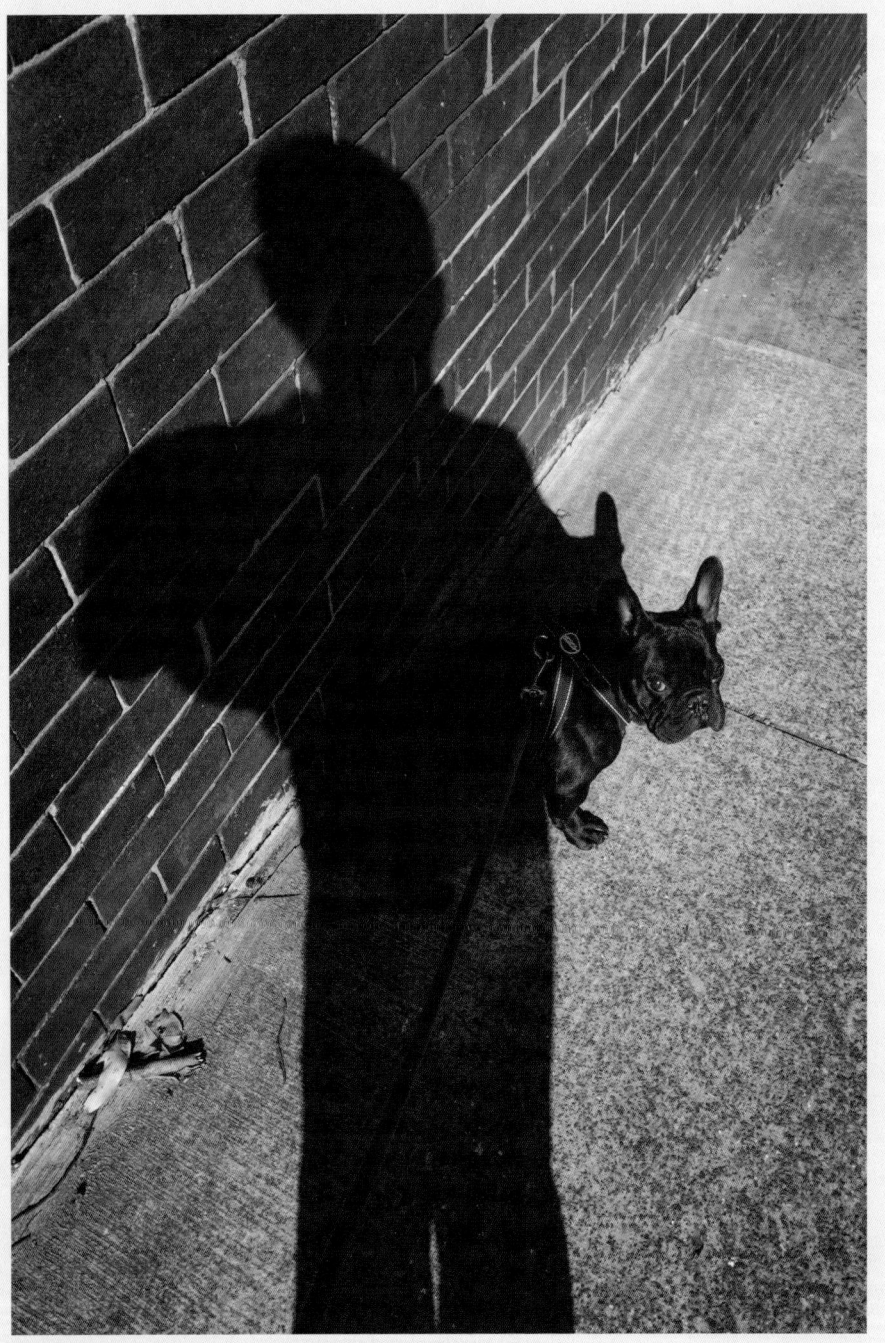

Introduction

When it was suggested that my next book focus on dogs, I was initially hesitant. Not because I don't love dogs; quite the contrary. I have the utmost respect for them – I believe they are the superior beings on this planet. As you've picked up this book, I'm sure you share that sentiment. The pressure to create something that reflected this was immense.

Based on my previous books, the obvious direction would have been to capture dogs in cute outfits and their equally stylish owners – Doggy Style – if you will. And although there's plenty of that in this book, I wanted to delve deeper.

What is it about these extraordinary beings that captures our hearts and forms unbreakable bonds that transform us for the better? I experienced this with my late dog Baxter and my current little French guy, Sebastian. I wanted to explore this incredibly layered relationship through other human-canine friendships.

I embarked on a journey around the world: Tokyo, Kyoto, New York City, London, Milan, Paris, Toronto, Melbourne, and my home town of Sydney. My mission was to document the unique ways in which dogs and their humans coexist in these concrete jungles. I encountered people with their four-legged companions and engaged them in a thought-provoking conversation: "If your dog could talk, what would they say about you?" This seemingly innocuous question sparked warm smiles and heartfelt responses, revealing the unique personalities and connections between dogs and their best friends.

Giuseppe Santamaria

"She can do anything. She's the only female that I can live with in my house. She's a year old now, and before Berta, there was Gina, she stayed with me for ten years."

Antonio and their dog Berta
Milan, Italy

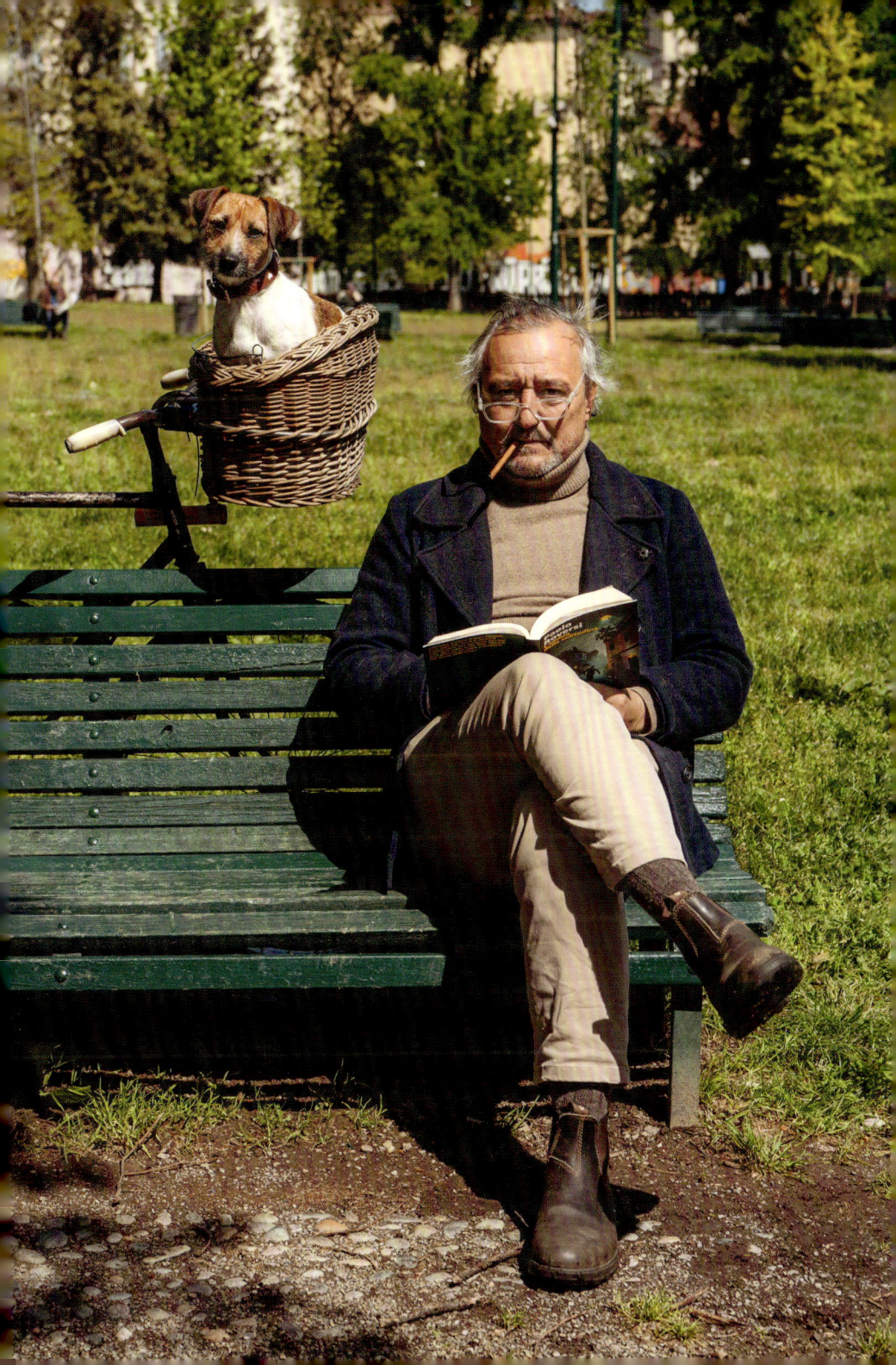

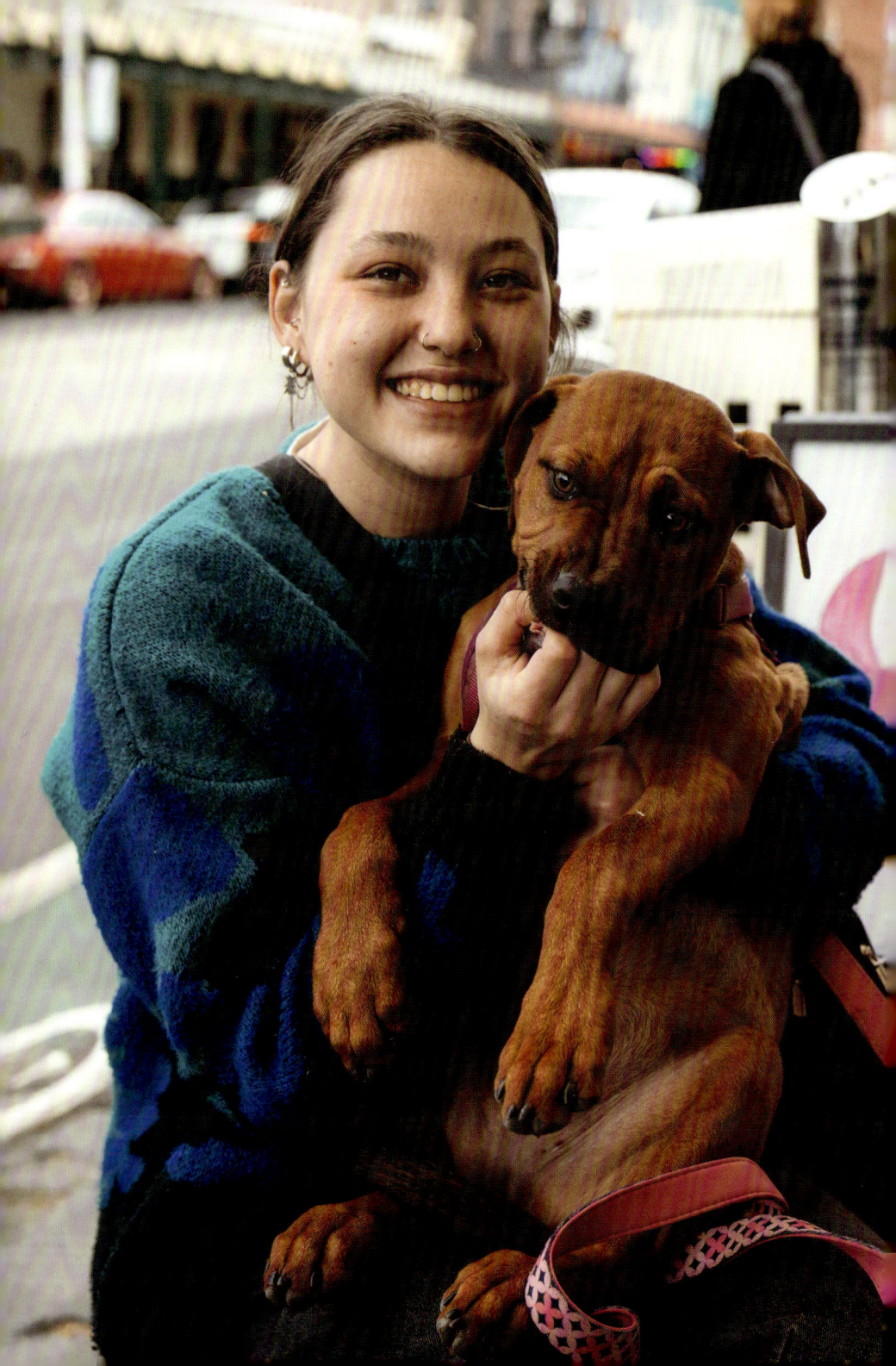

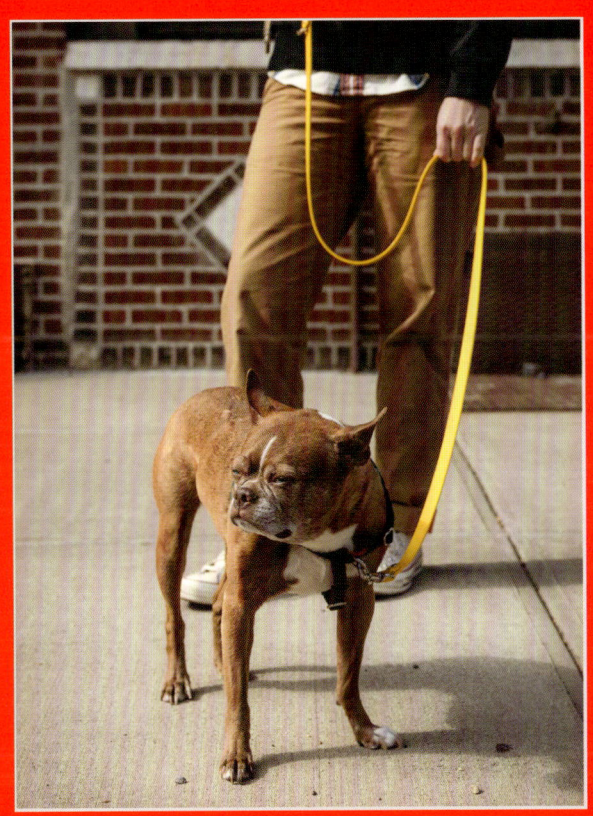

New York City, USA

"She's only about 6 months old, so she's really into chewing my fingers right now."

Cass and their dog Roo
Melbourne, Australia

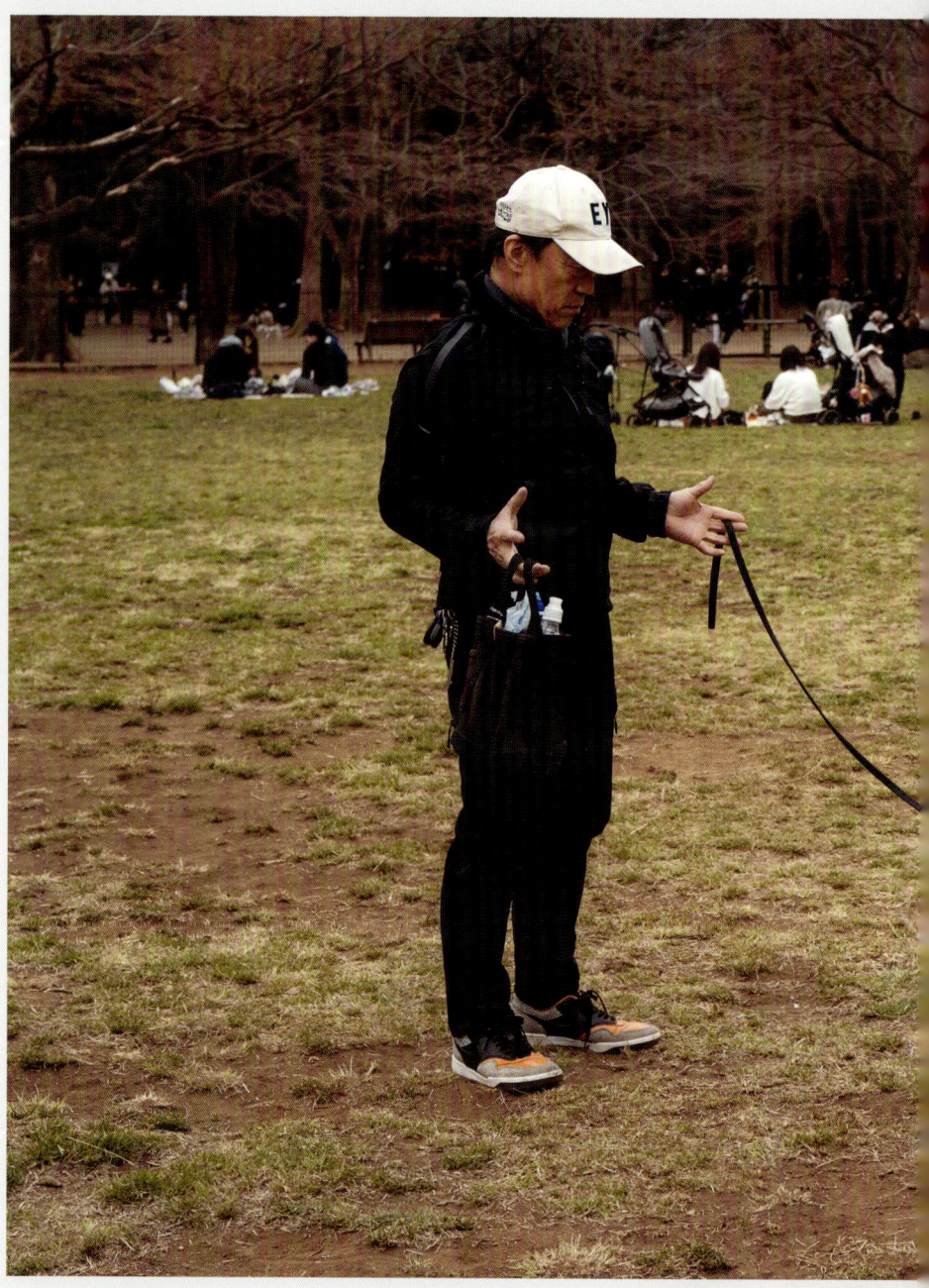

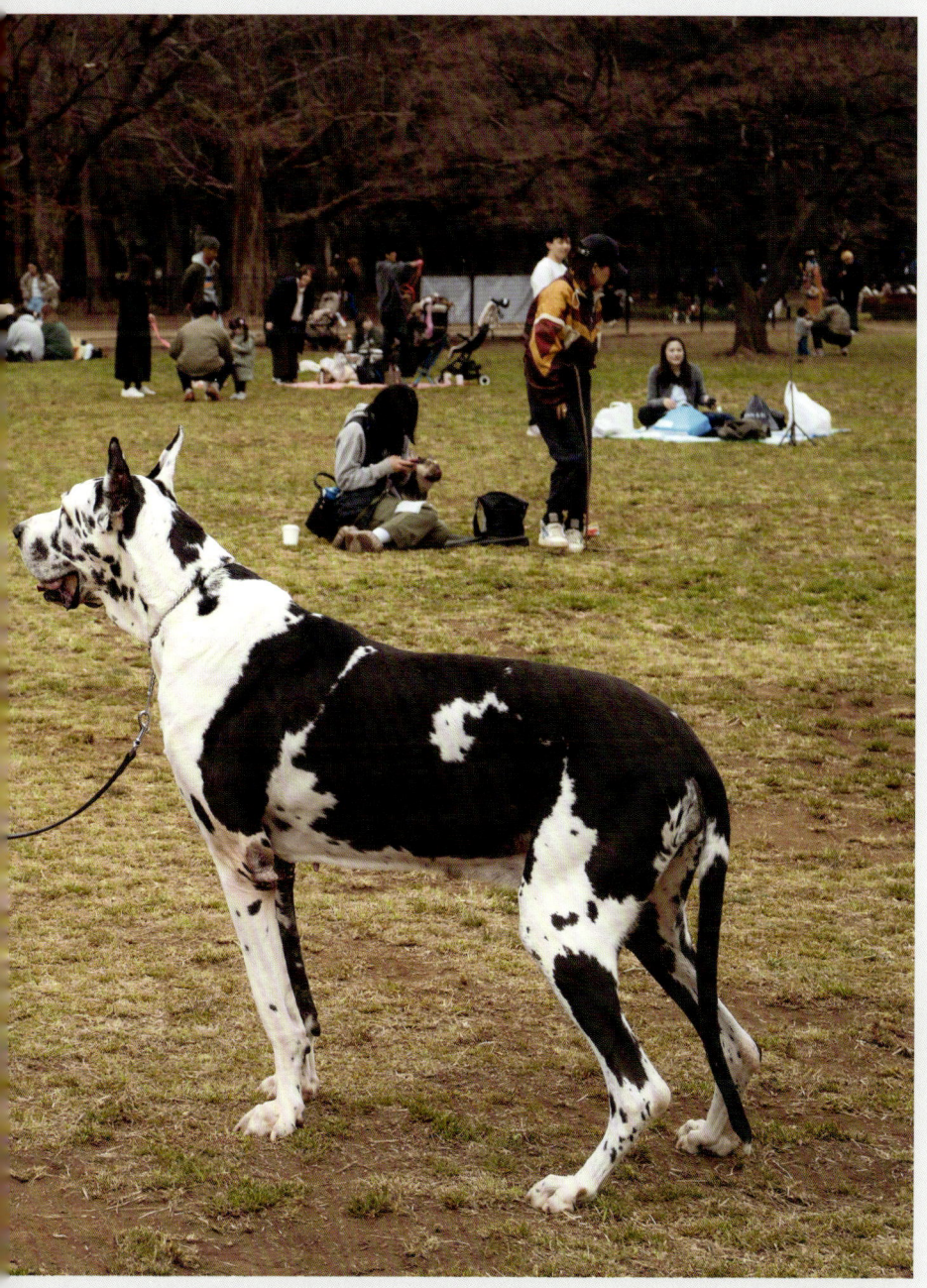

Tokyo, Japan

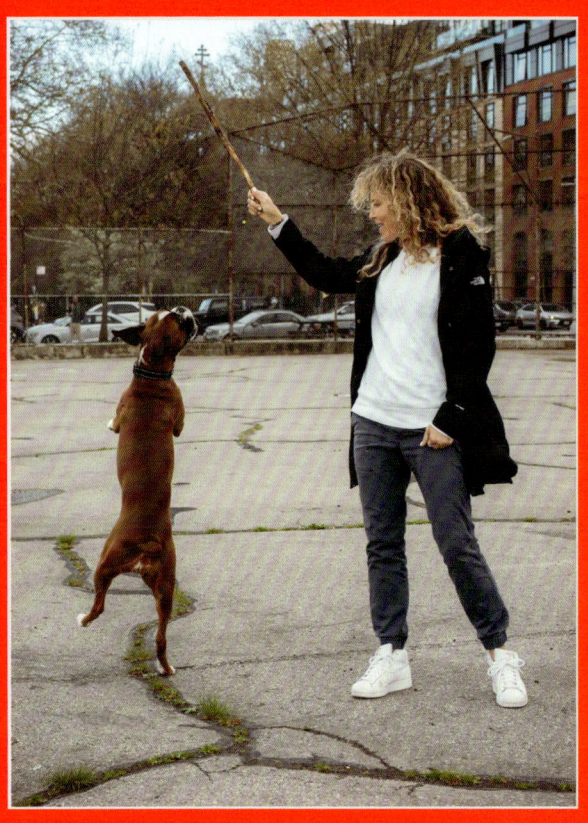

"She's my third boxer.
They're just the sweetest."

Meissa and their dog Cuckoo
New York City, USA

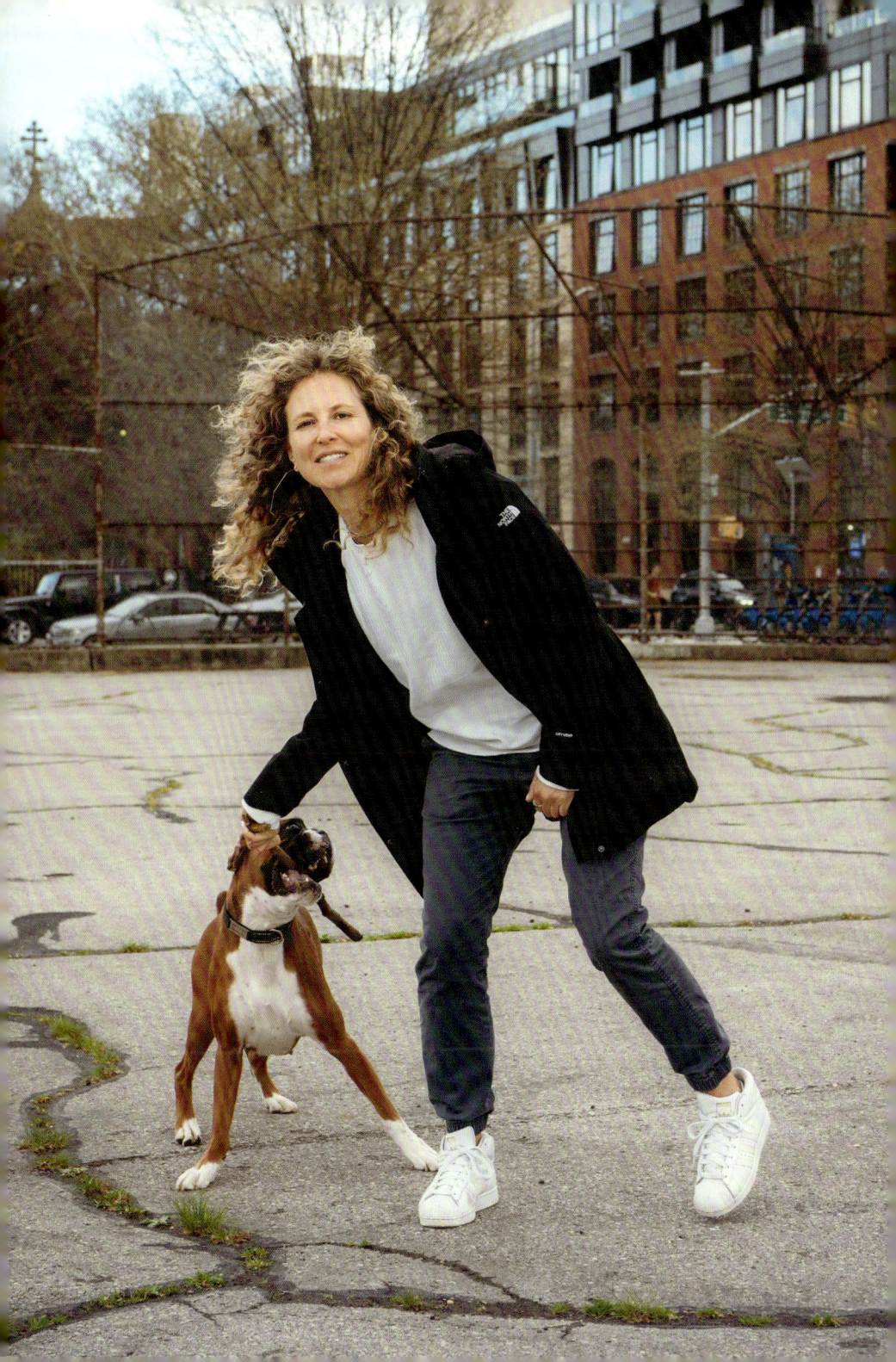

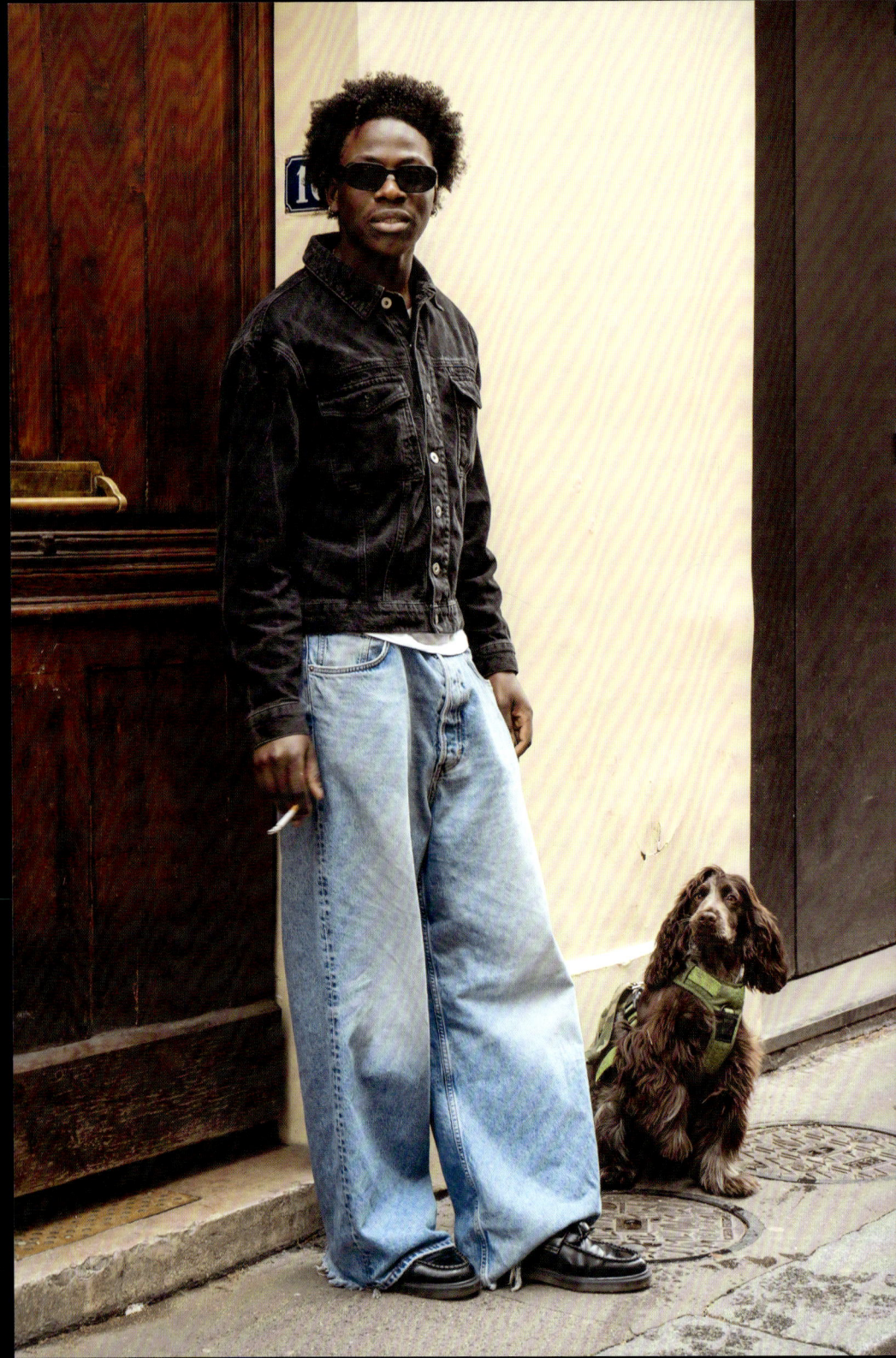

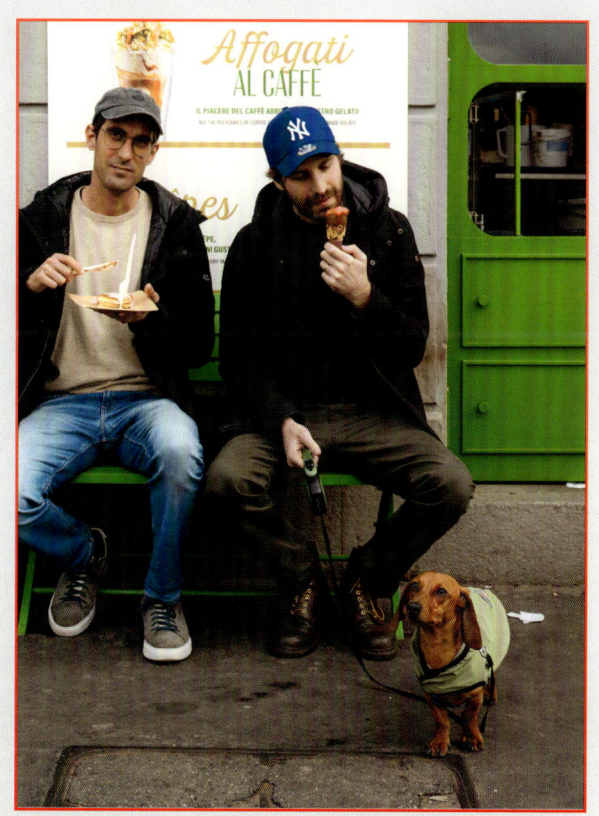

Milan, Italy

"She thinks I'm very very lovely.
I'm the one who sneaks her food
when we are having dinner."

Franklin and their dog Lilou
Paris, France

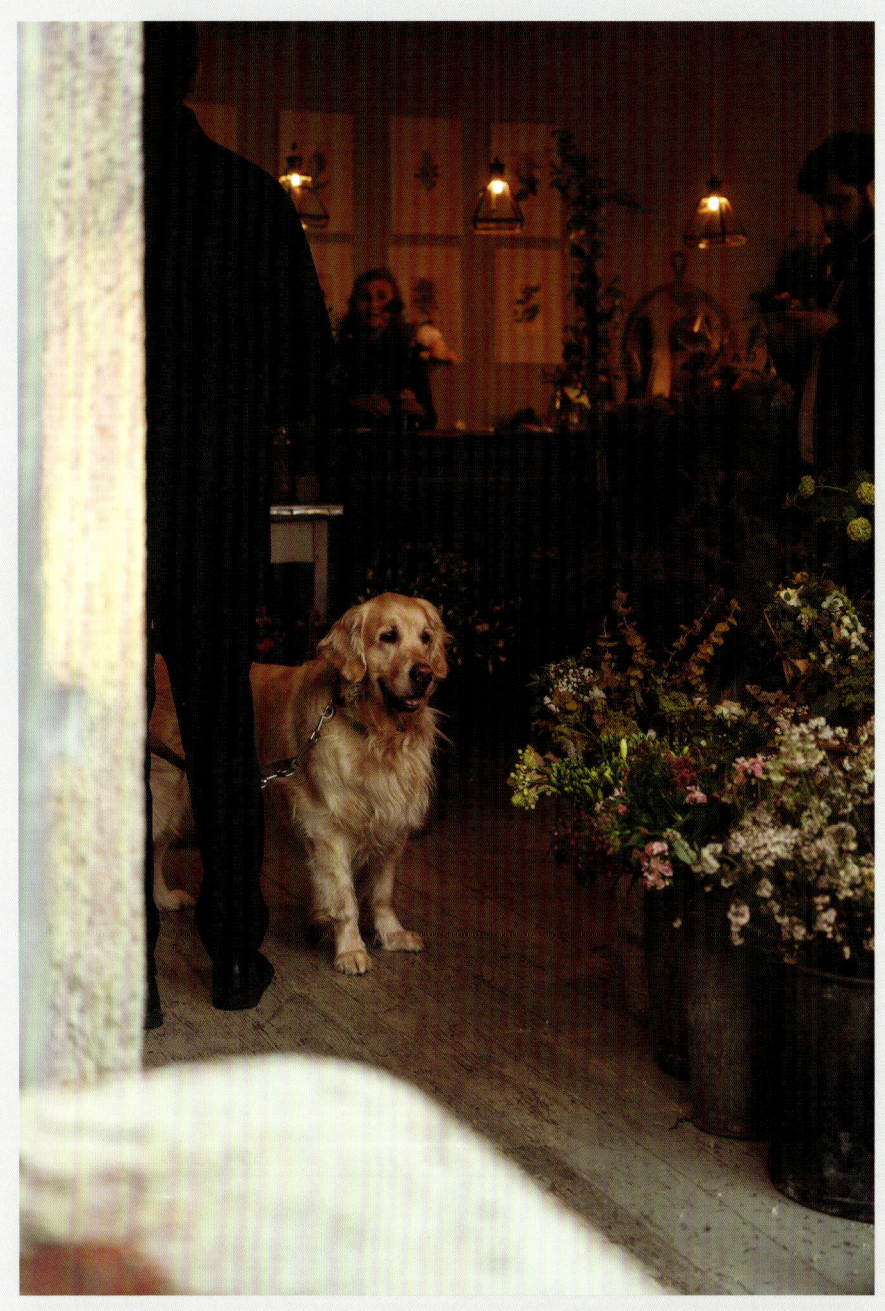

Milan, Italy | Milan, Italy

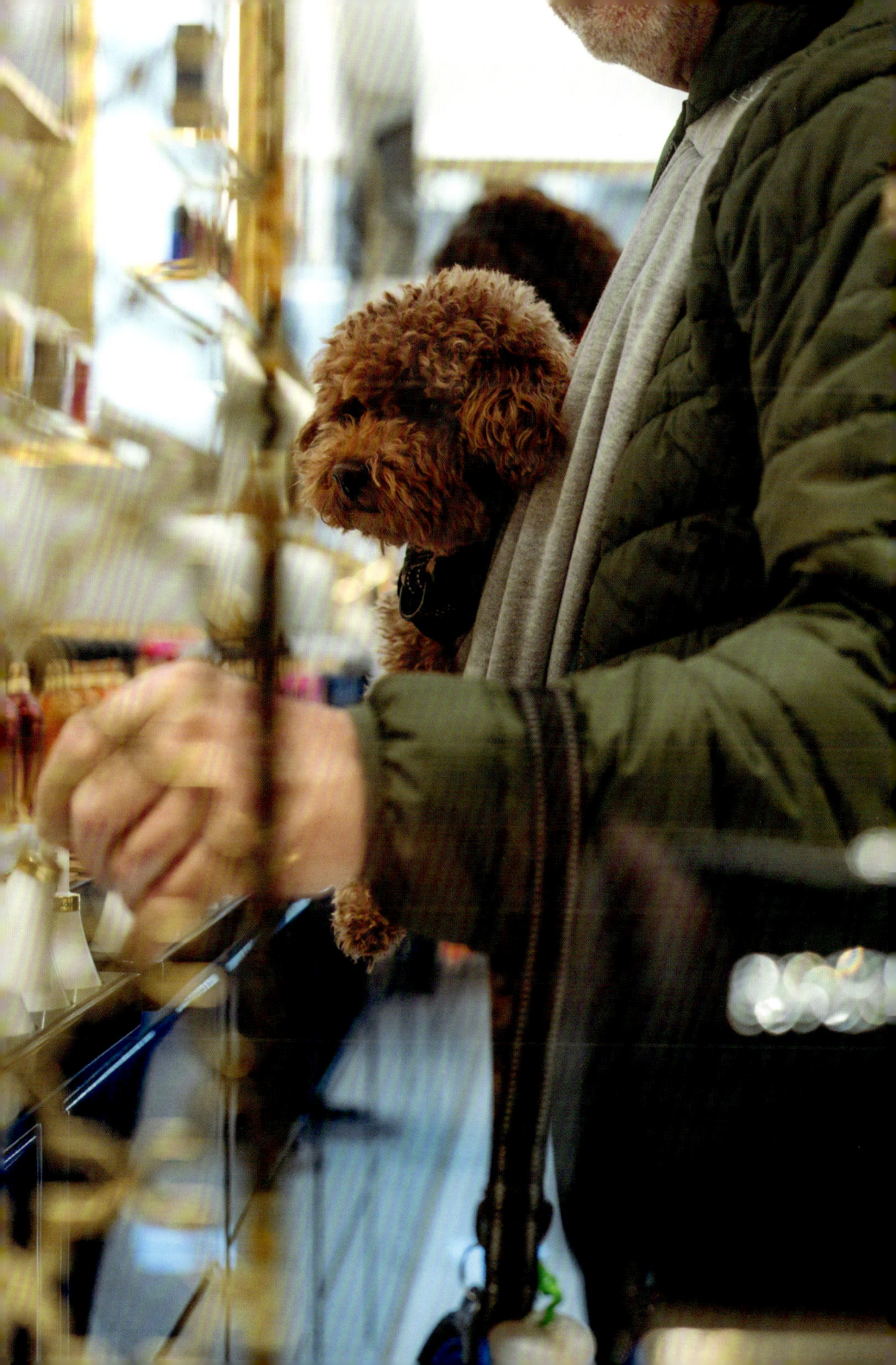

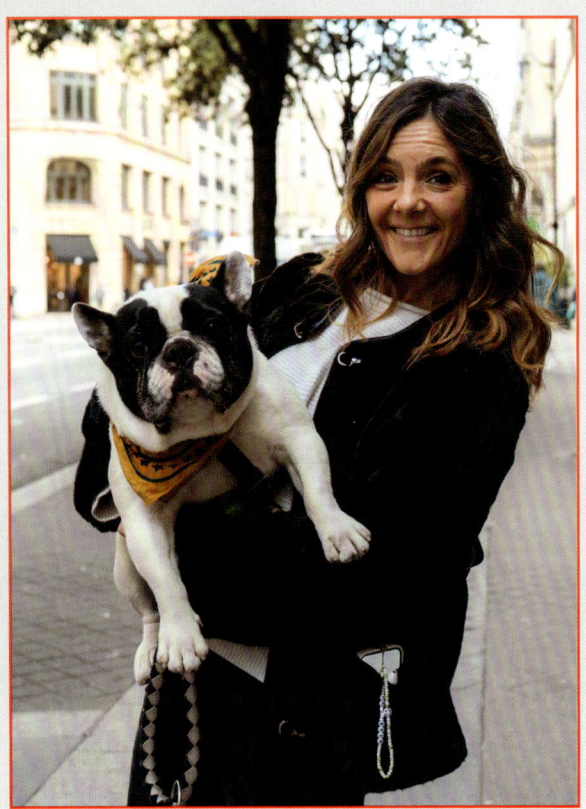

"I feel like I'm in a toxic relationship. He's very demanding but I still love him."

Nanaka (left) and their dog Doughnut with dog friend Bon
Tokyo, Japan

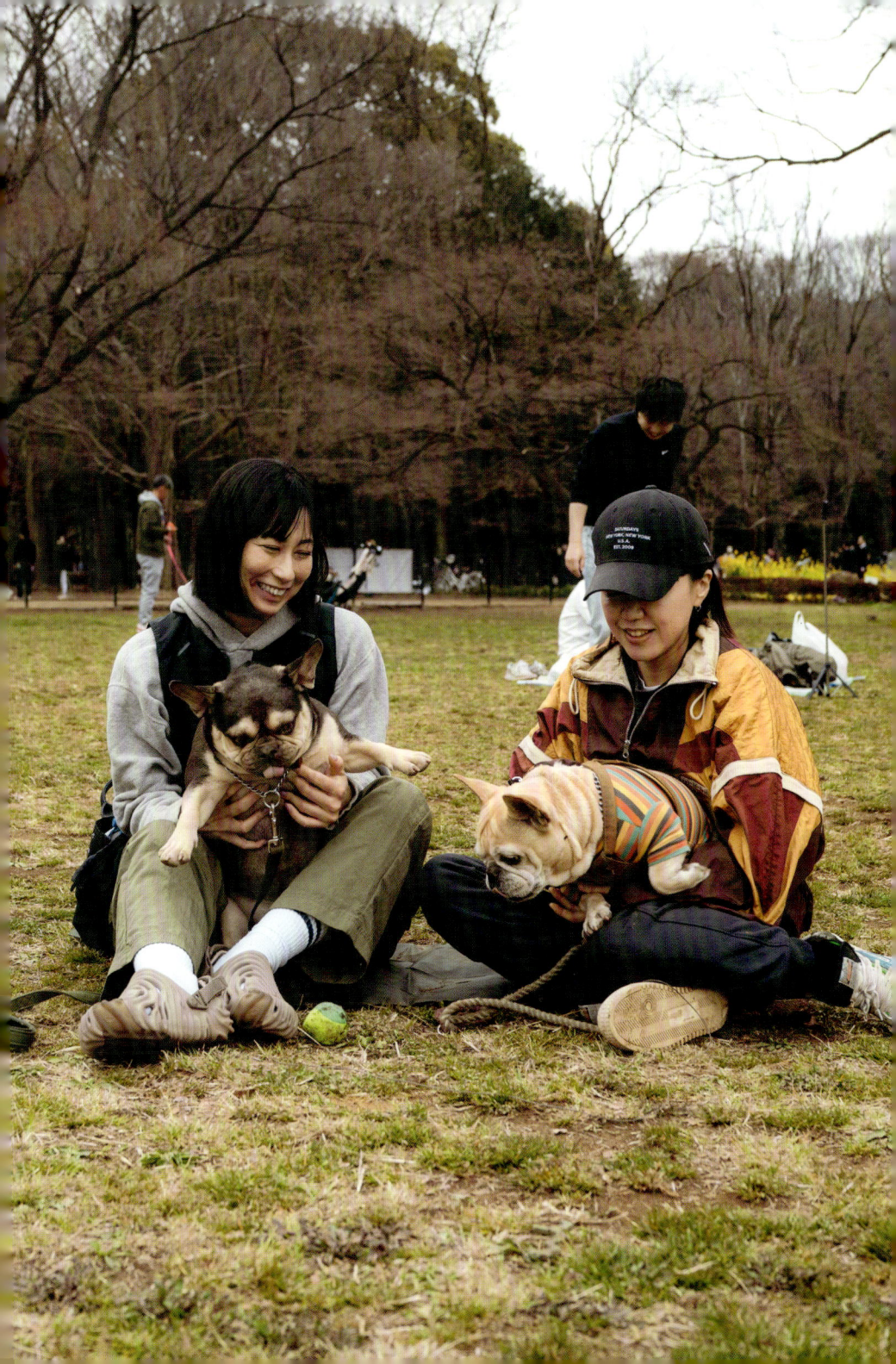

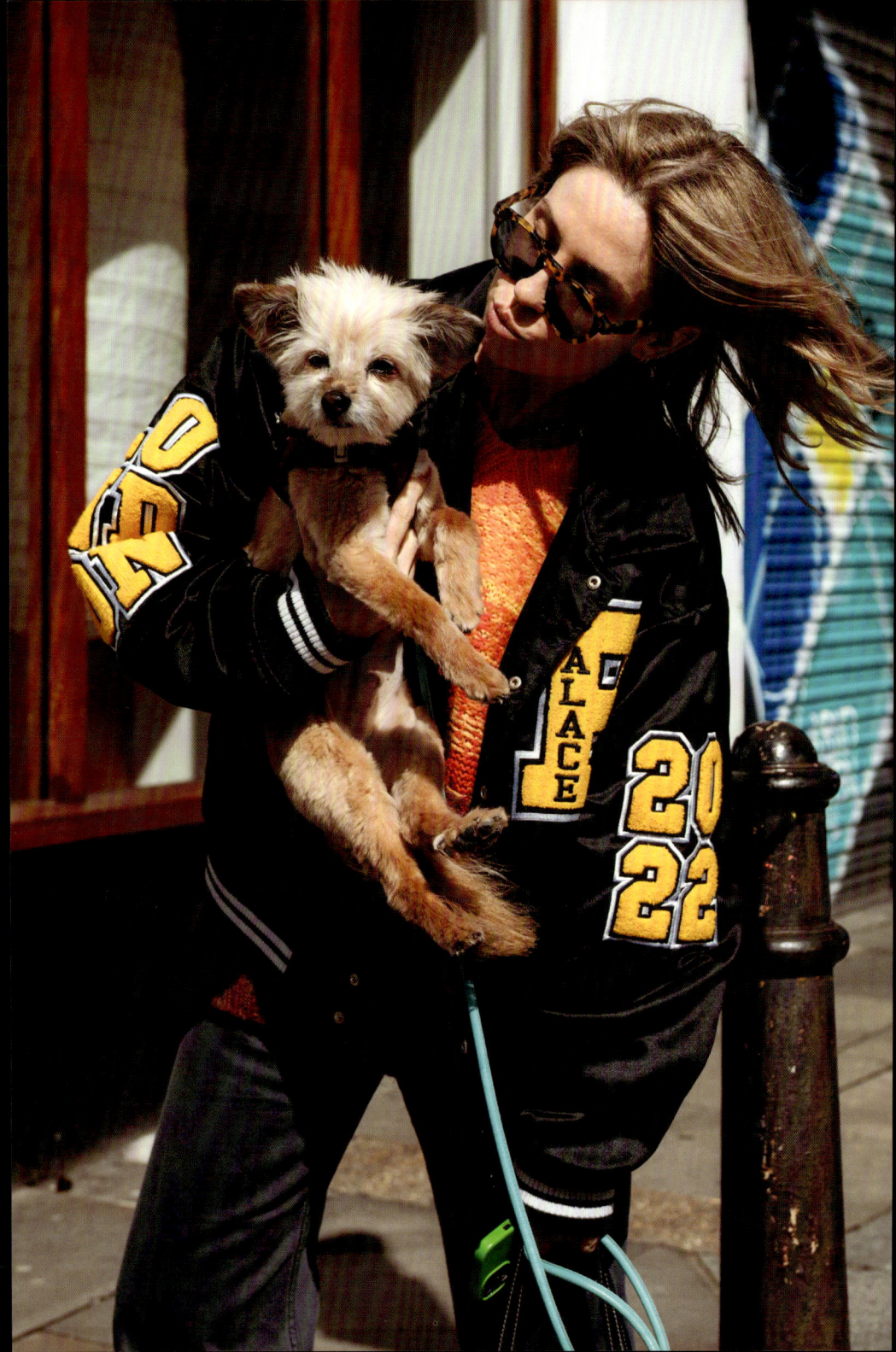

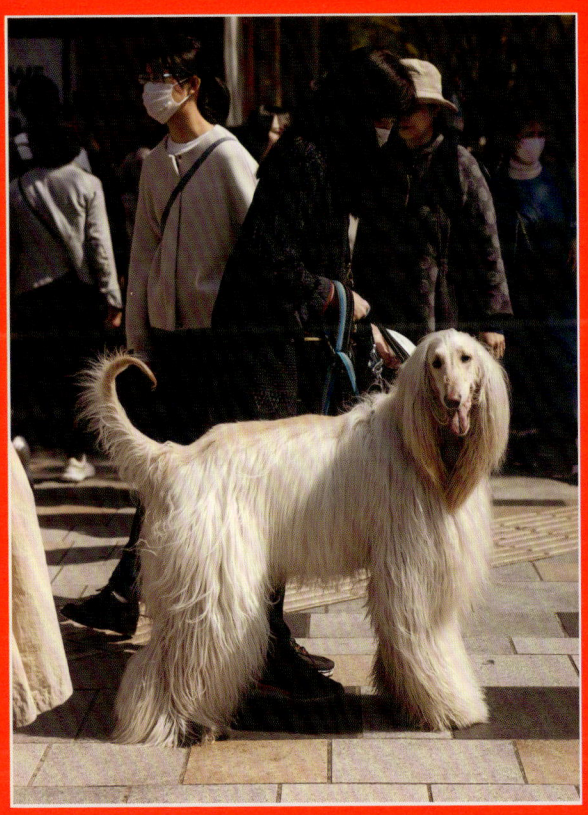

Tokyo, Japan

"I'm sure he thinks I'm a mental bitch."

Emmy and their dog Gino
London, England

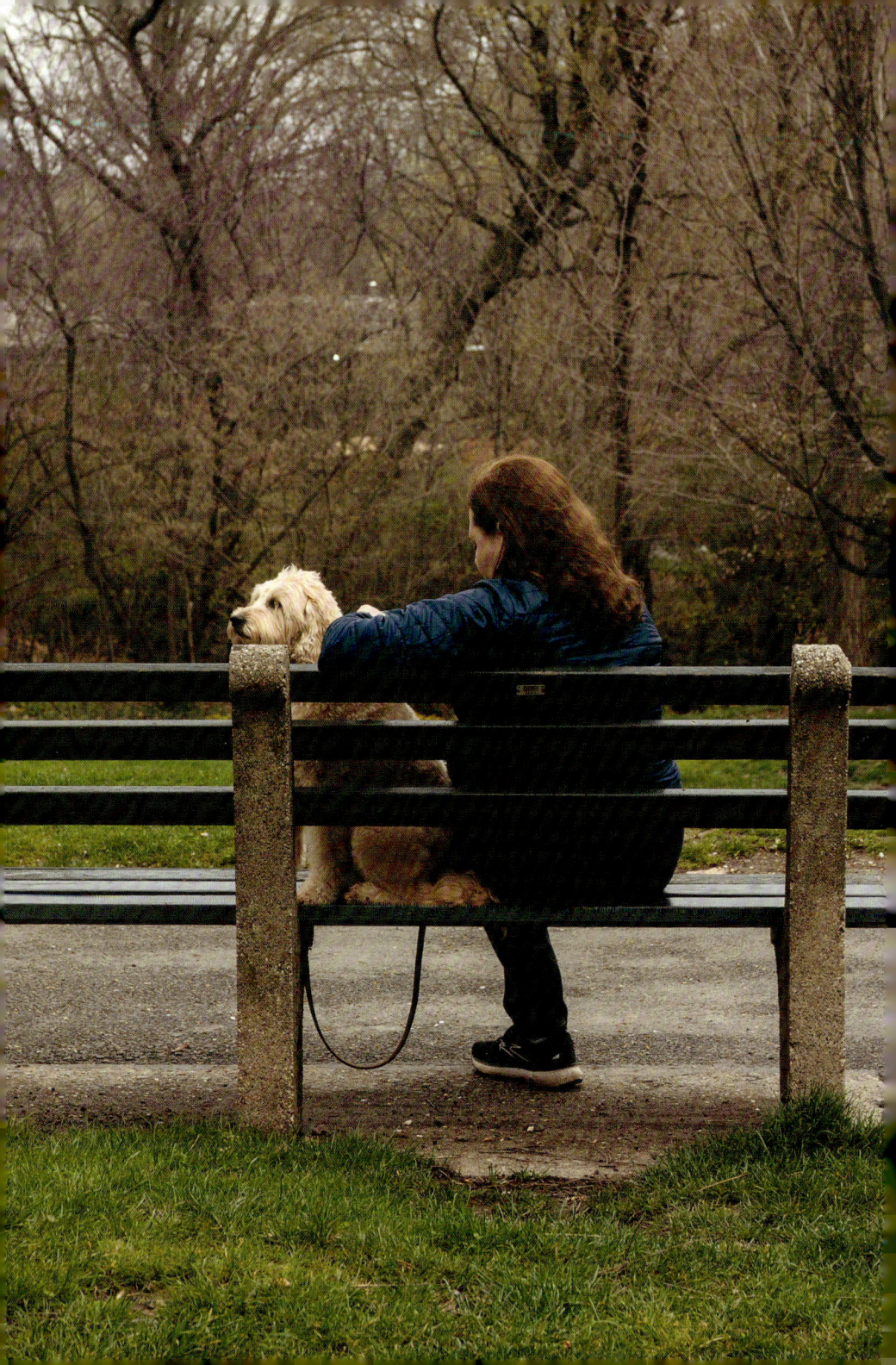

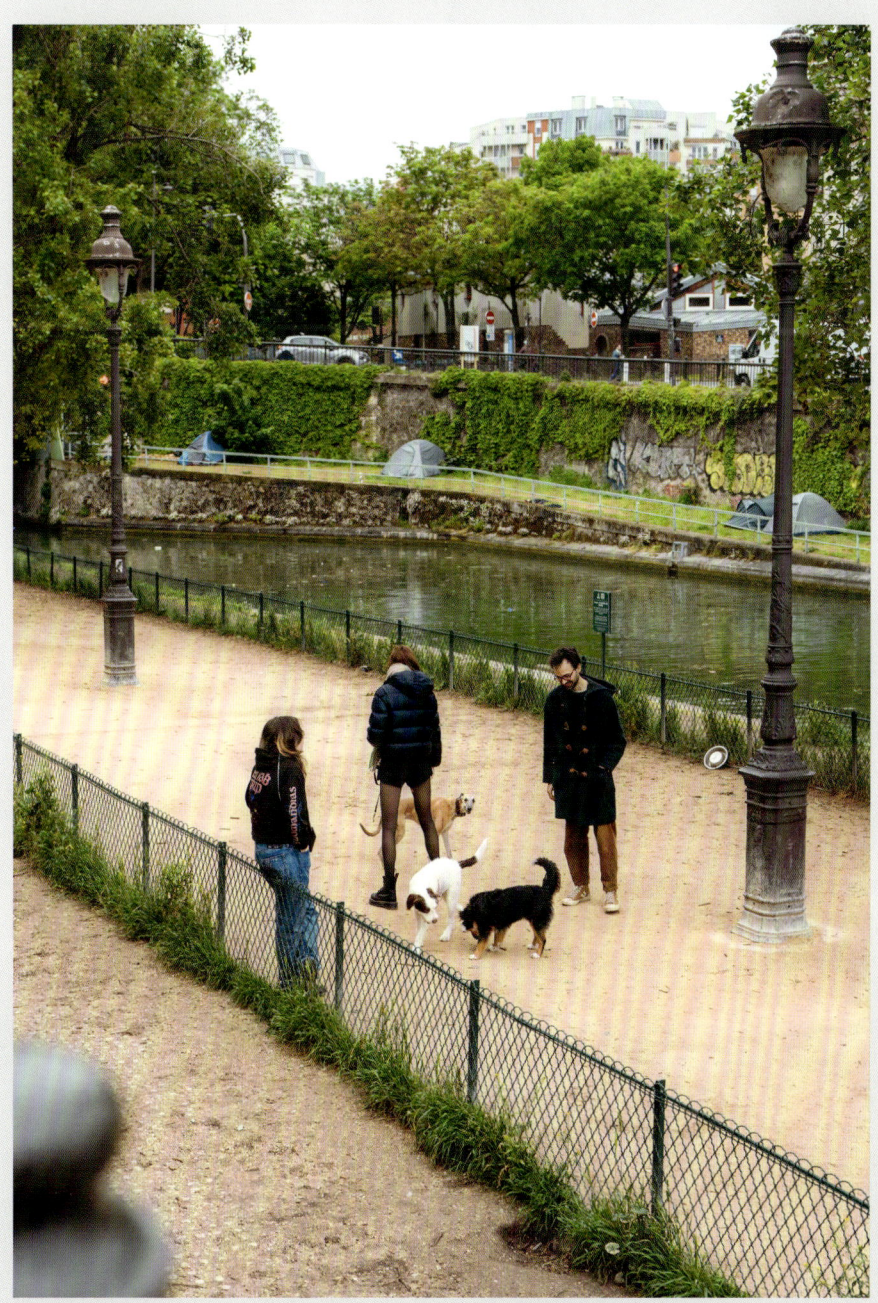

New York City, USA | Paris, France

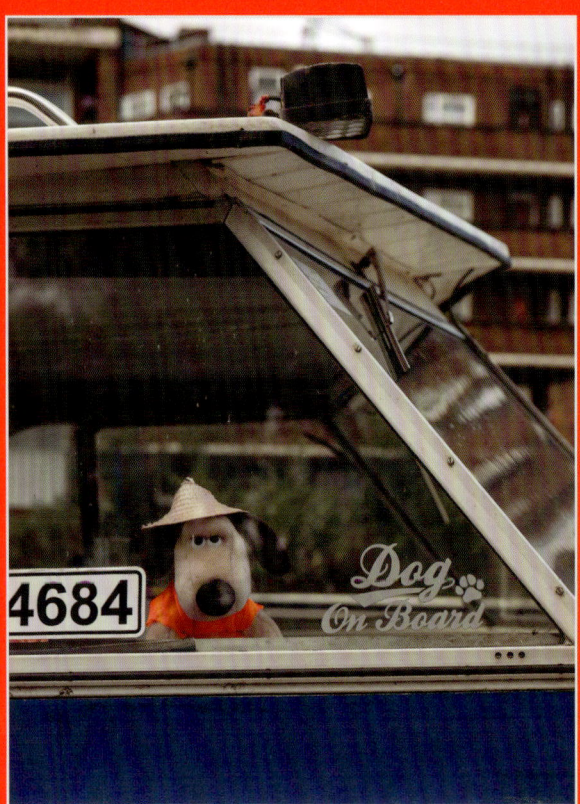

London, England

"I think we do a lot for each other. It's a very therapeutic relationship."

Adrian and their dog Bubos
Sydney, Australia

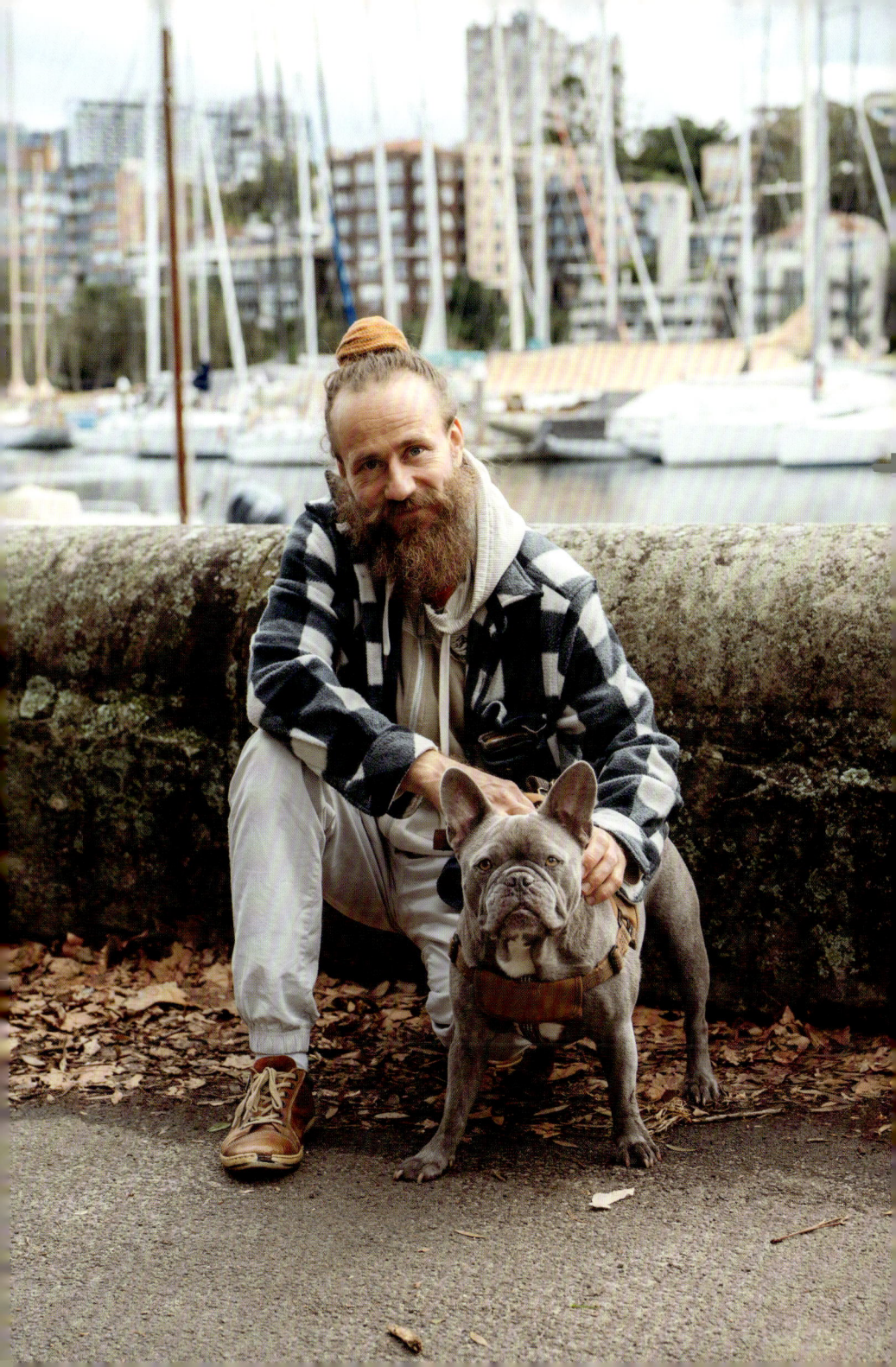

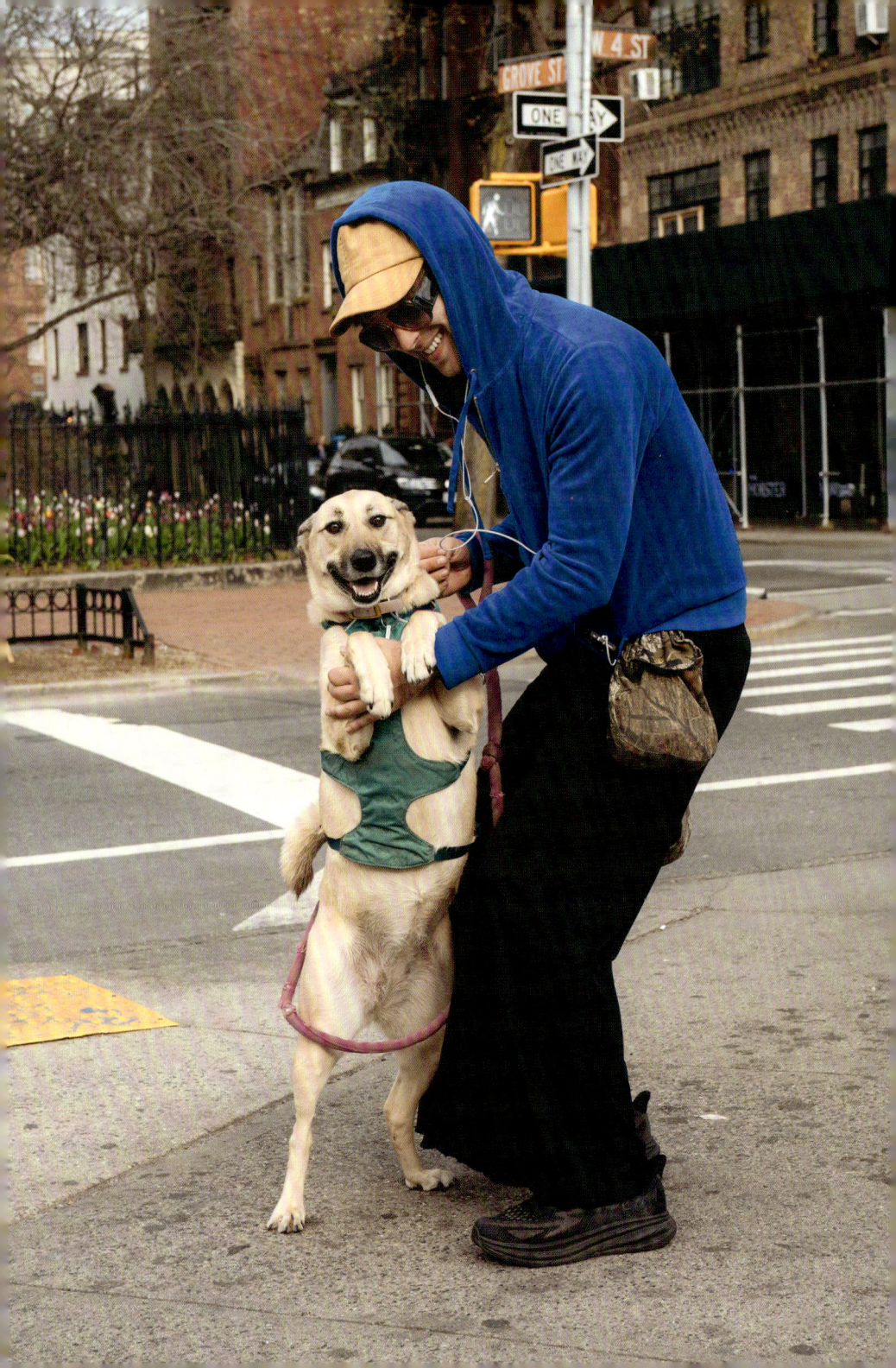

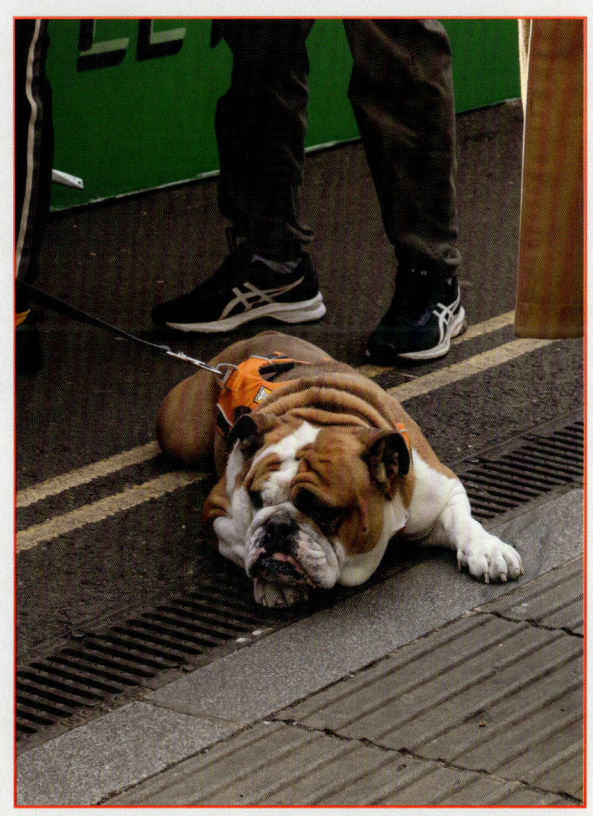

"I'm always in a hurry with her, I think she would prefer if we slowed it down."

Keith and their dog Sabina
New York City, USA

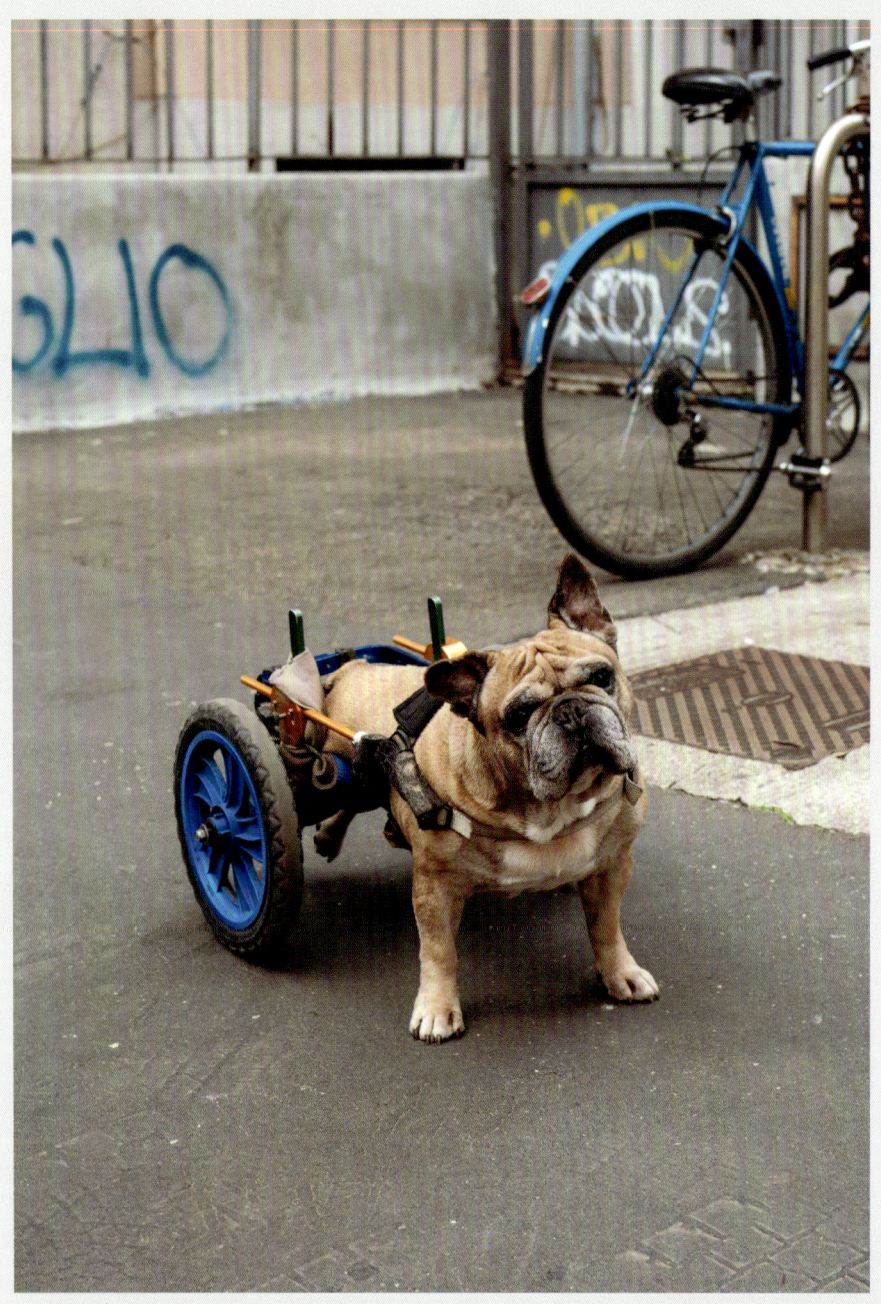

Milan, Italy | Tokyo, Japan

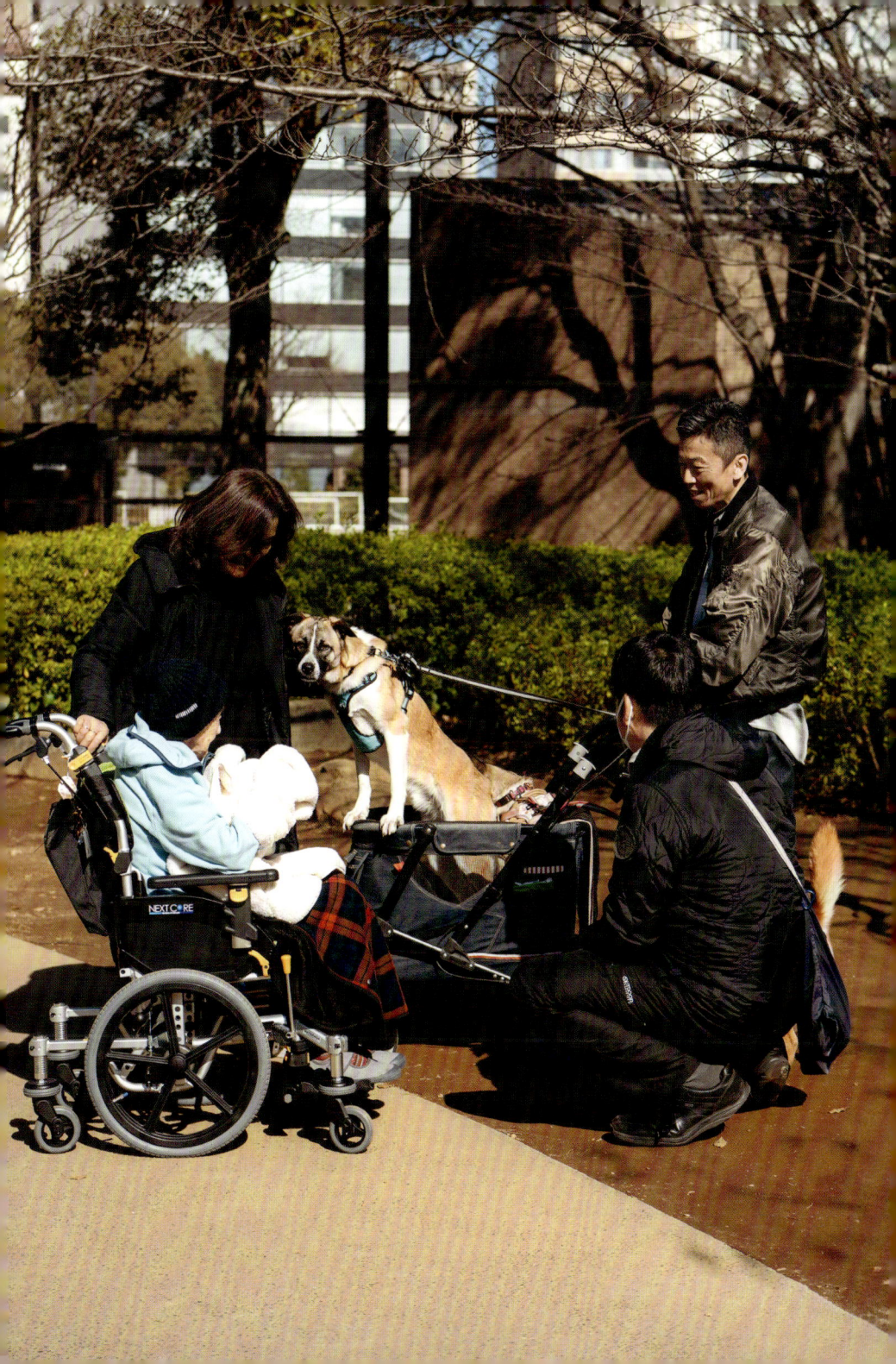

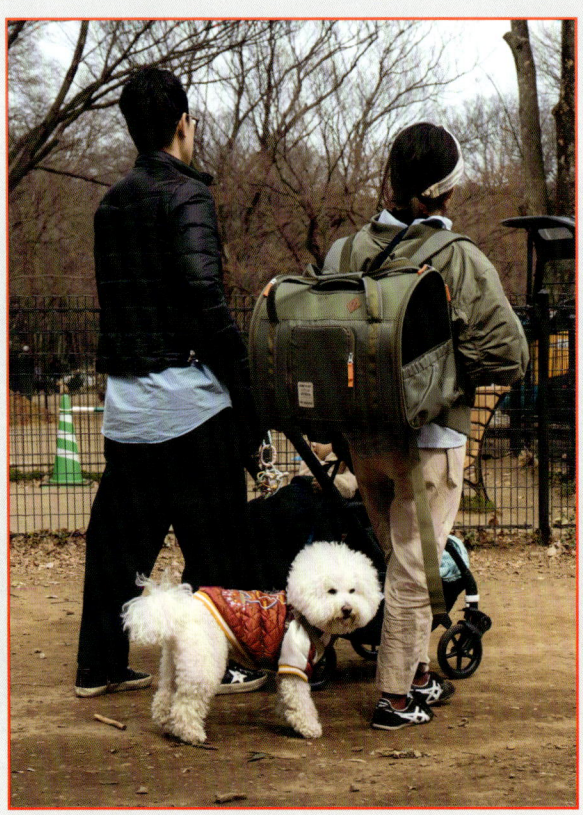

Tokyo, Japan

"He is the central point of our family, with my wife and kids."

Jean-Philippe and their dog Naoussa
Paris, France

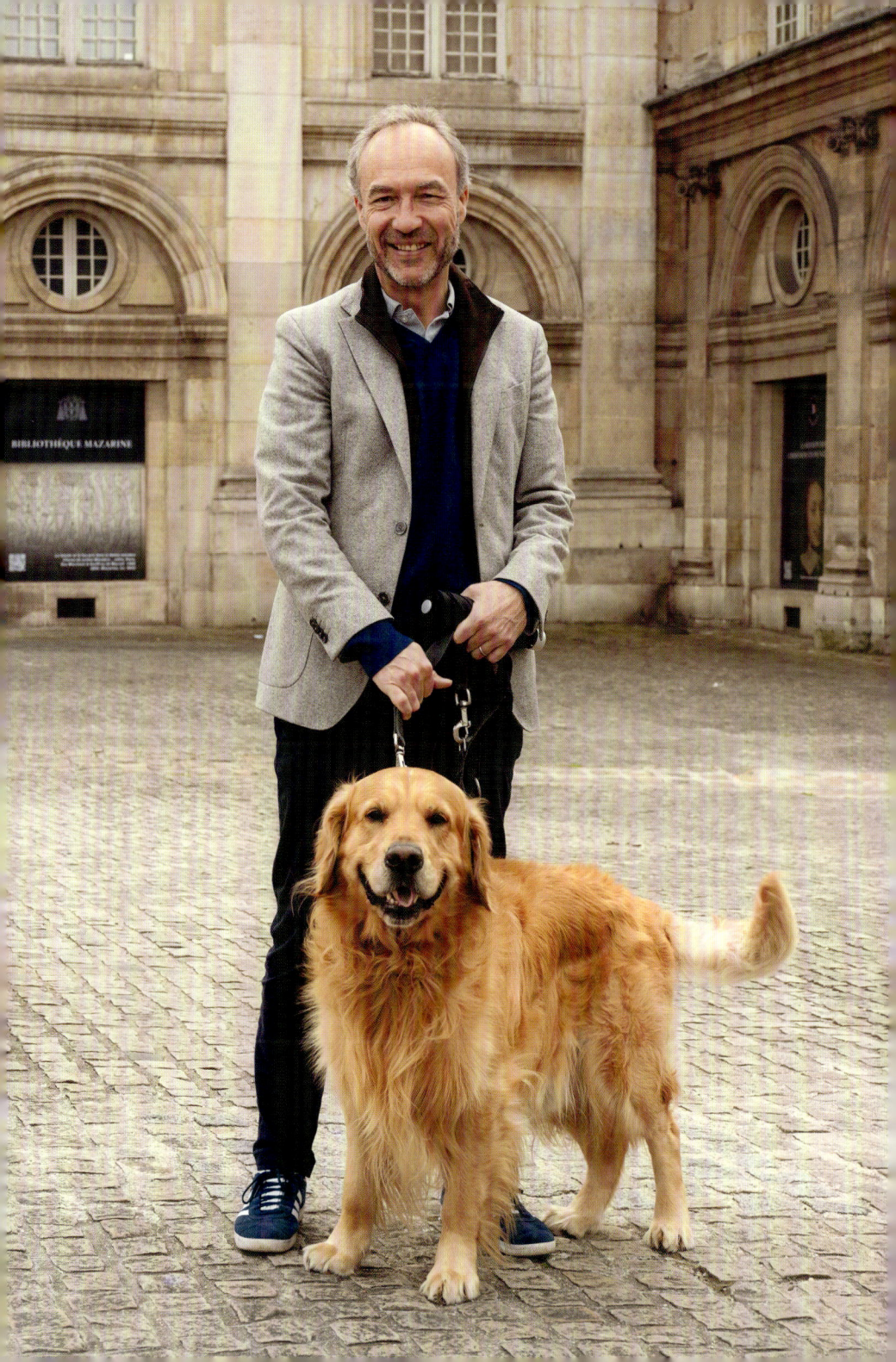

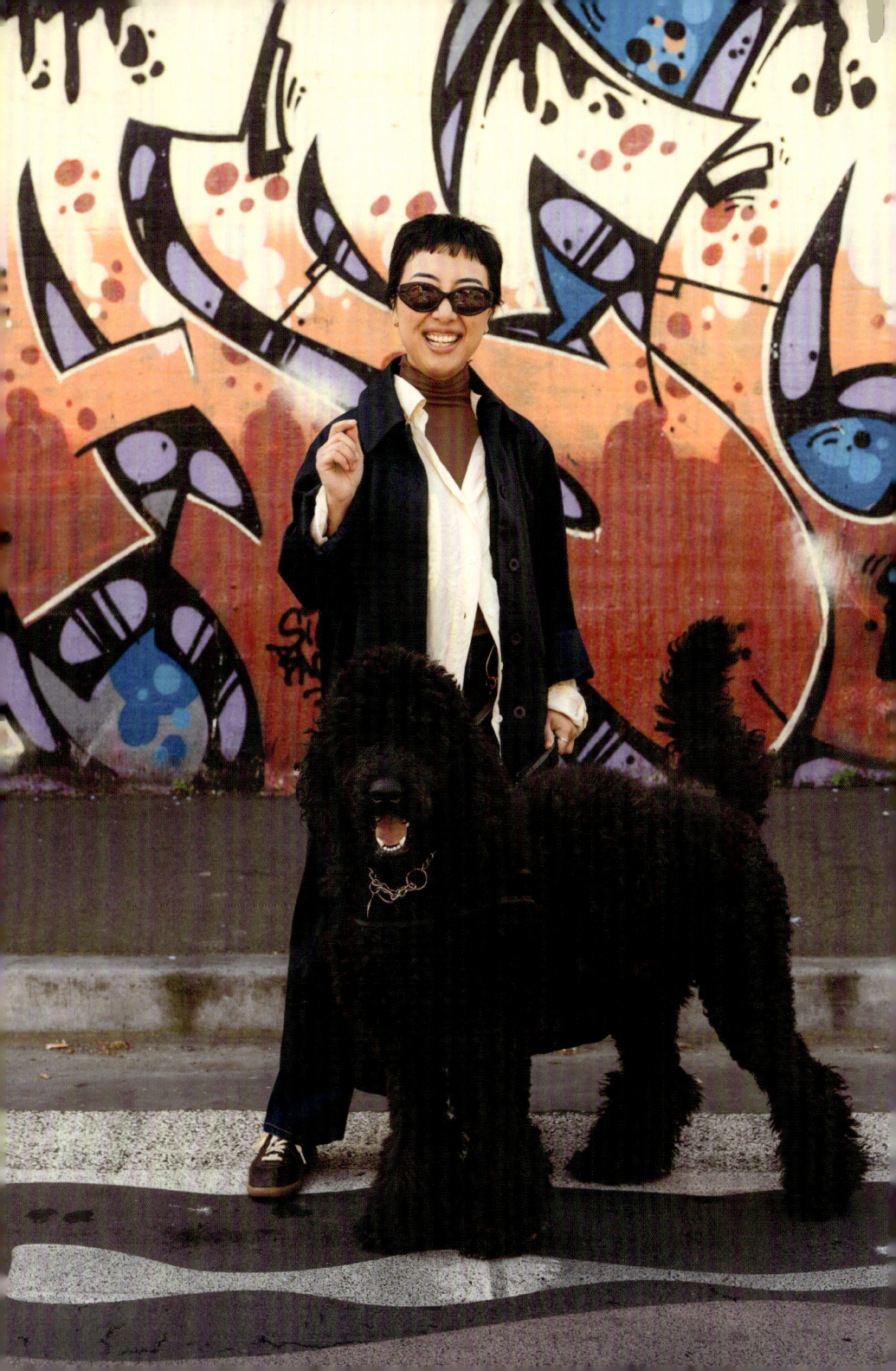

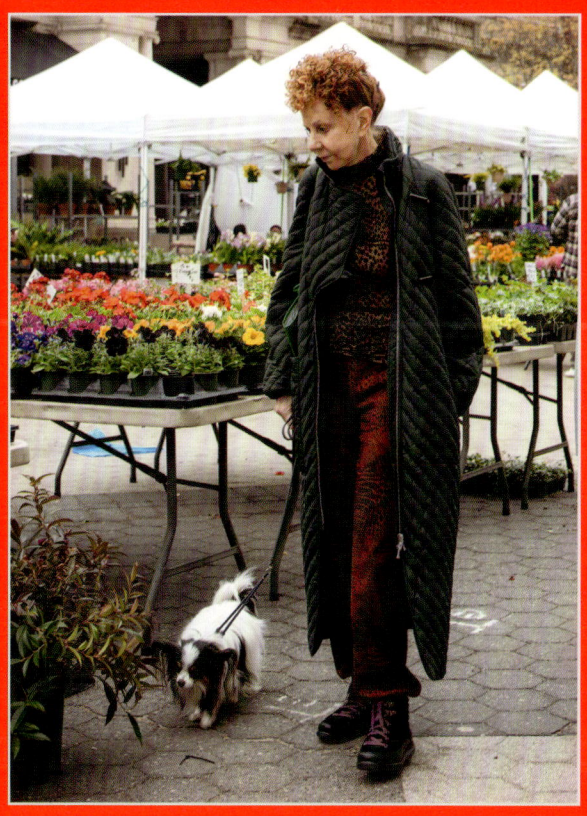

New York City, USA

"I feel like we coexist in
a way that we both just get."

Diletta and their dog Gaspard
Melbourne, Australia

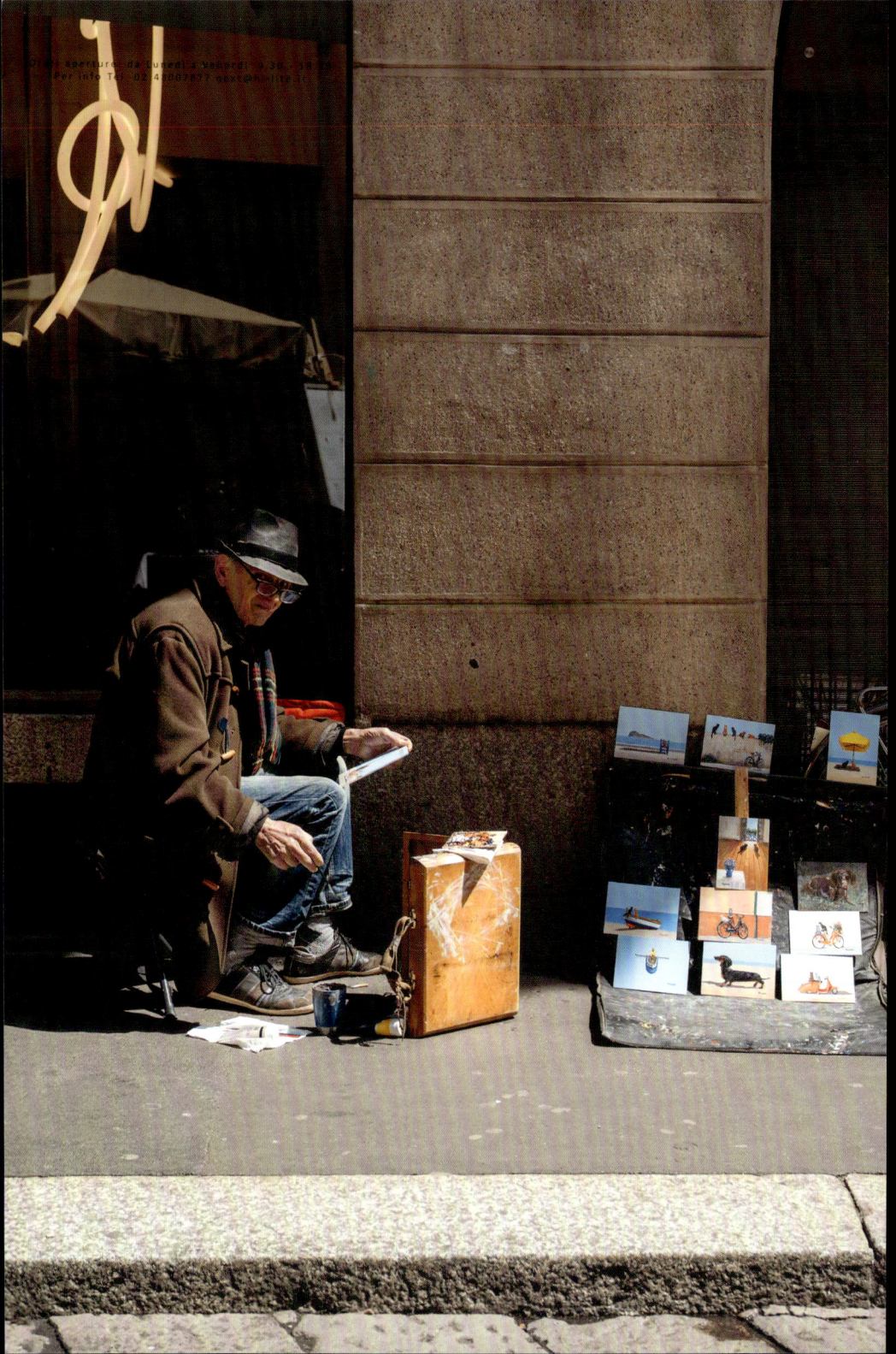

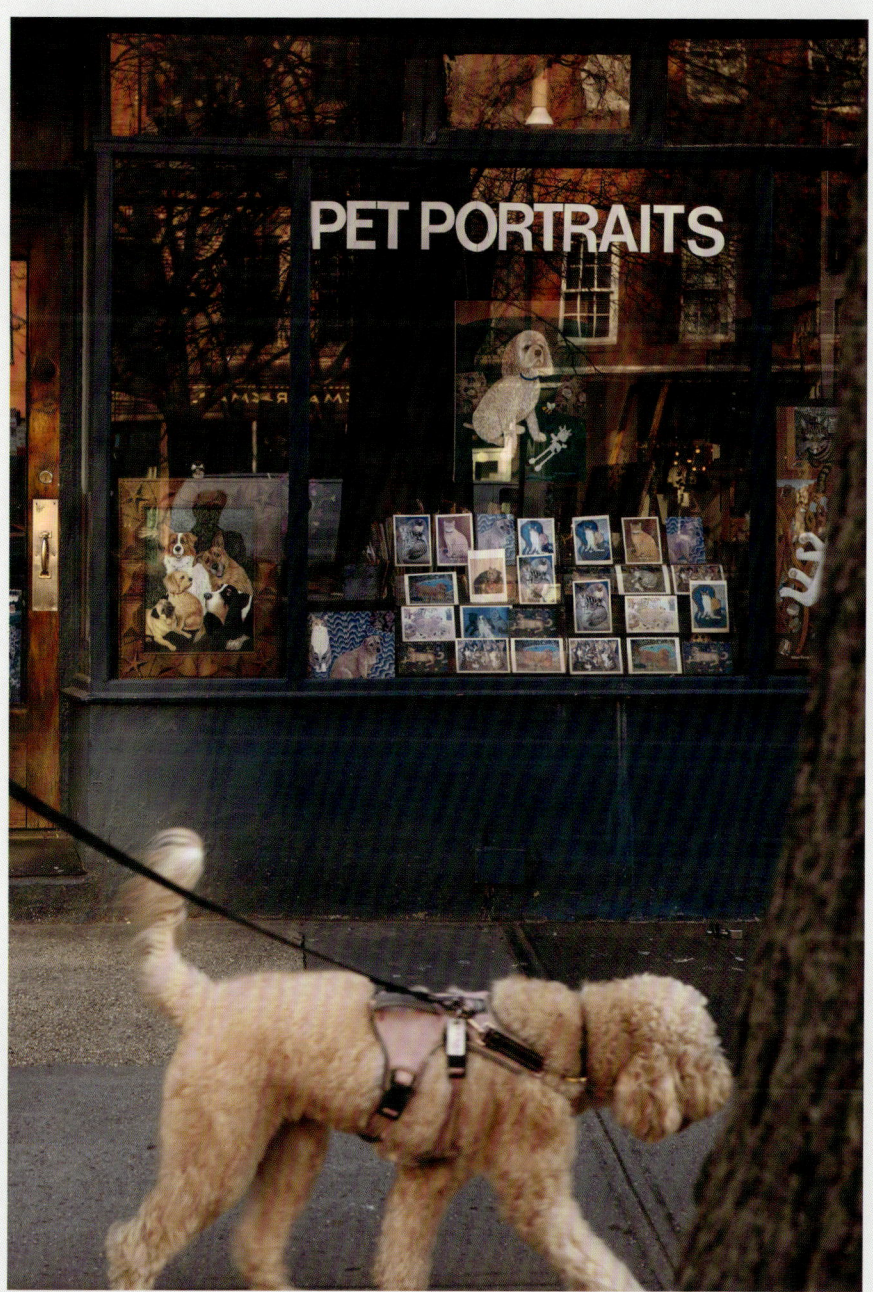

Milan, Italy | New York City, USA

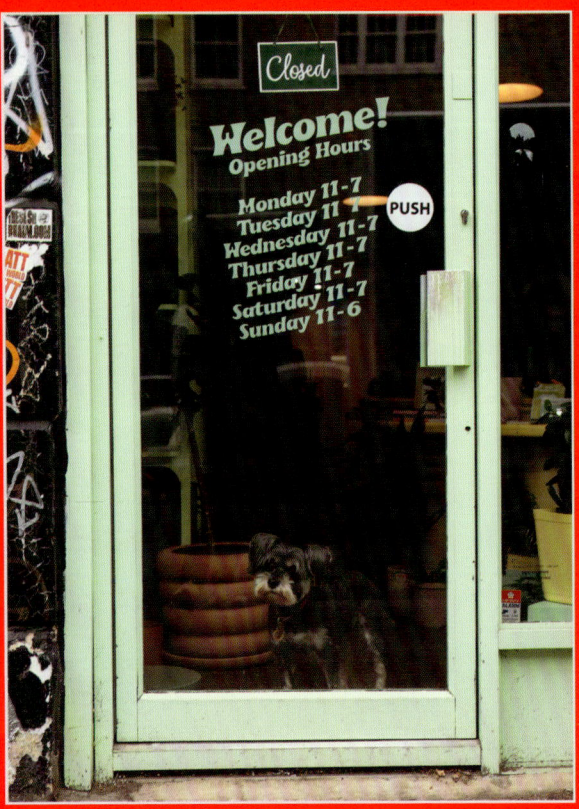

"He works with me in my shop. But he grows tired of it and just wants me to take him out."

Emma and their dog Walnut
London, England

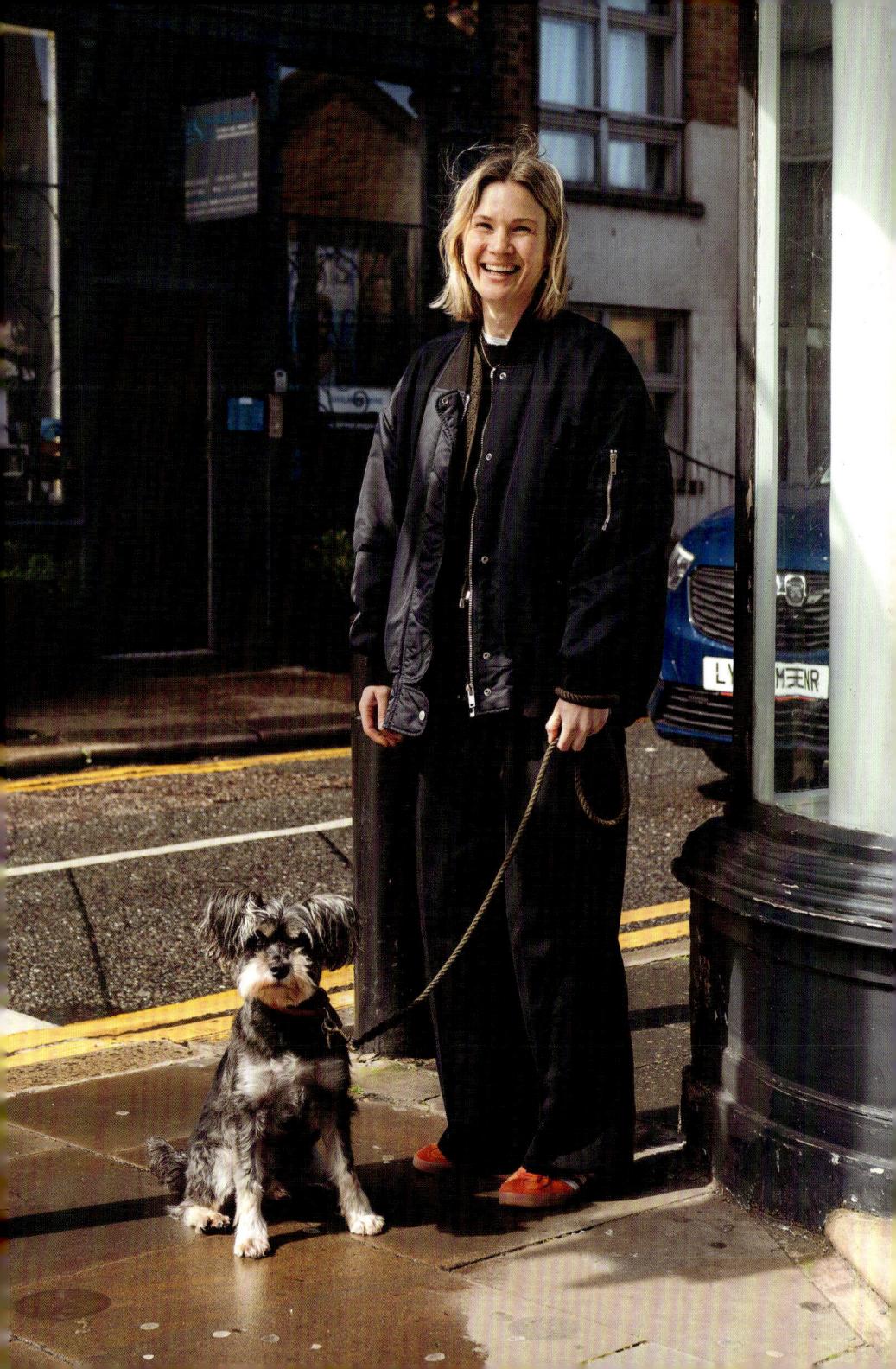

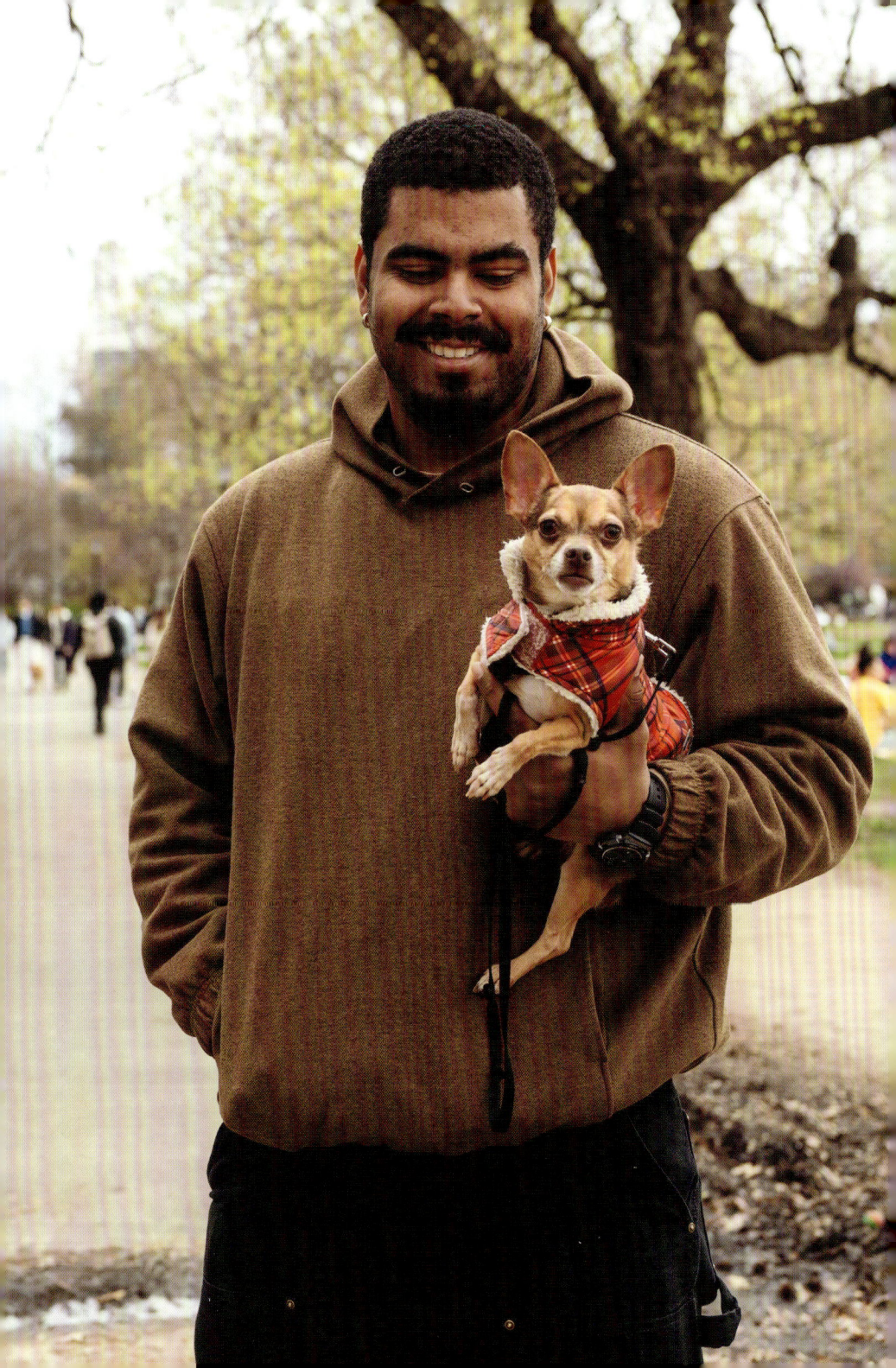

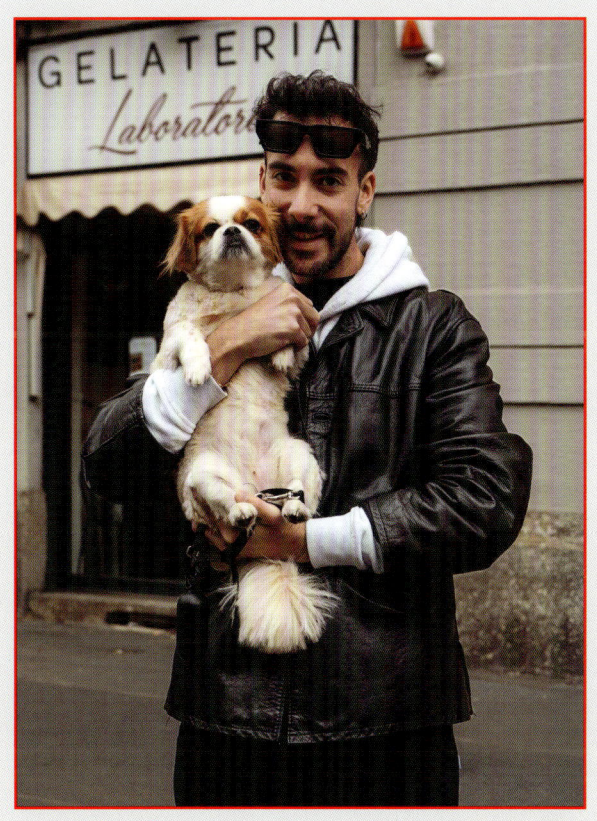

Milan, Italy

"He doesn't eat dog food so I cook for him every day. Mostly ground beef, some sweet potato, sprinkled with some vitamins."

Saul and their dog Duey
New York City, USA

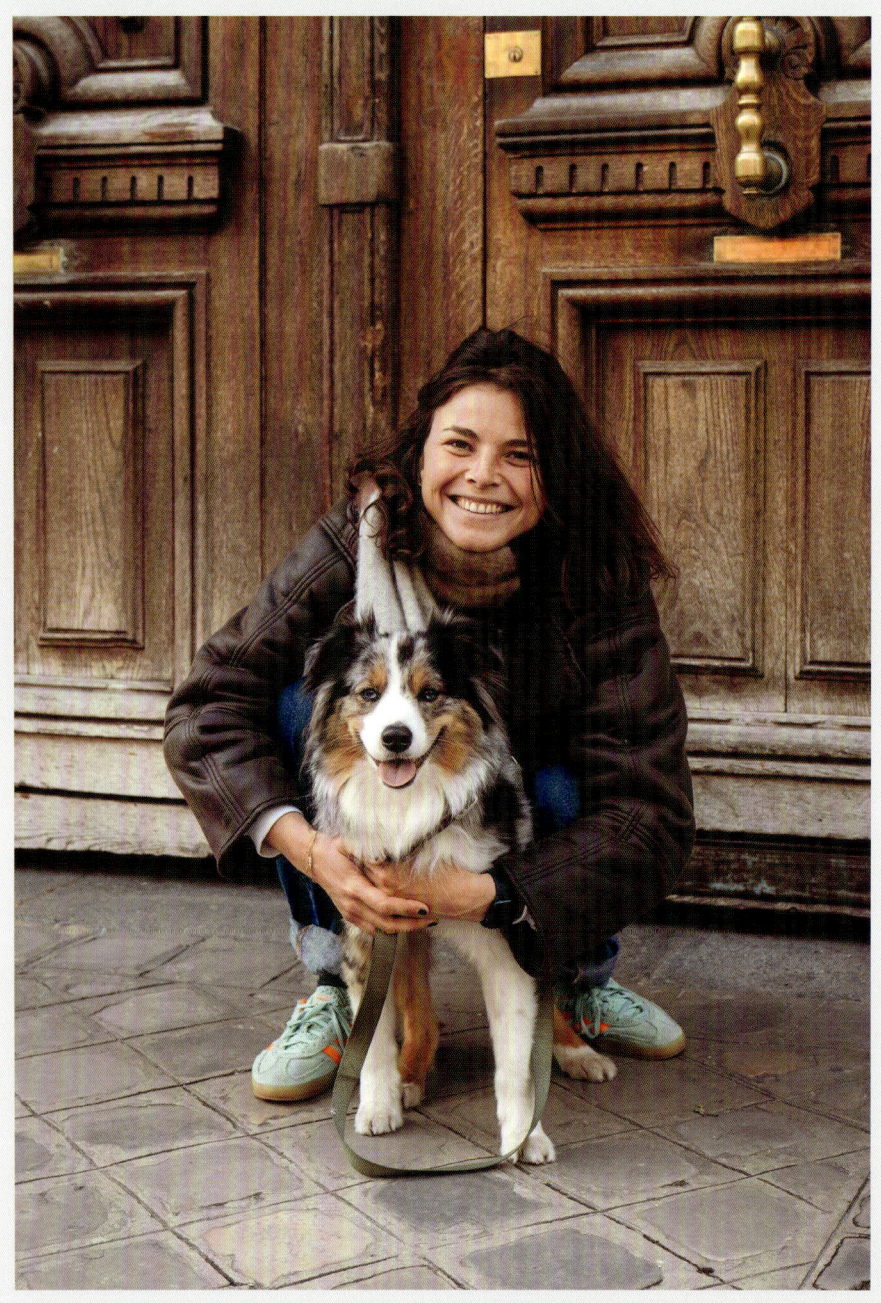

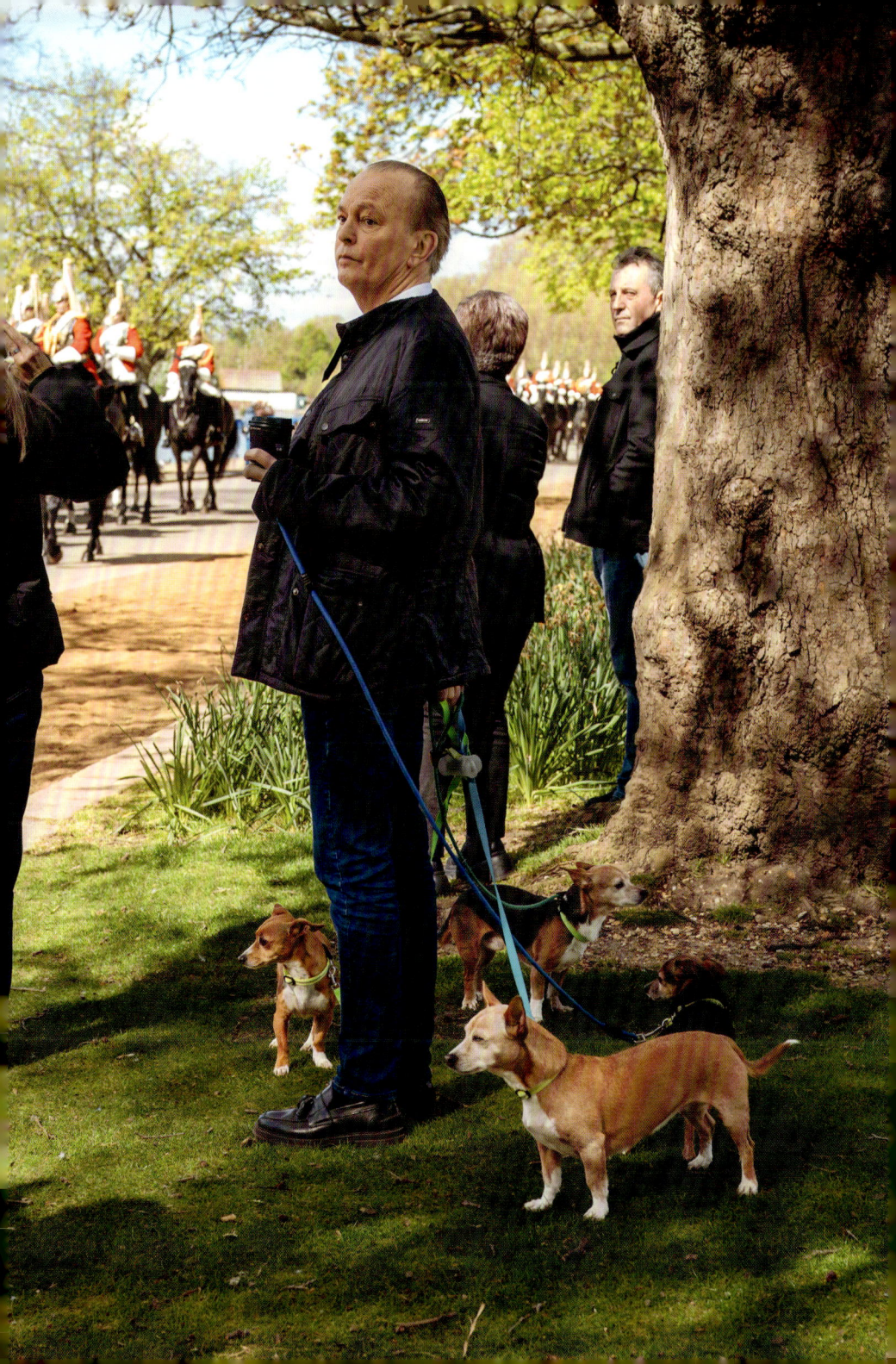

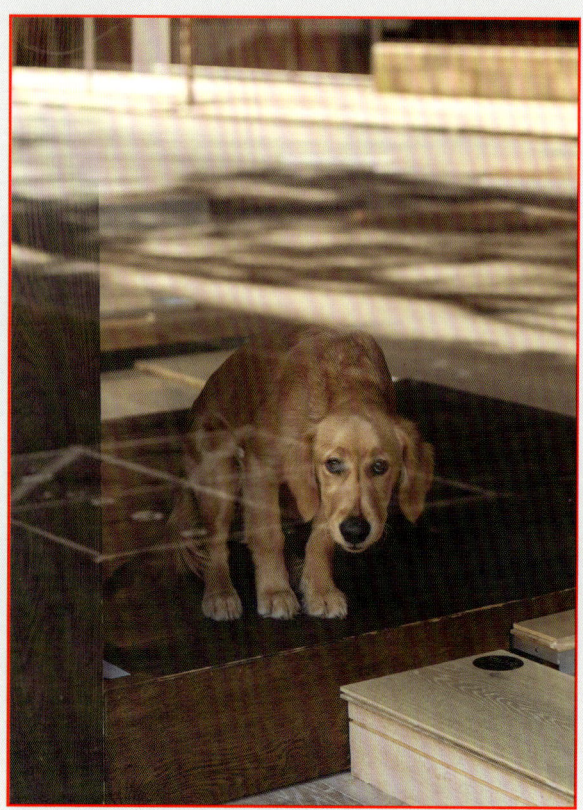

Sydney, Australia

"He's my father's dog.
He calls him my brother."

Jules and his father Claude and his dog Lino
Paris, France

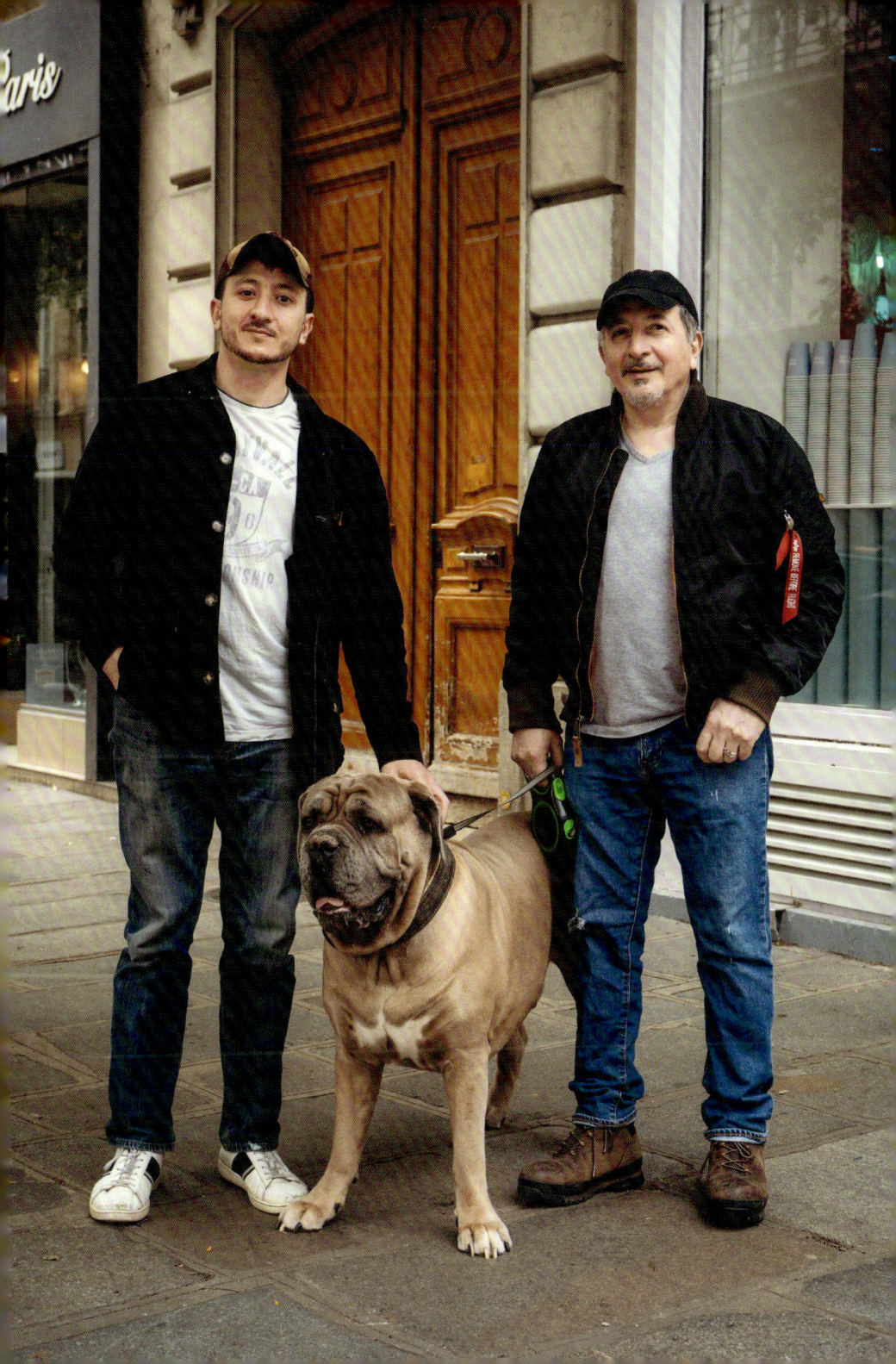

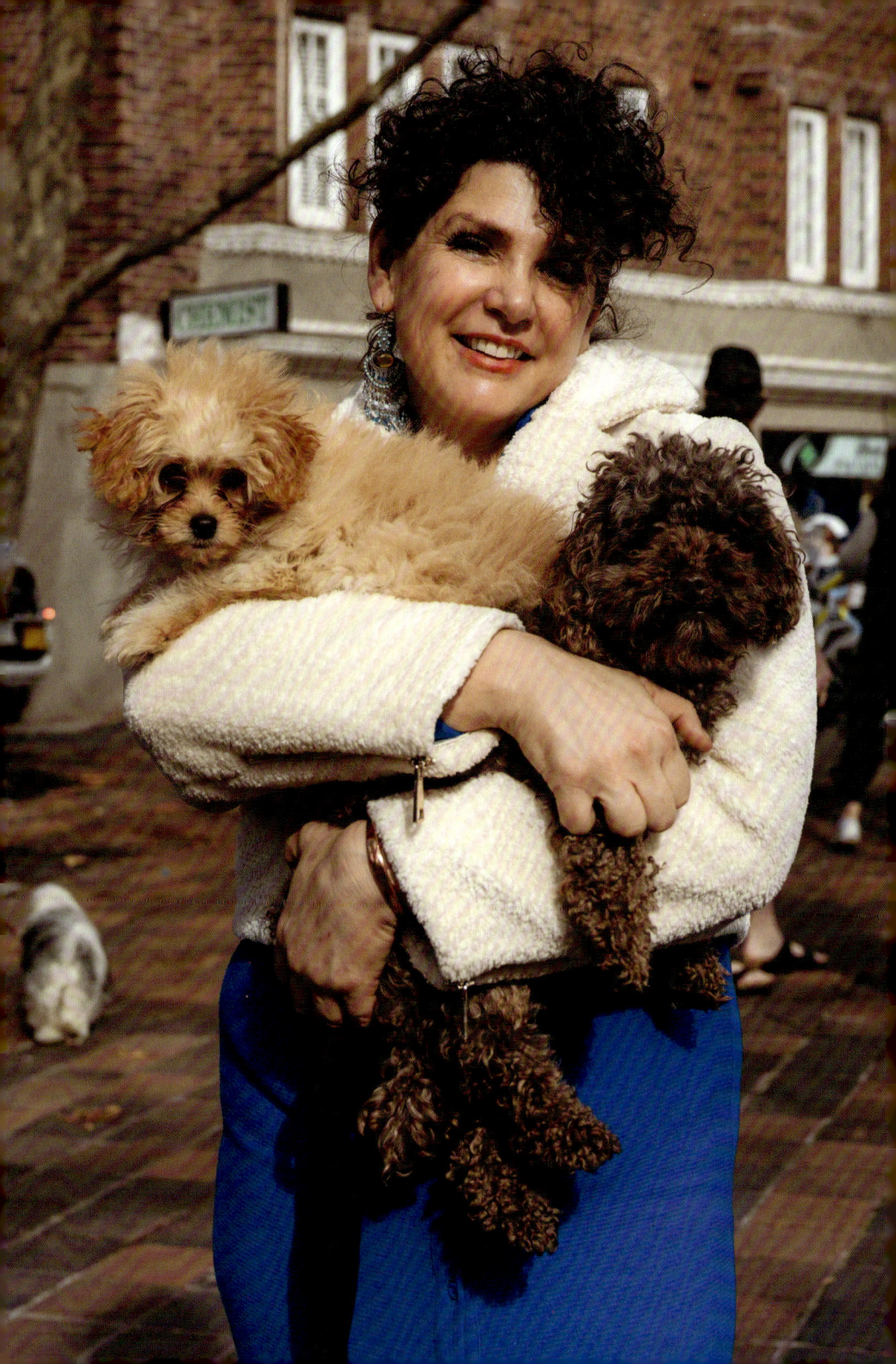

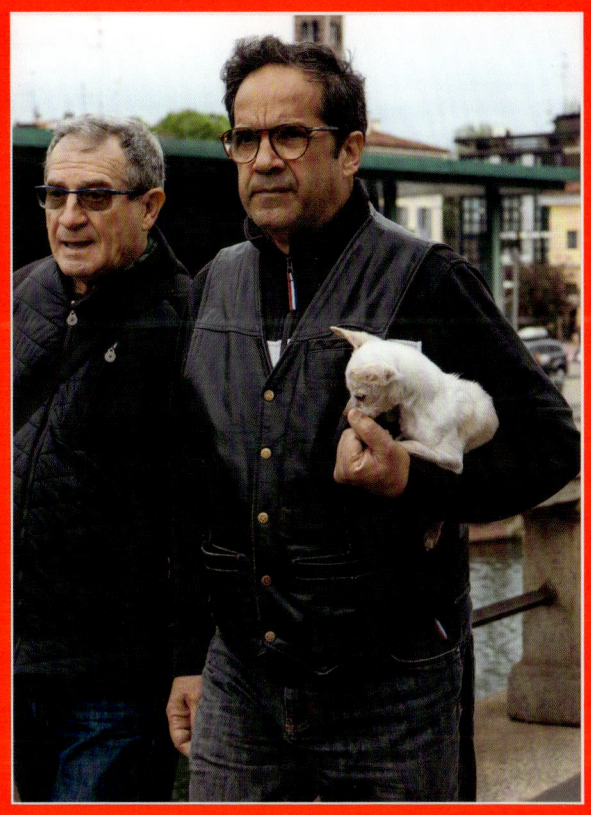

Milan, Italy

"They love to be with me wherever I go. And they love chicken necks."

Helena and their dogs Ponyo and Don Gato
Sydney, Australia

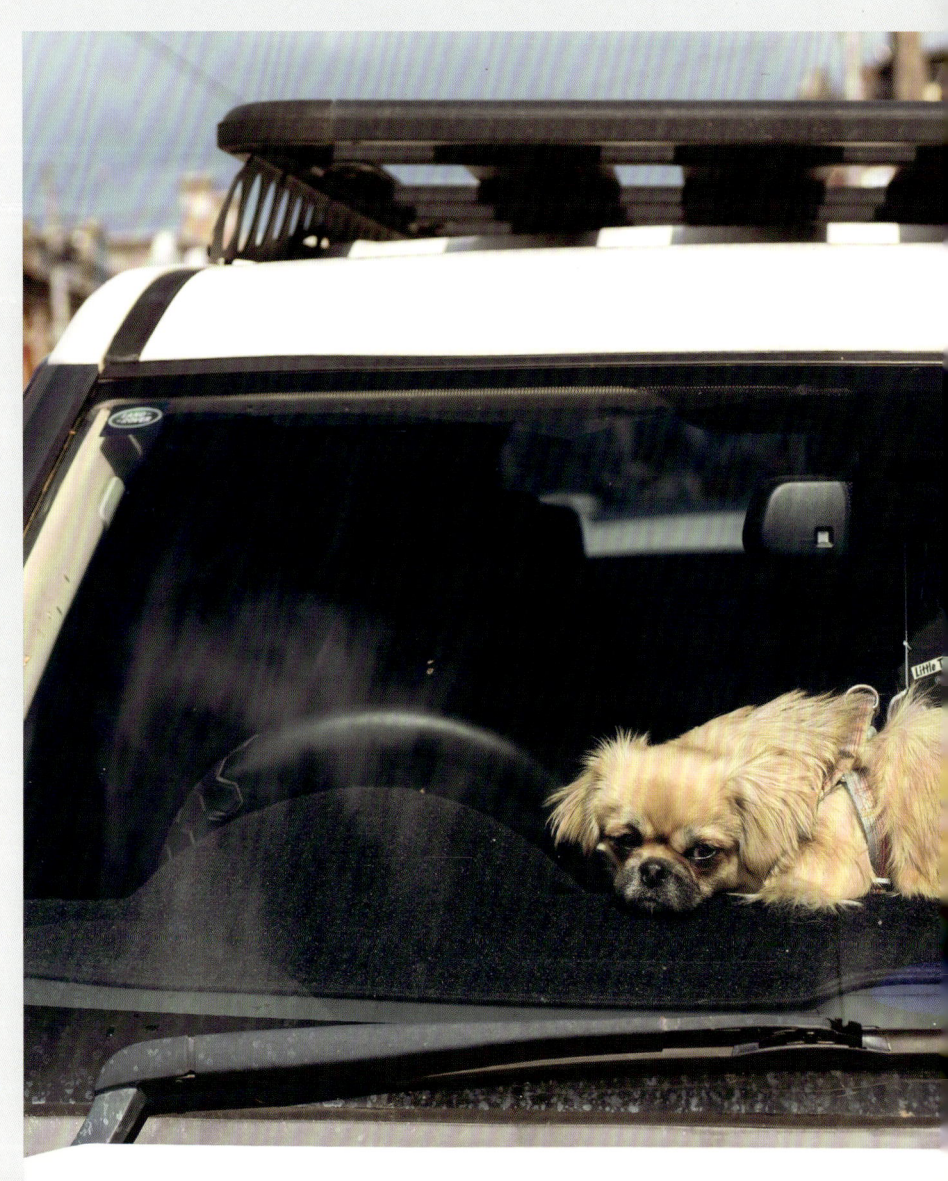

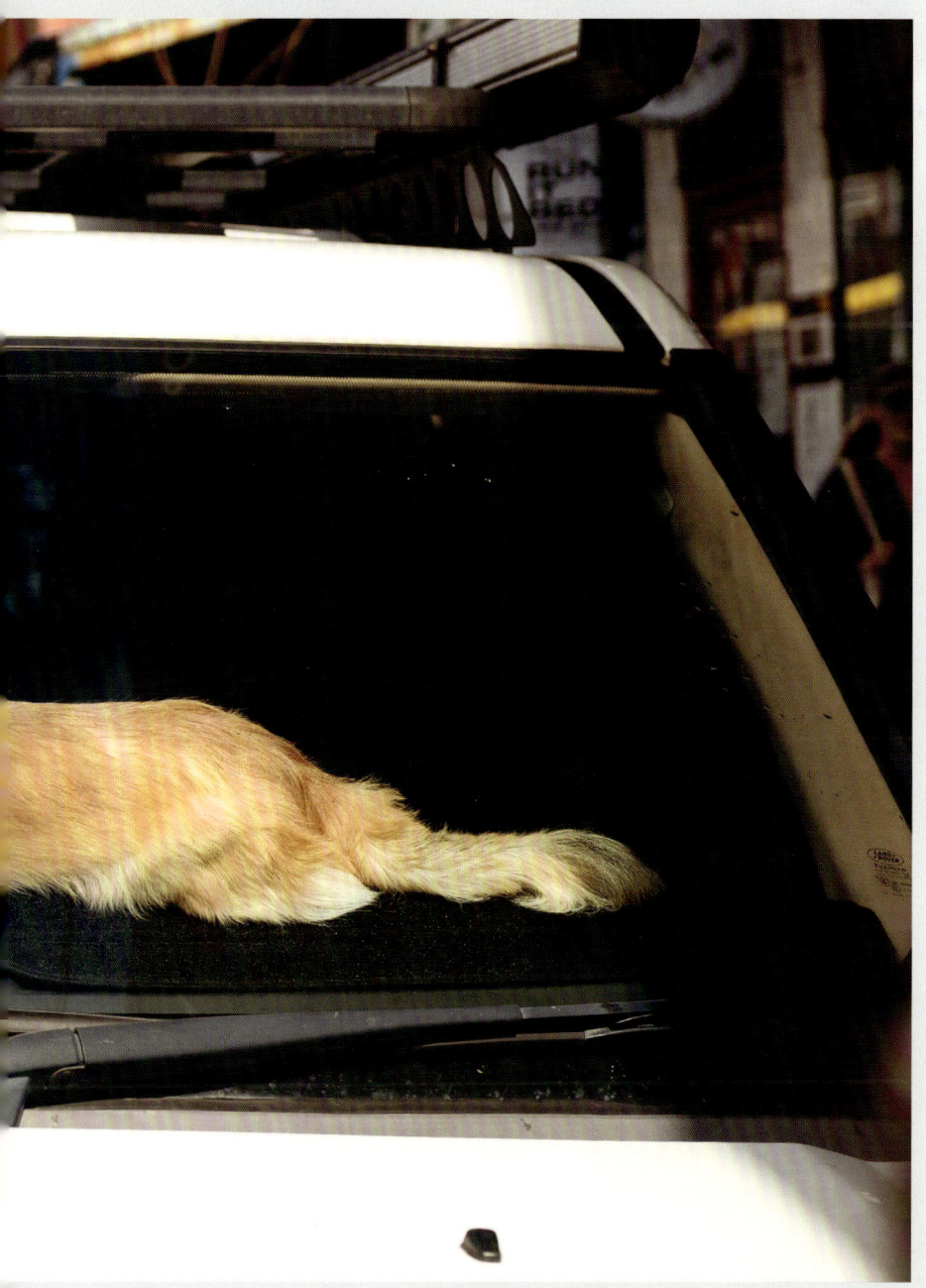

Melbourne, Australia

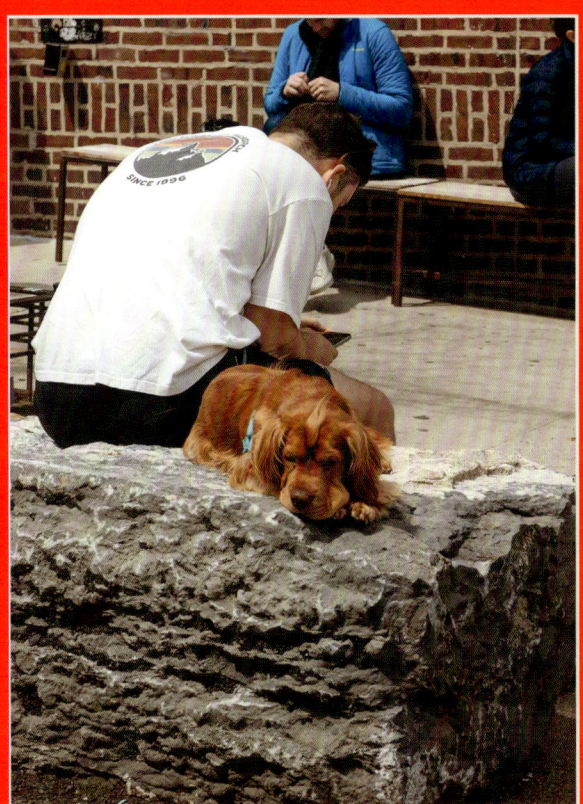

New York City, USA

"He doesn't know why I discipline him.
Hopefully he gets it when he's older."

Andrew and their dog Louie
Sydney, Australia

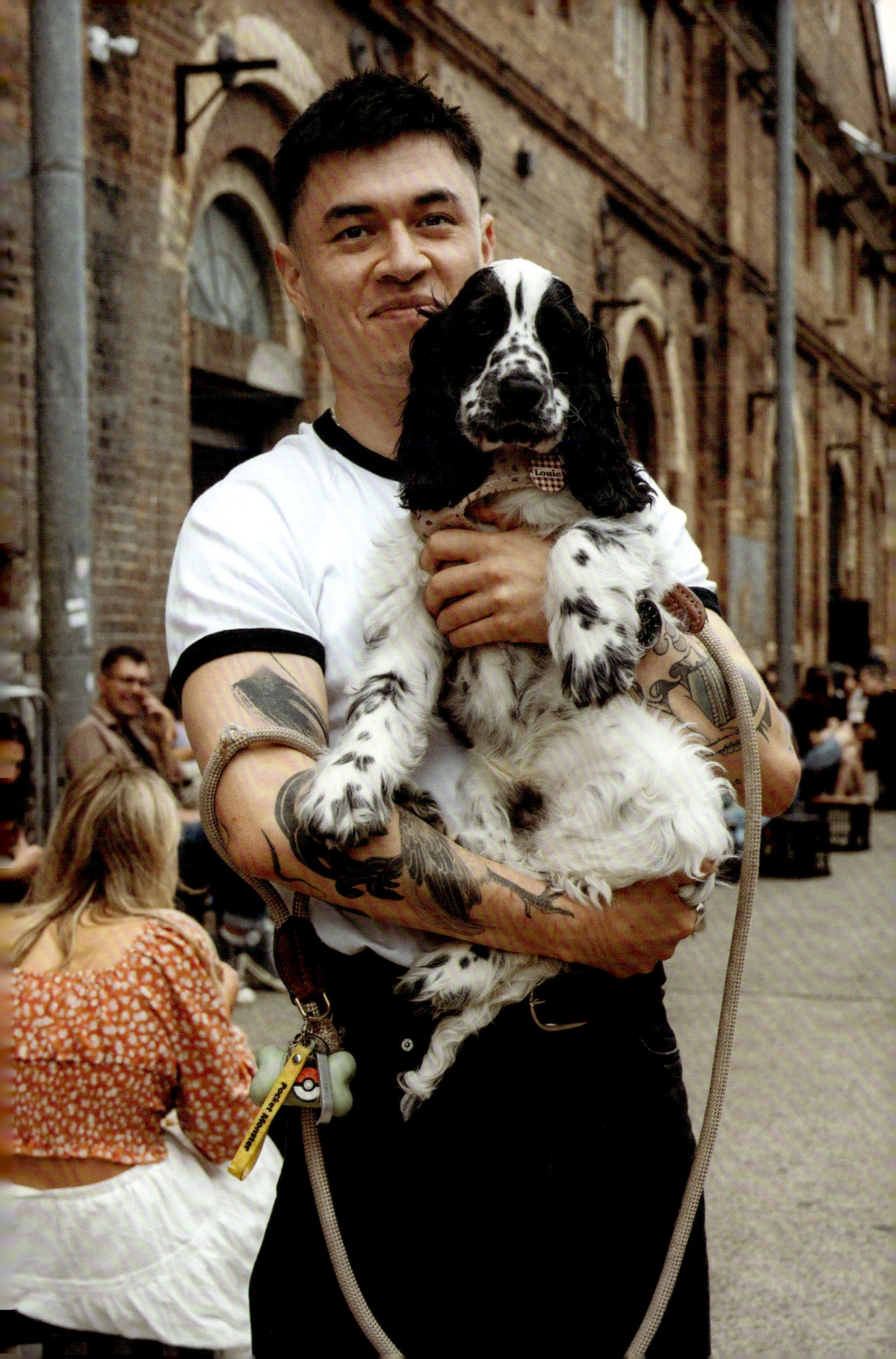

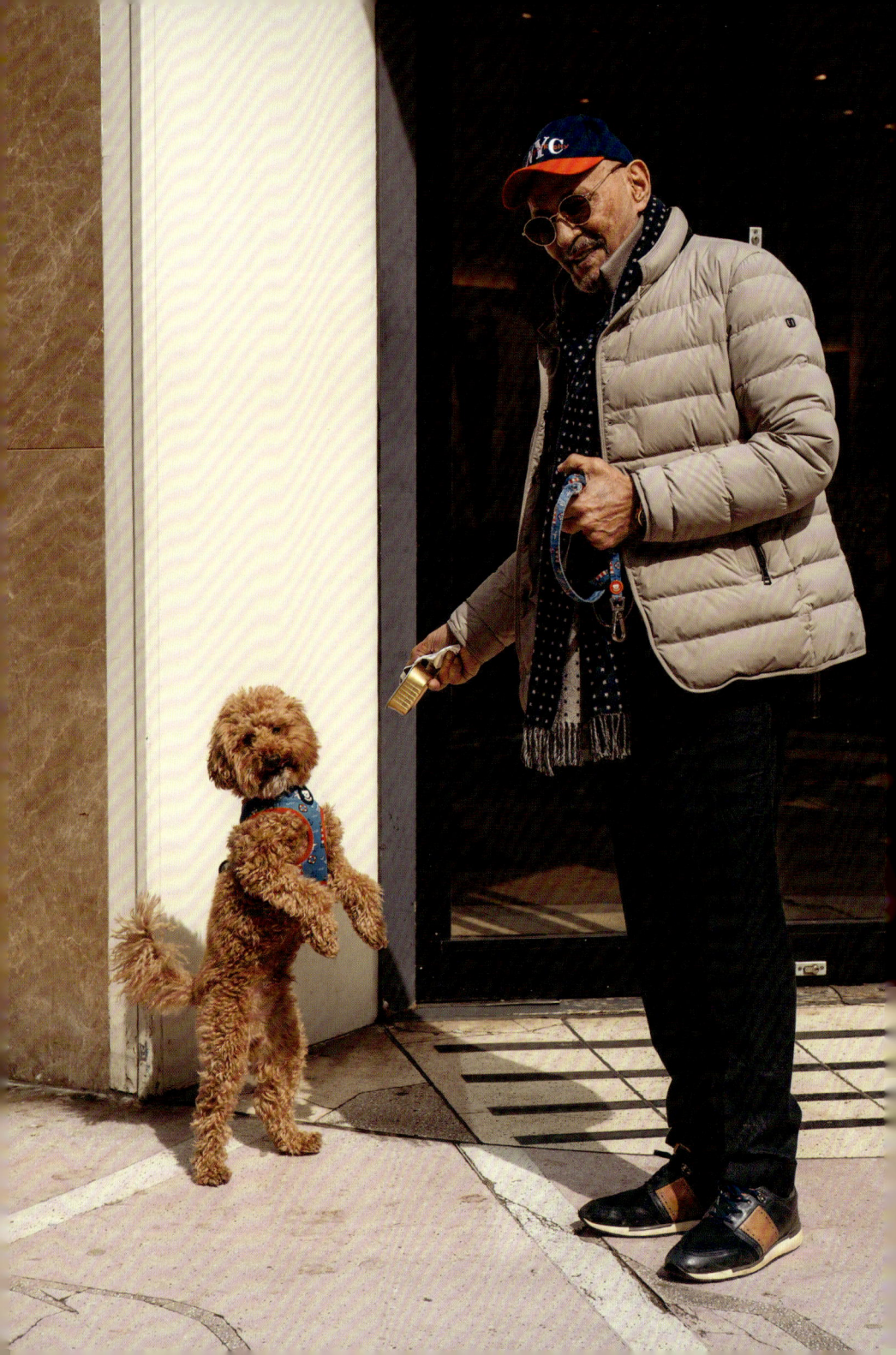

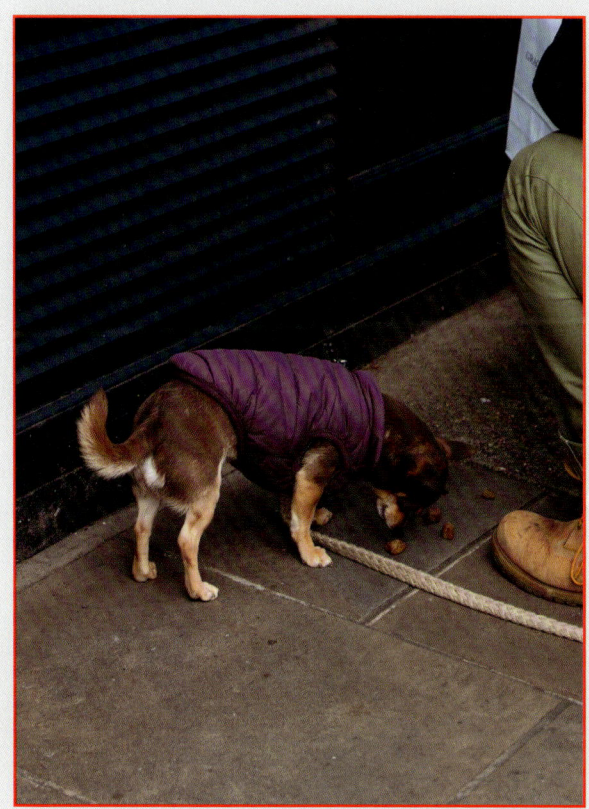

London, England

"He thinks I'm a lovely man."

Alex and their dog Romeo
London, England

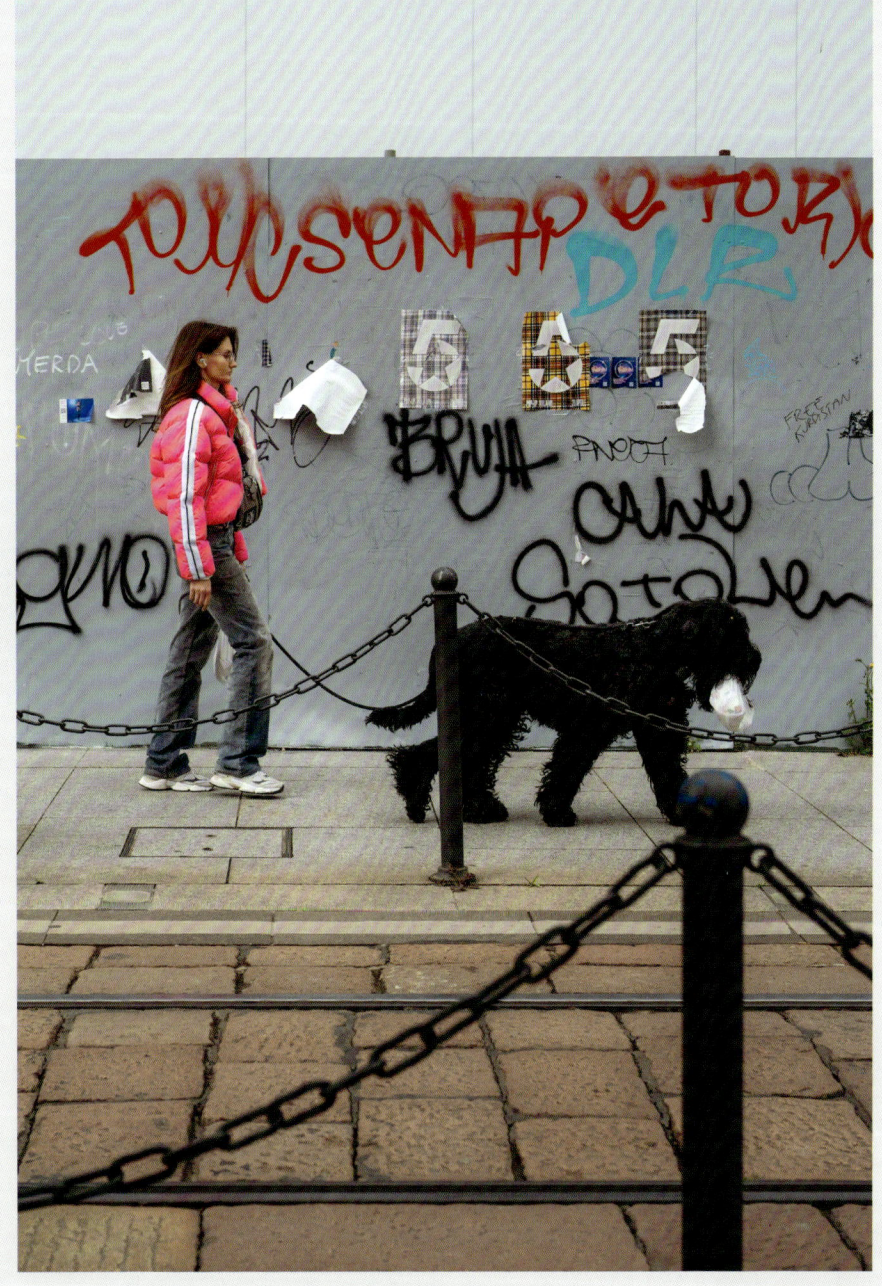

Milan, Italy | Paris, France

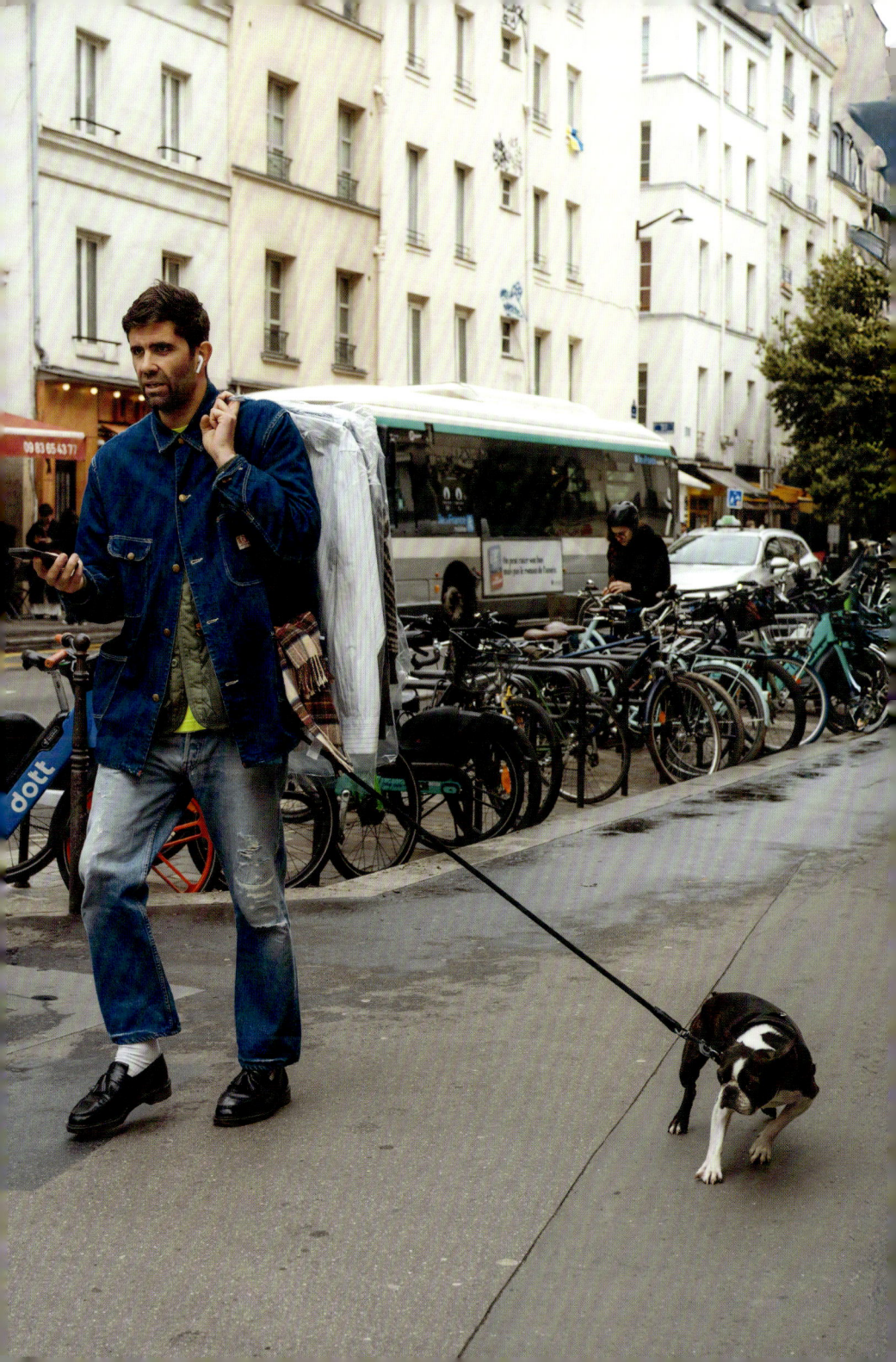

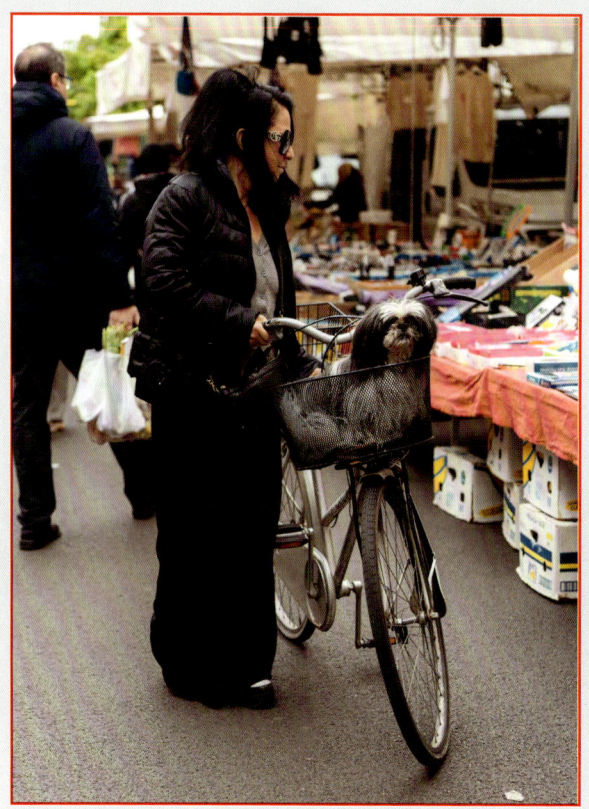

Milan, Italy

"She has travelled the world with me.
And I hope she thinks everything is
just how it should be."

Jeni and their dog Spruce
Melbourne, Australia

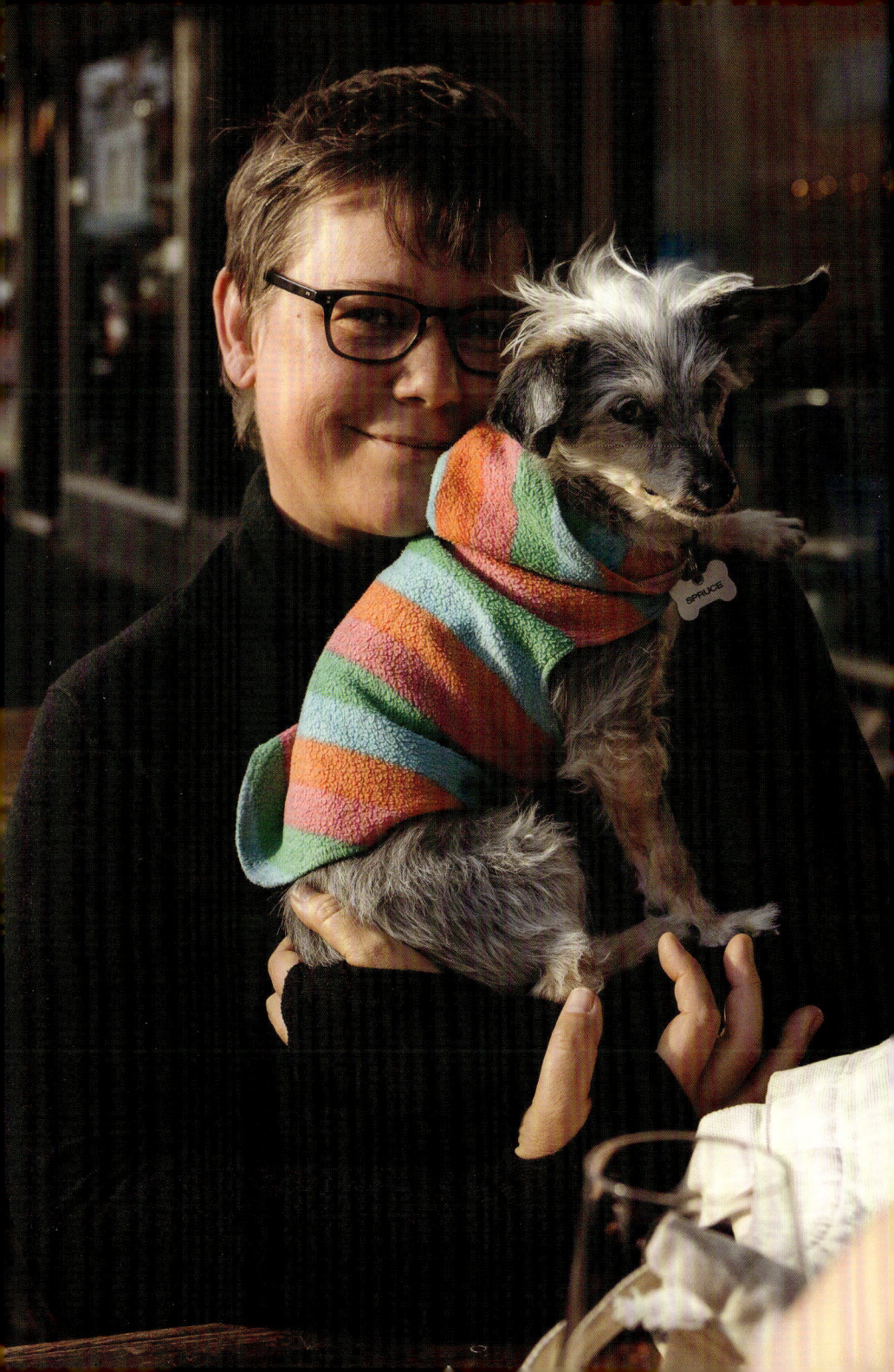

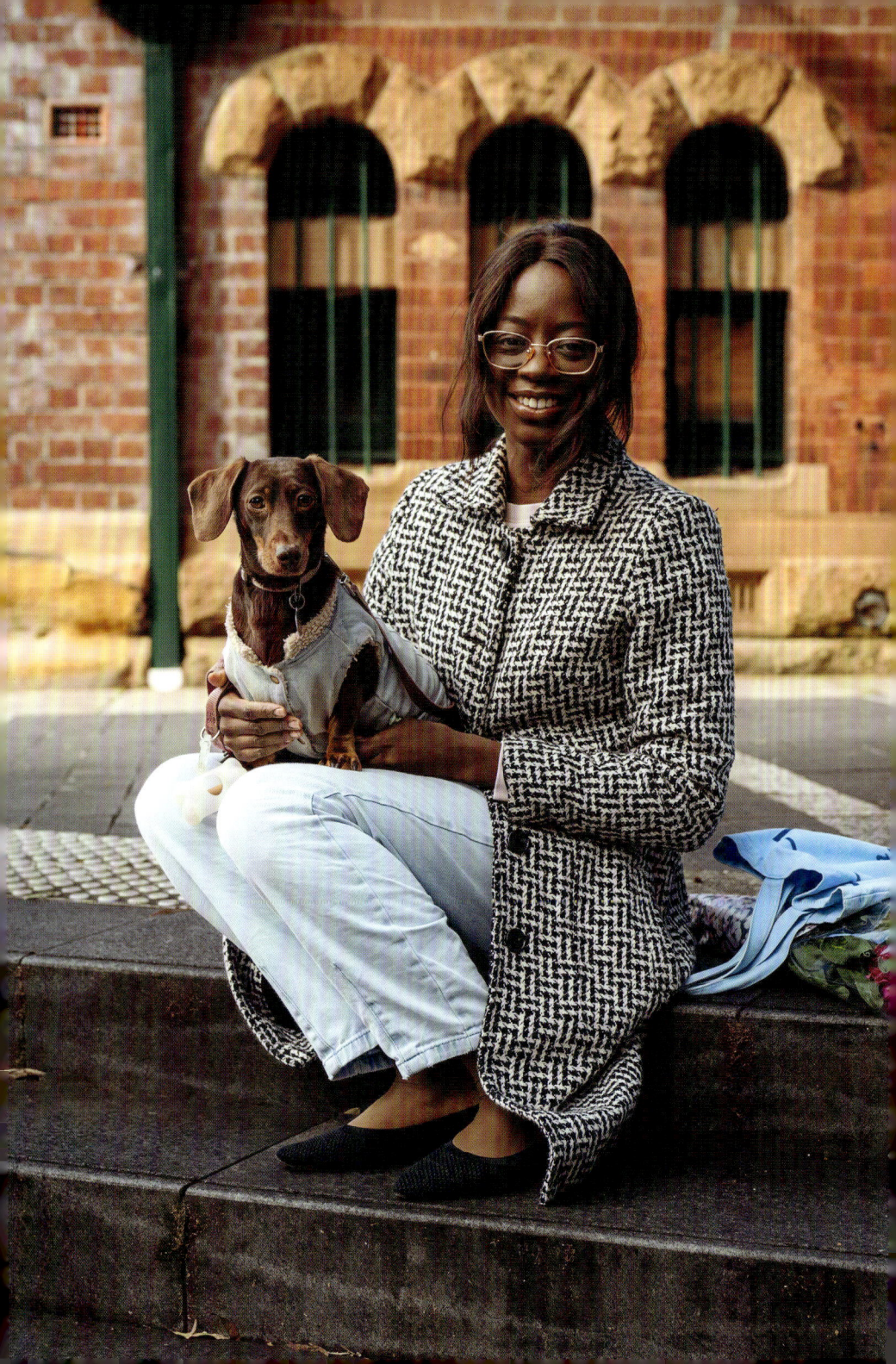

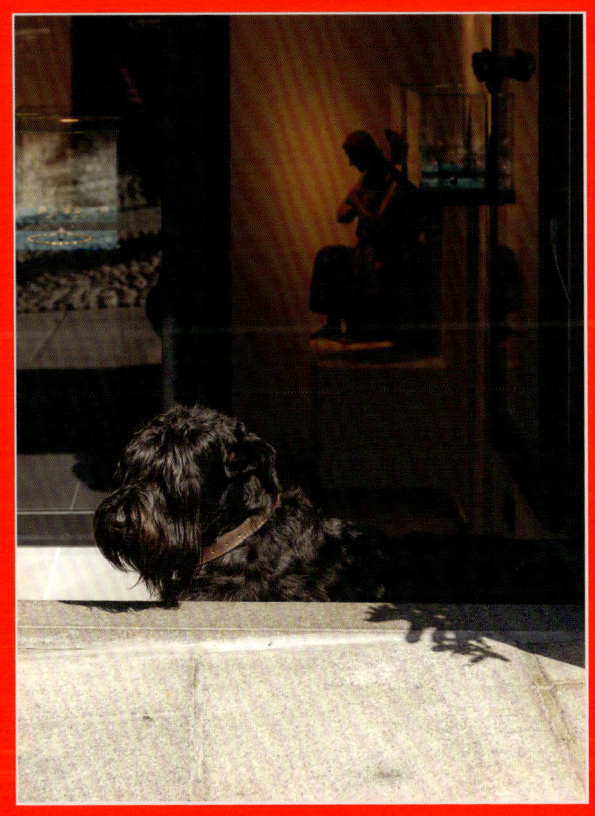

Milan, Italy

"She's quite short, so she needs assistance to reach certain places. For instance her stool, so she can sit in the sun."

Fifi and their dog Effie
Sydney, Australia

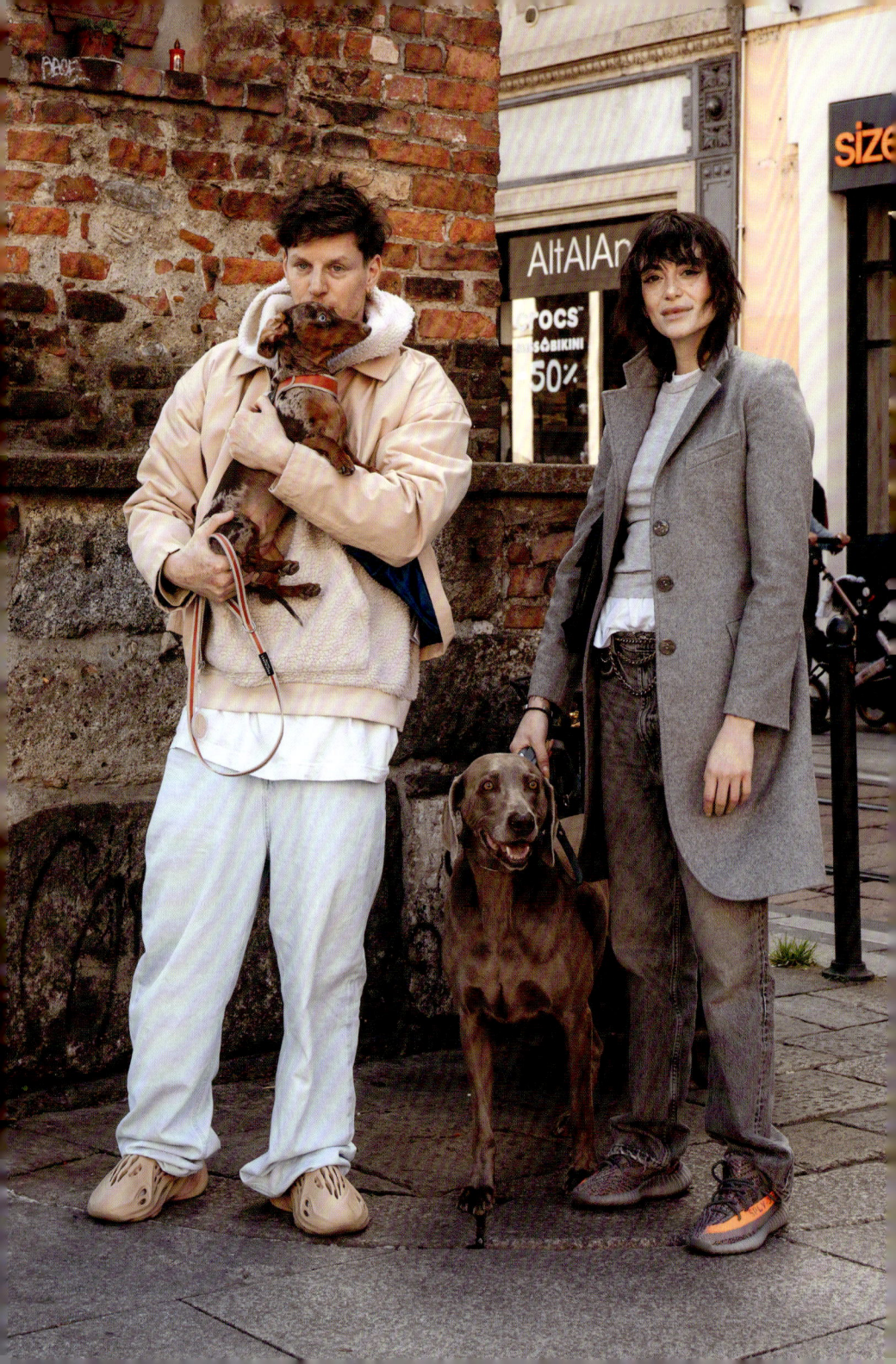

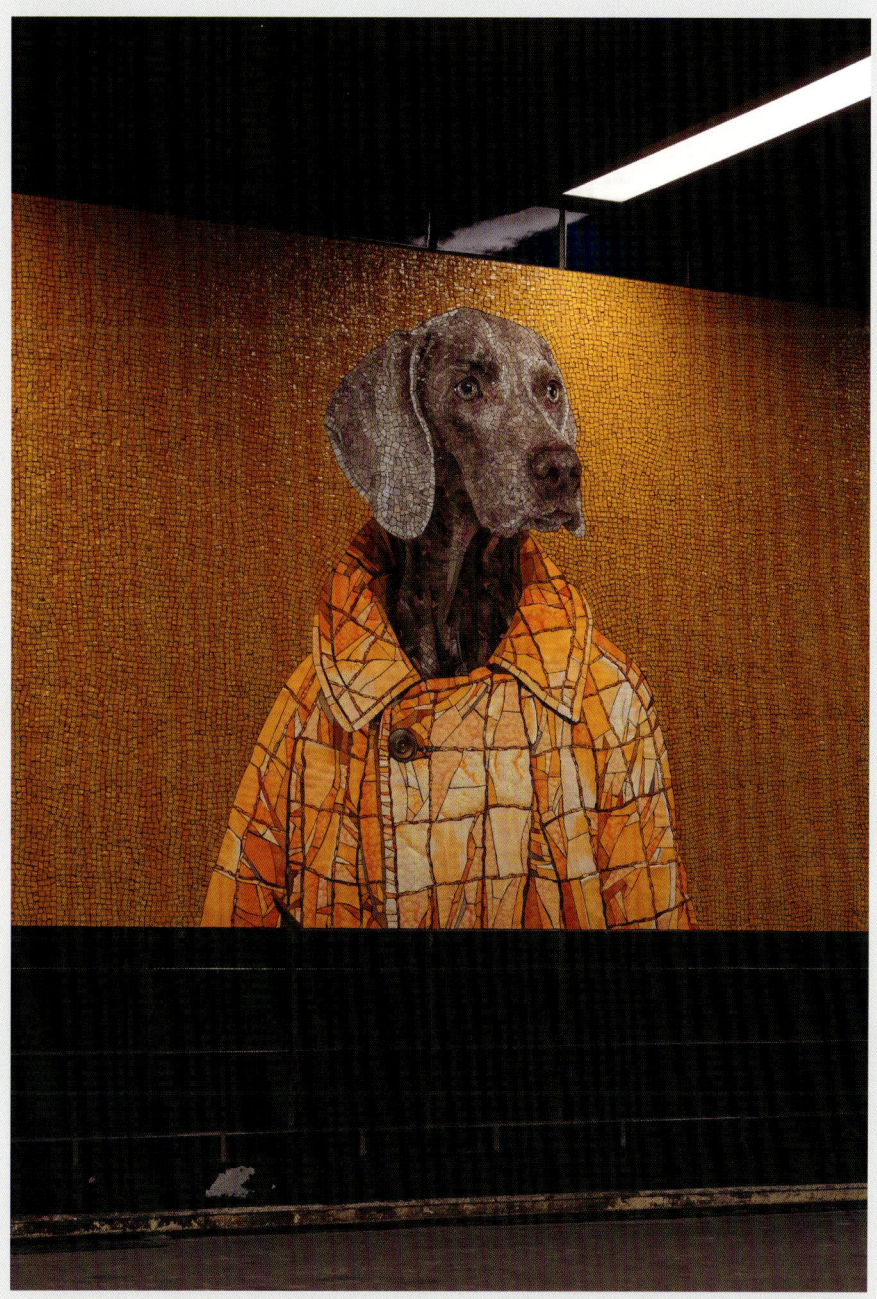

Milan, Italy | New York City, USA

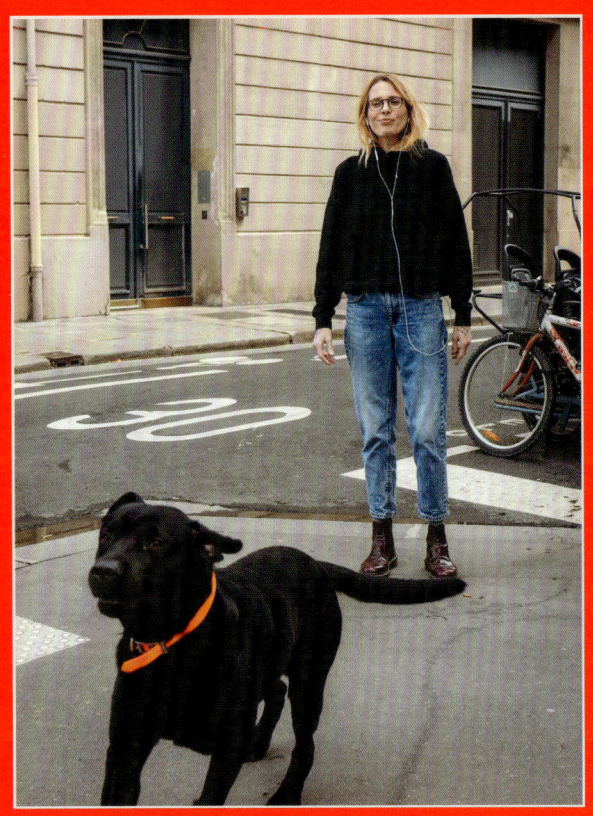

"She's really funny and tries to be happy.
But sometimes she gets really pissed off."

Marion and their dog Sonic
Paris, France

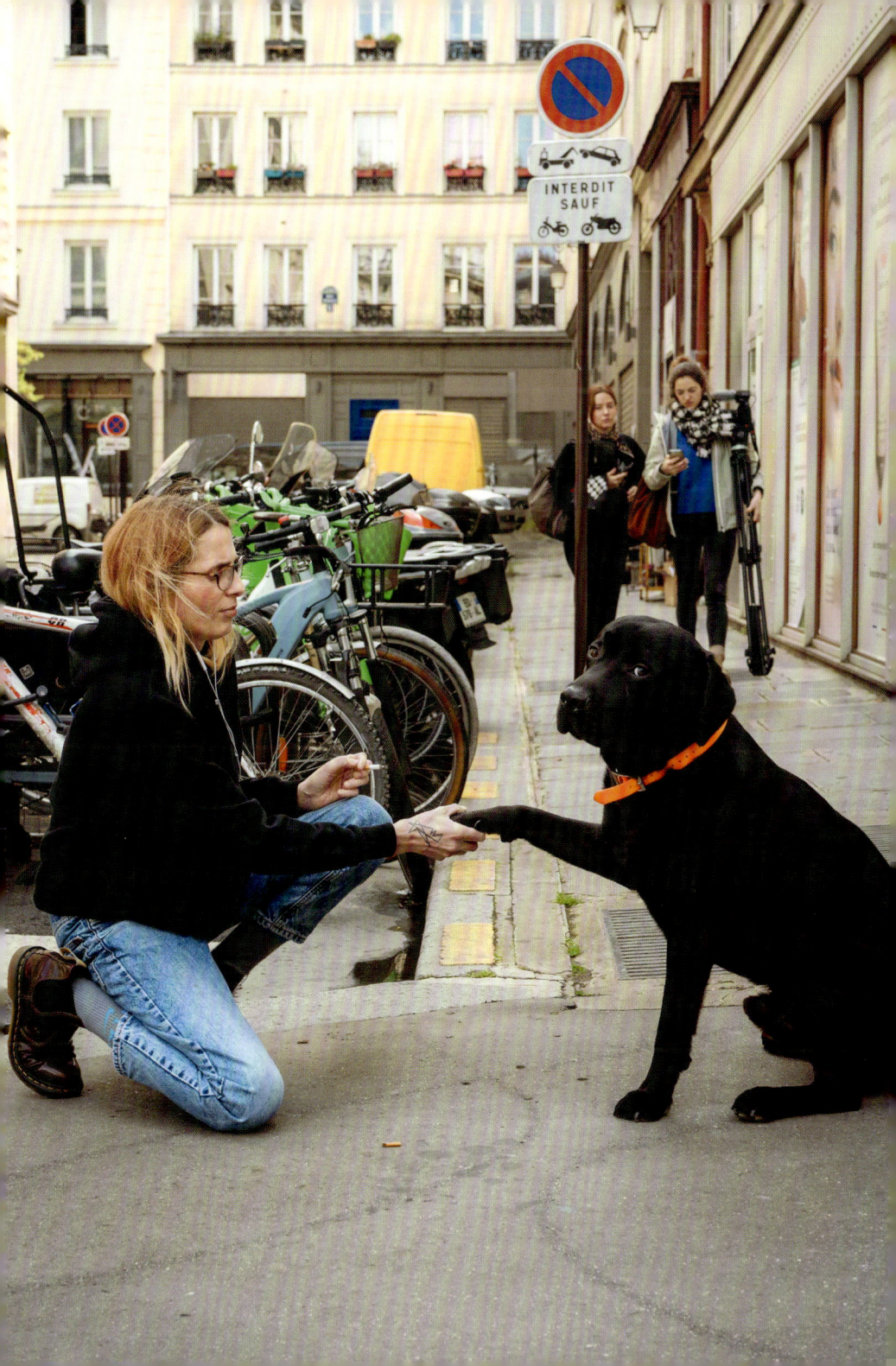

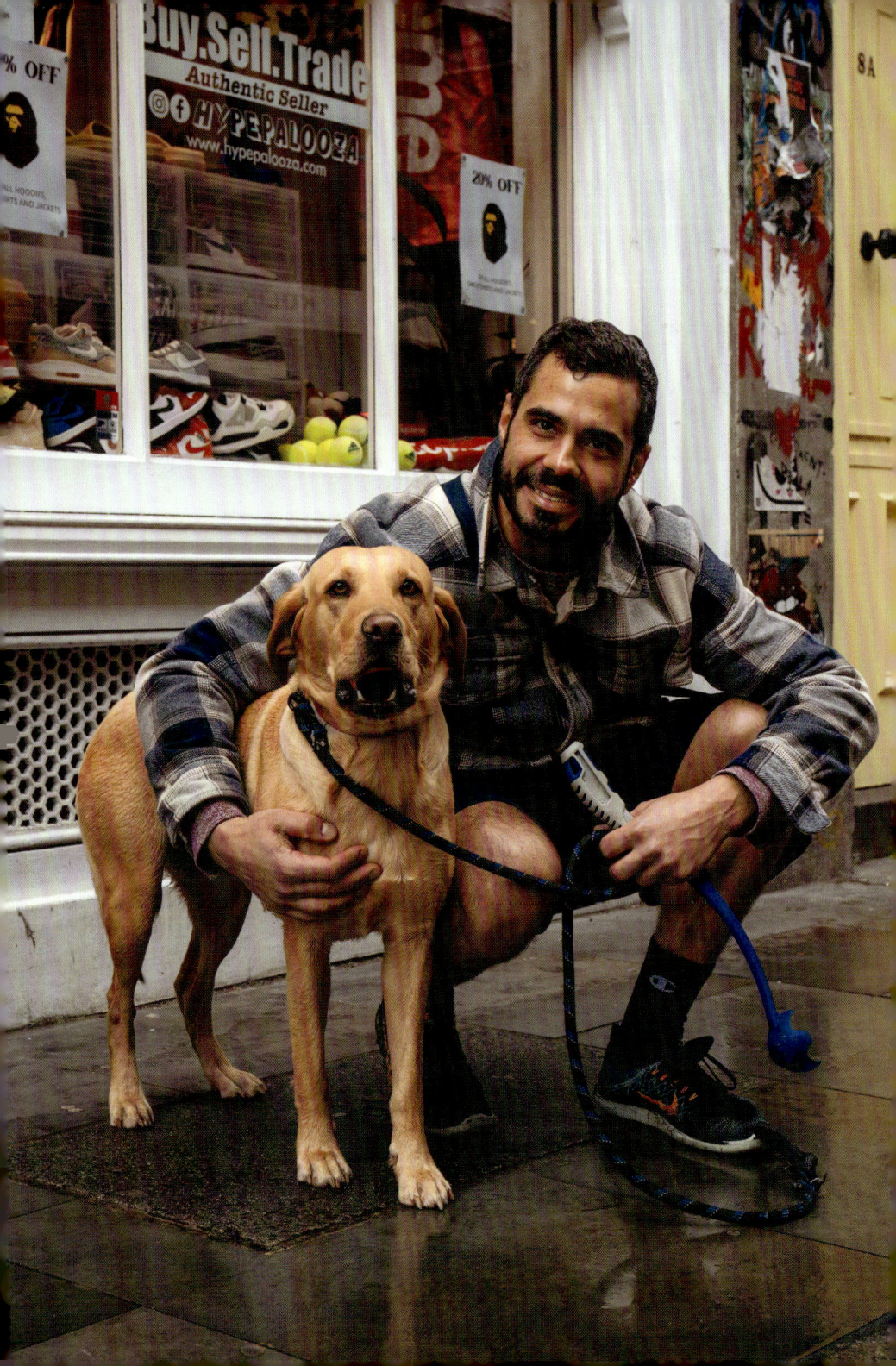

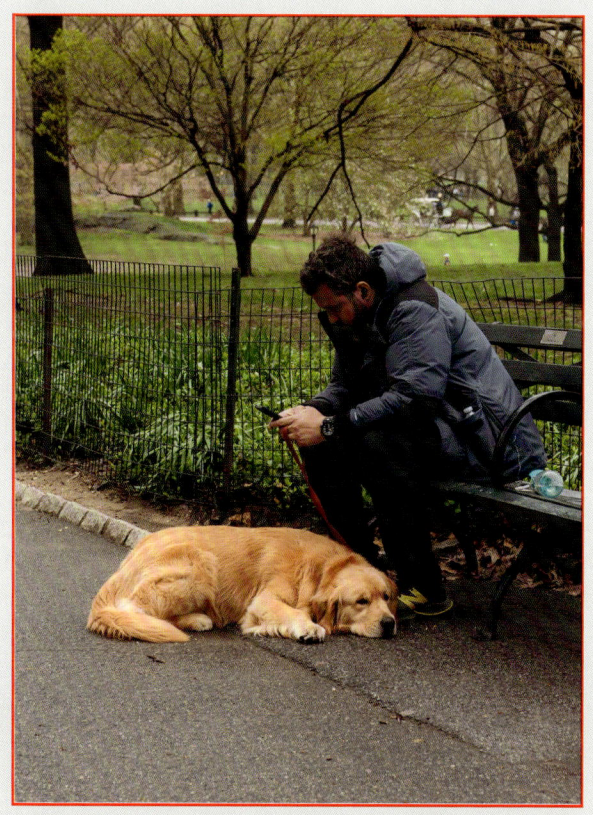

New York City, USA

"I can be a bit tough on her sometimes, but that's just me and my stress."

Fransisco and their dog Betsy
London, England

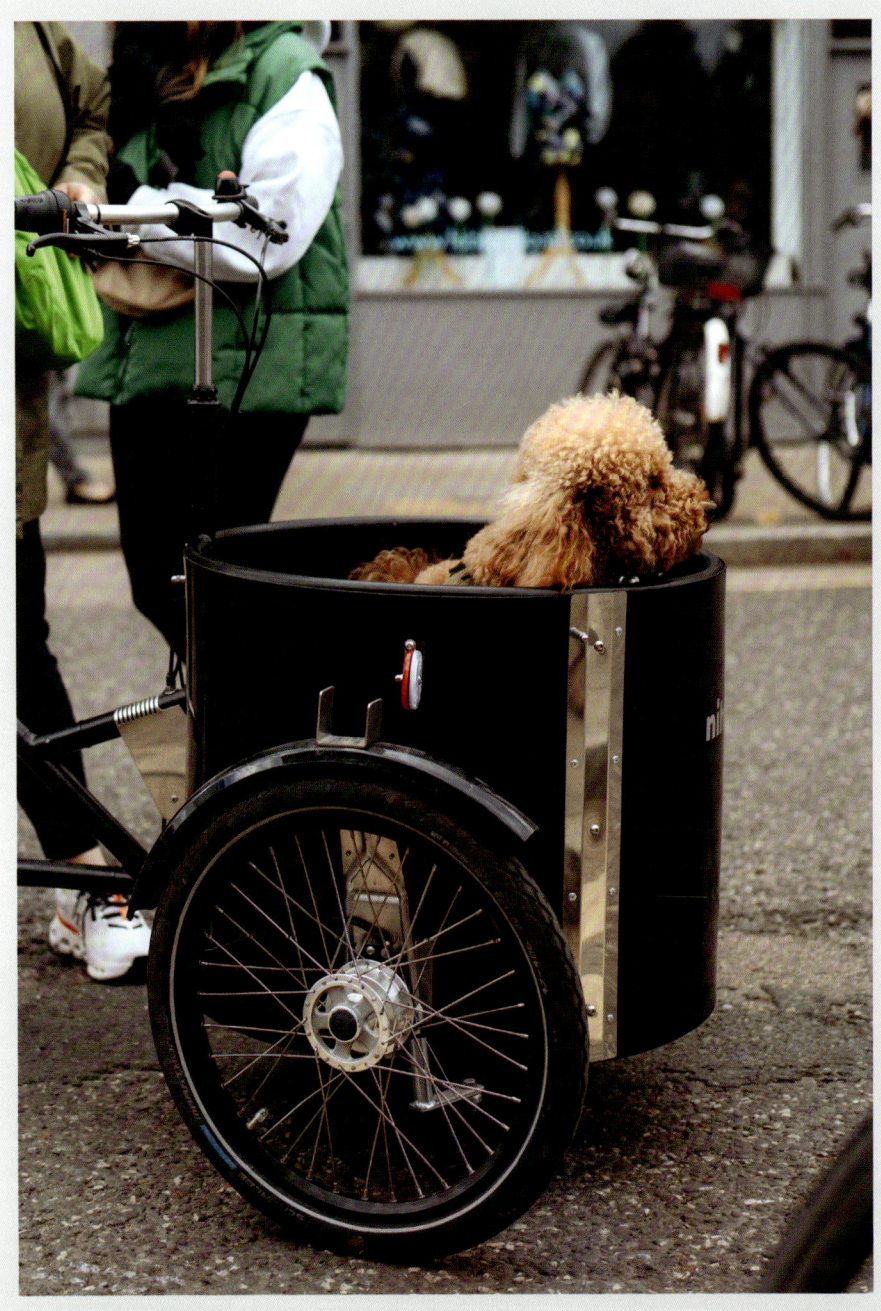

London, England | Tokyo, Japan

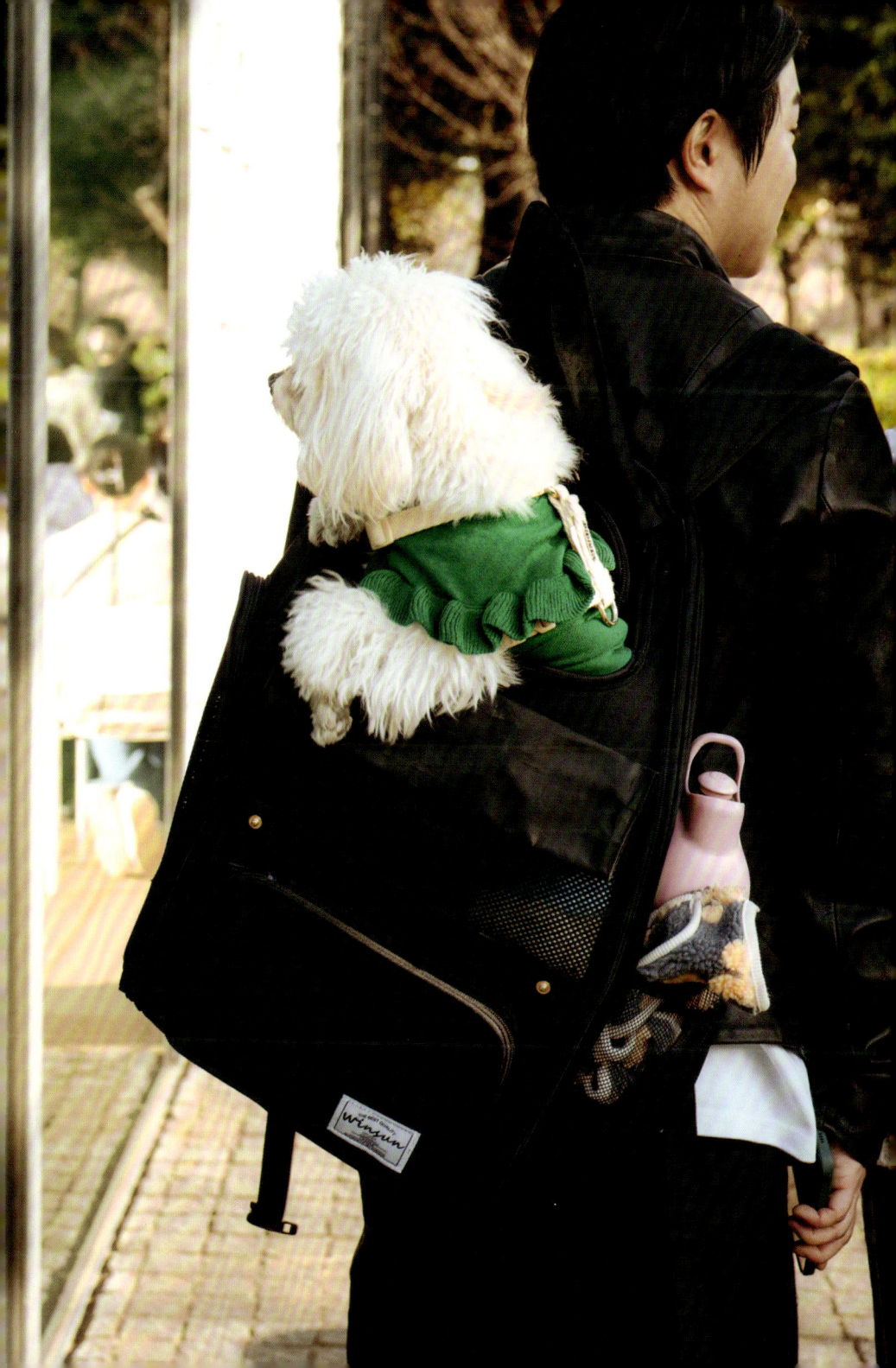

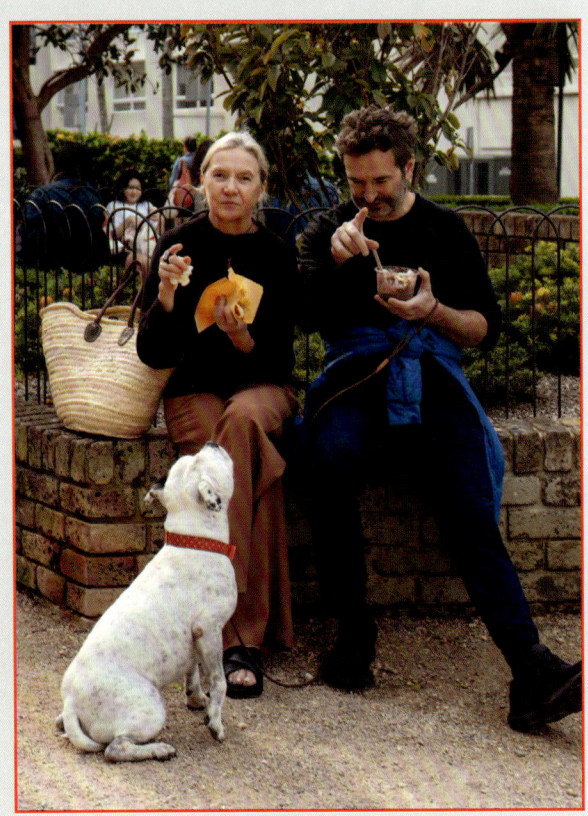

Sydney, Australia

"He's always looking for his next meal. He loves my mom, we call her the food lady."

Fernanda and their dog Toulouse
New York City, USA

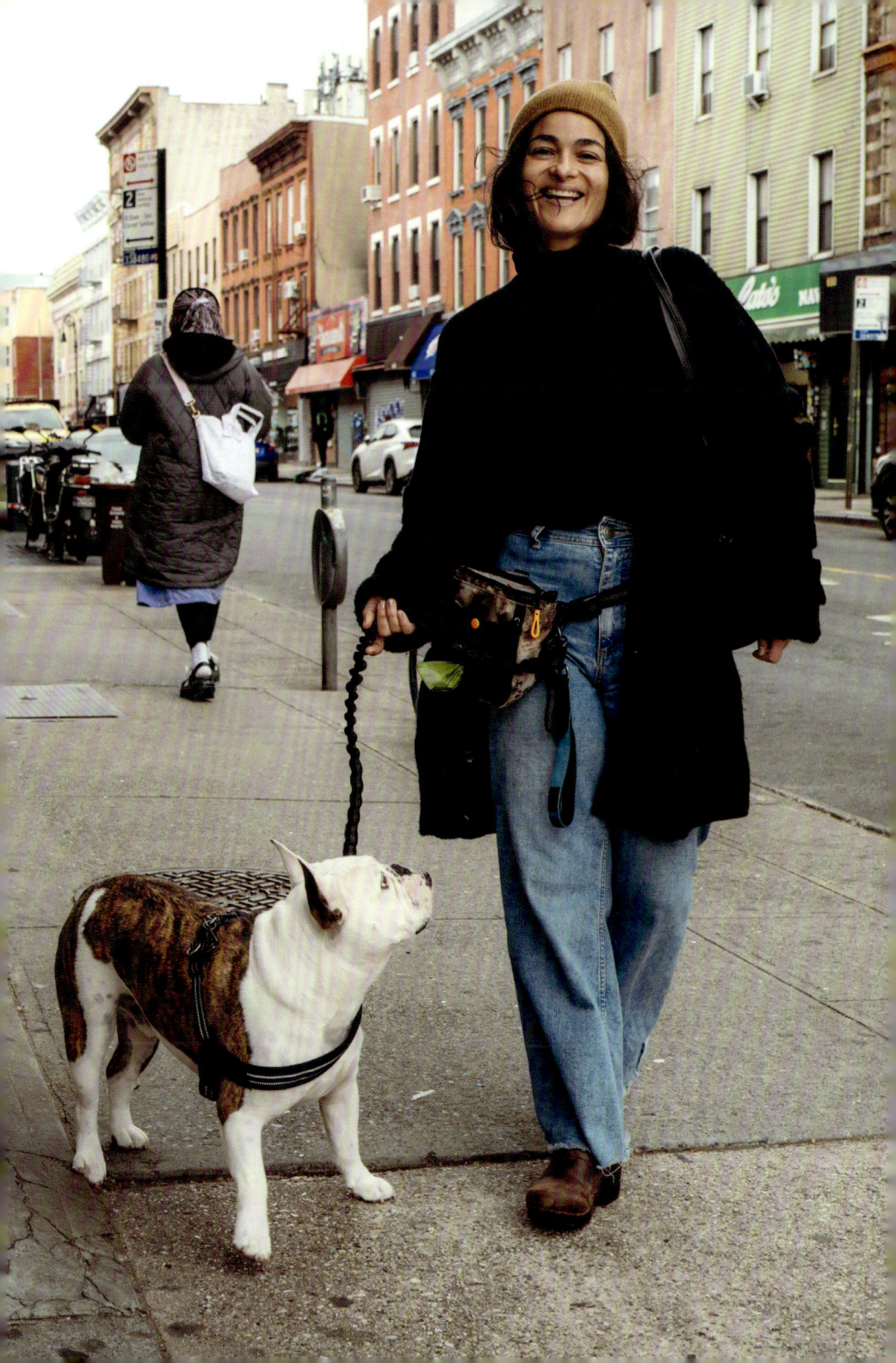

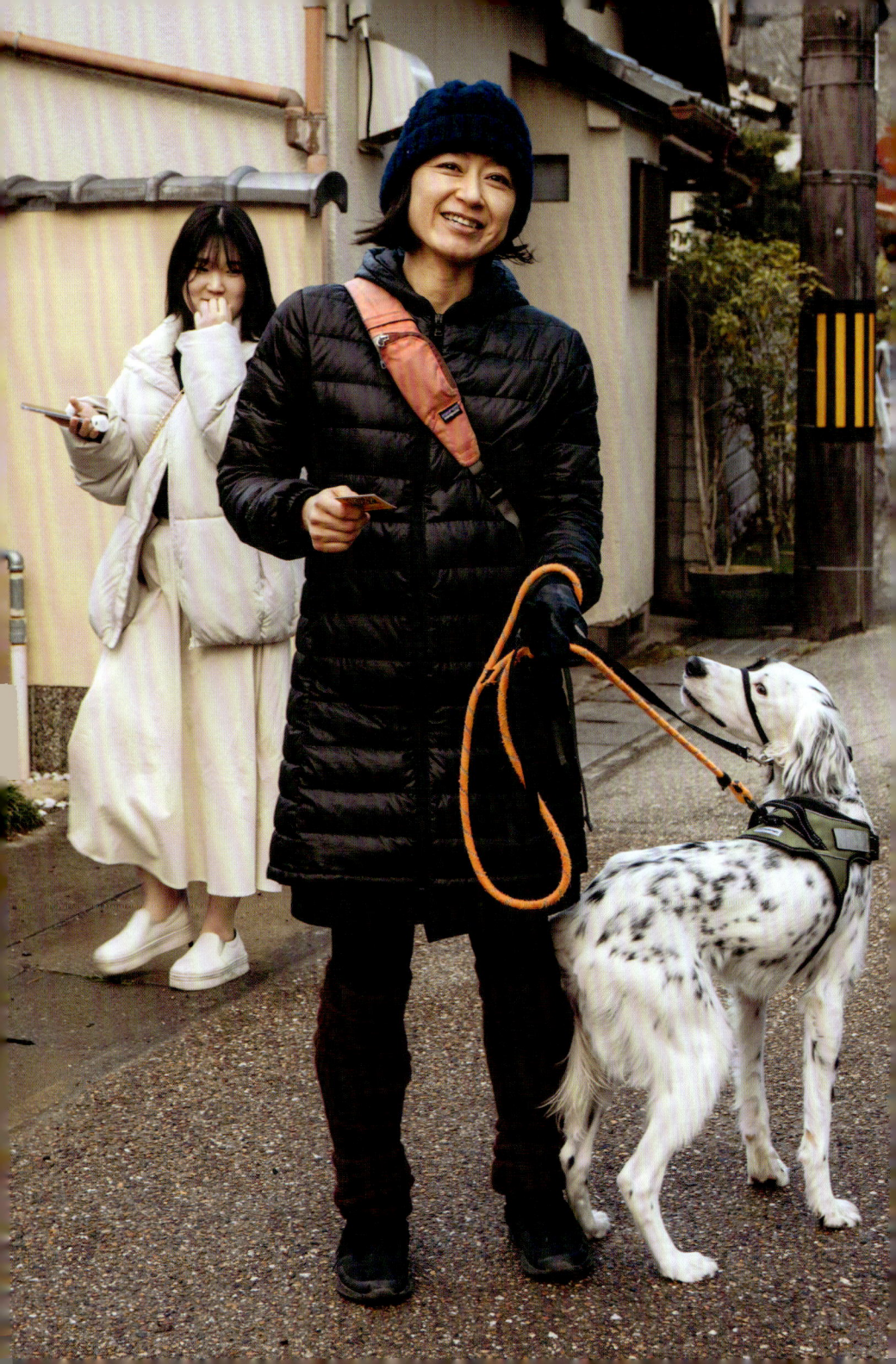

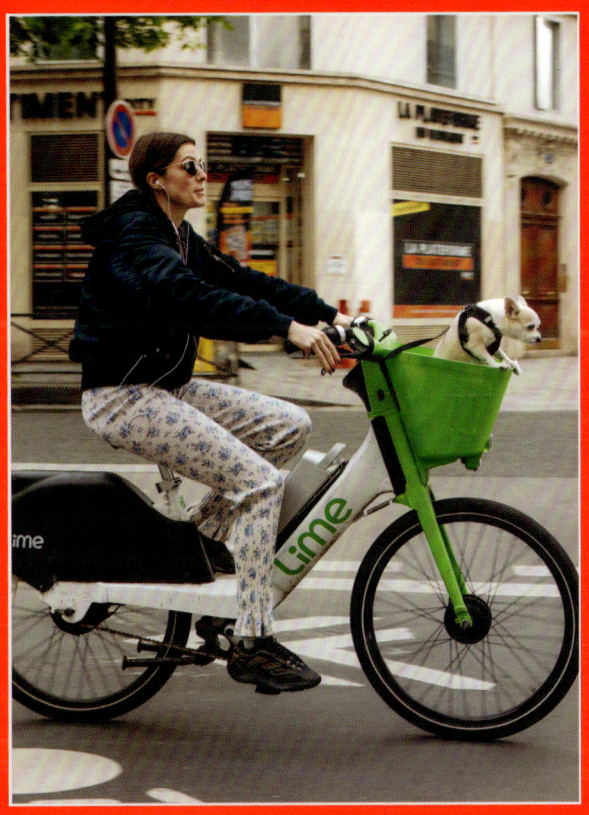

Paris, France

"She likes to go her way,
I'm just along for the ride."

Ryoko and their dog Yukichi
Kyoto, Japan

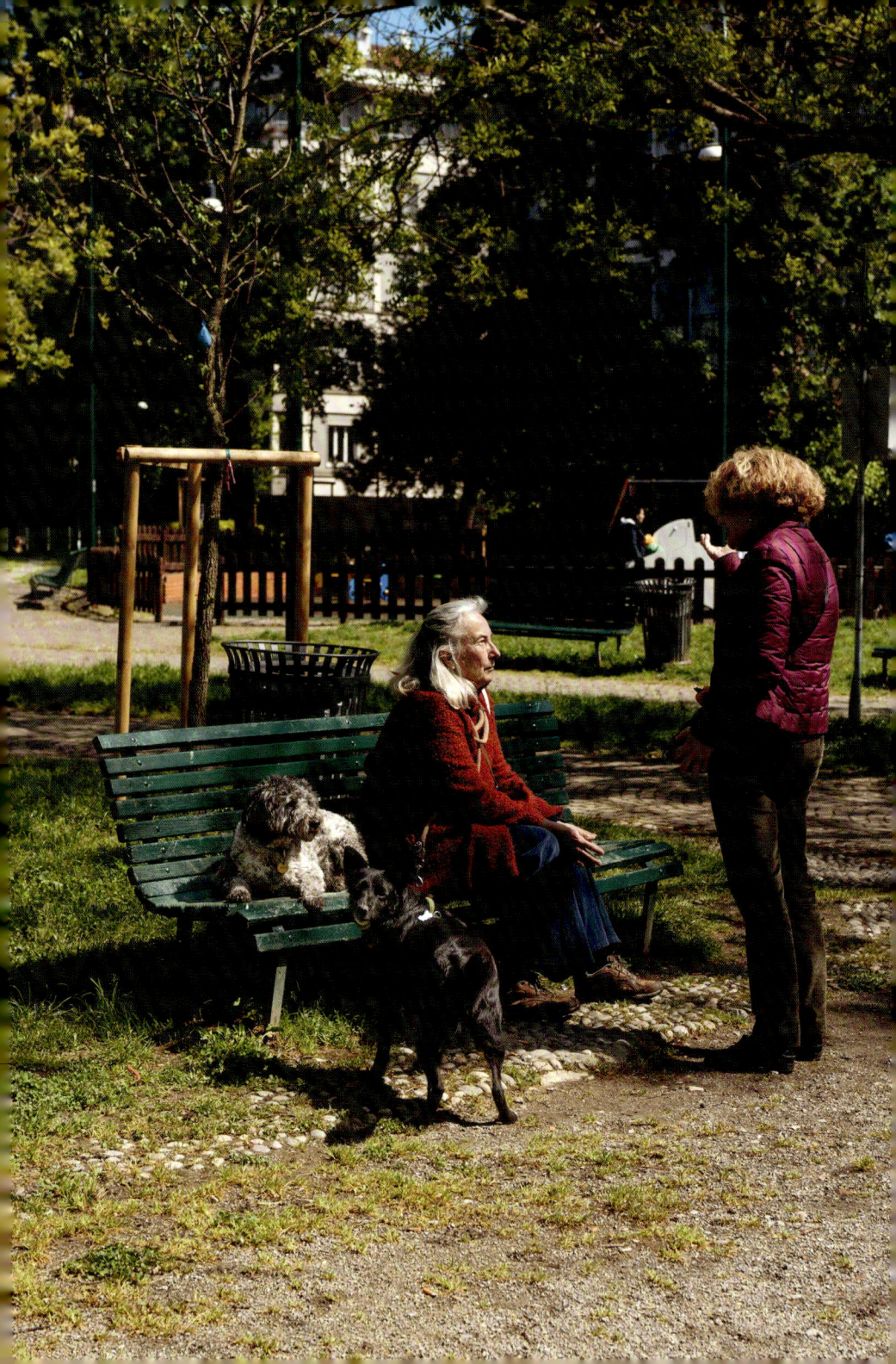

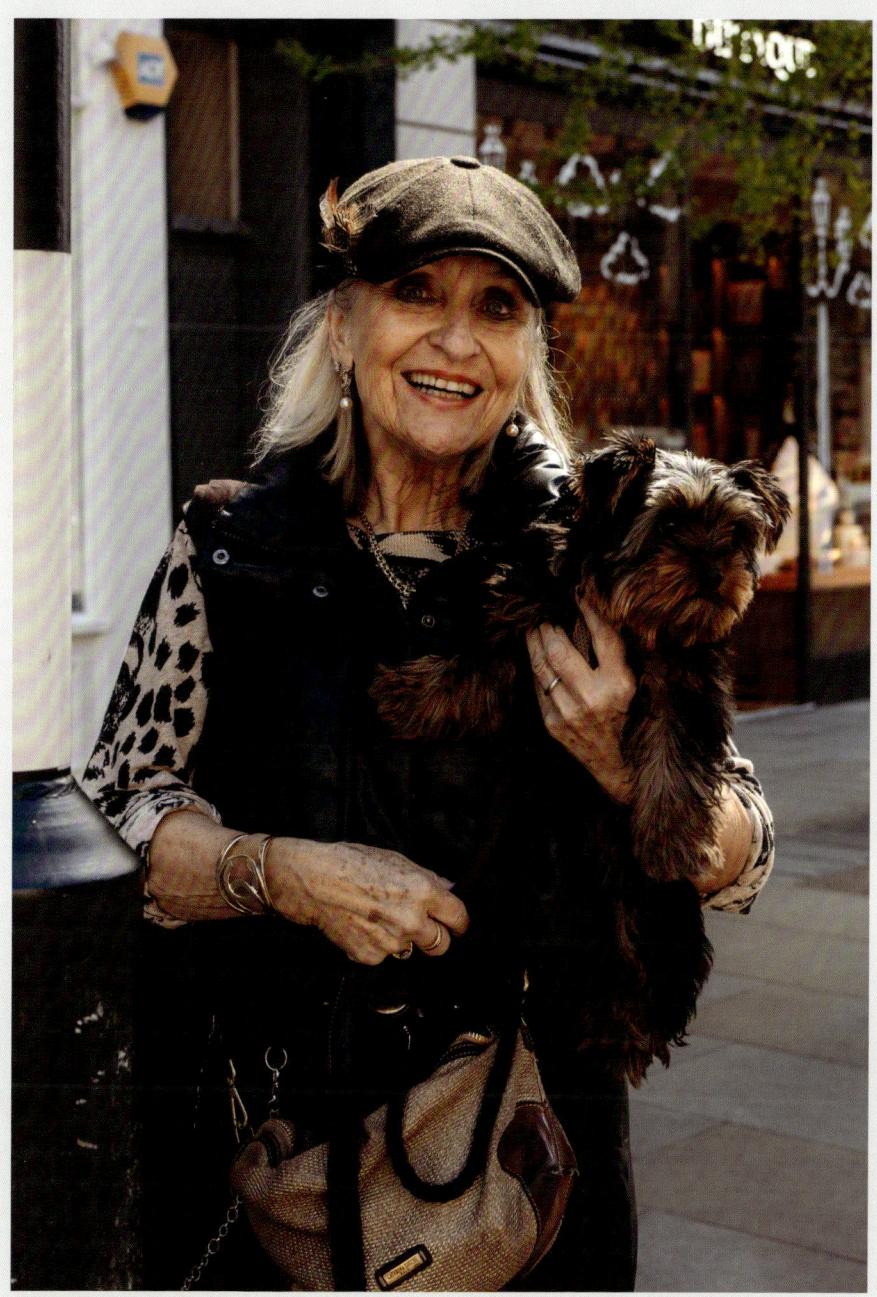

Milan, Italy | London, England

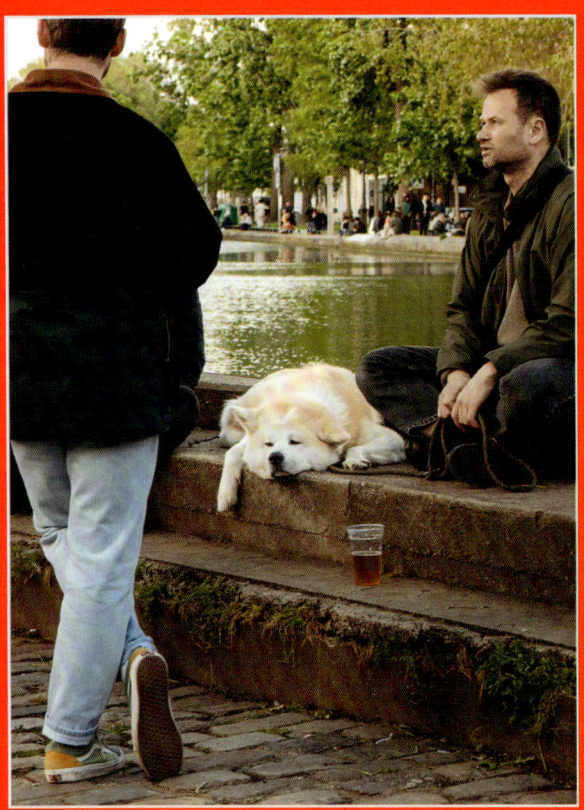

Paris, France

"She thinks I'm lazy. I know it."

Giovanni and their dog Leila
Milan, Italy

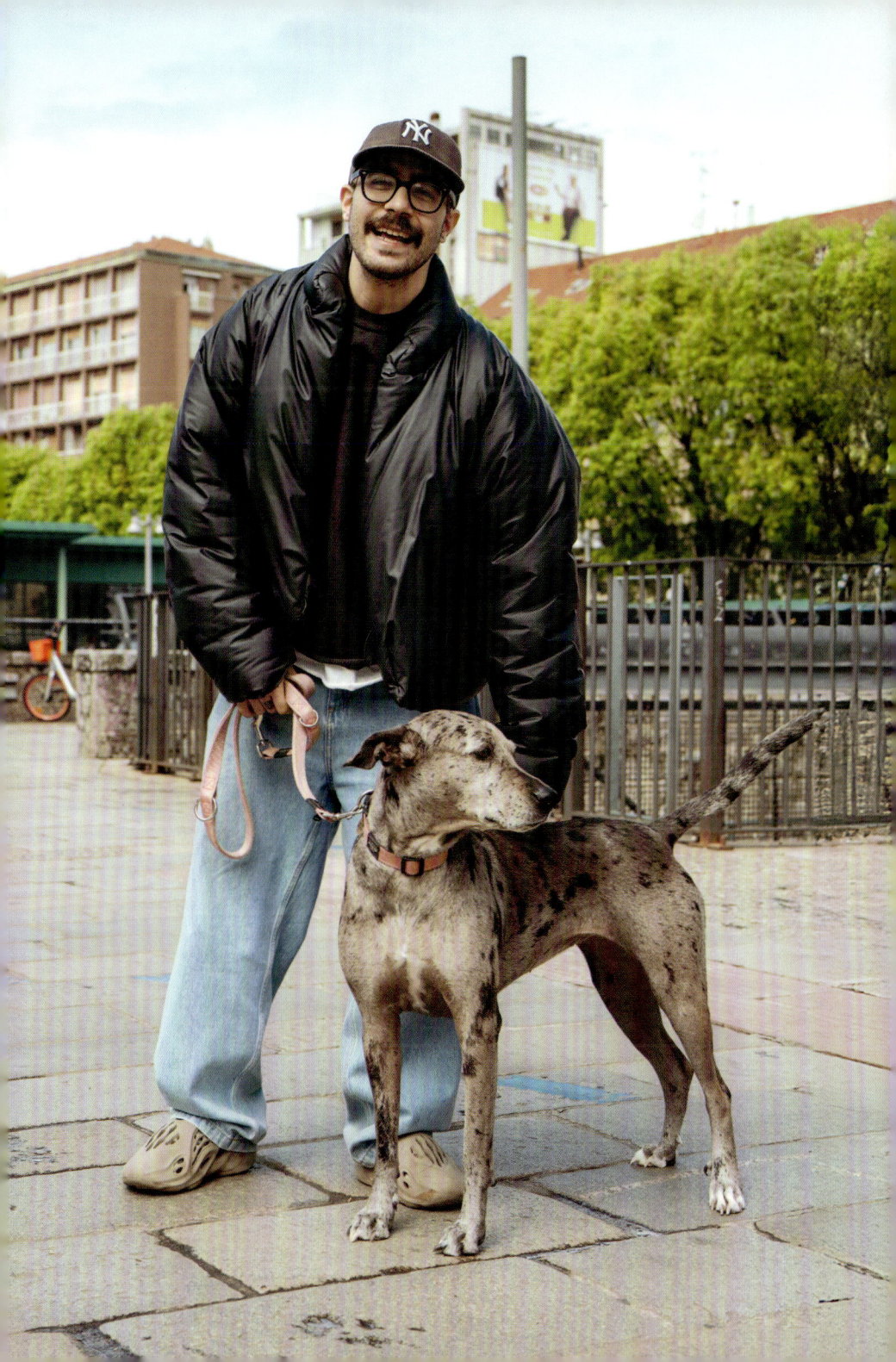

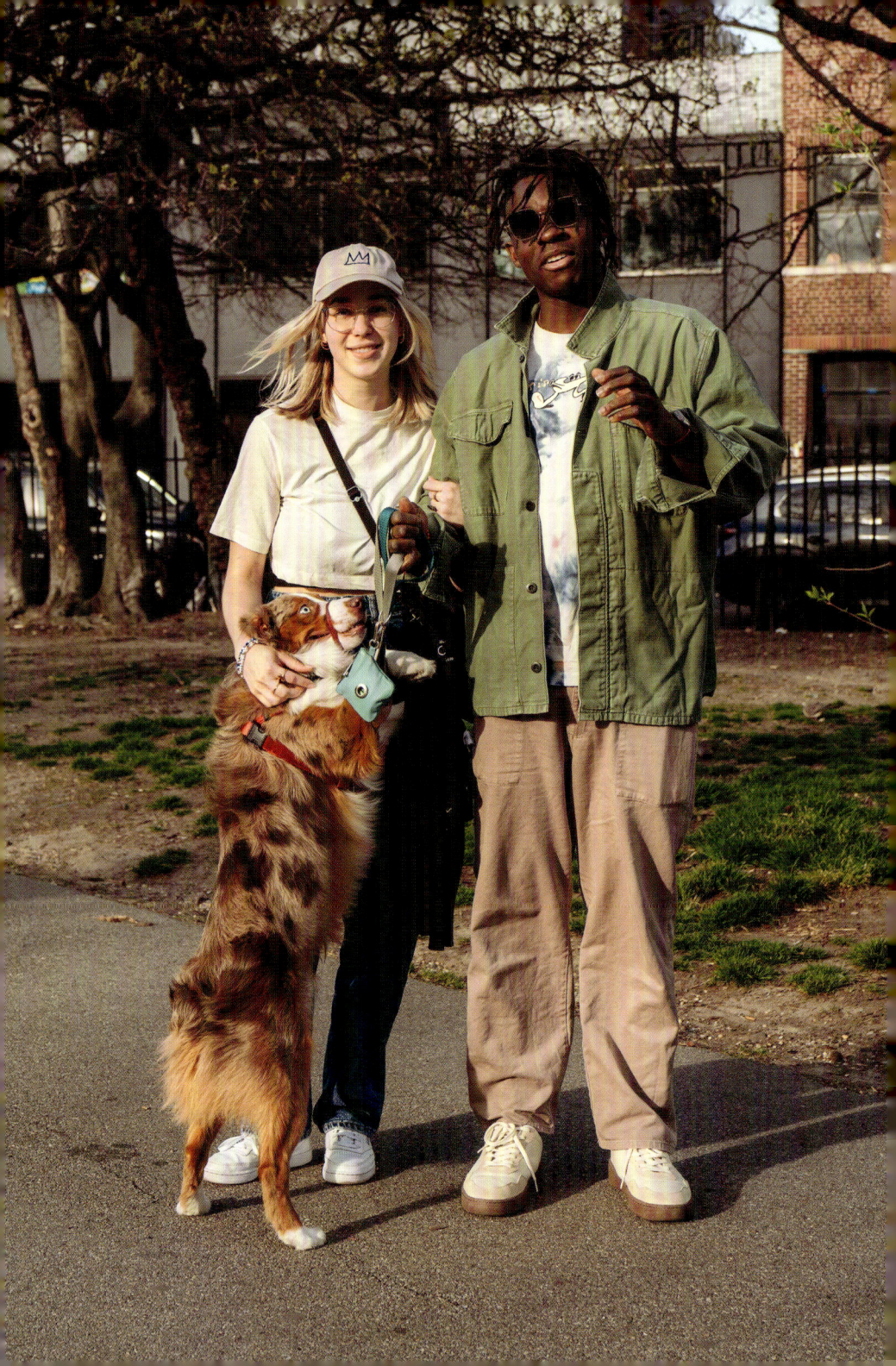

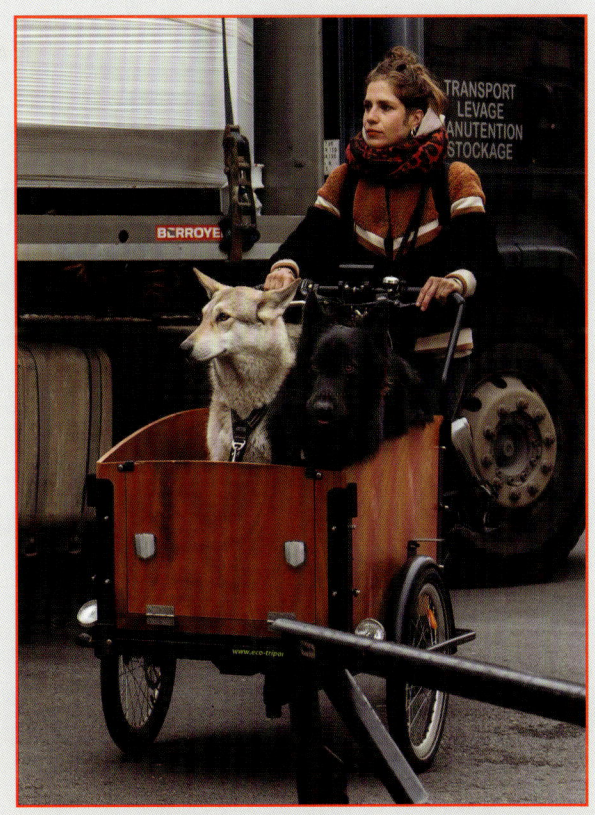

"I'm either a tyrant or a king."

Yohan and Sasha and their dog Jasper
New York City, USA

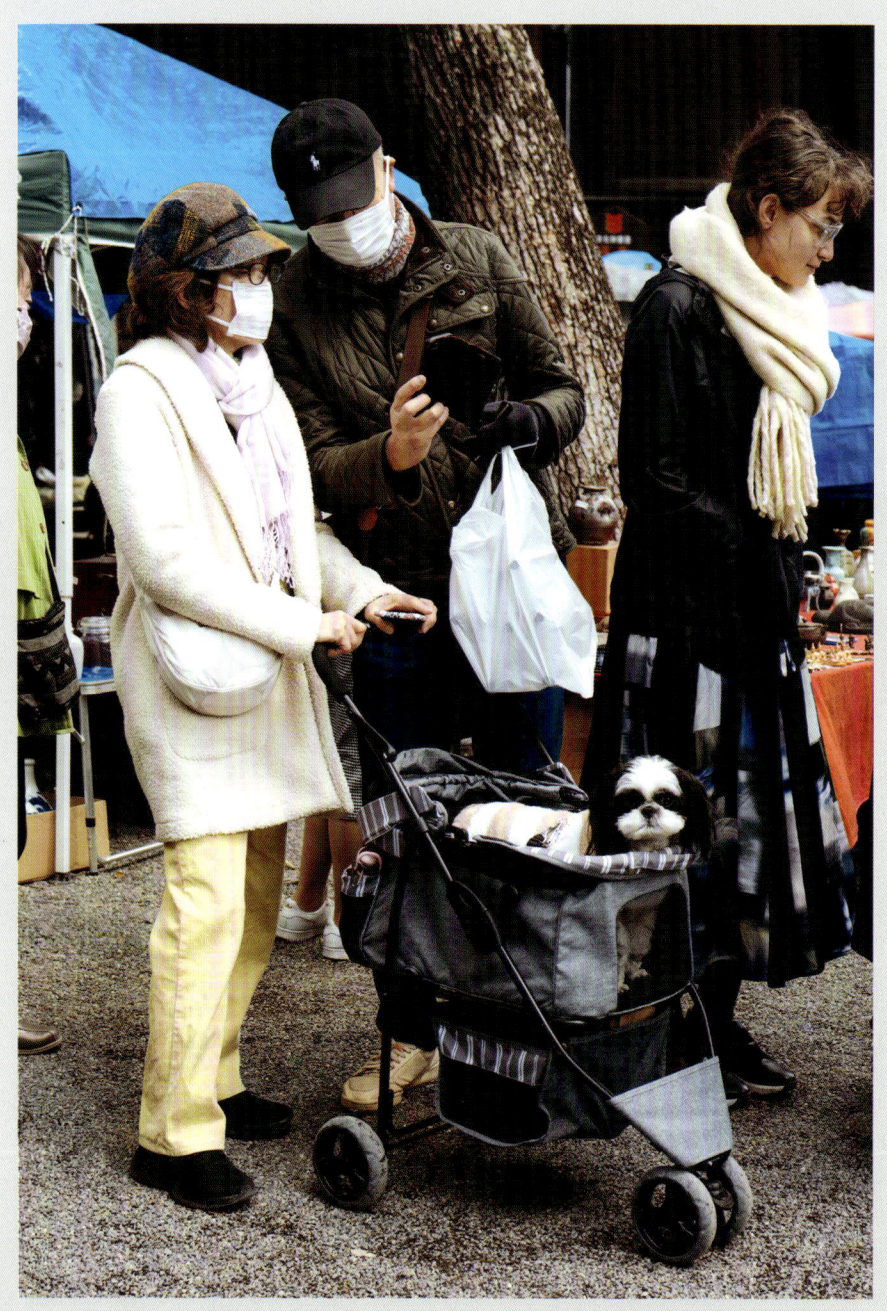

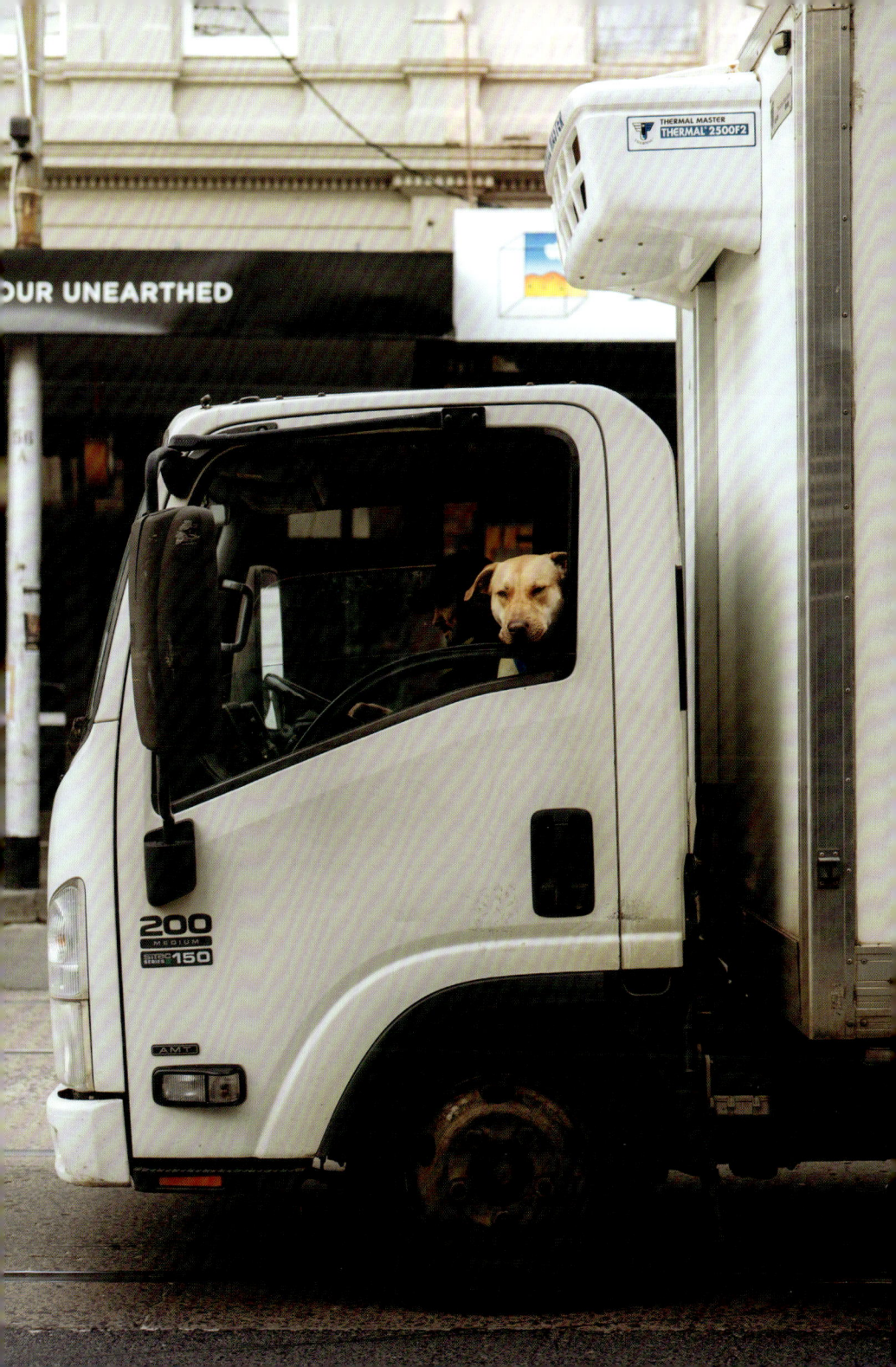

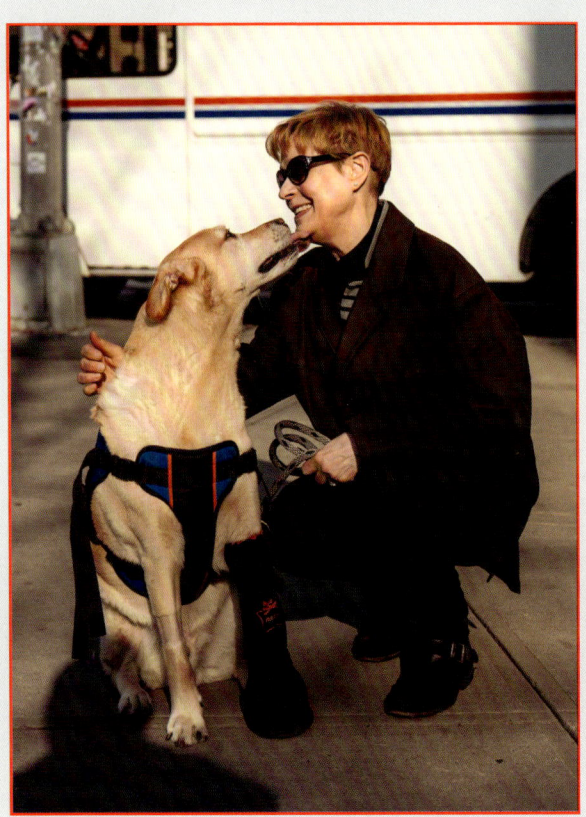

New York City, USA

"I know he loves me,
he tells me everyday!"

Narek and their dog Pablo
London, England

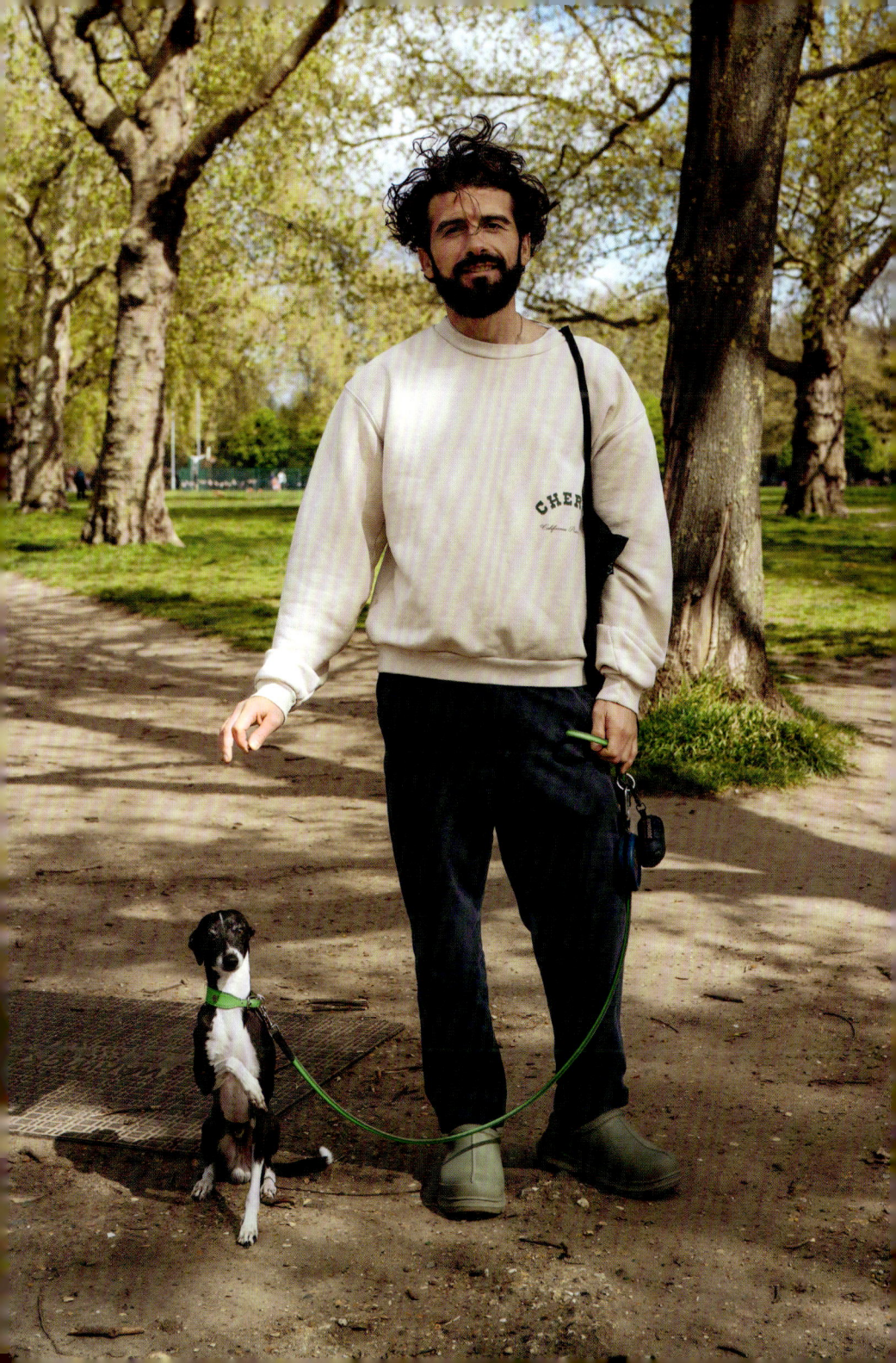

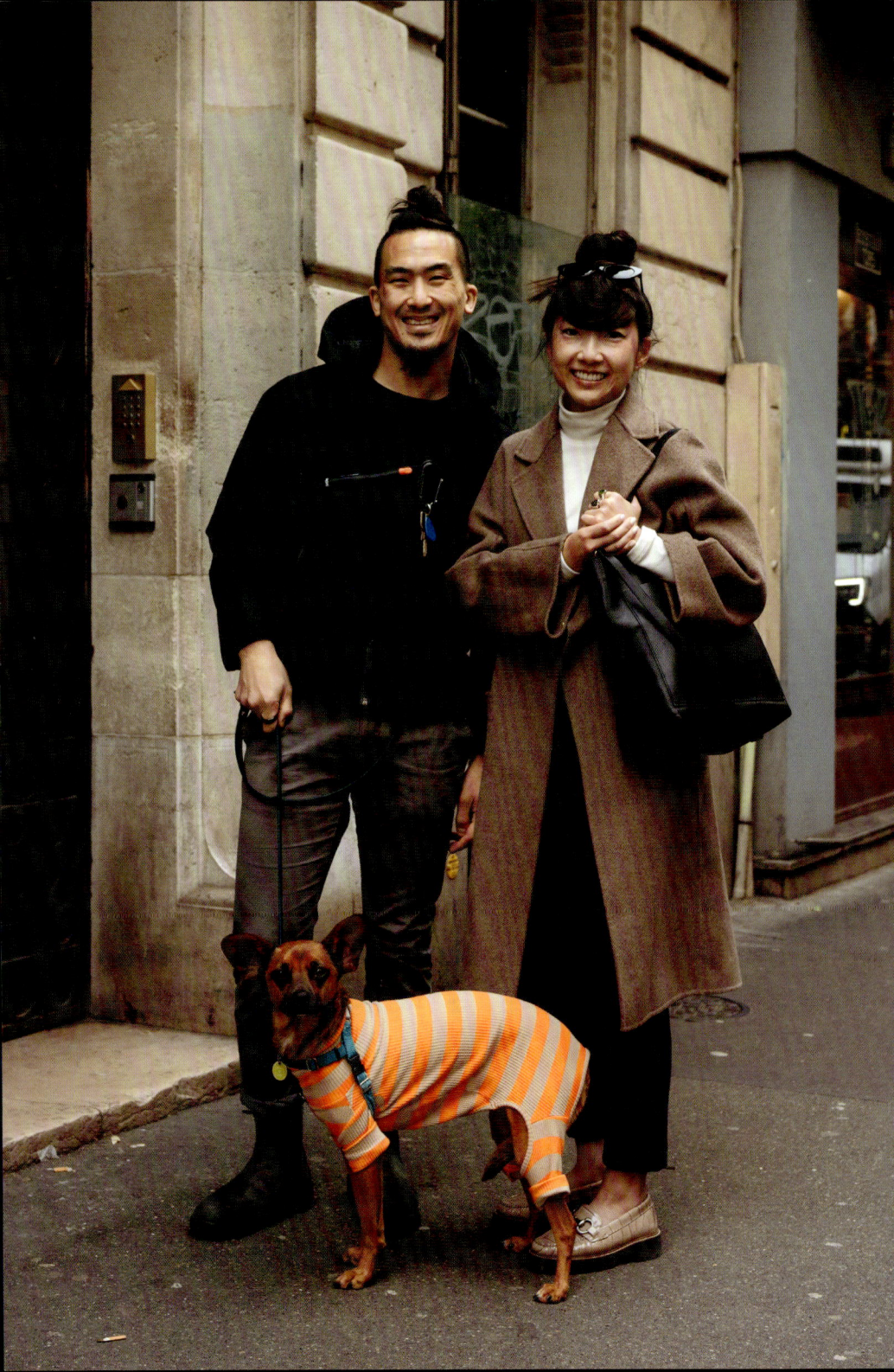

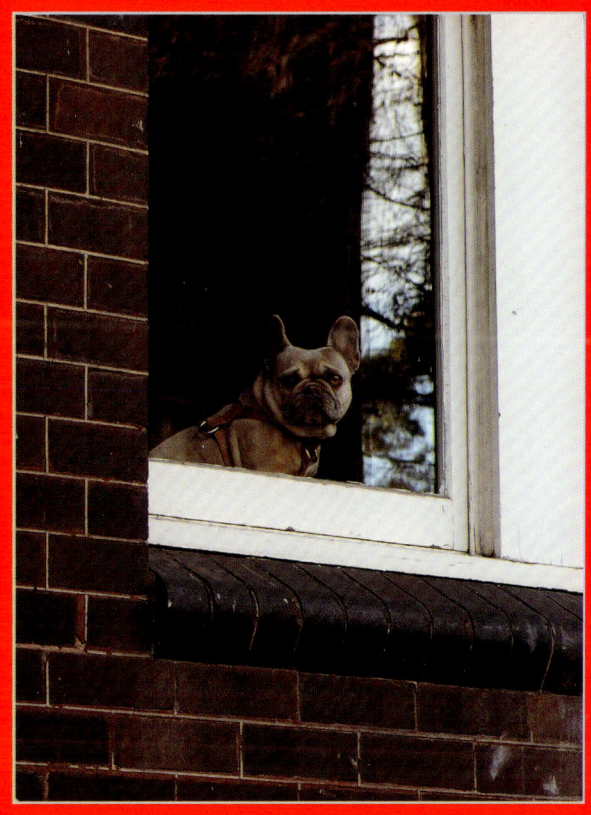

Sydney, Australia

"He doesn't like Paris. He's very introverted, and would rather always be at home with us, and no one else."

Amy and Frank and their dog Speck
Paris, France

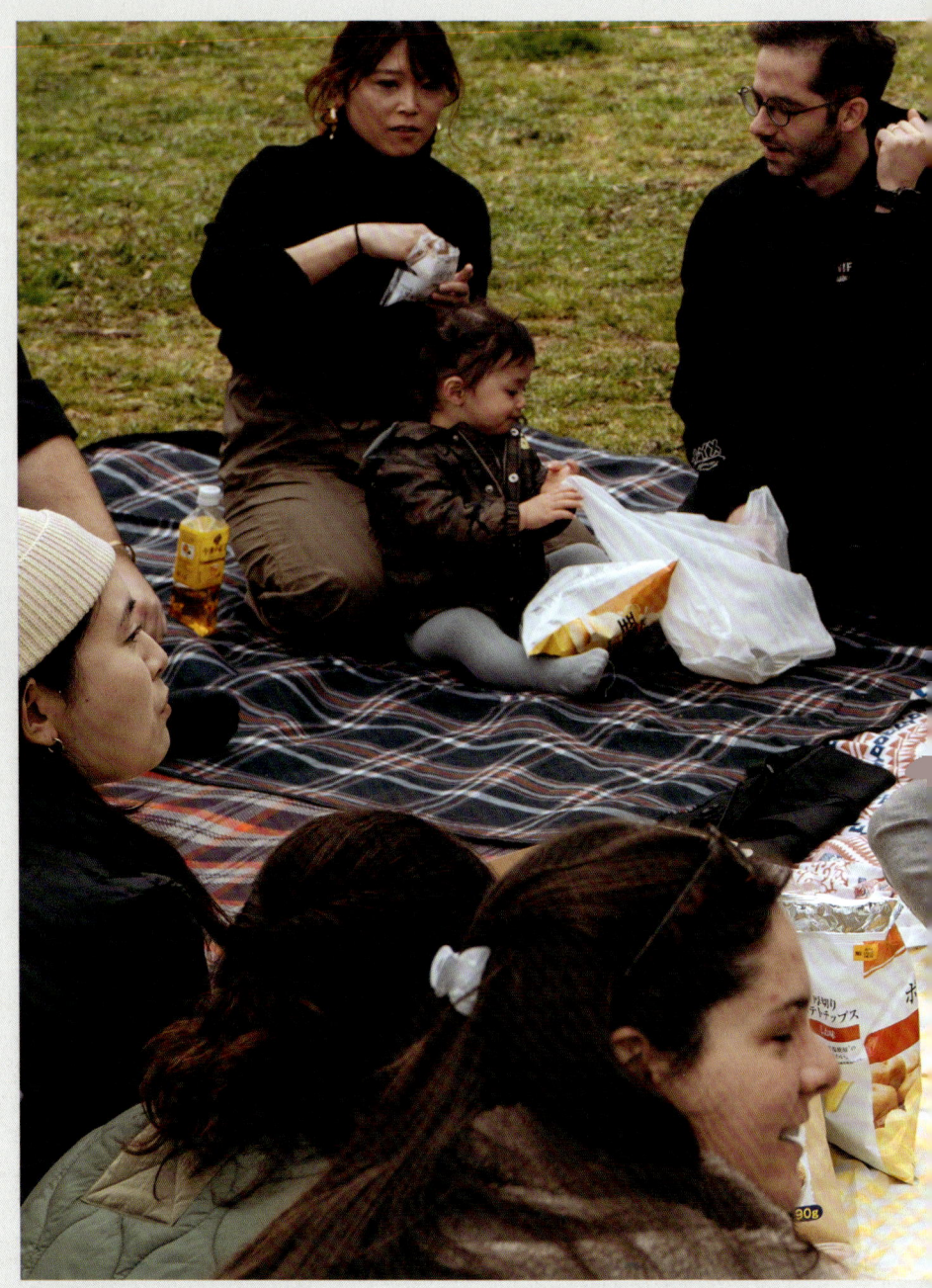

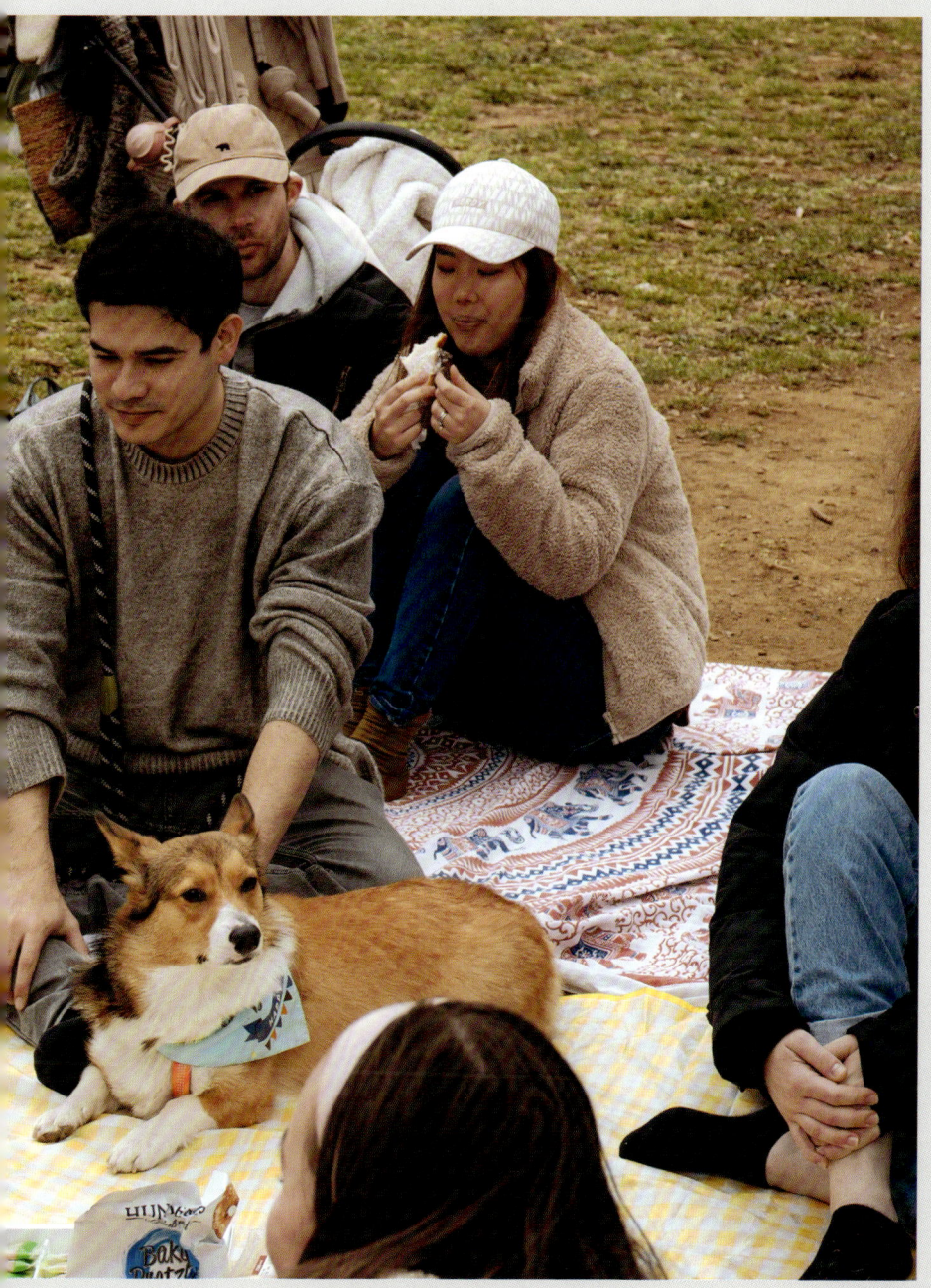

Tokyo, Japan

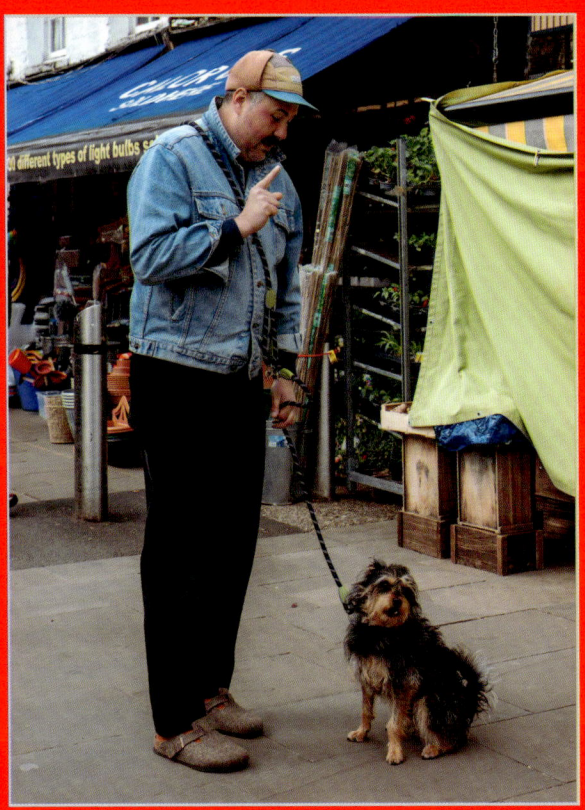

London, England

"He talks a lot, he's very talkative.
Always asking for food."

Mae and their dog Oliver
Paris, France

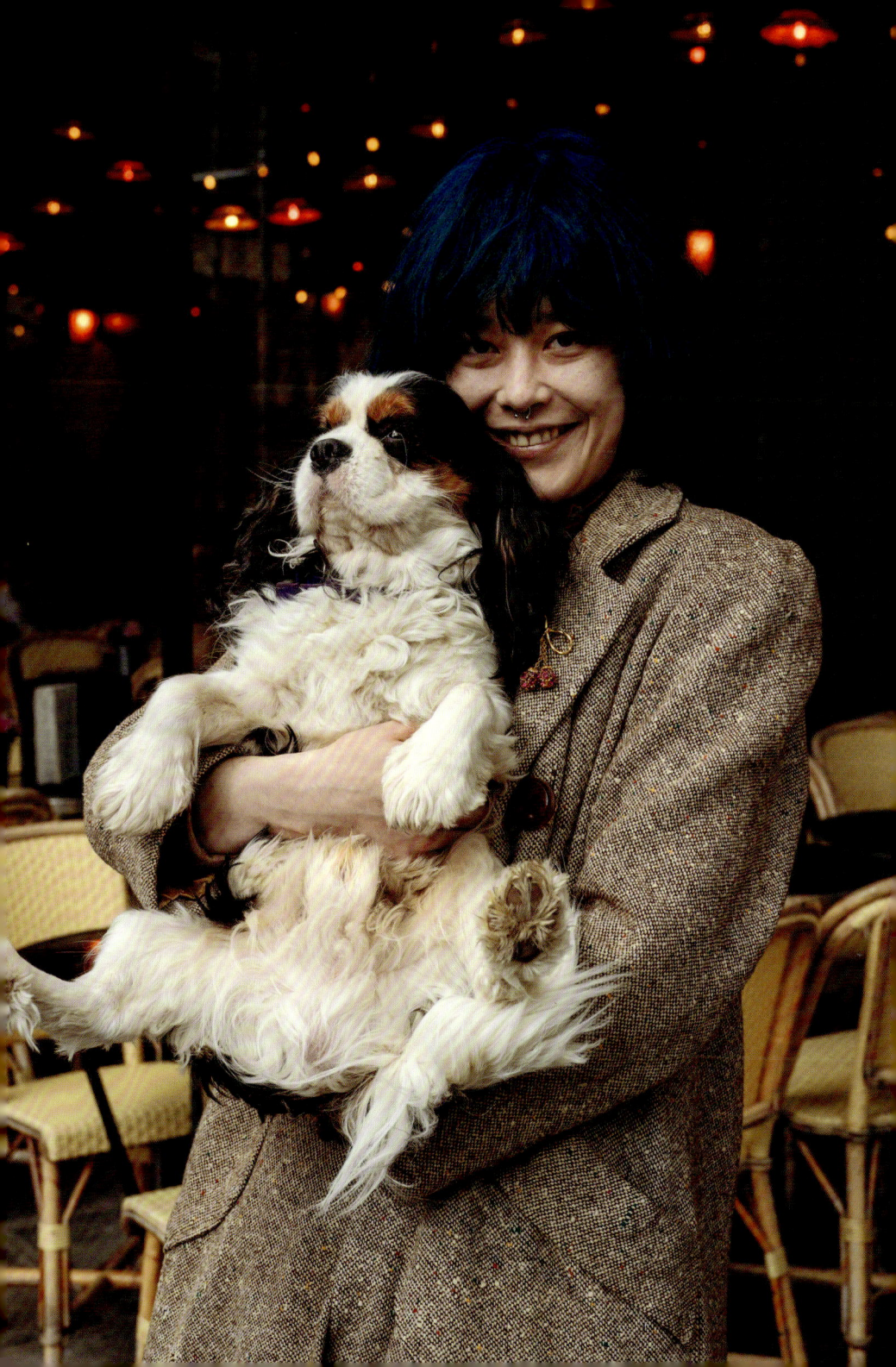

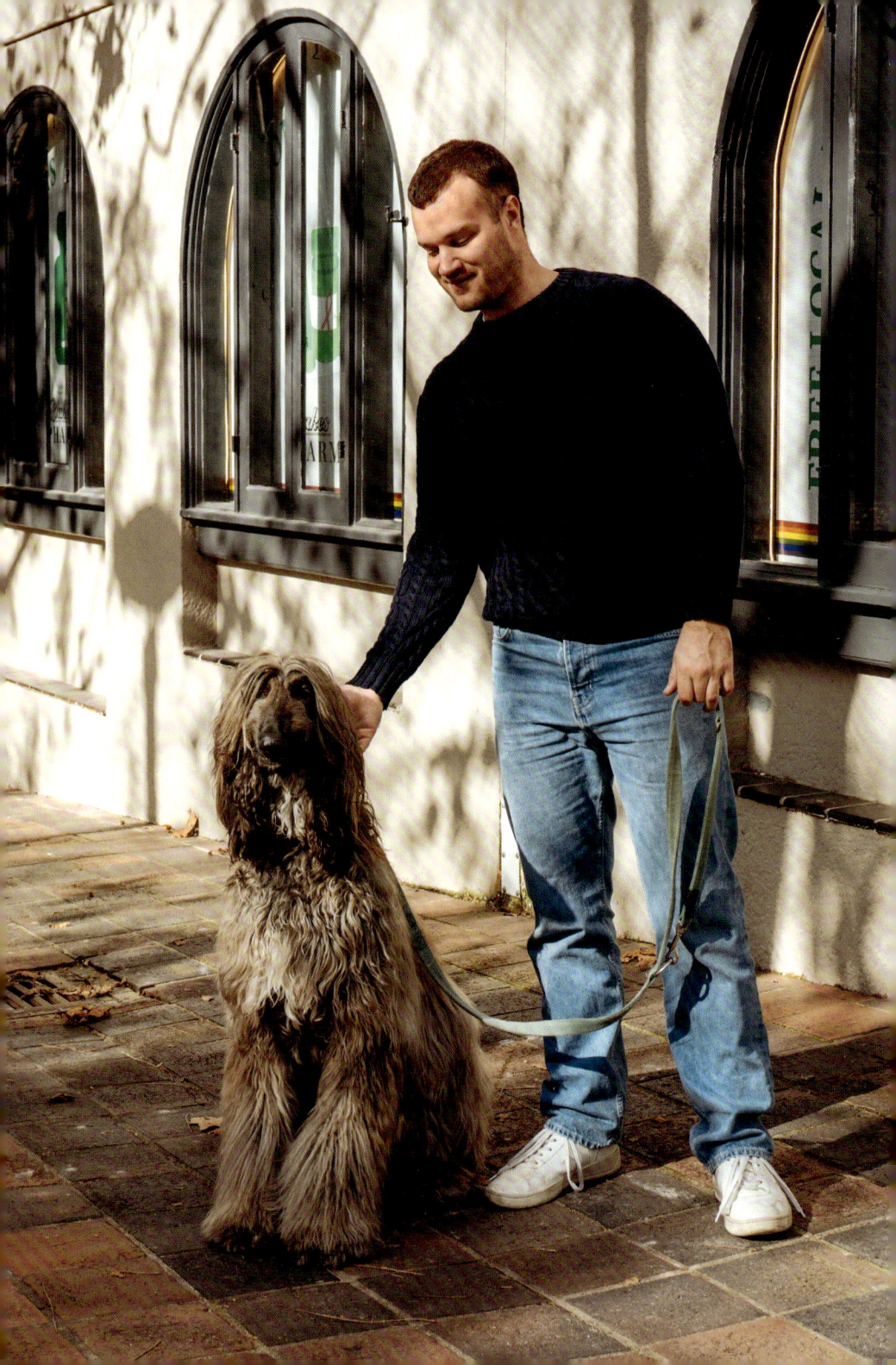

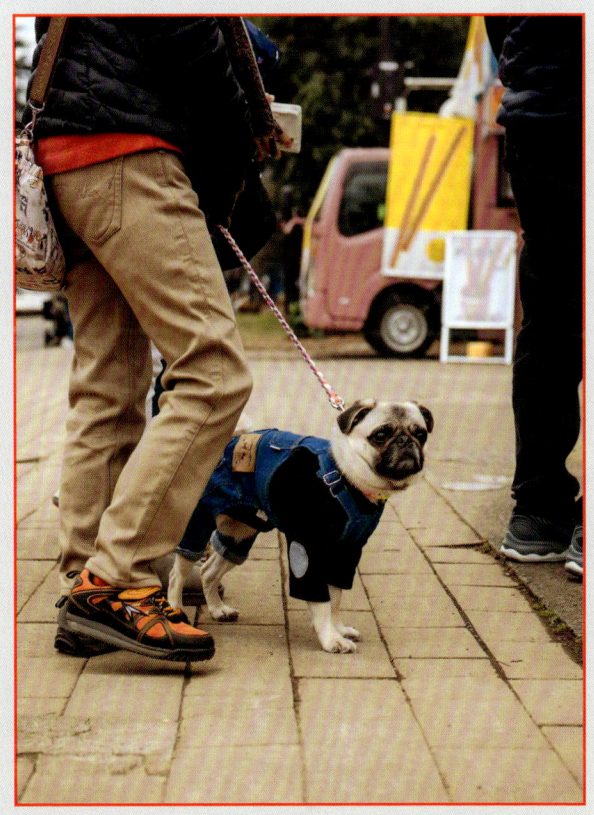

Tokyo, Japan

"He's very judgmental. I don't even want to know what he thinks of me."

Henry and their dog Freddie
Sydney, Australia

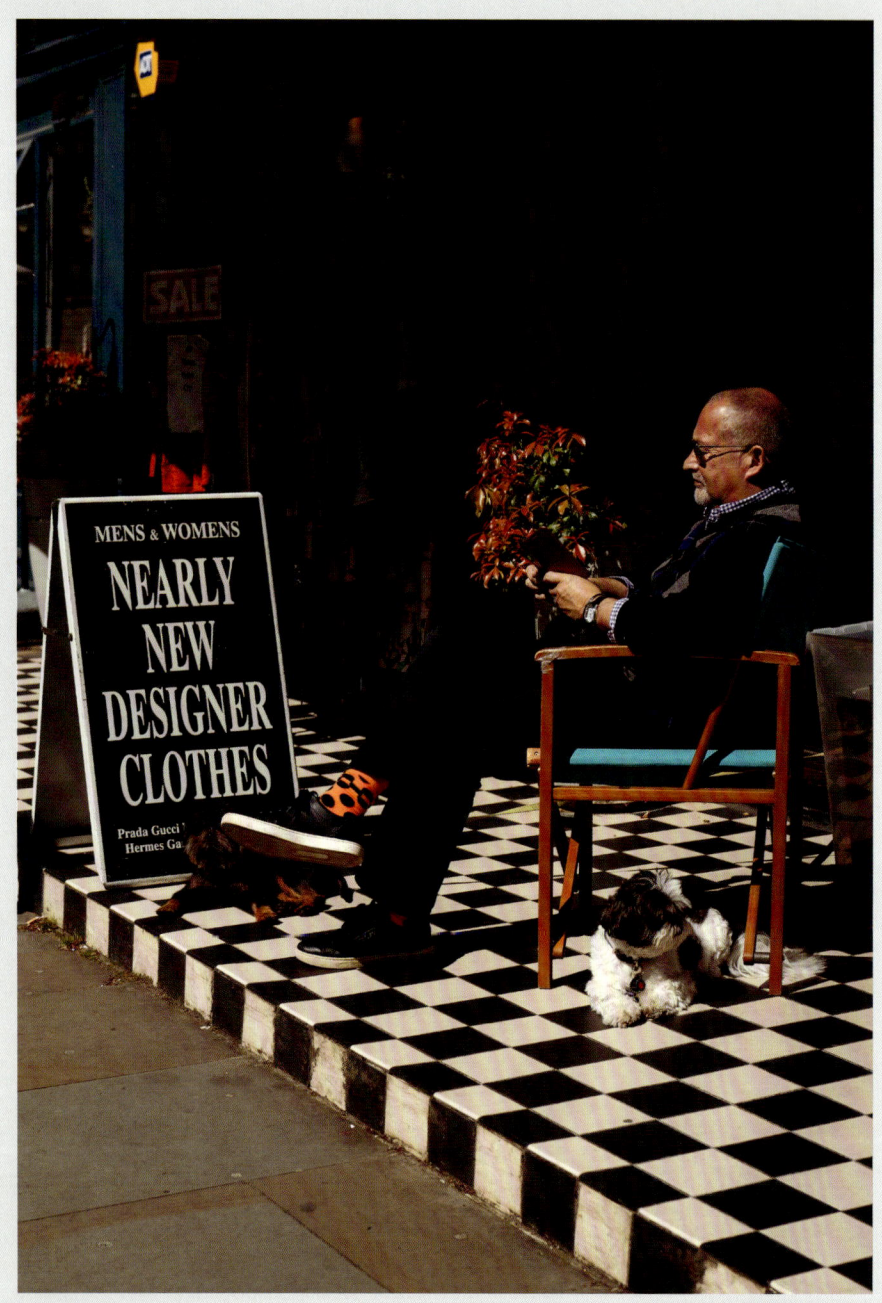

London, England | New York City, USA

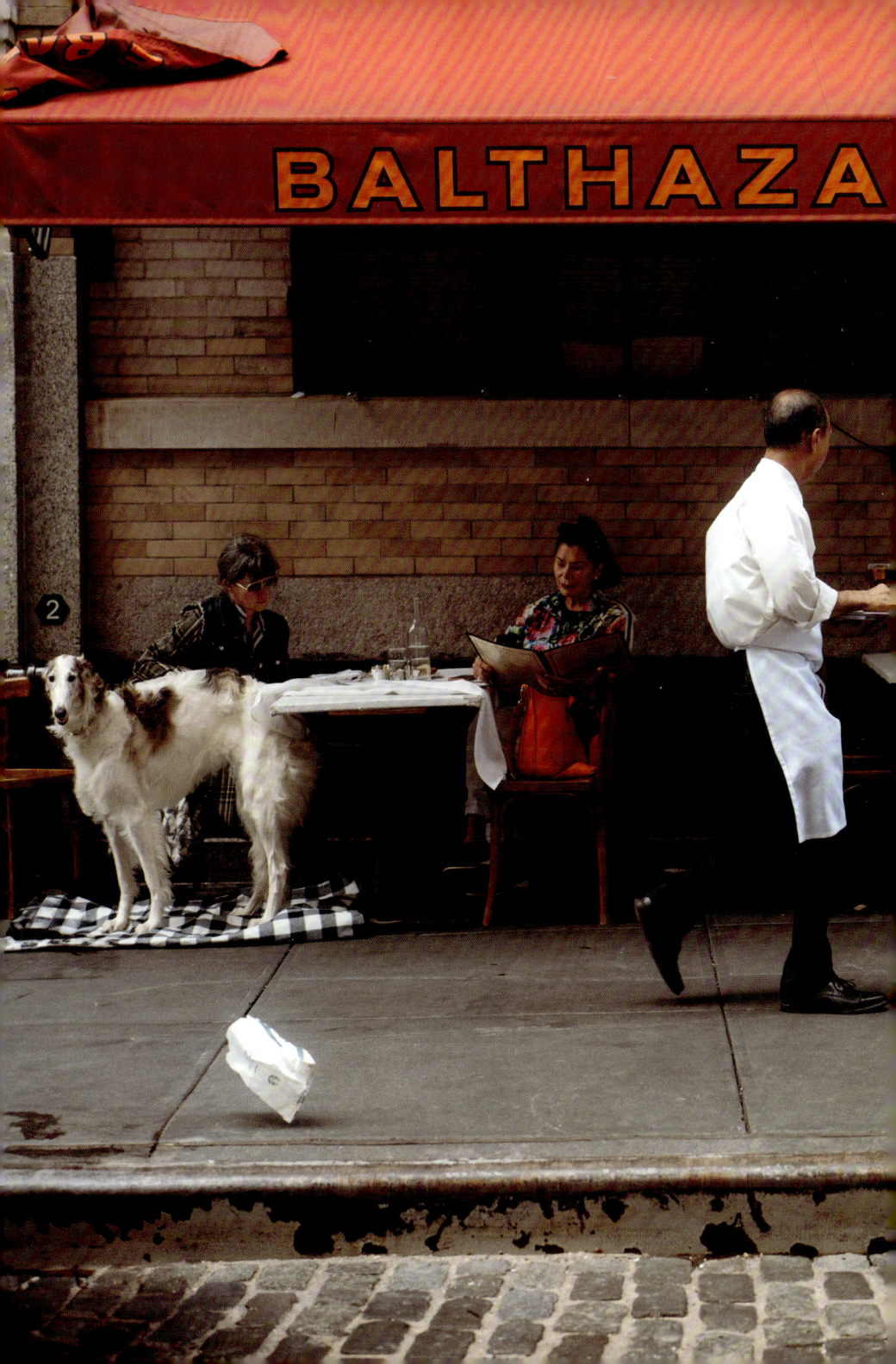

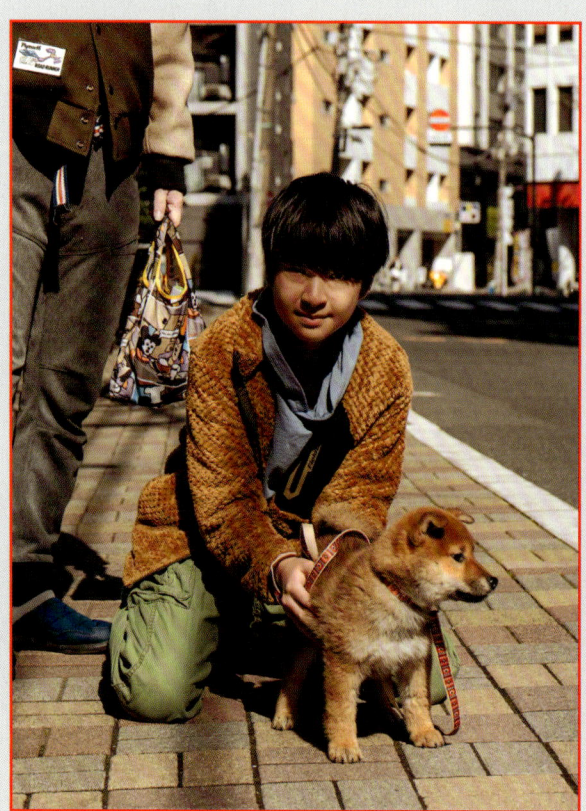

"We've been together for 14 years. She's seen me through everything!"

Jen and their dog Lily
New York City, USA

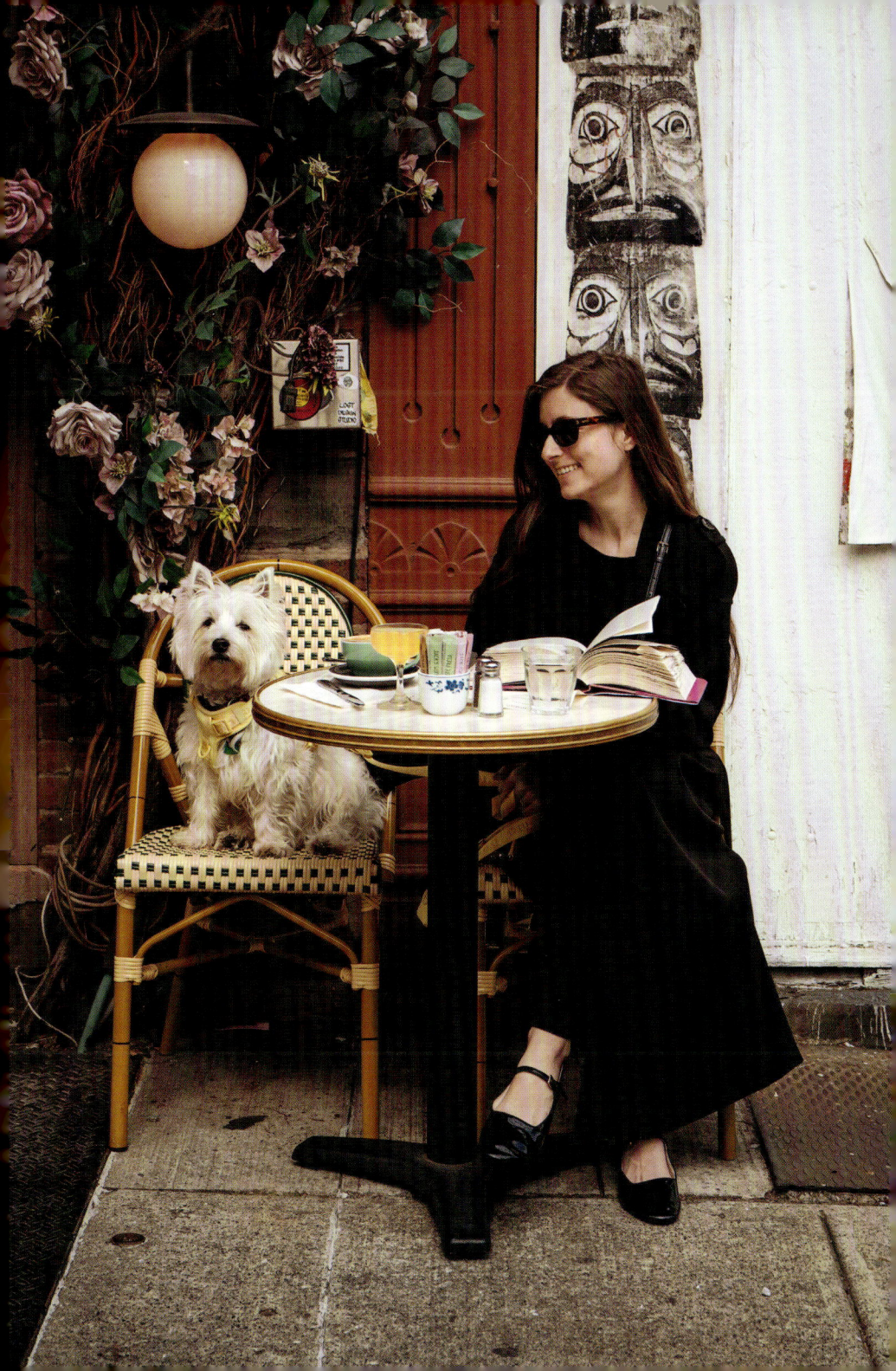

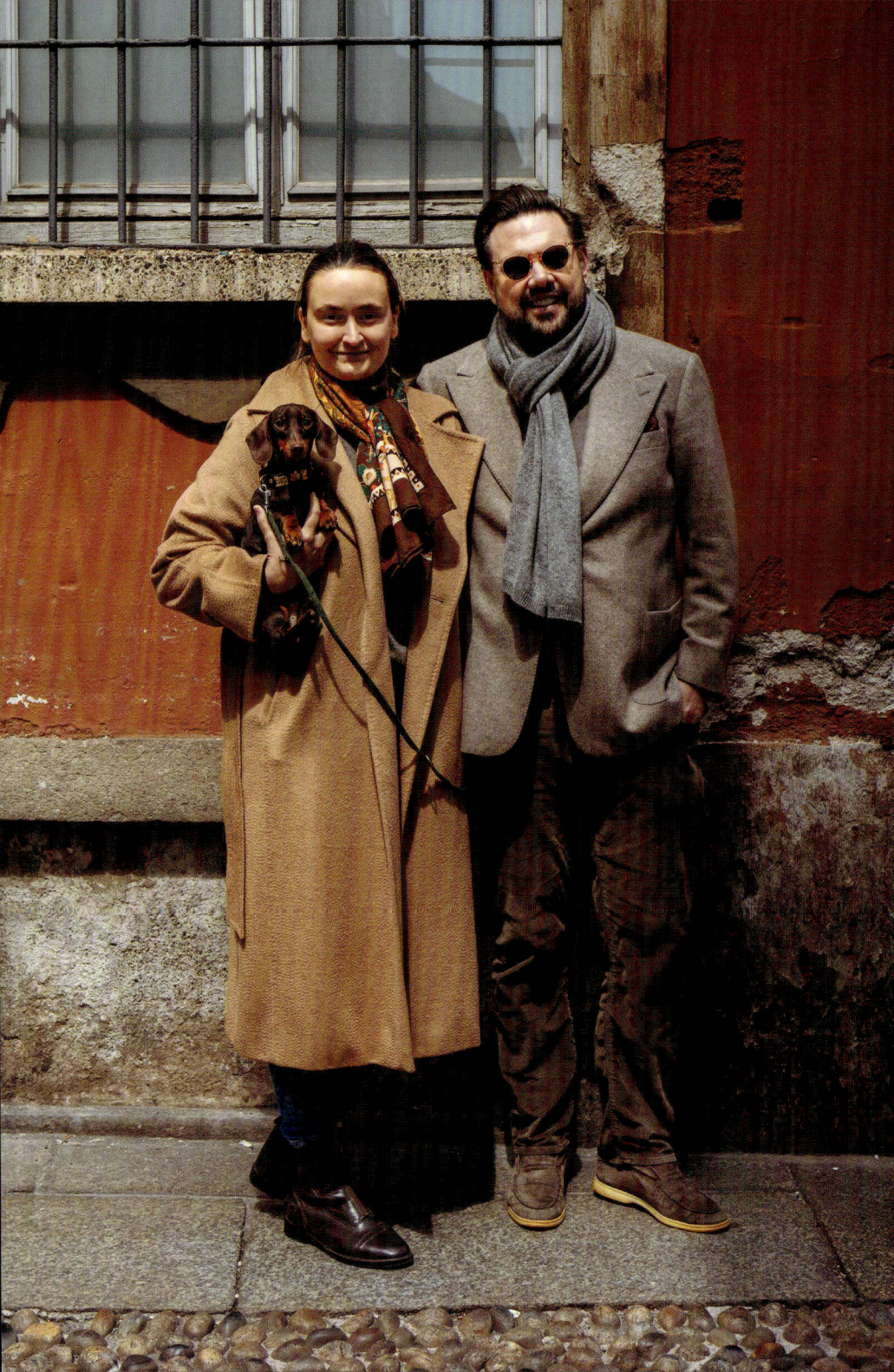

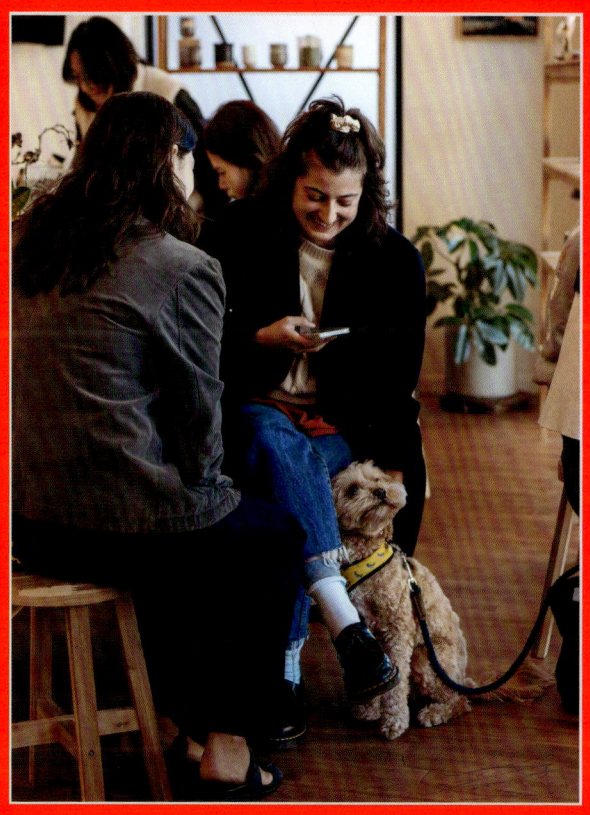

Sydney, Australia

"We give her all our attention but she always wants more."

Estelle and Karl and their dog Toffee
Milan, Italy

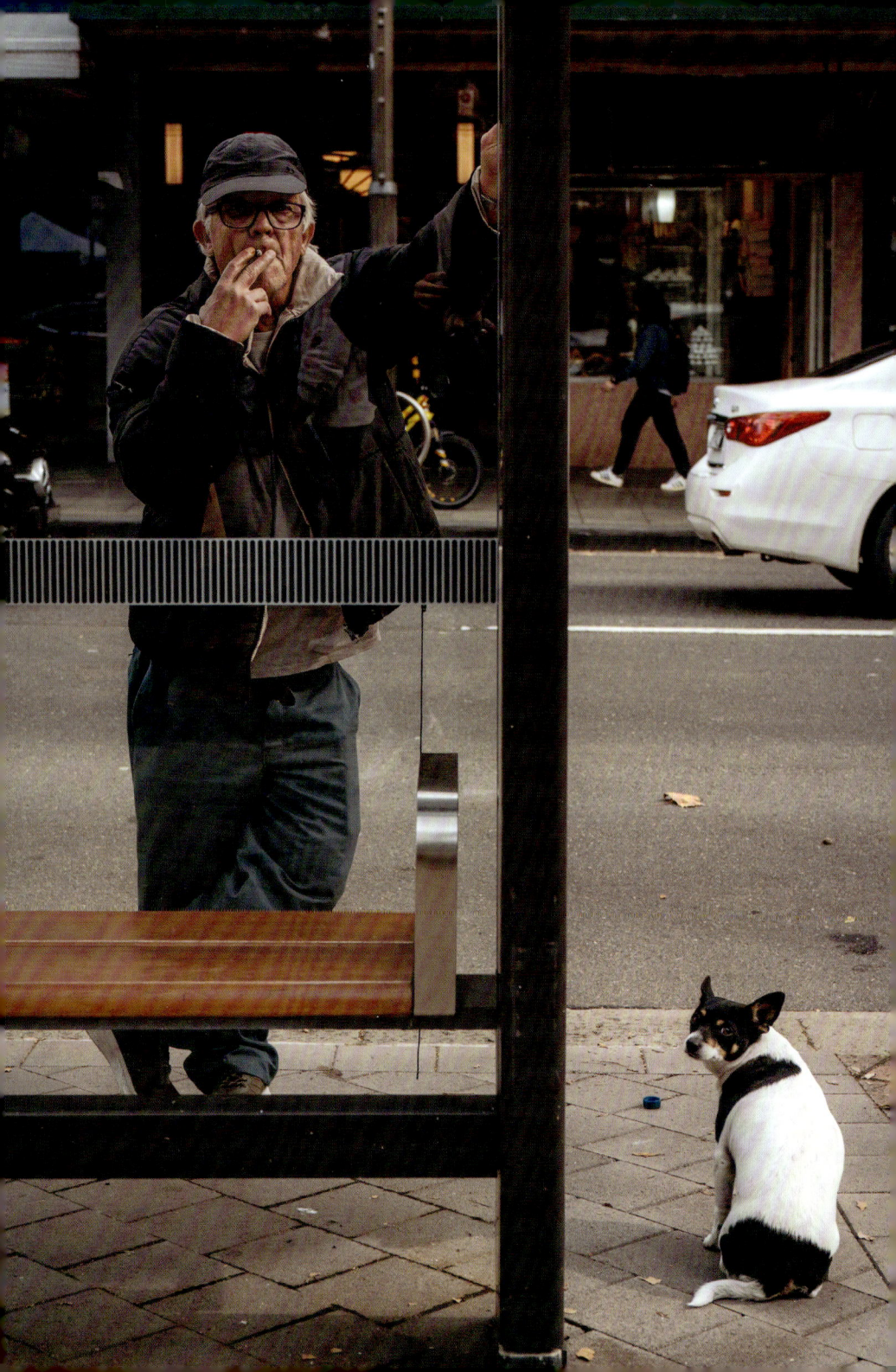

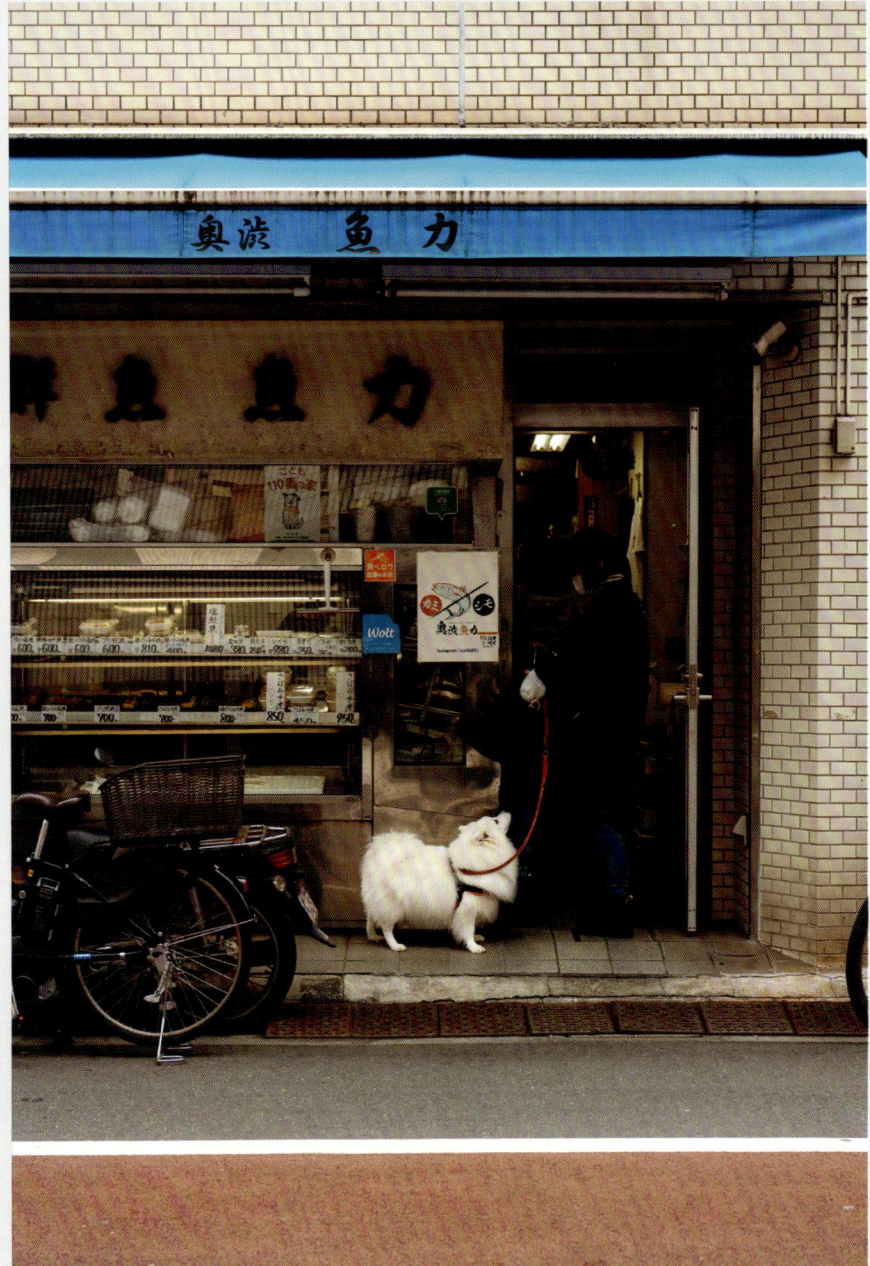

Sydney, Australia | Tokyo, Japan

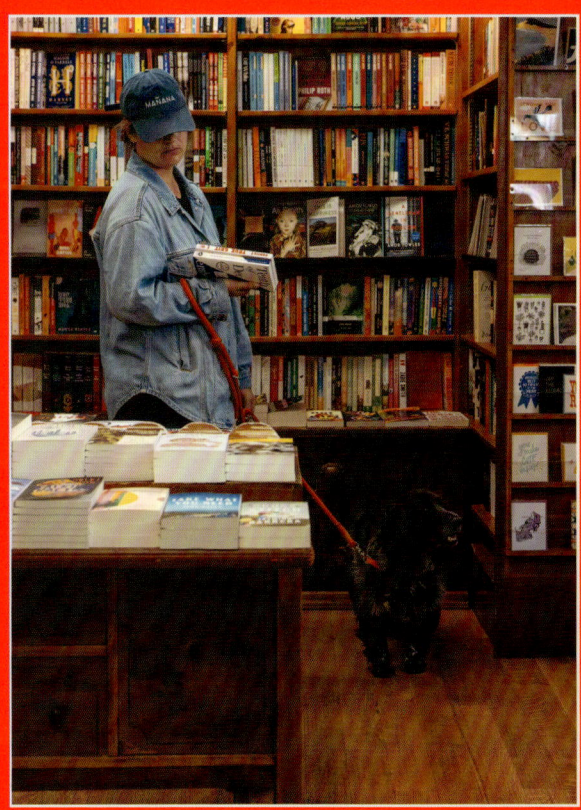

New York City, USA

"I'm his absolute hero! I've taken him everywhere with me, since day two."

Tim and their dog Flash
London, England

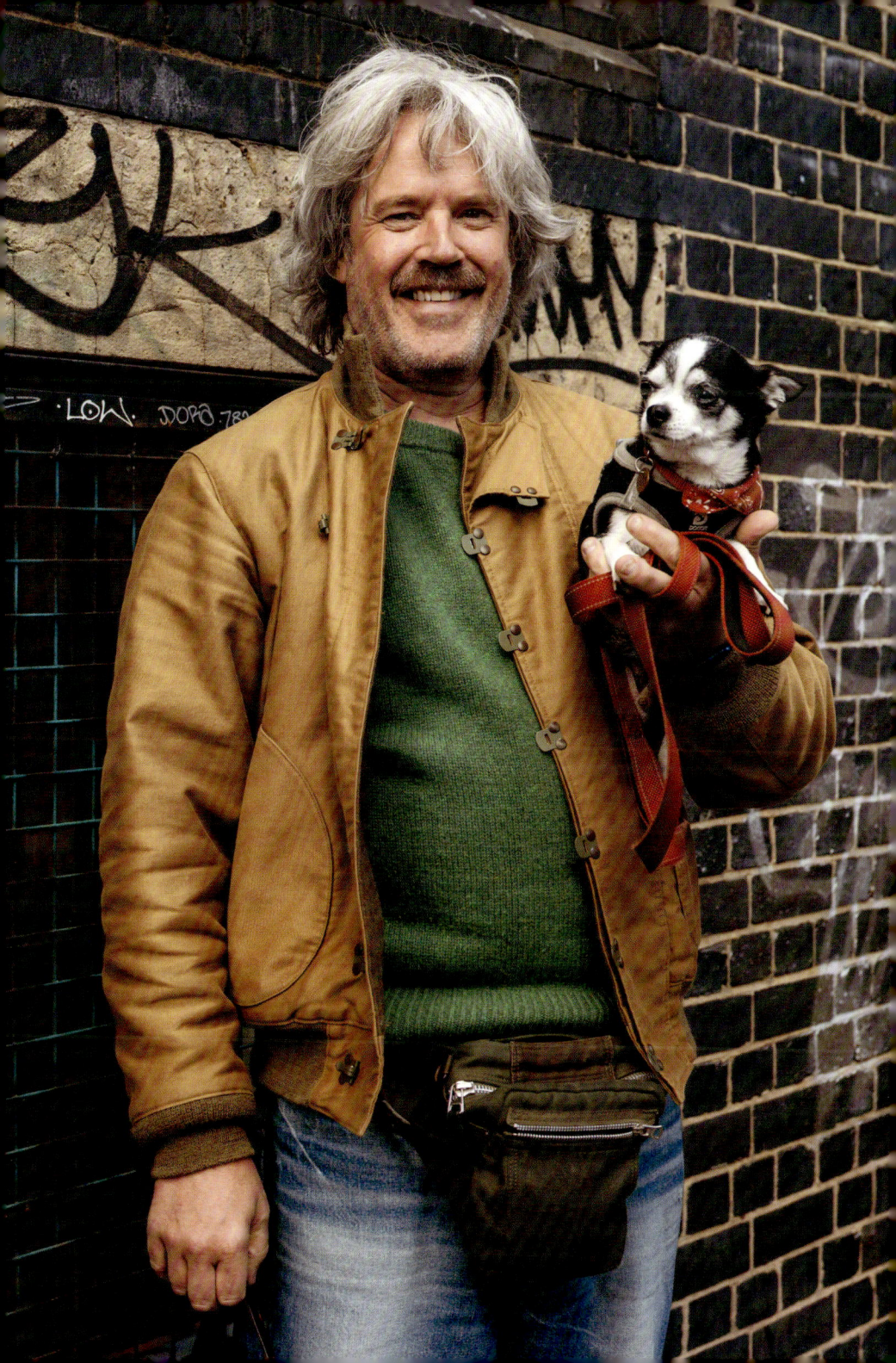

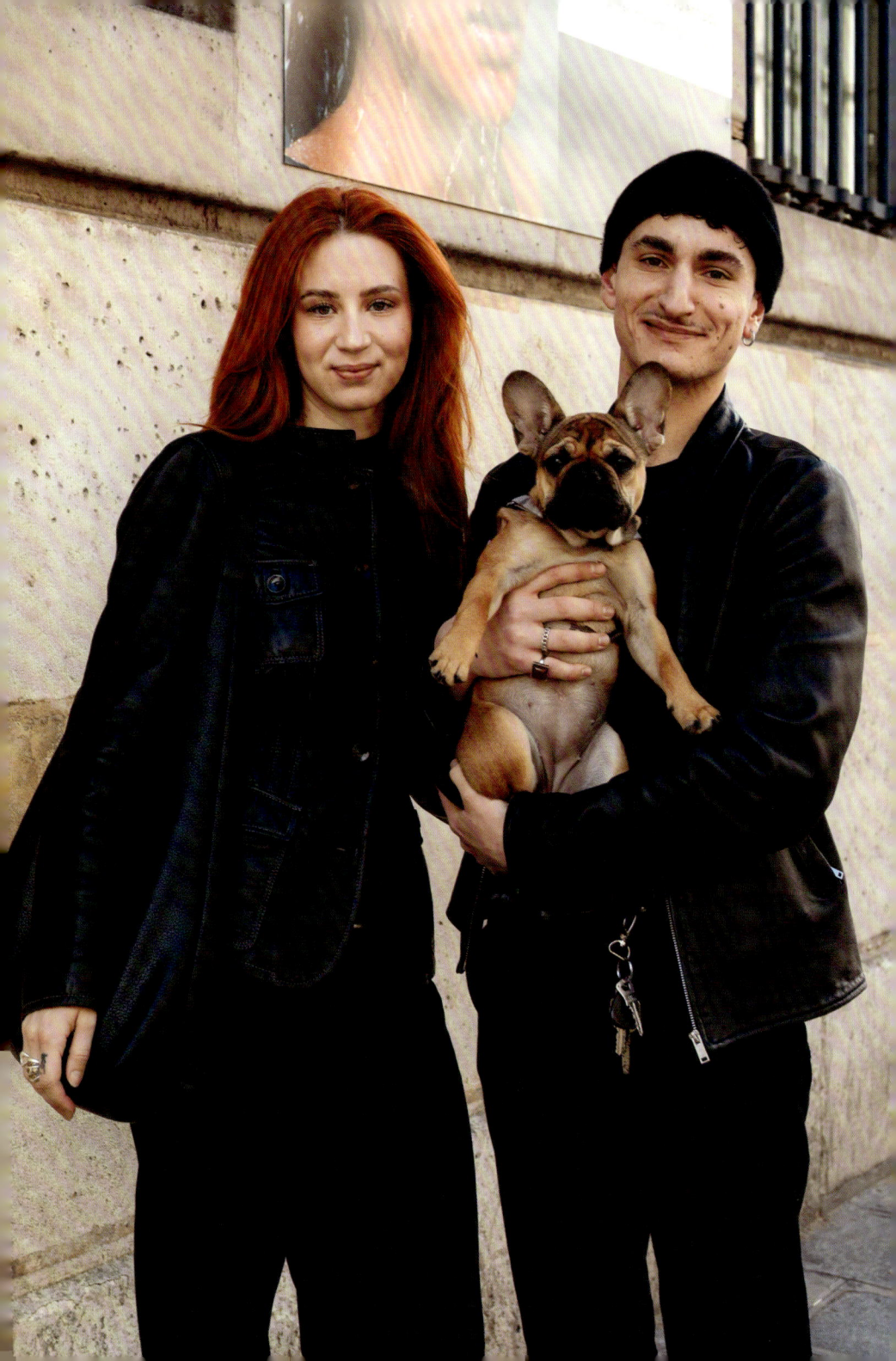

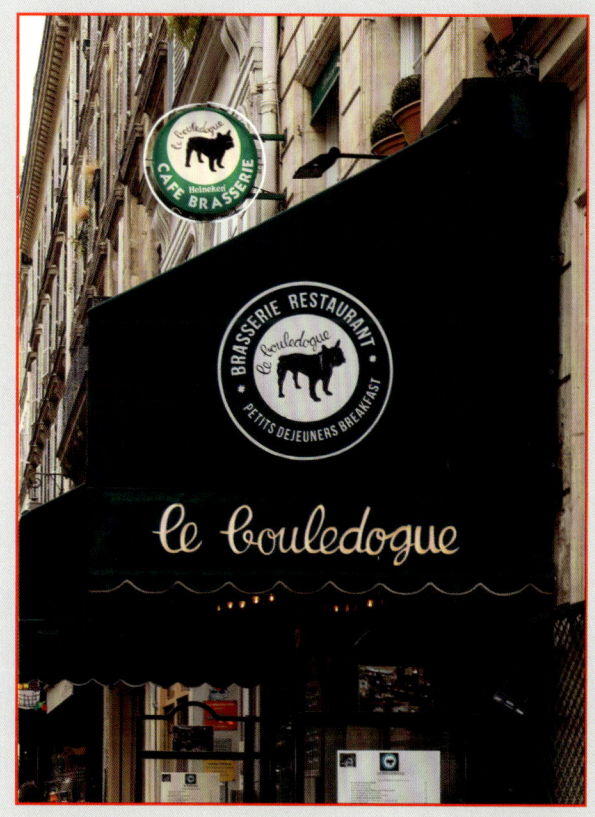

Paris, France

"She rules our house. She can do anything she wants."

Chloe and Julien and their dog Sweeny
Paris, France

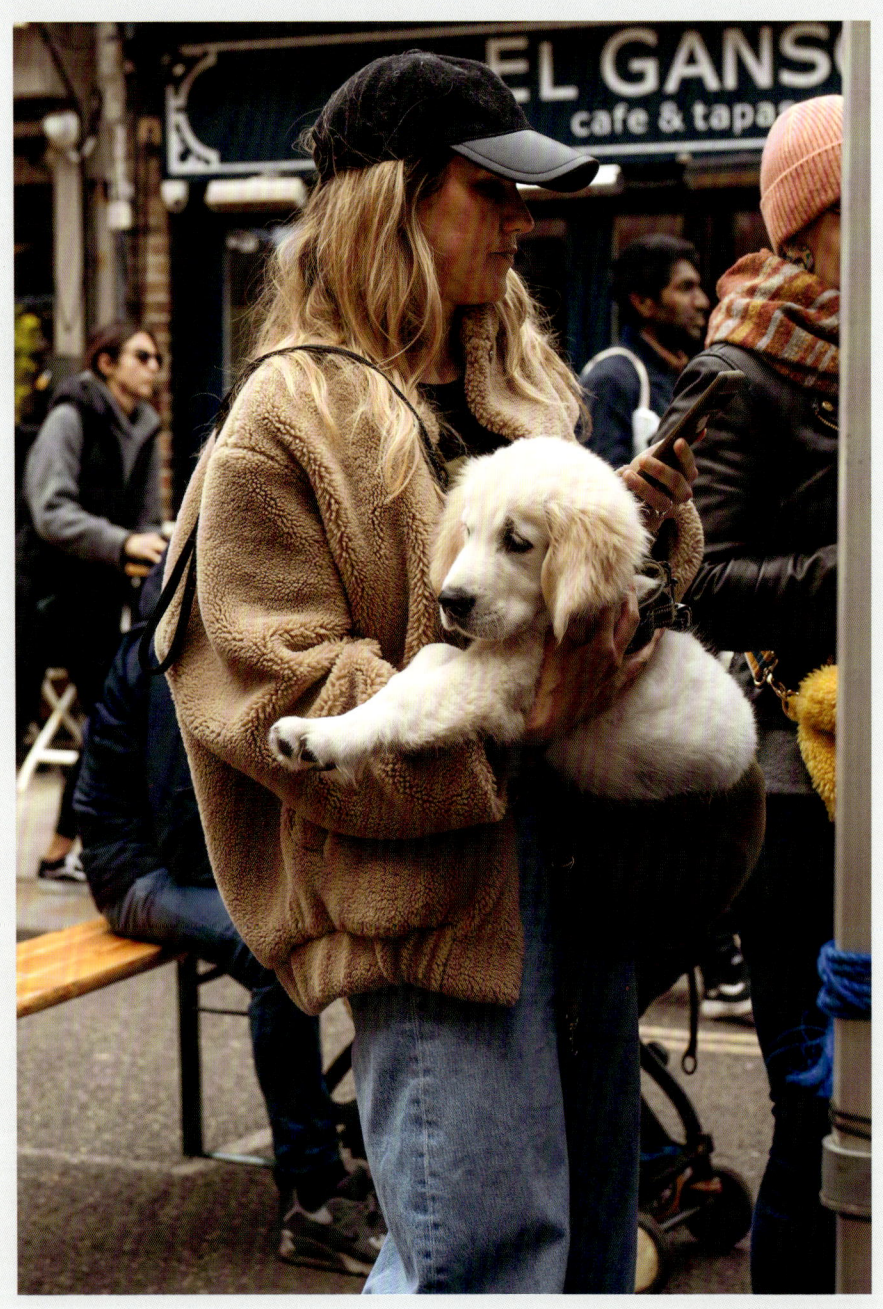

London, England | New York City, USA

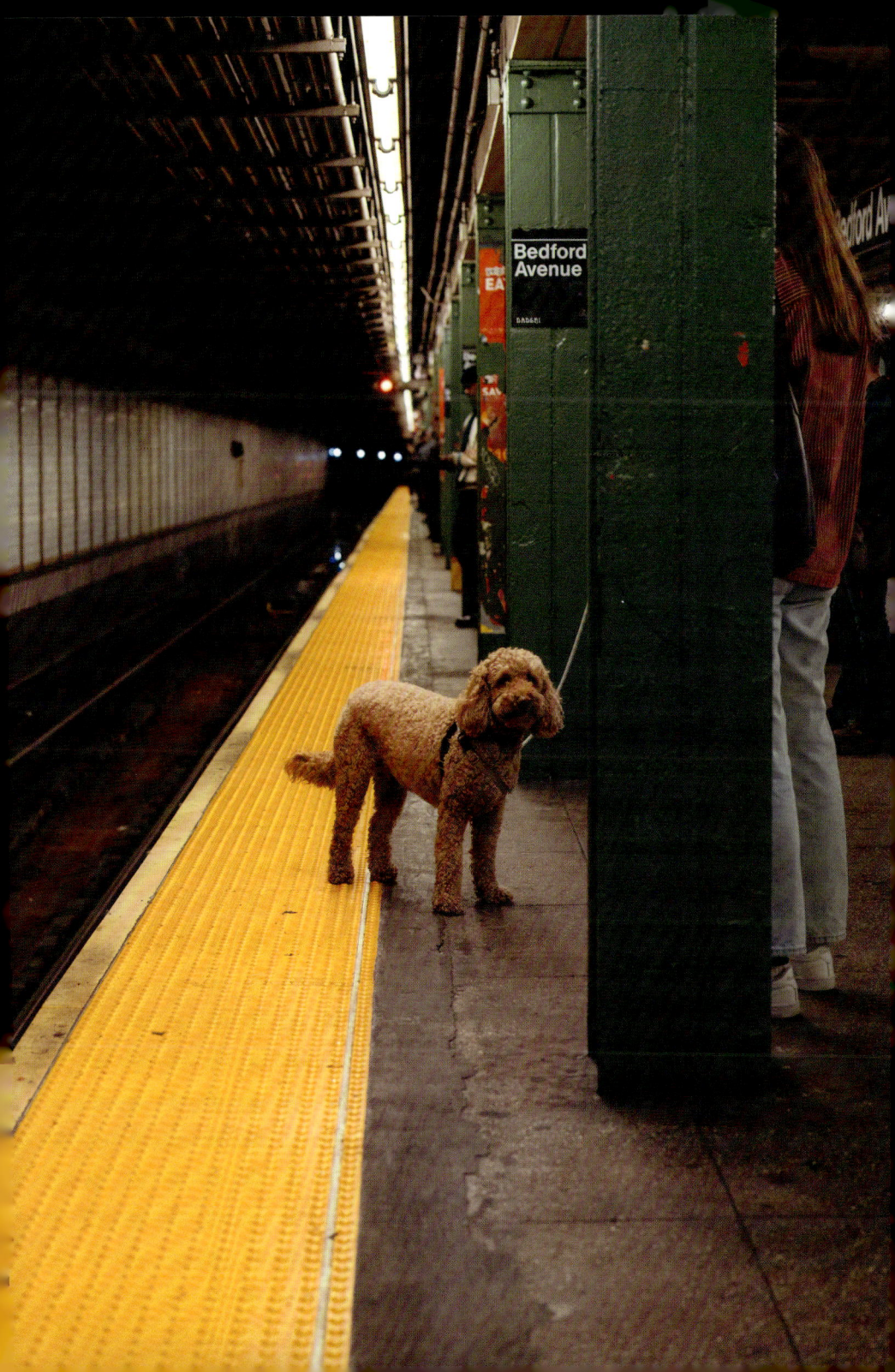

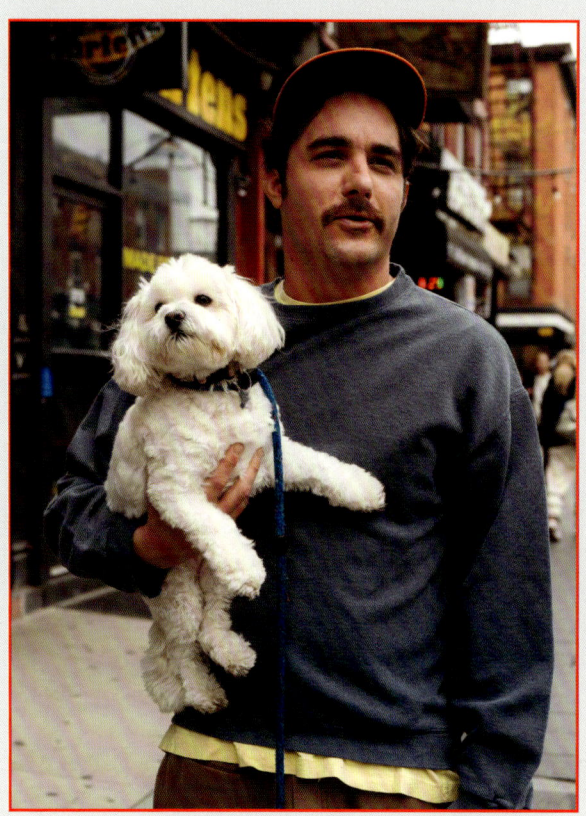

New York City, USA

"I've had her since I was 11.
She loves a good bum scratch."

Stella and their dog Ava
Sydney, Australia

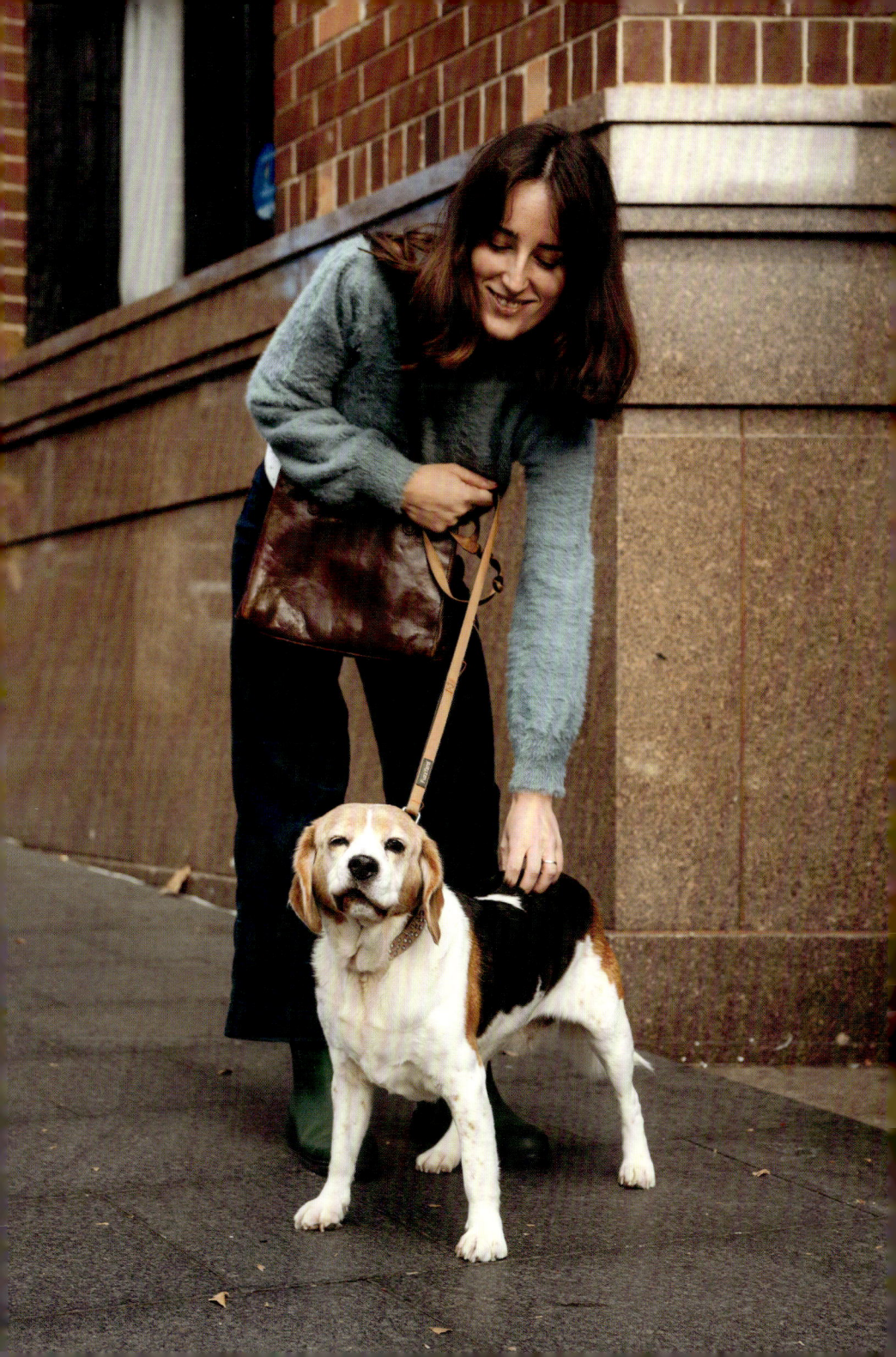

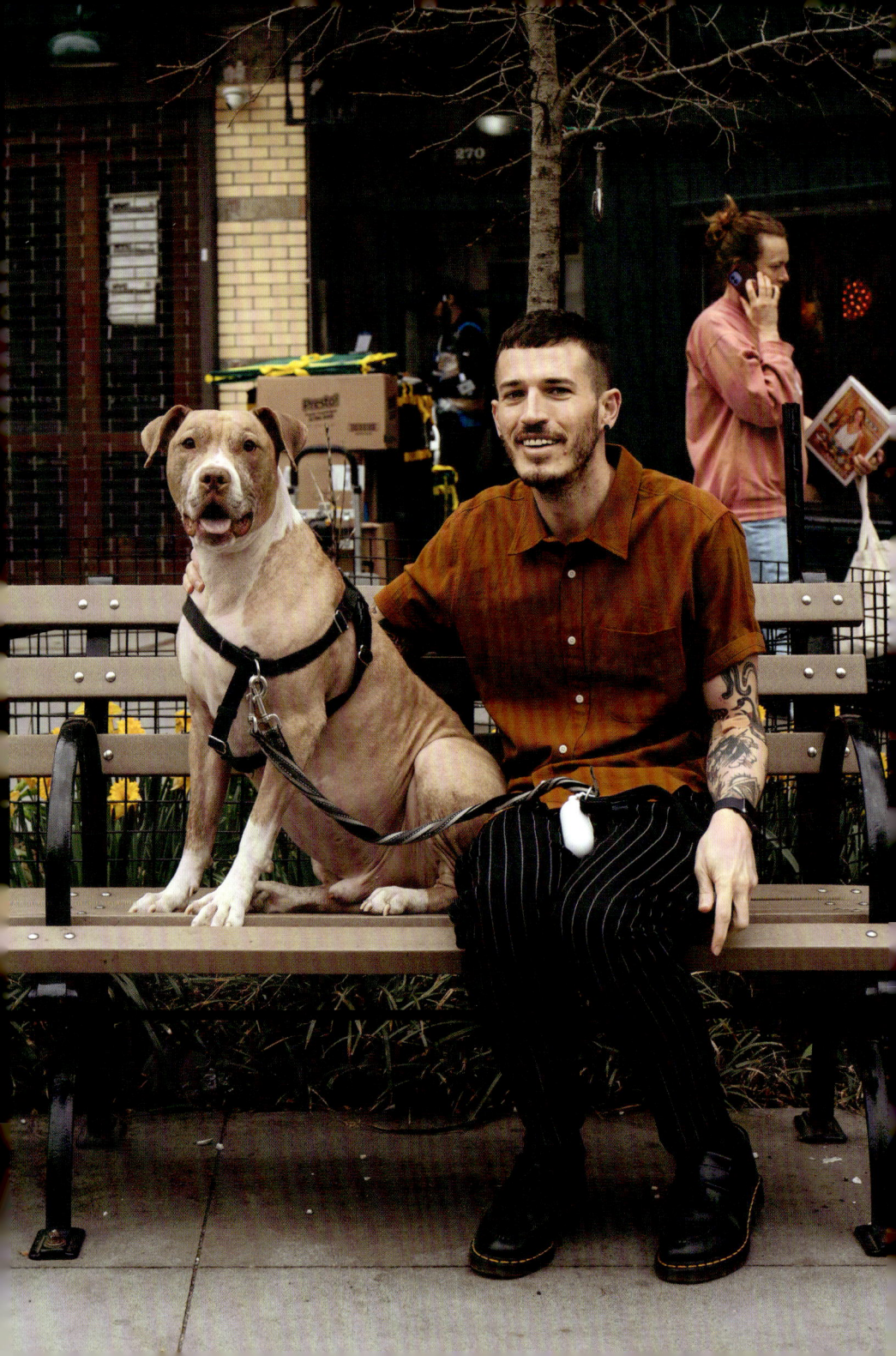

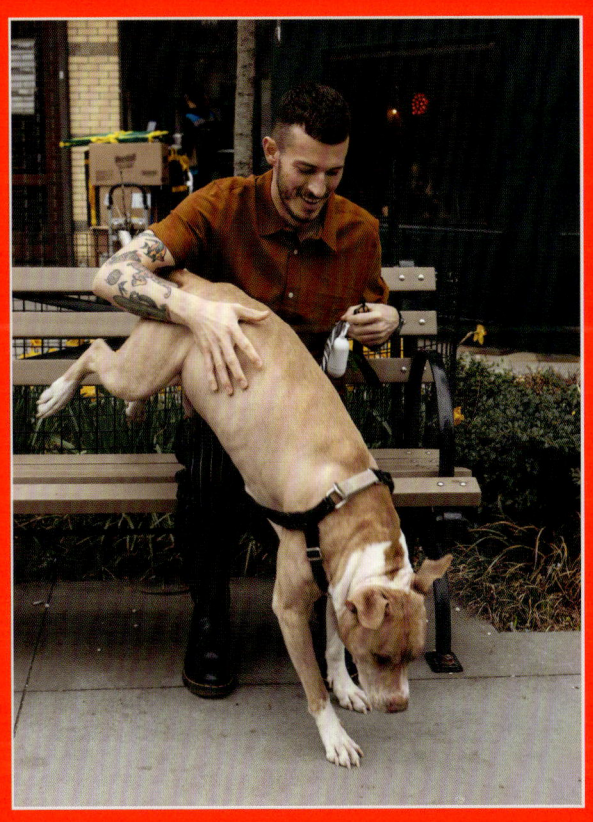

"He's recovering from a brain tumour. So I think he's very grateful that he's doing better. I know I am."

Matt and their dog Theo
New York City, USA

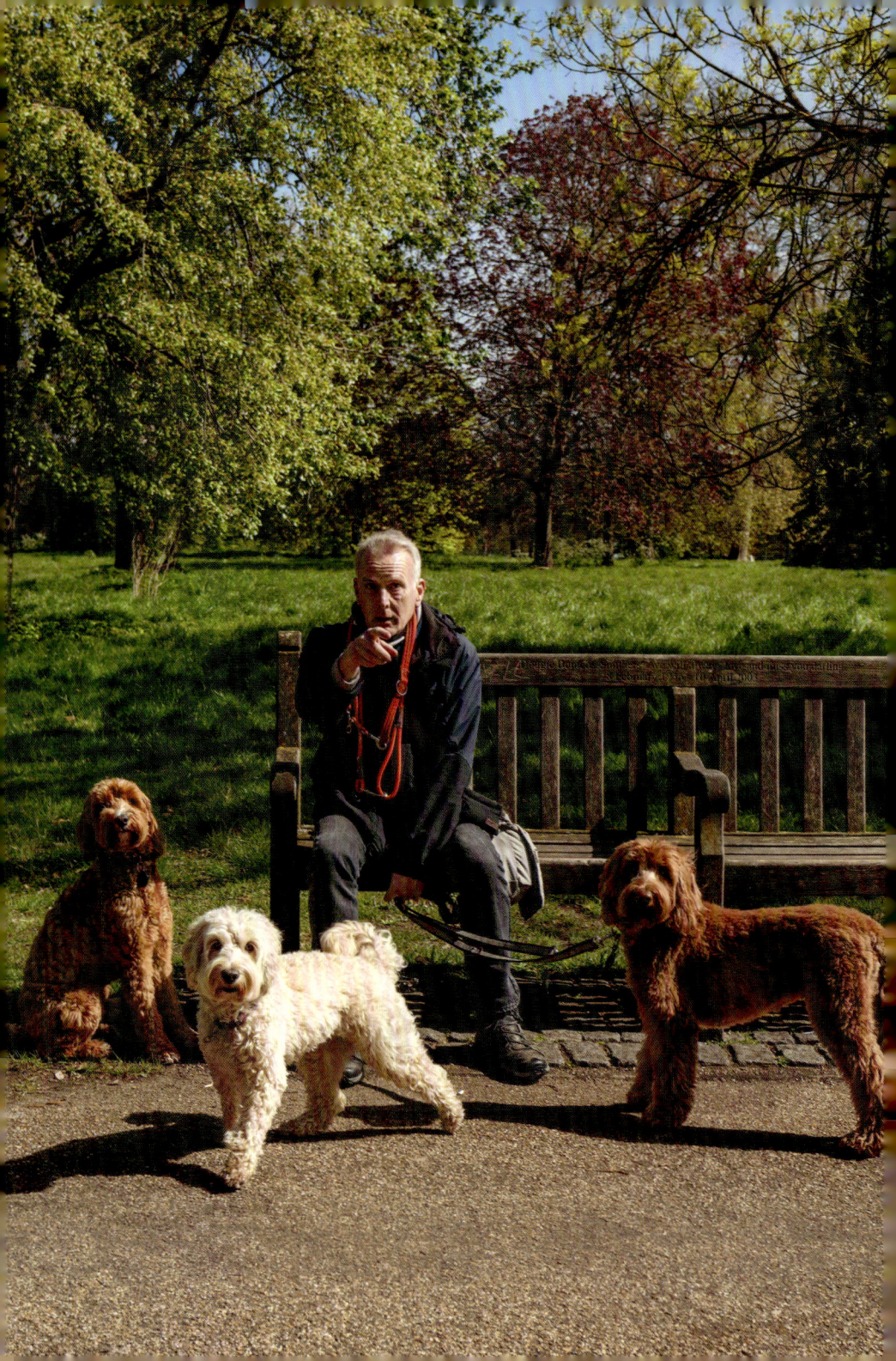

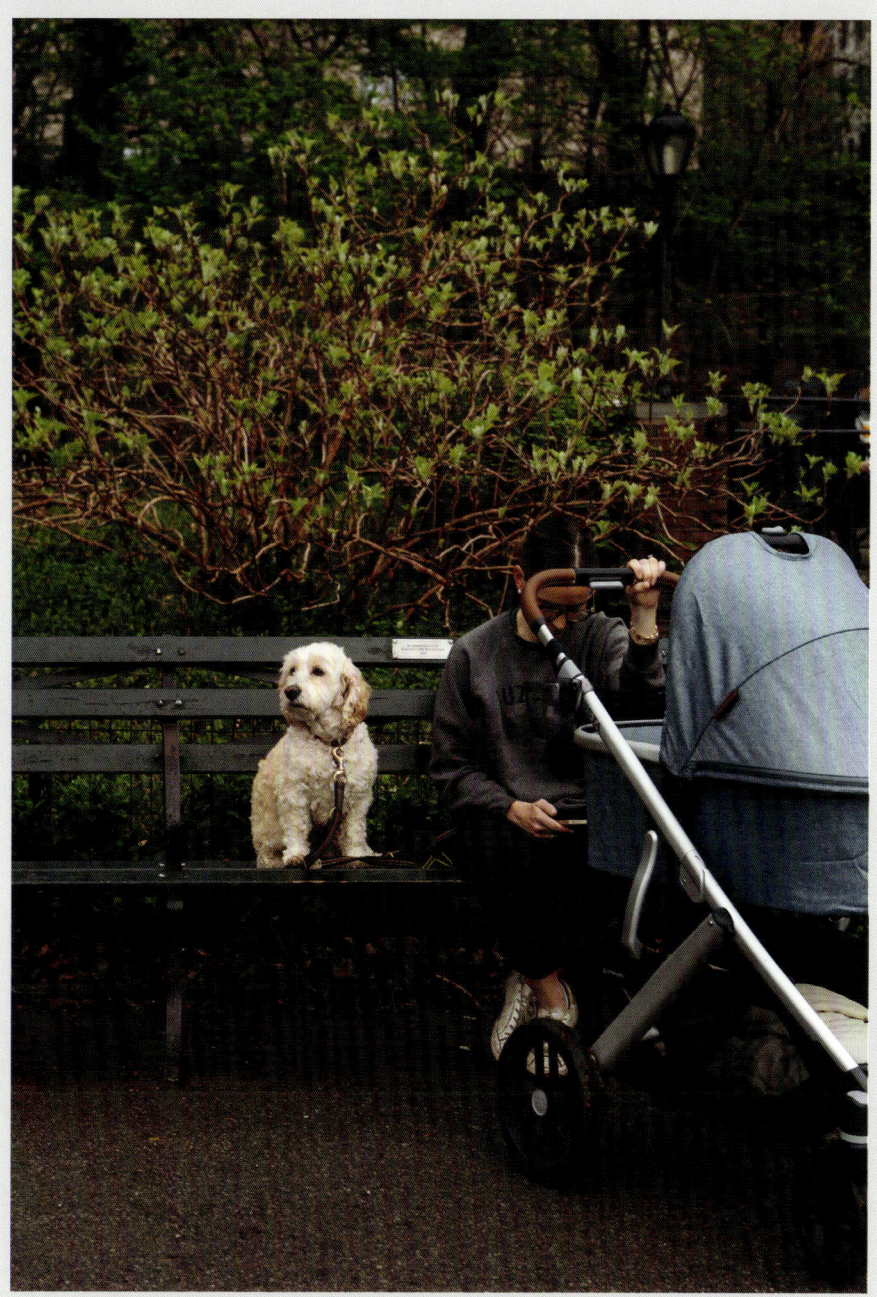

London, England | New York City, USA

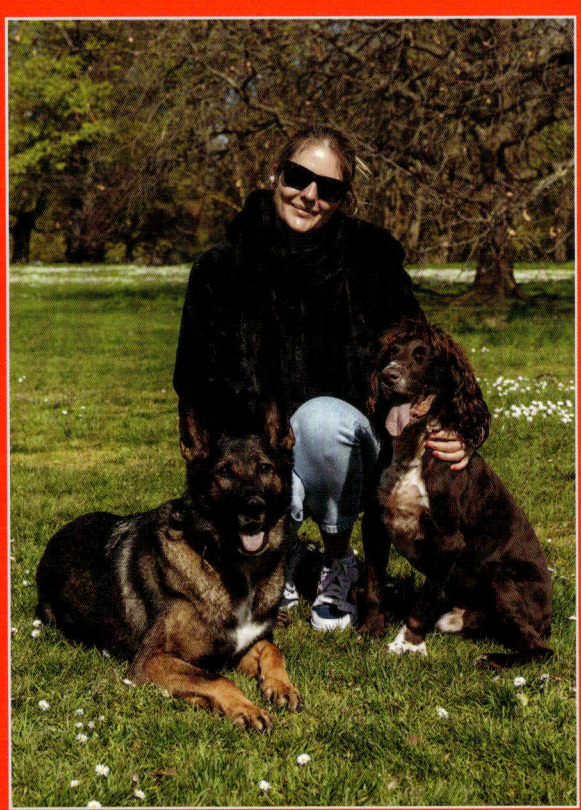

London, England

"She loves a day at the salon."

Shuichi and their dog Anne
Tokyo, Japan

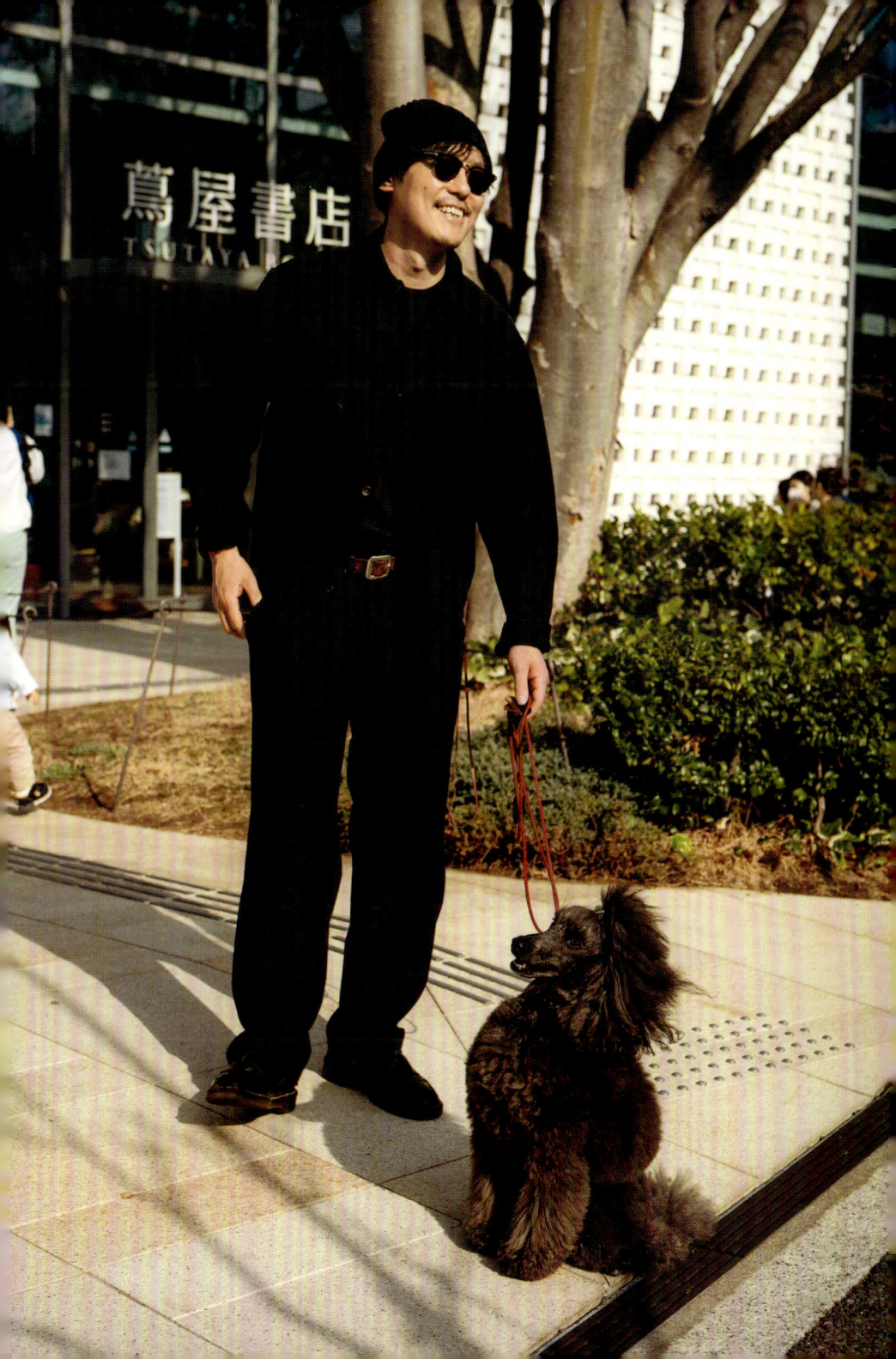

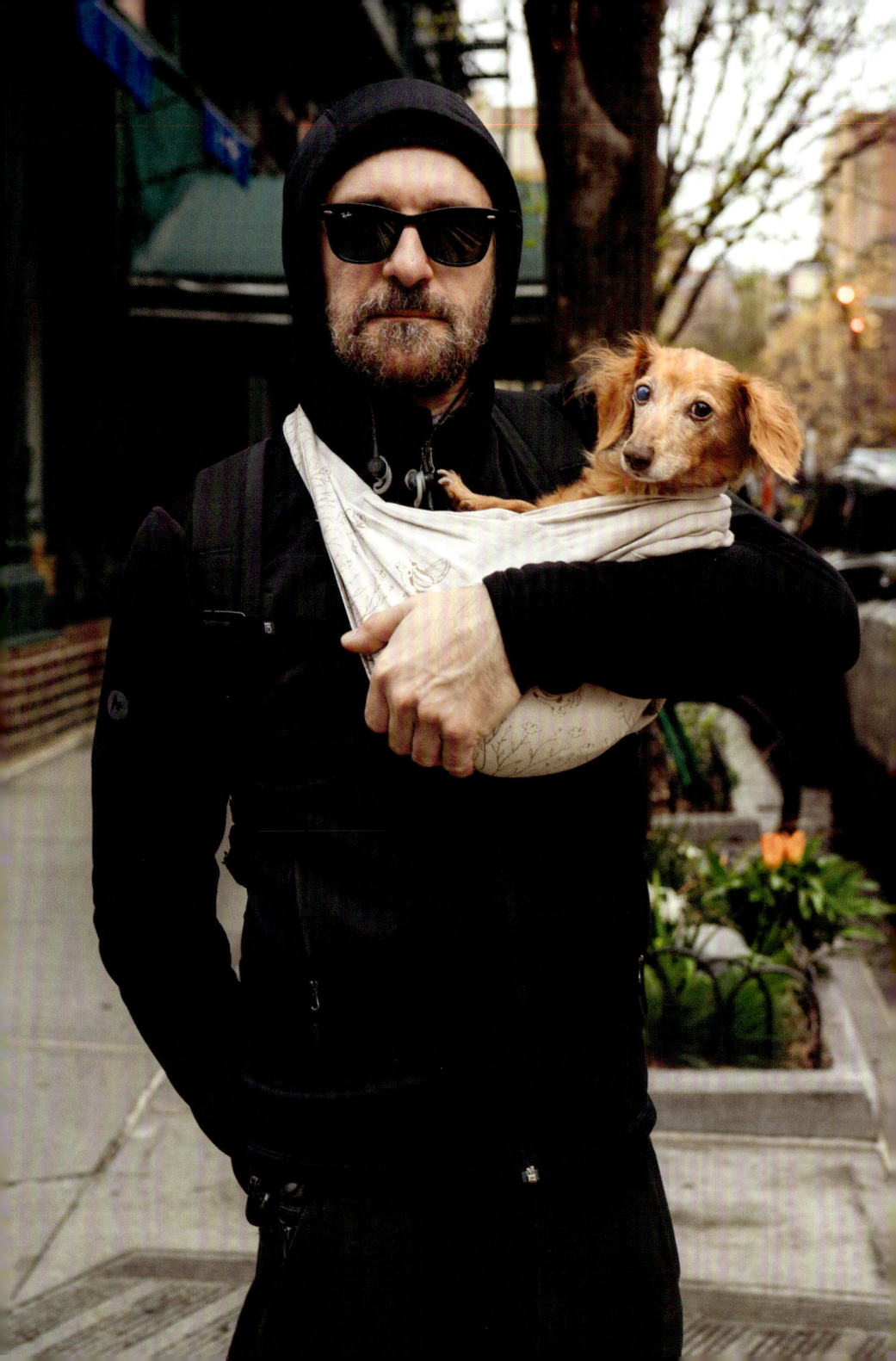

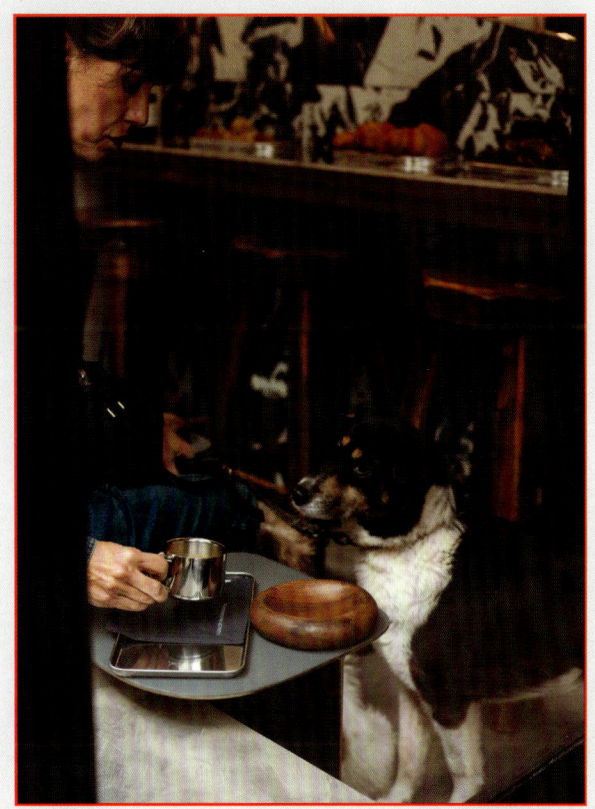

"He would say I don't feed him enough."

Pete and their dog Macy
New York City, USA

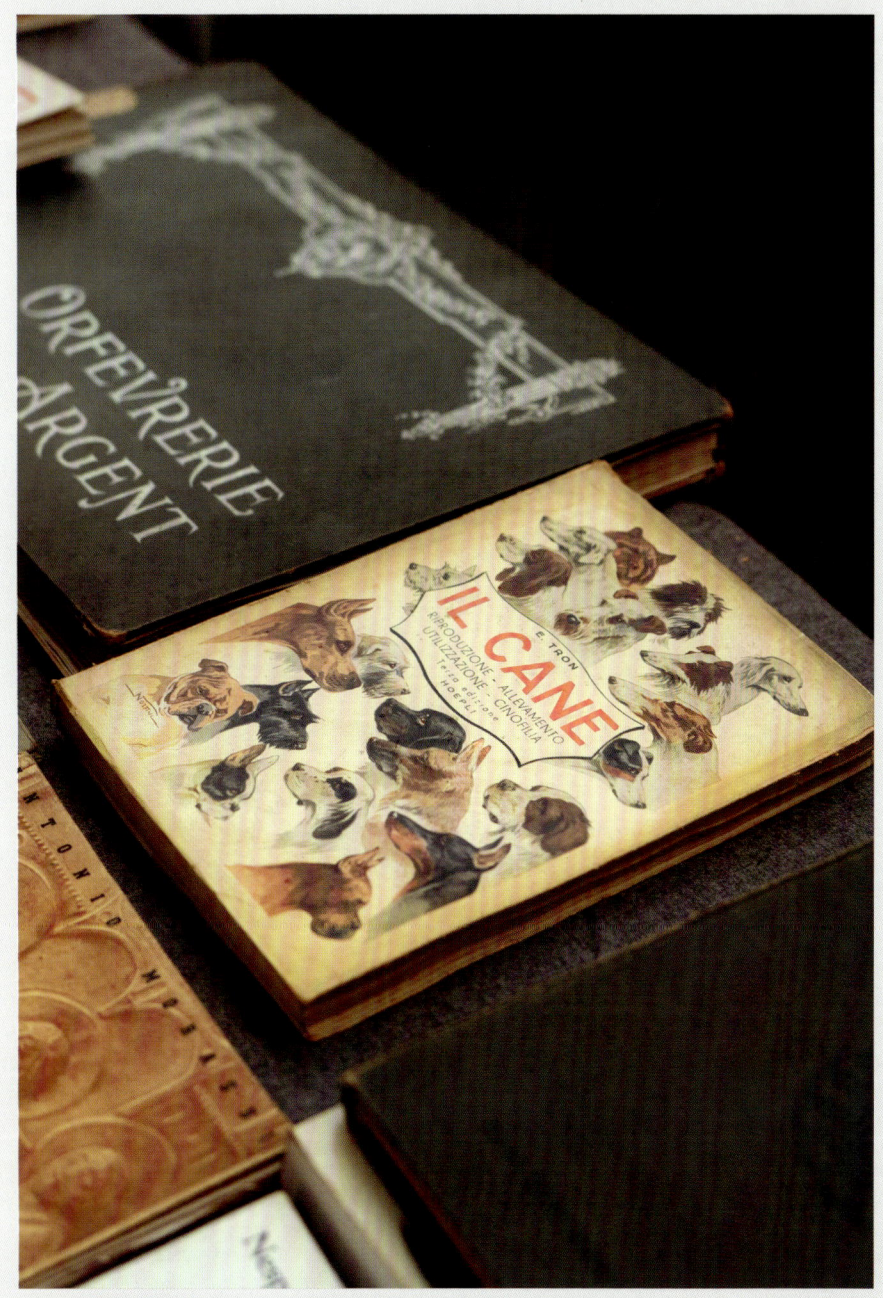

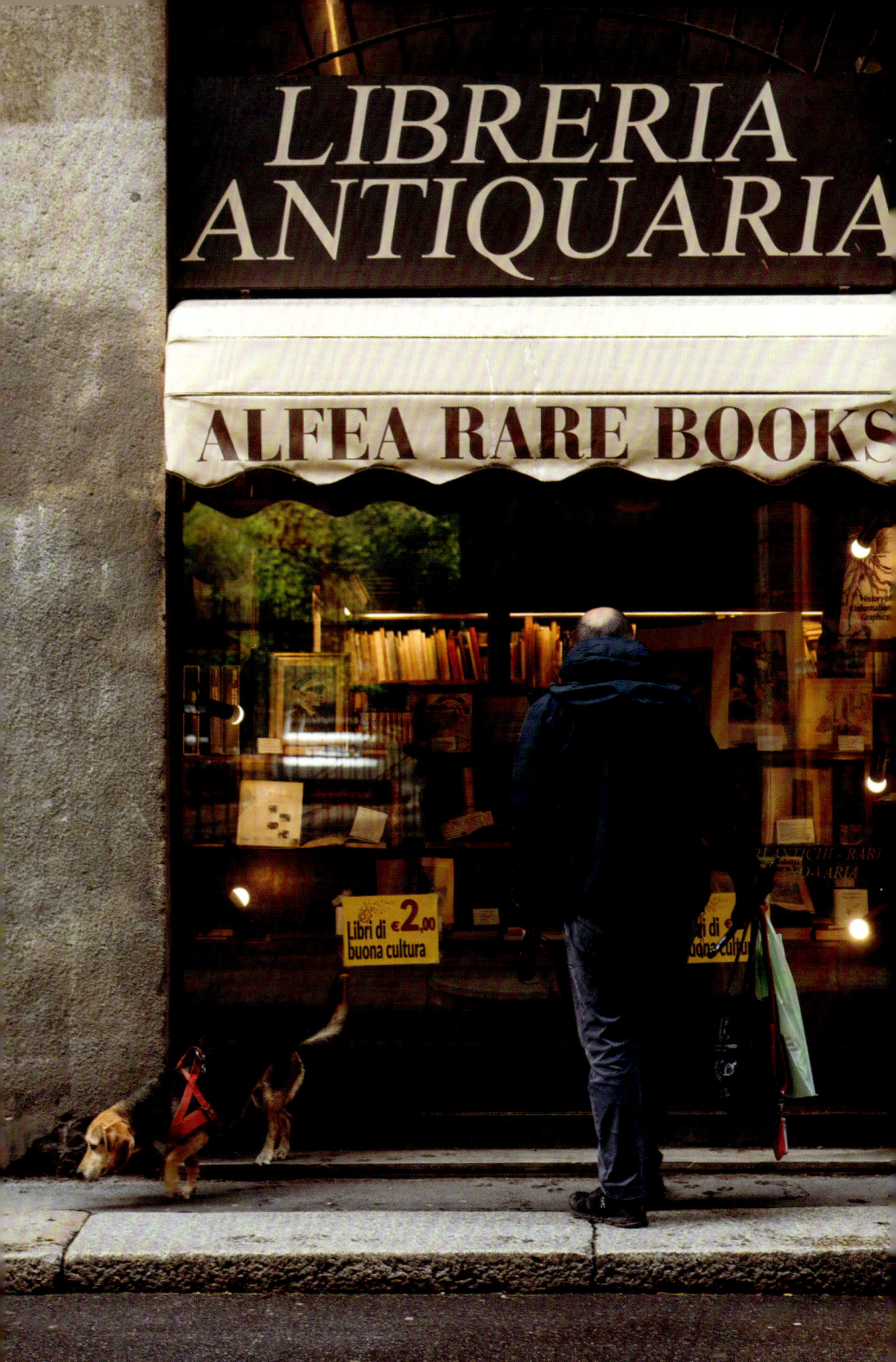

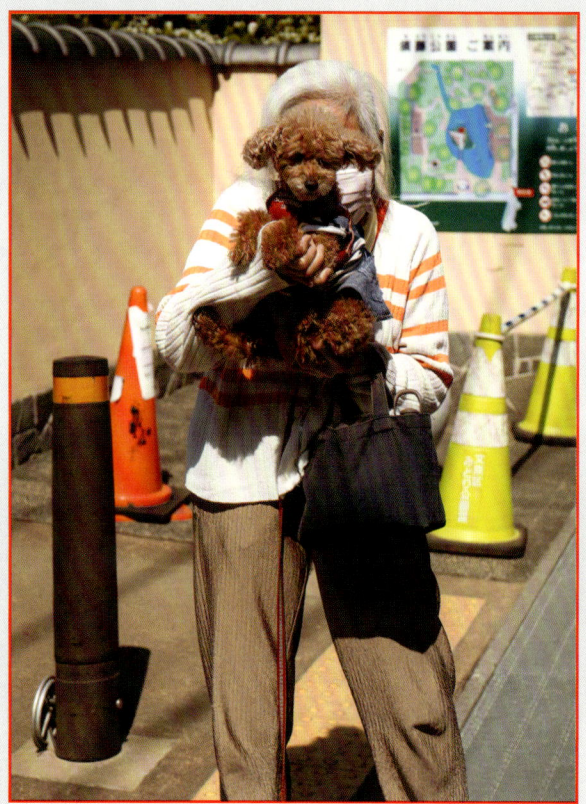

Tokyo, Japan

"She loves me very much."

Marina and their dog Fidel
Milan, Italy

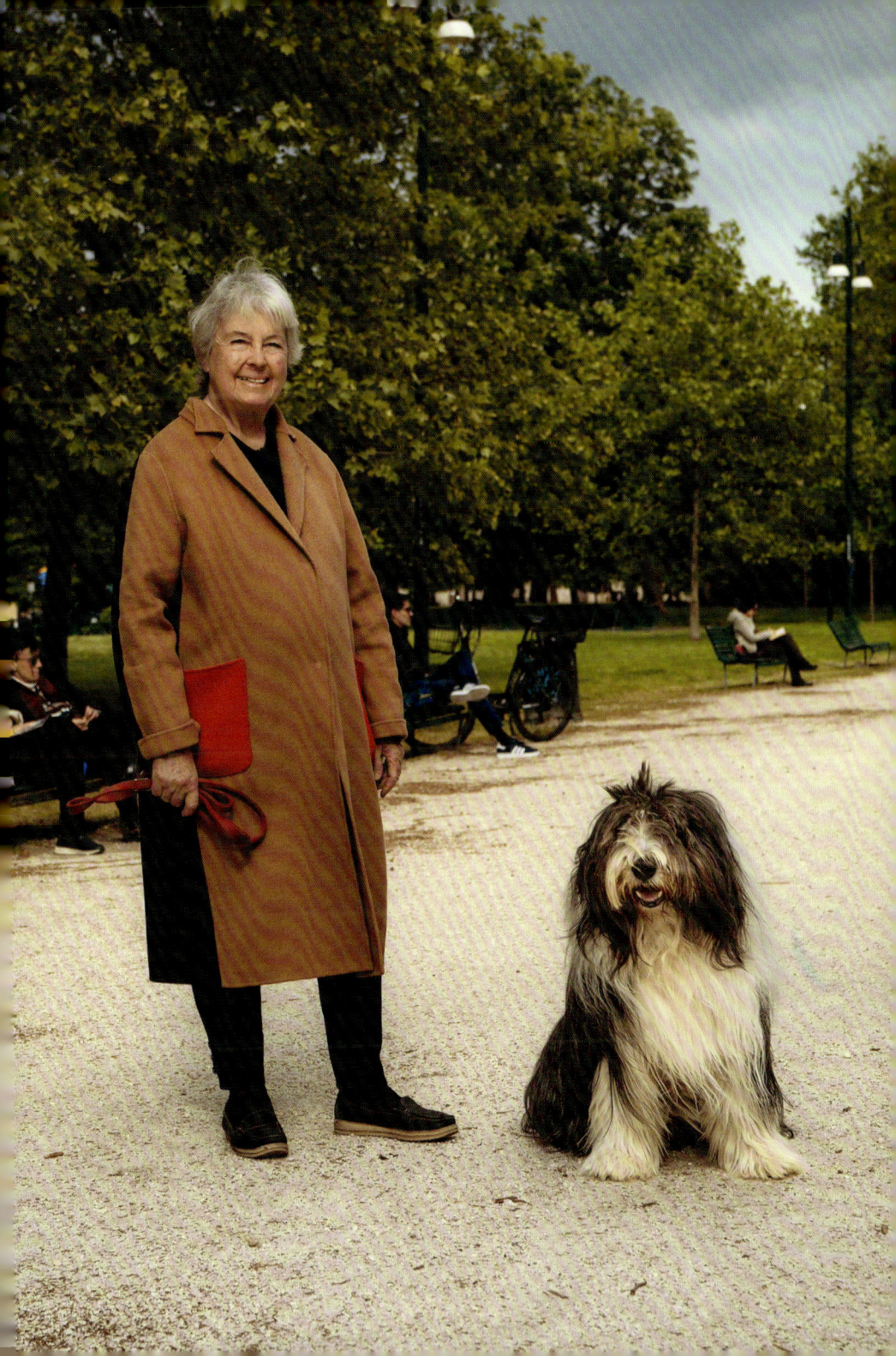

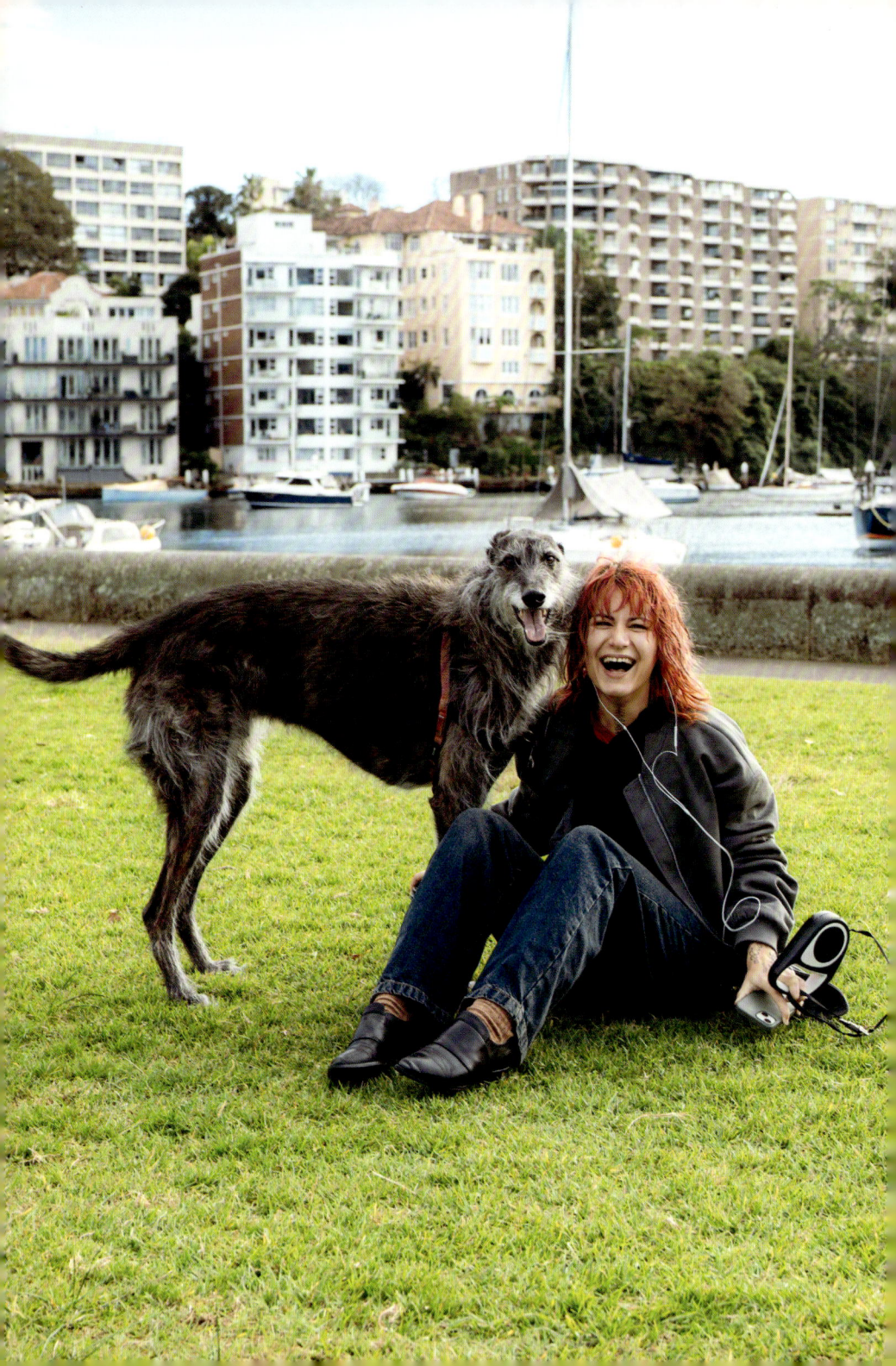

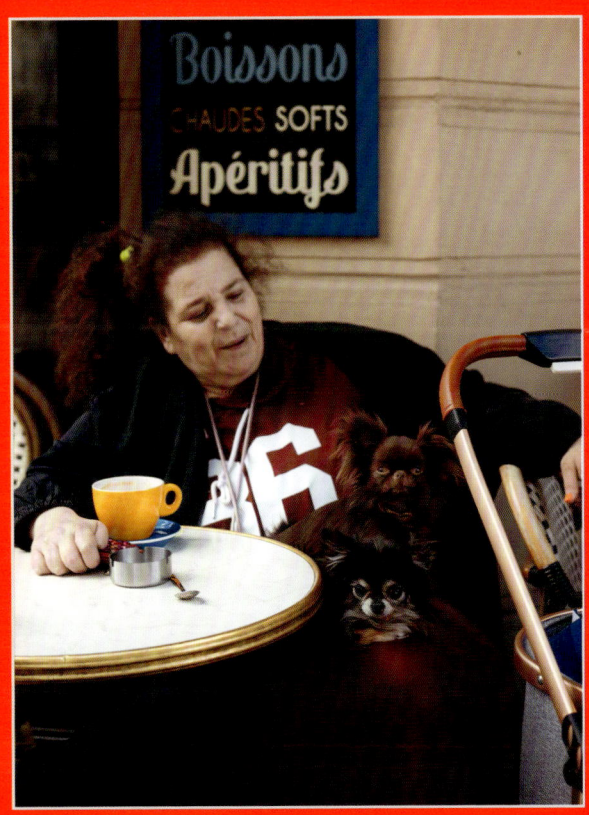

Paris, France

"He's very much a human in my eyes. He enjoys our morning routine and his daily puppuccino."

Madison and their dog Phil
Sydney, Australia

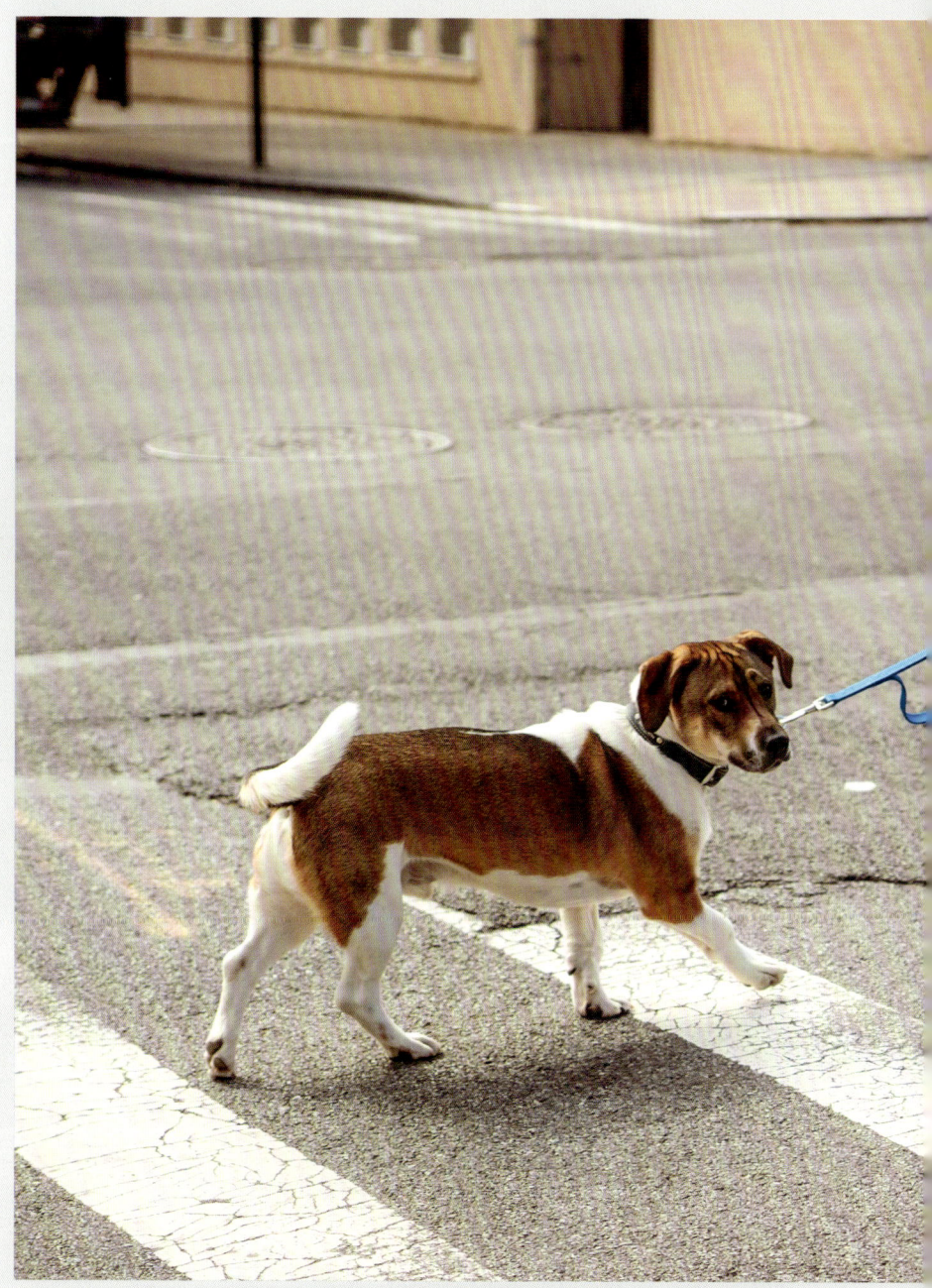

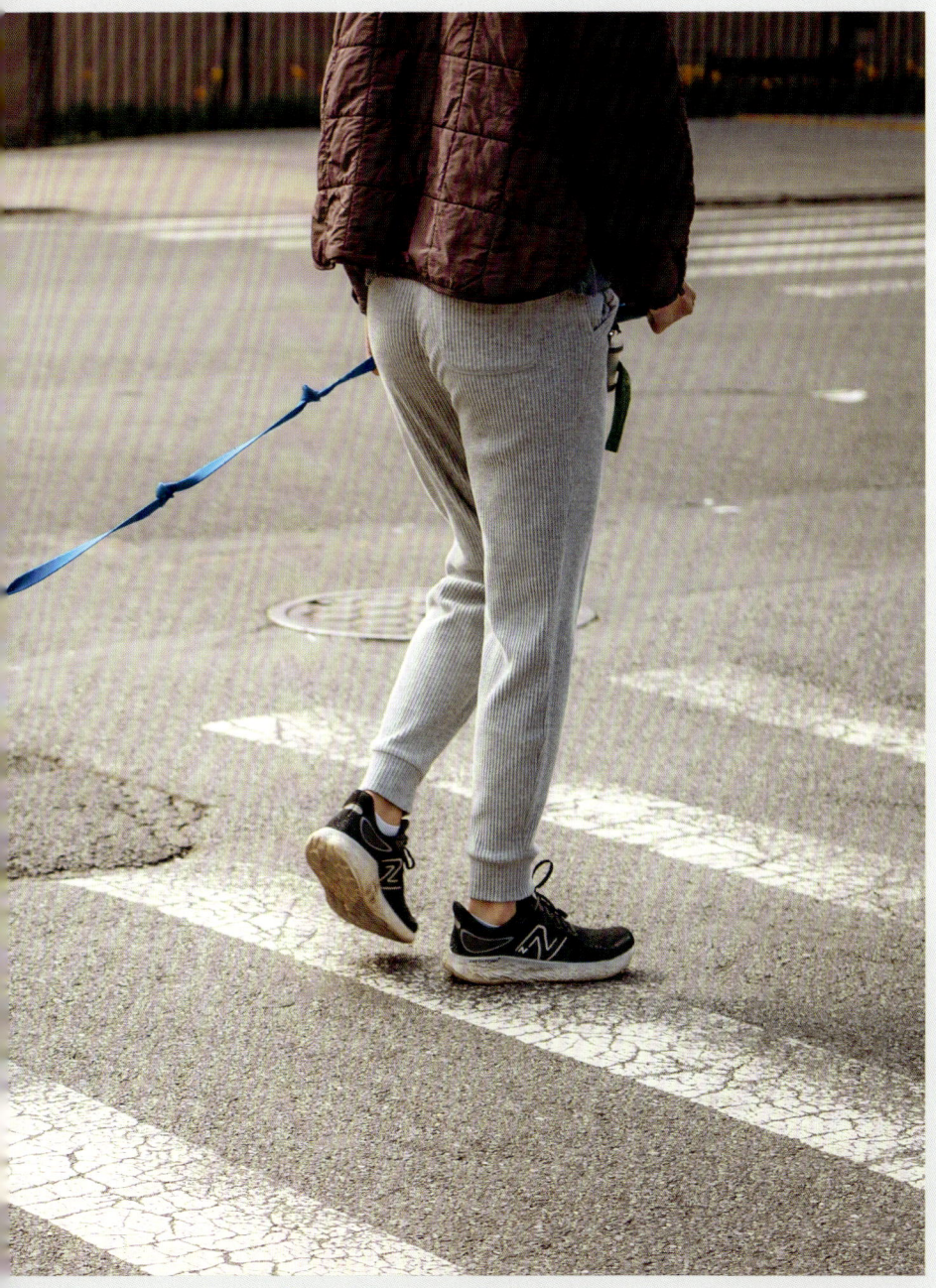

New York City, USA

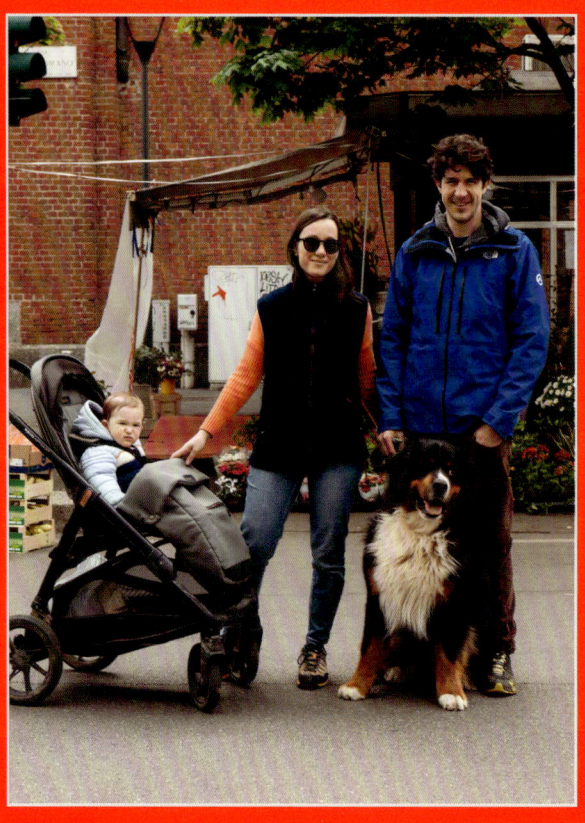

"He was my cuddle buddy before the baby, now he's a bit jealous."

Thomaso and their dog Giorgio
Milan, Italy

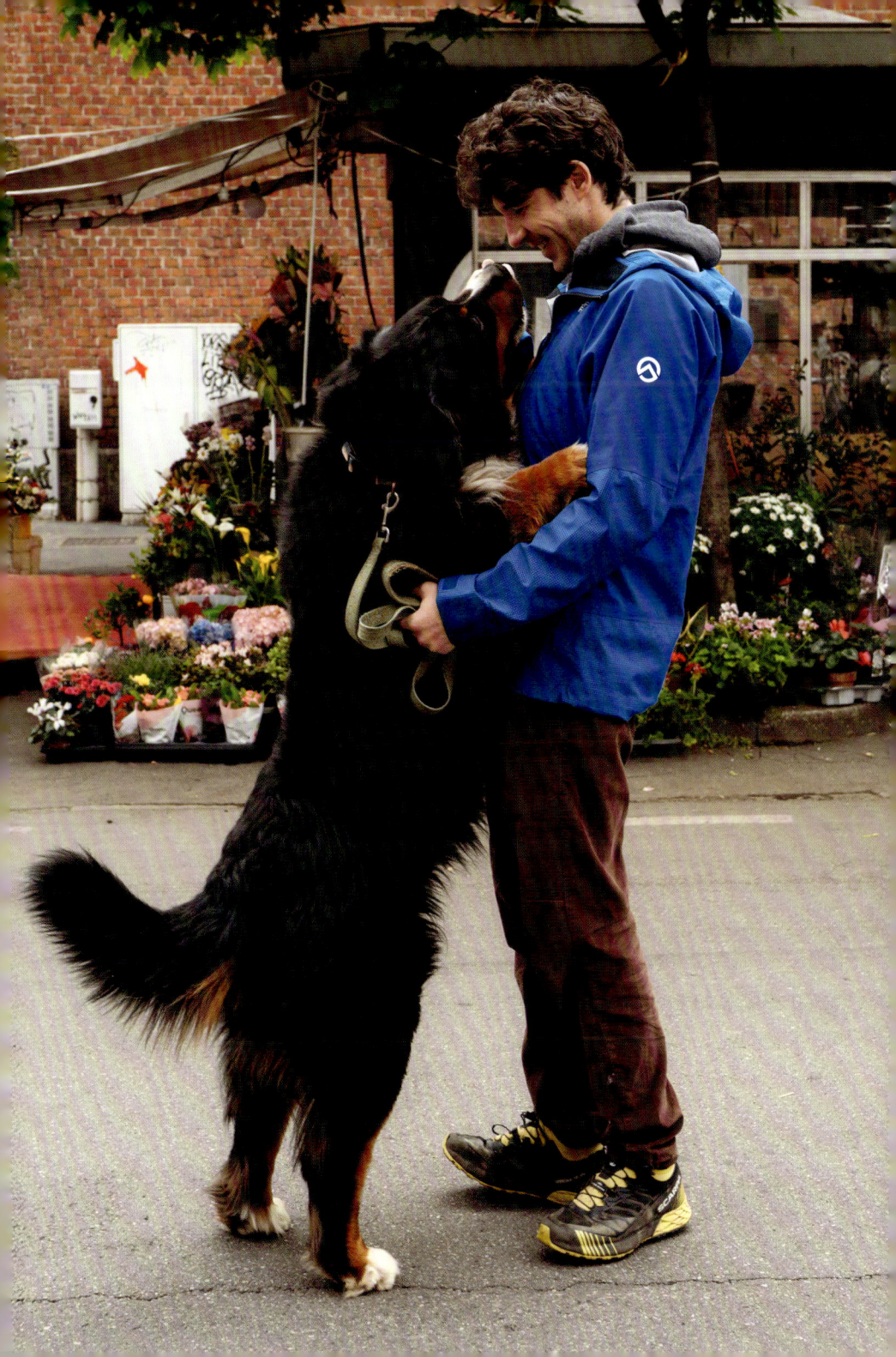

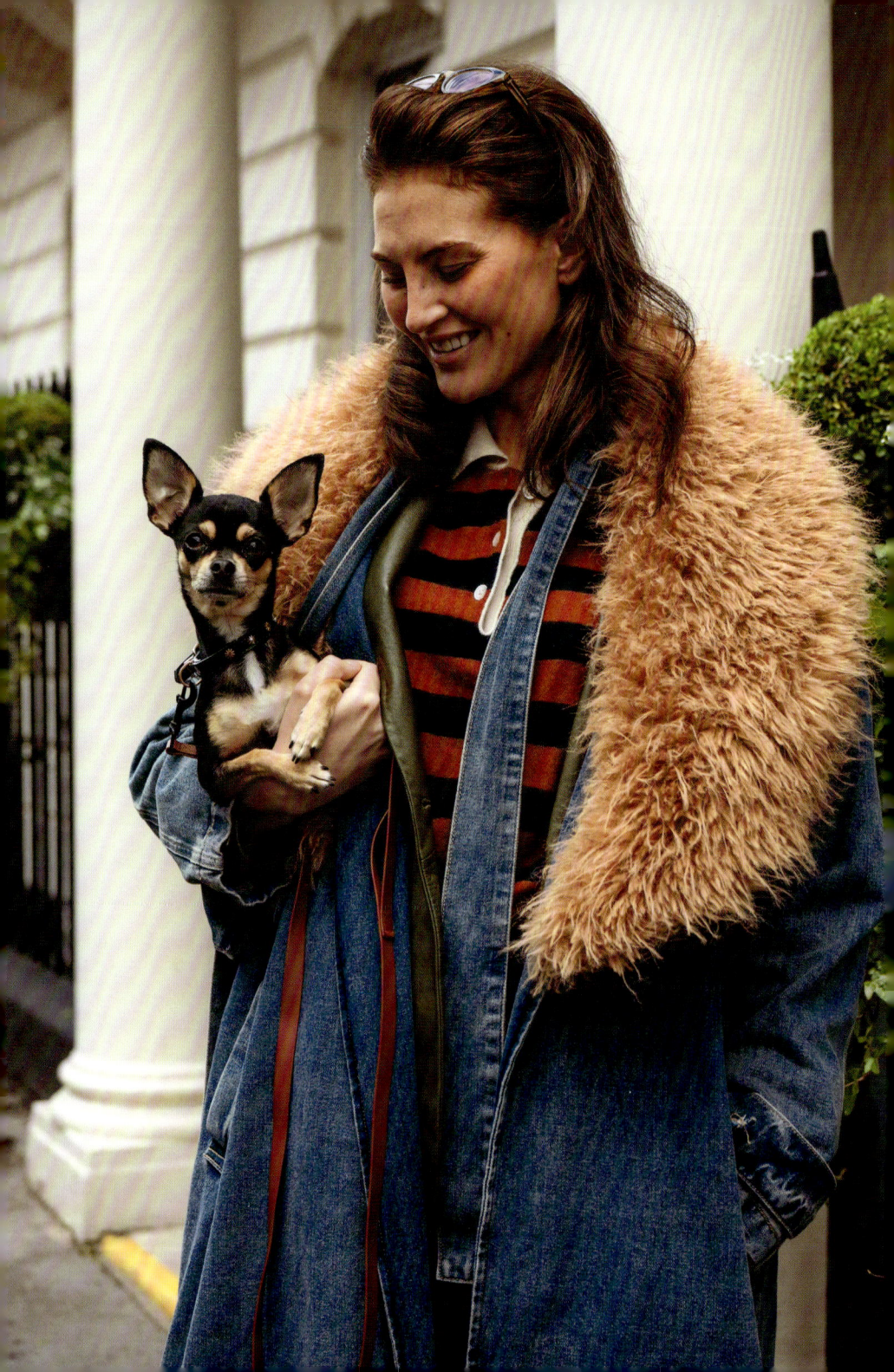

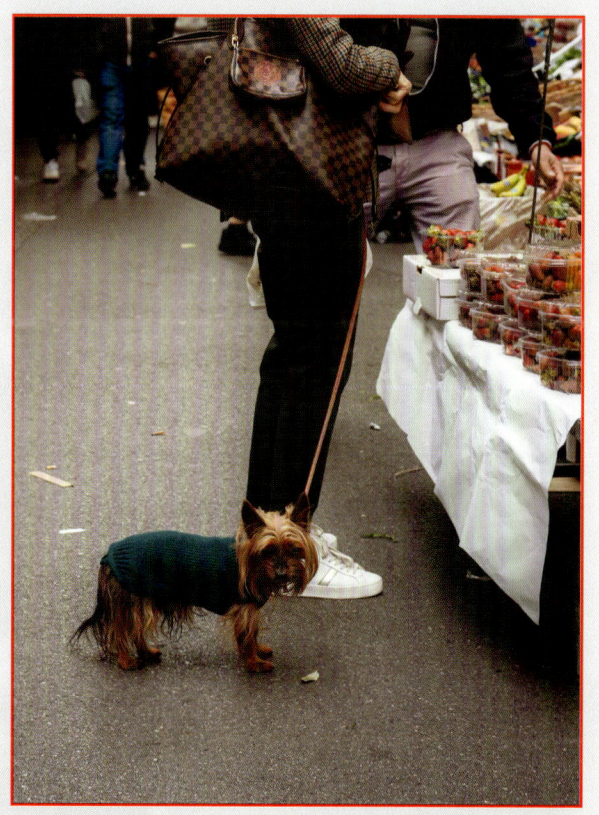

Milan, Italy

"She thinks I'm wonderful because she gets three meals a day."

Riquelle and their dog Disco
London, England

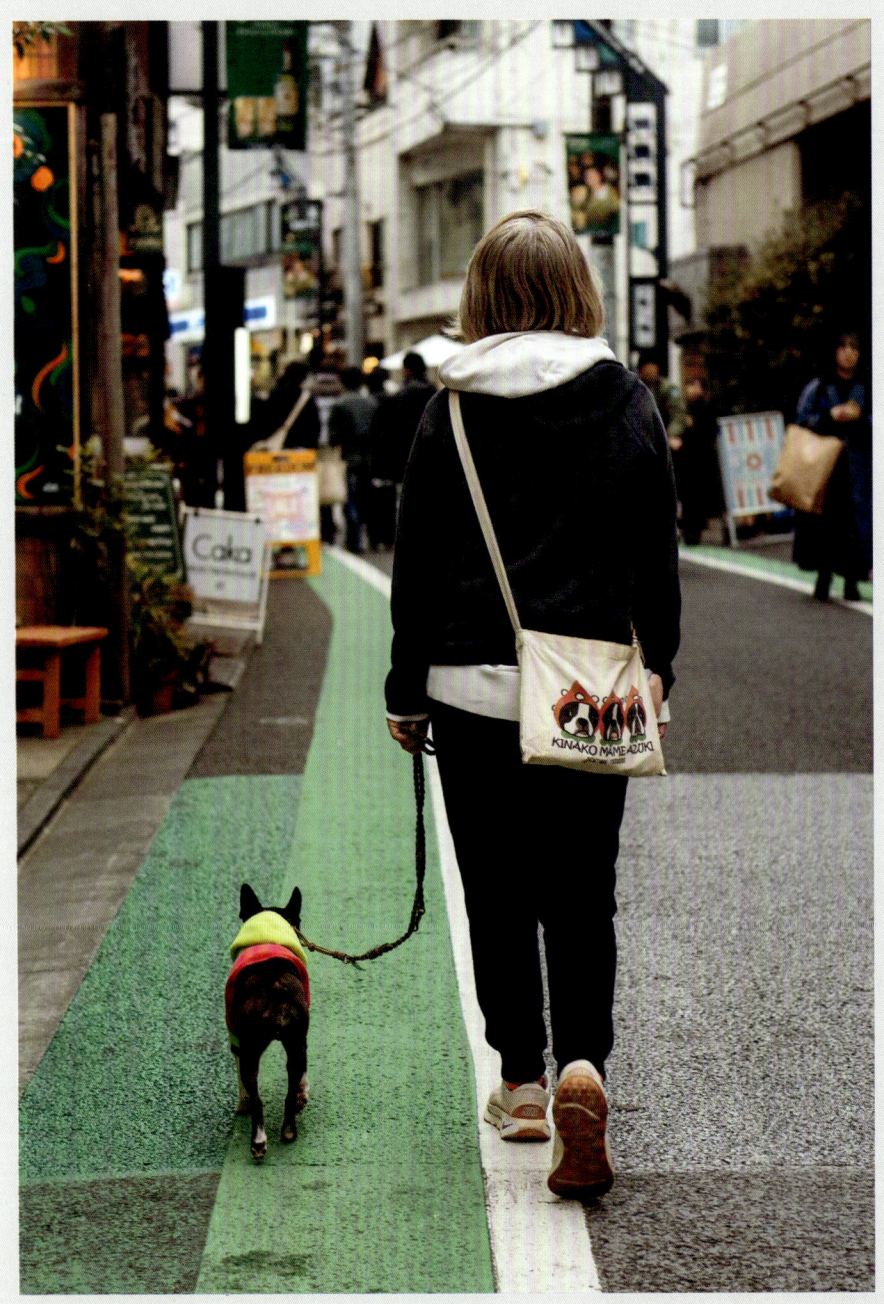

Tokyo, Japan | London, England

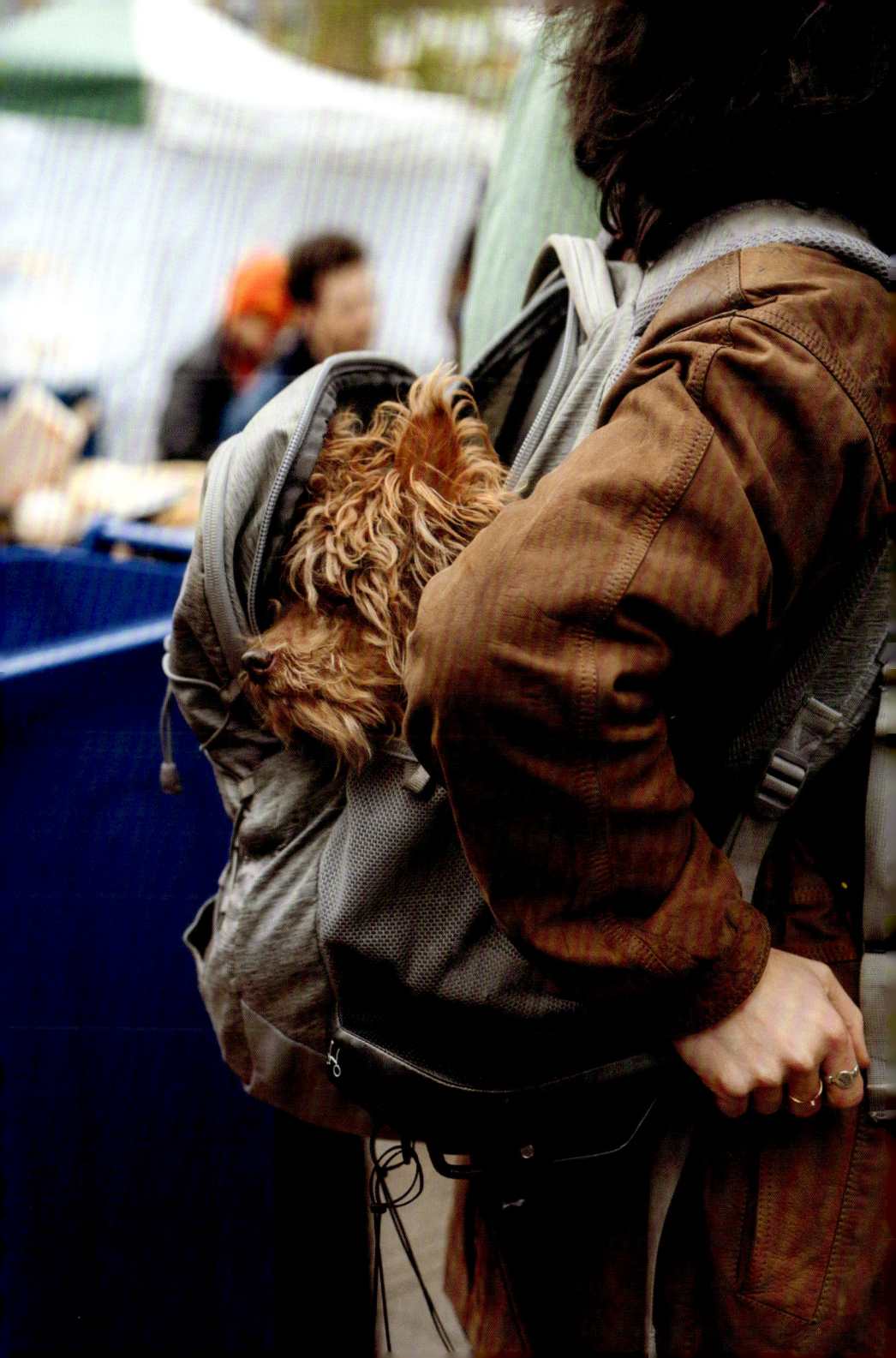

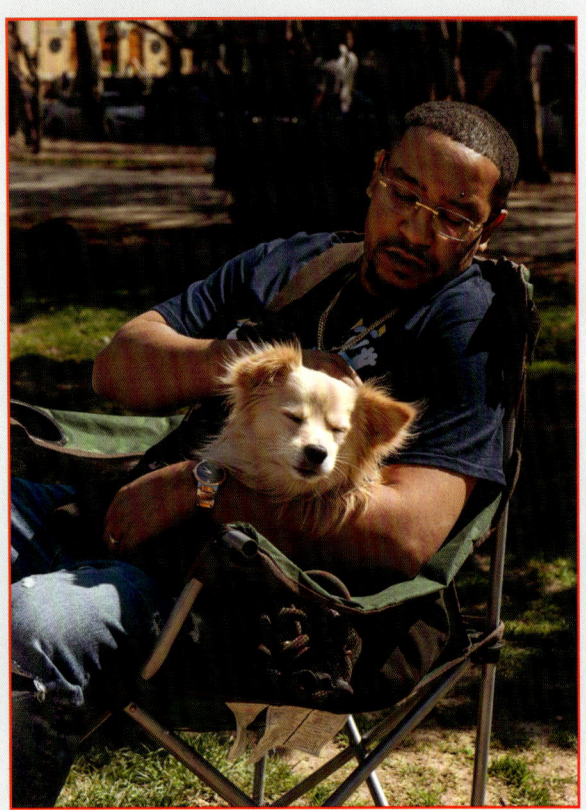

New York City, USA

"She's daddy's little girl."

Shusuke and their dog Rose
Kyoto, Japan

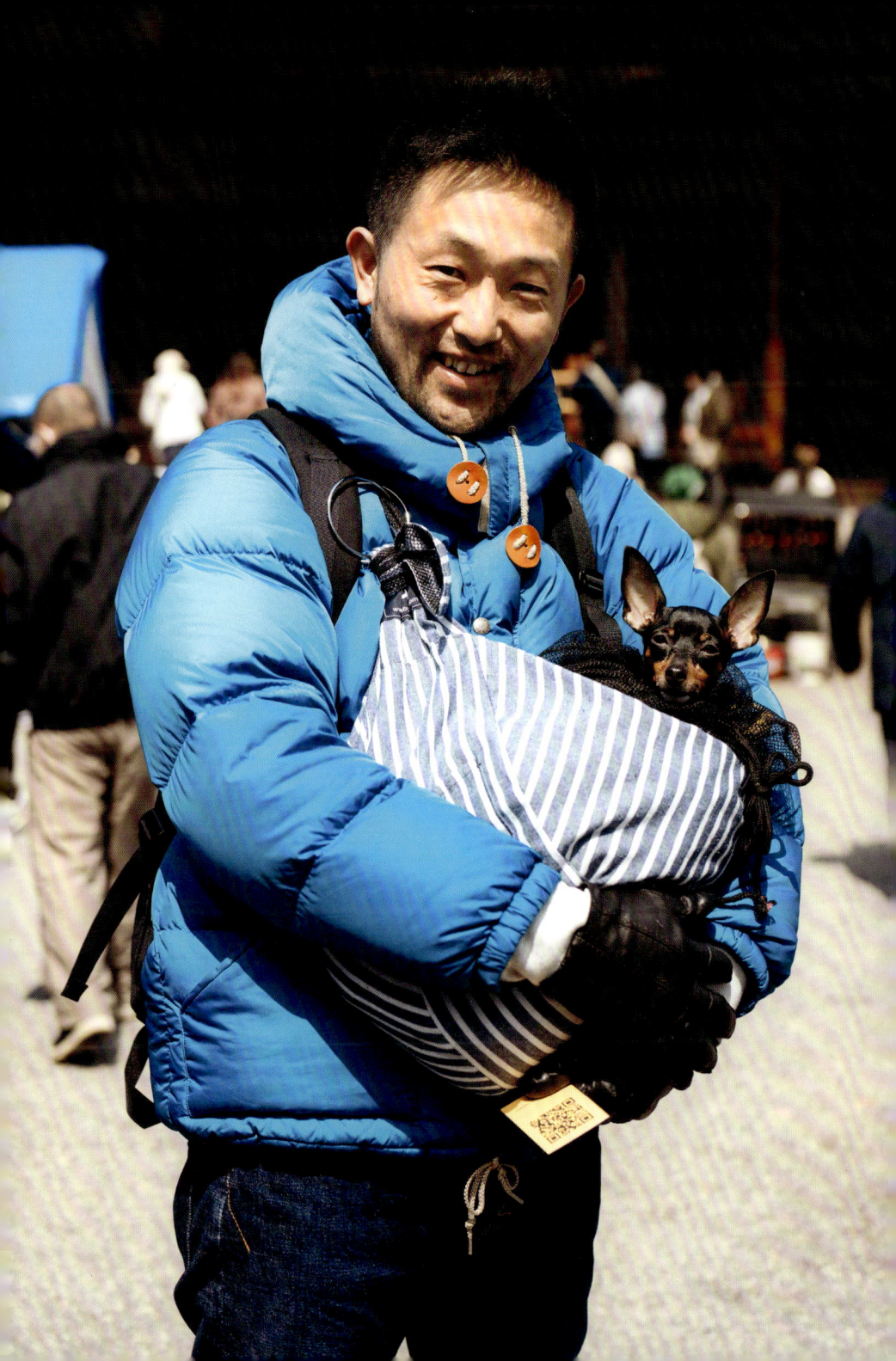

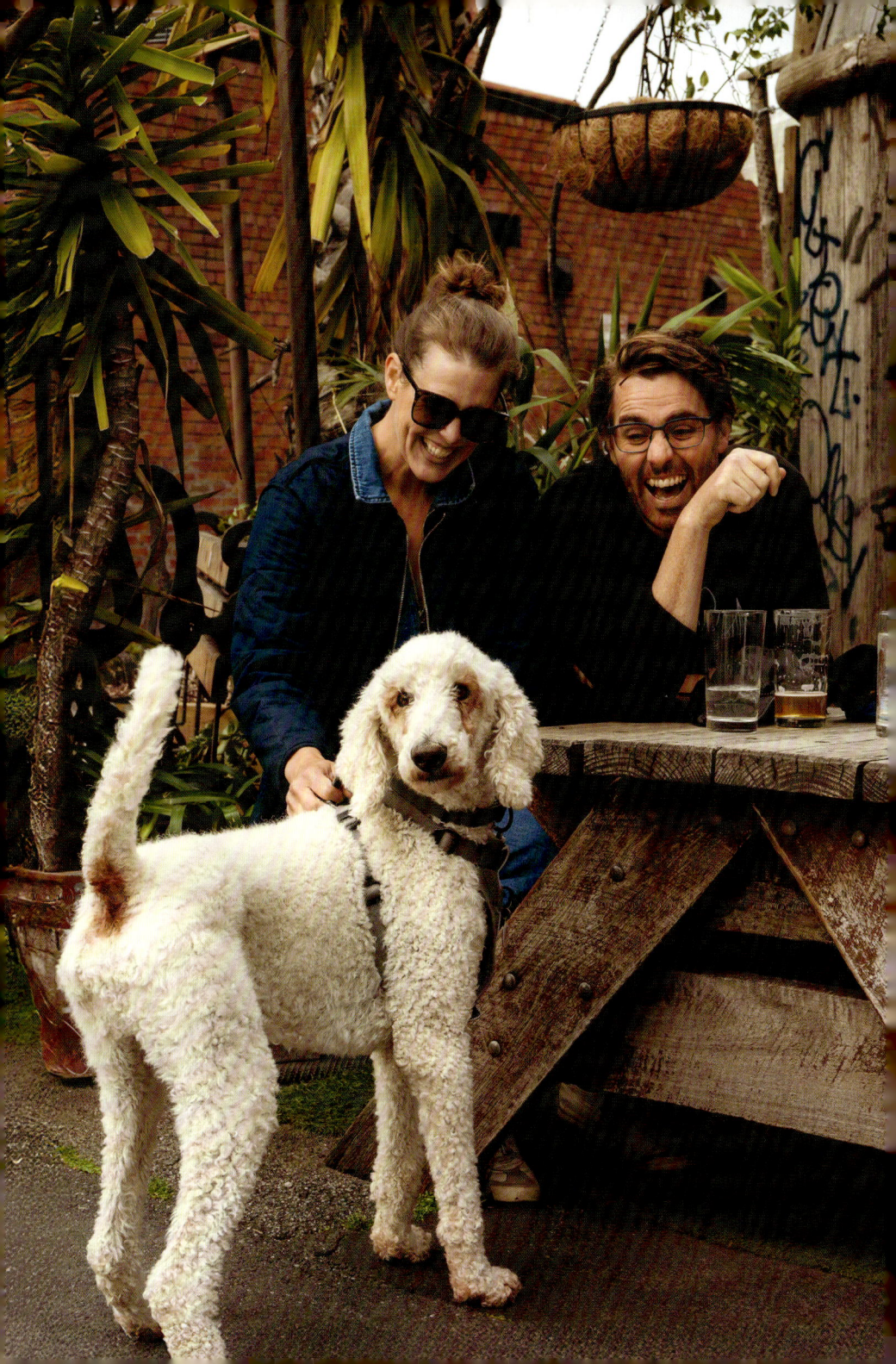

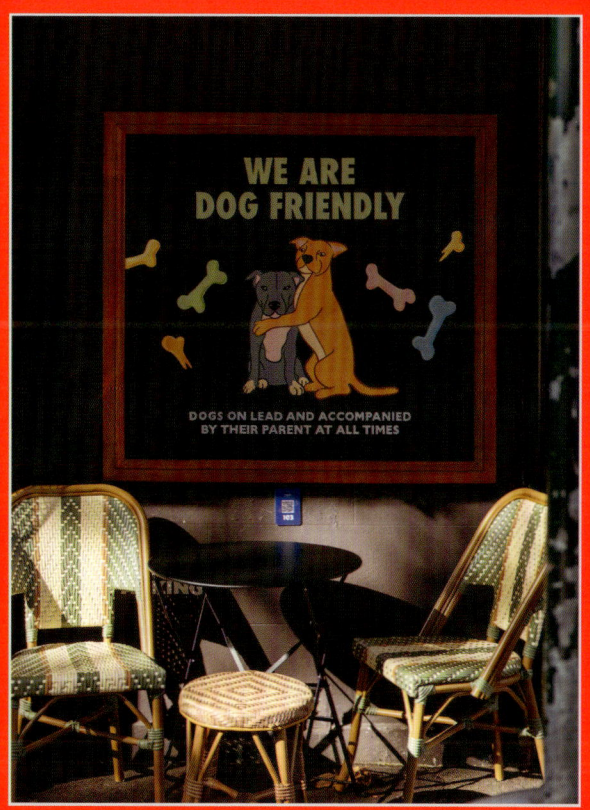

Sydney, Australia

"We recently introduced him to kangaroo meat and he loves it."

Mark and Sarah and their dog Remi
Melbourne, Australia

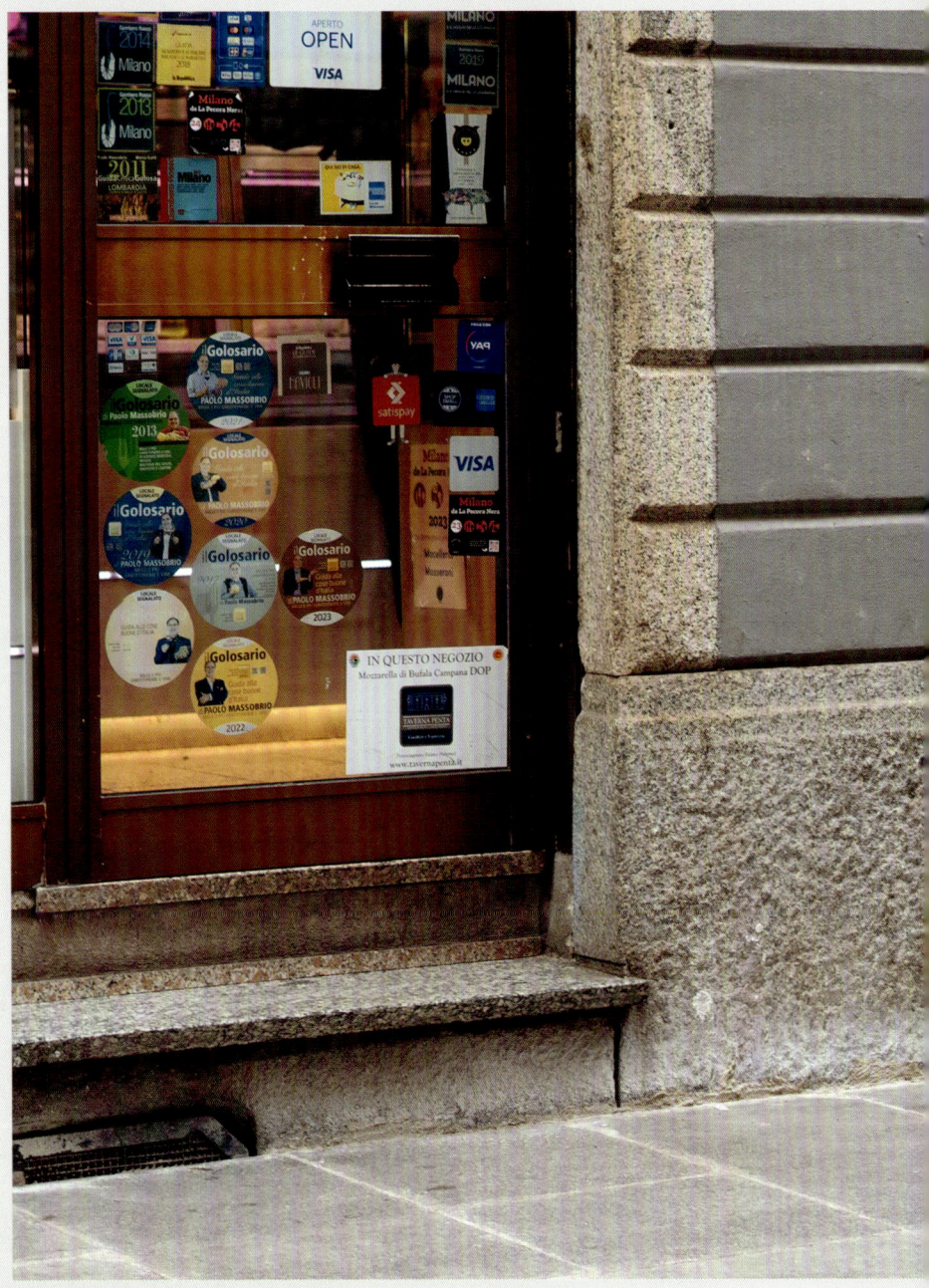

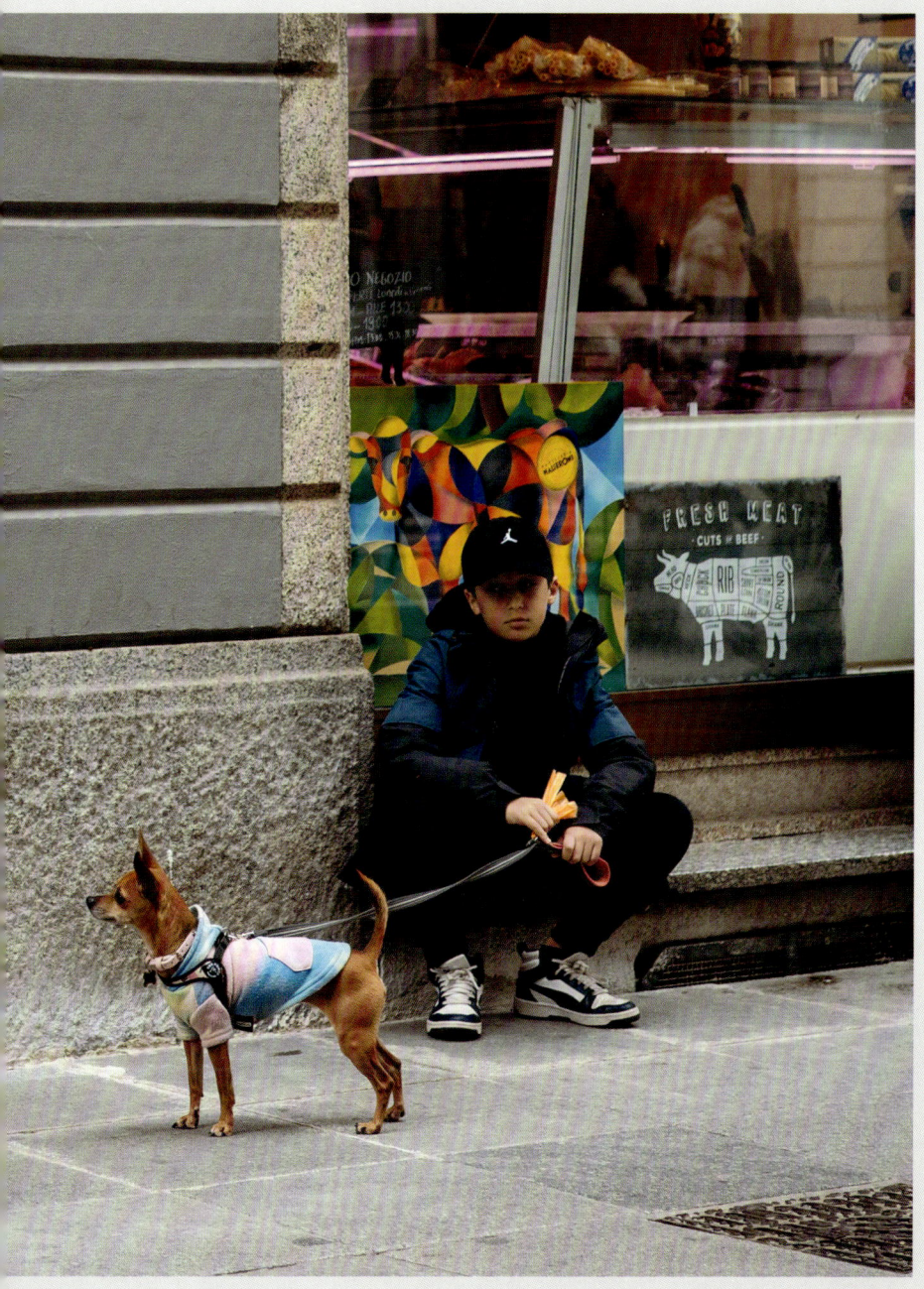

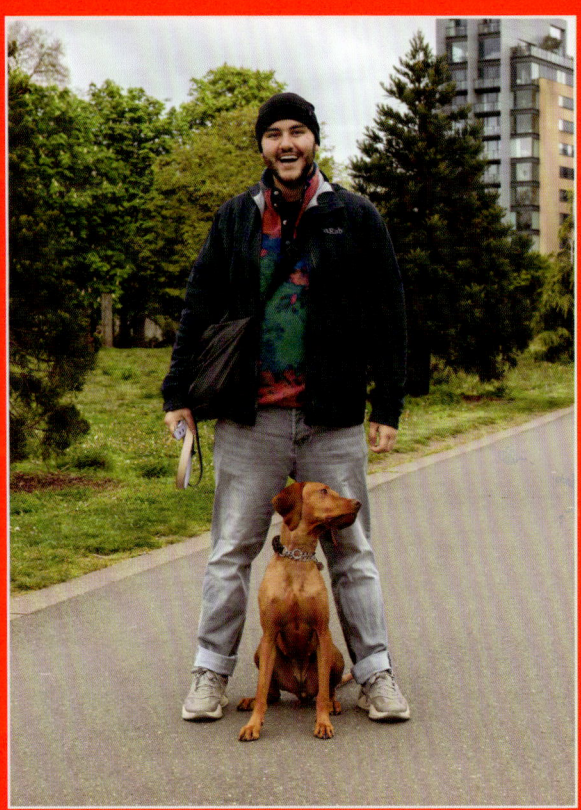

London, England

"We're attached at the hip, unless he sniffs something more interesting."

Anaïs and their dog Guinness
Sydney, Australia

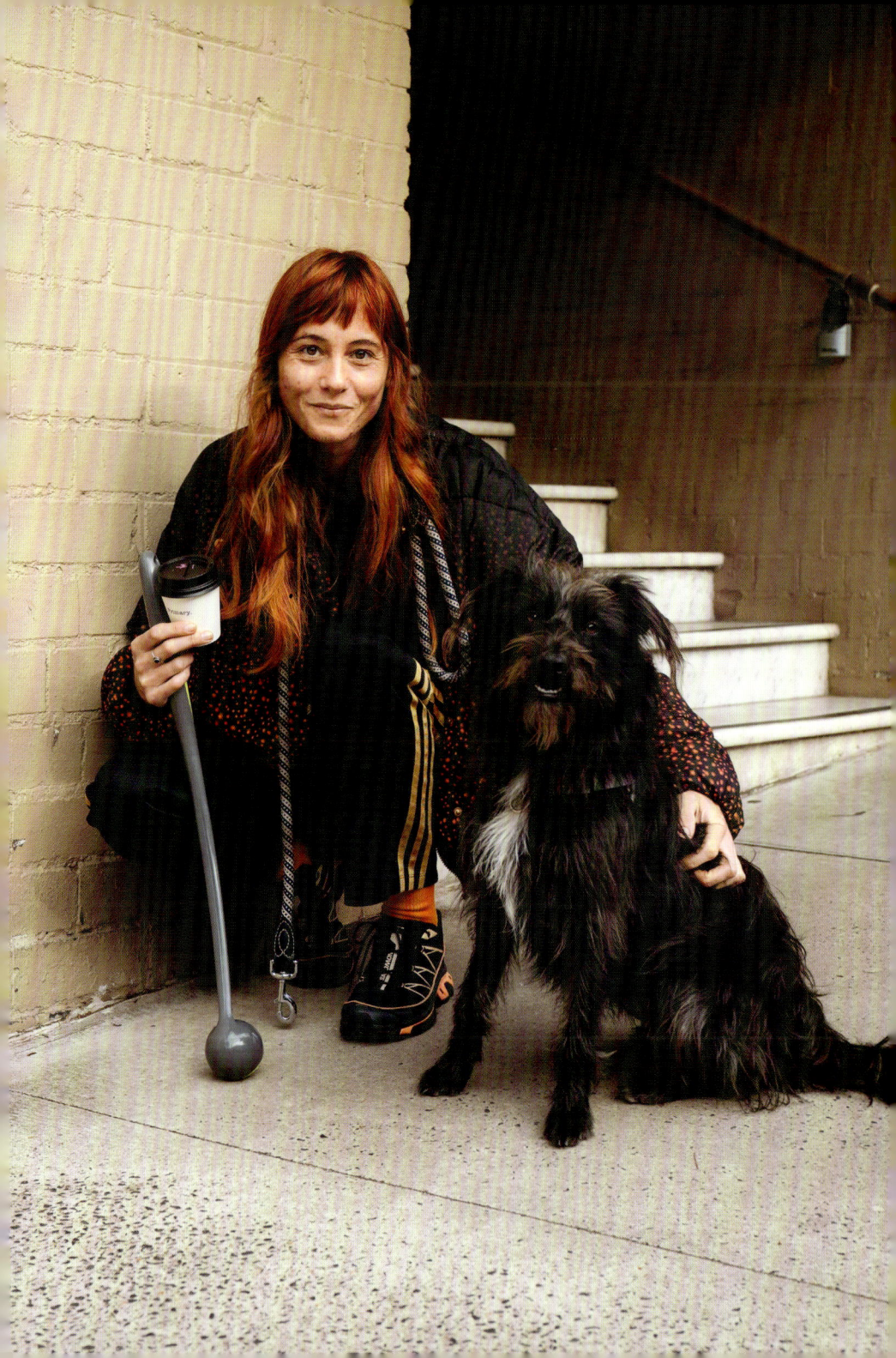

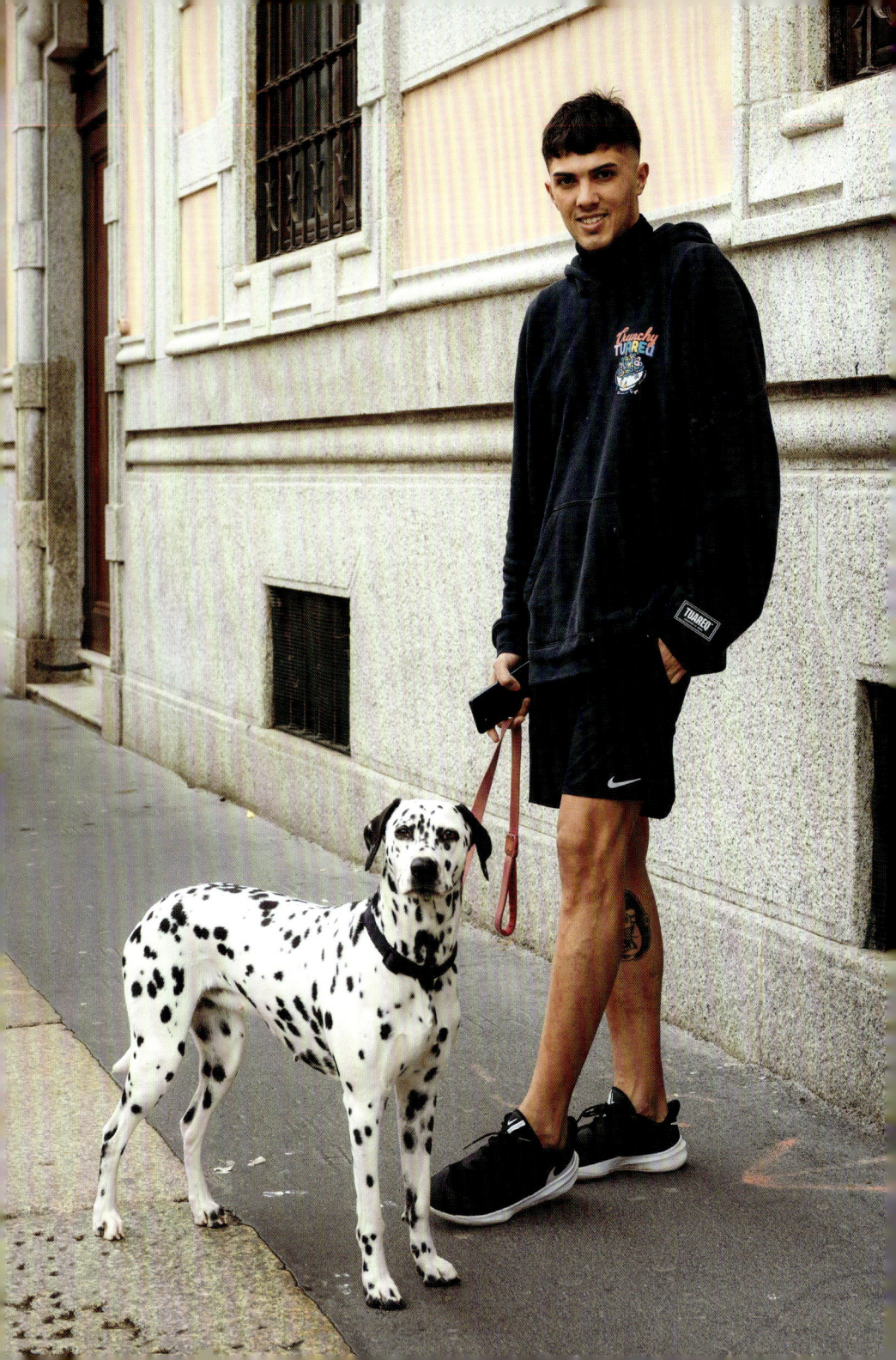

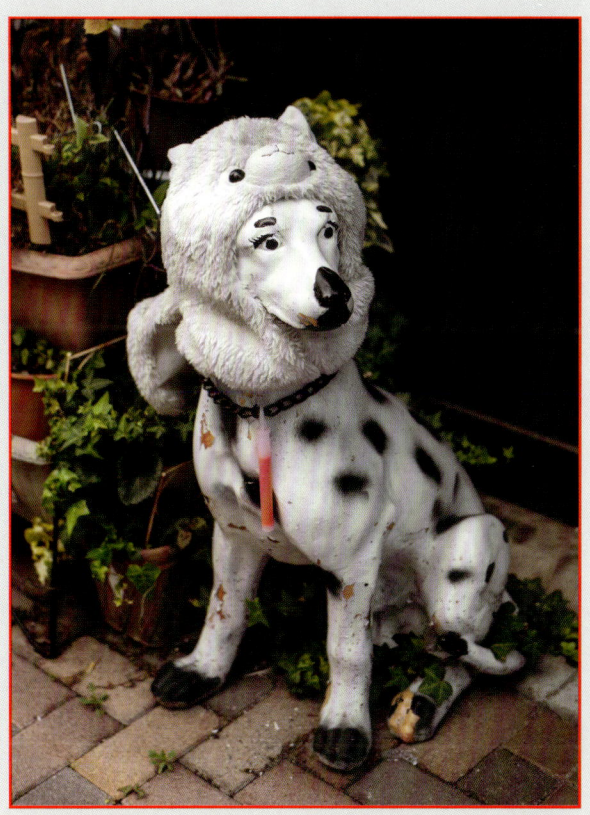

Tokyo, Japan

"She's deaf, so I don't know what she would say. But I know she loves me."

Gaston and their dog Sade
Milan, Italy

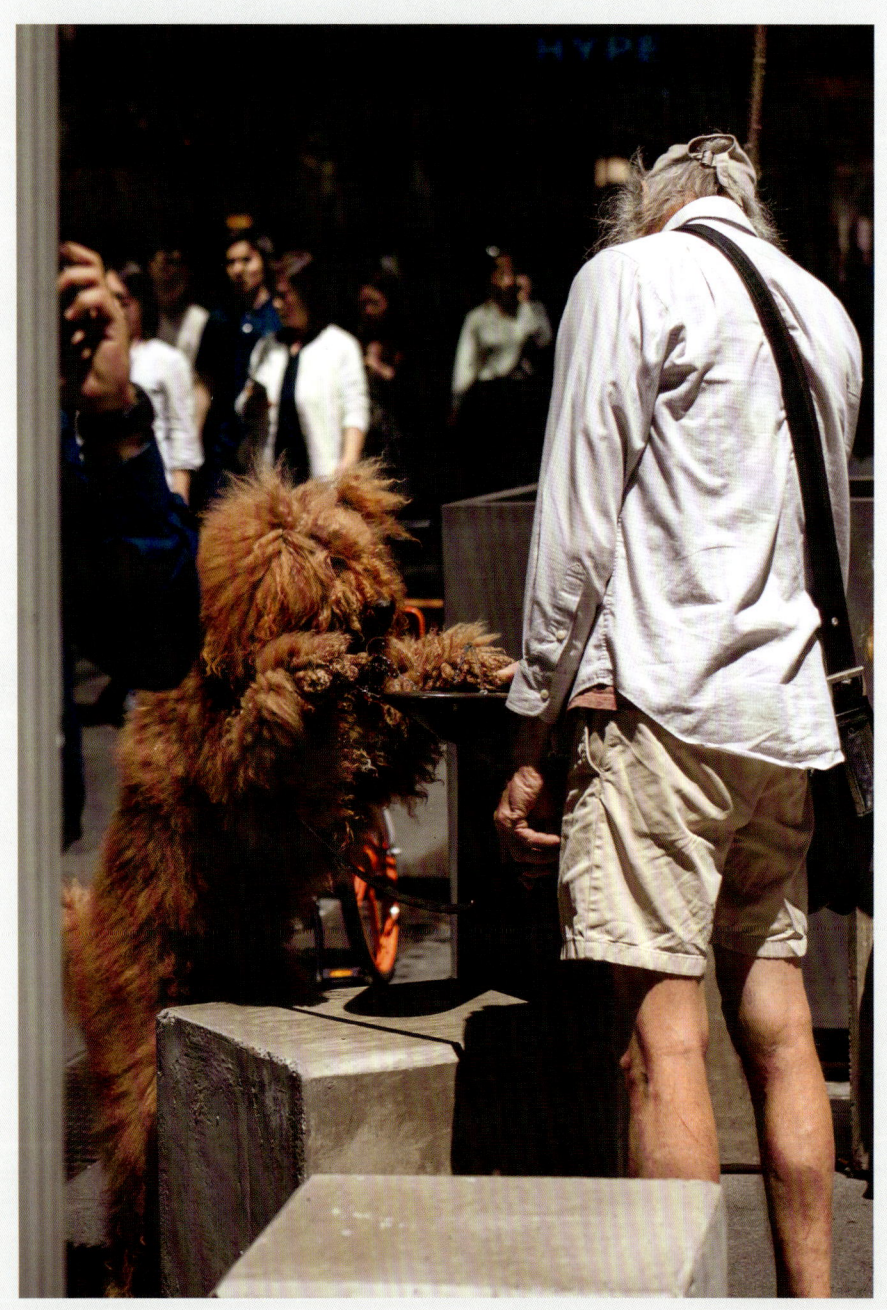

Sydney, Australia | Milan, Italy

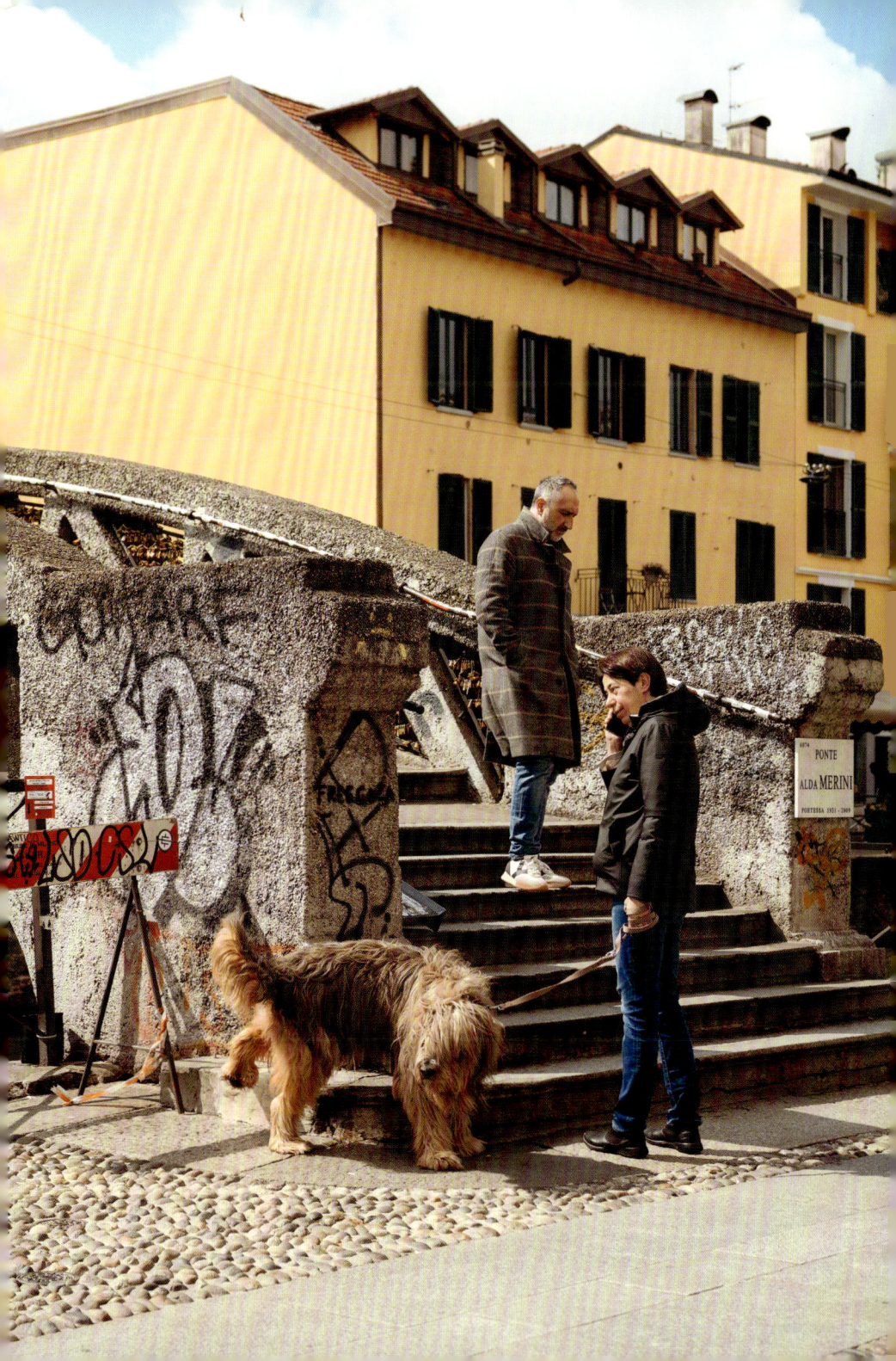

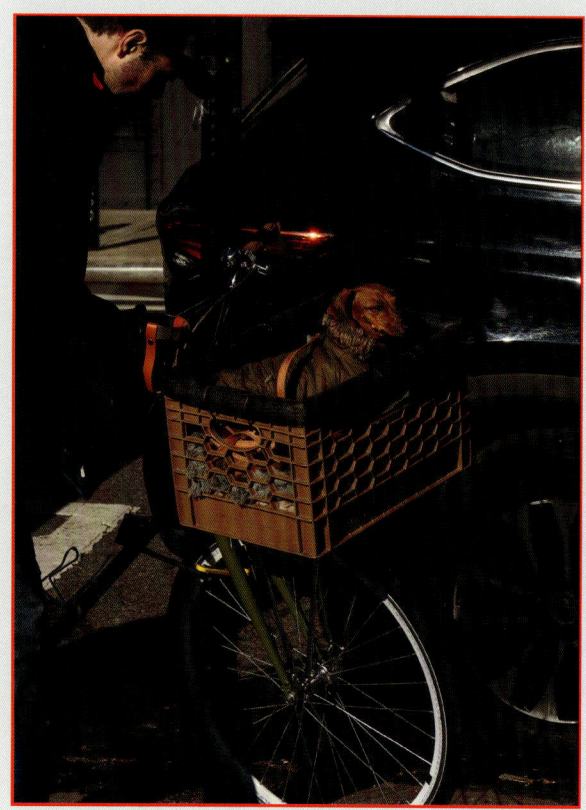

New York City, USA

"I'm her humble servant and wait on her hand and foot."

Jake and their dog Ziggy
Paris, France

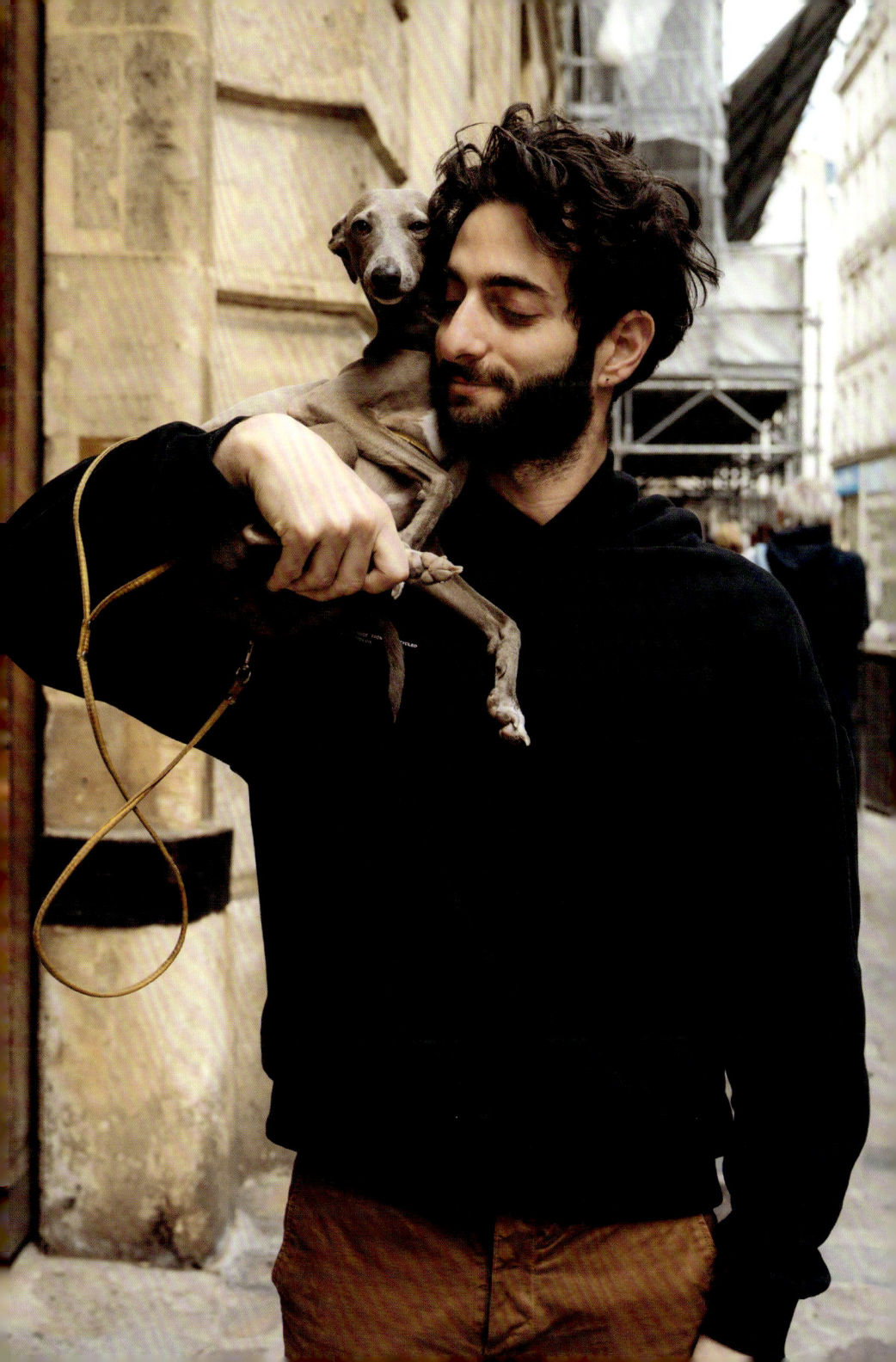

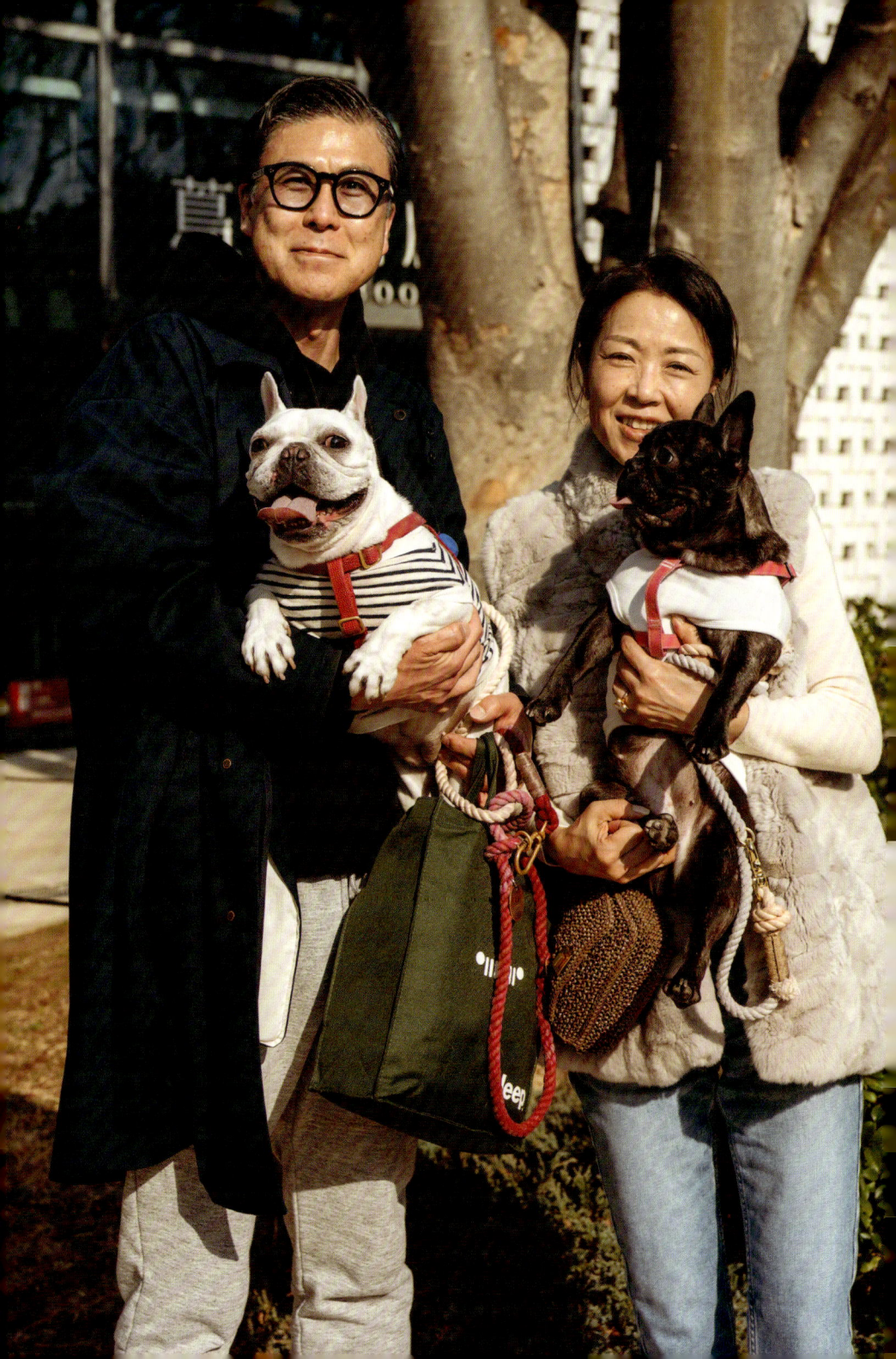

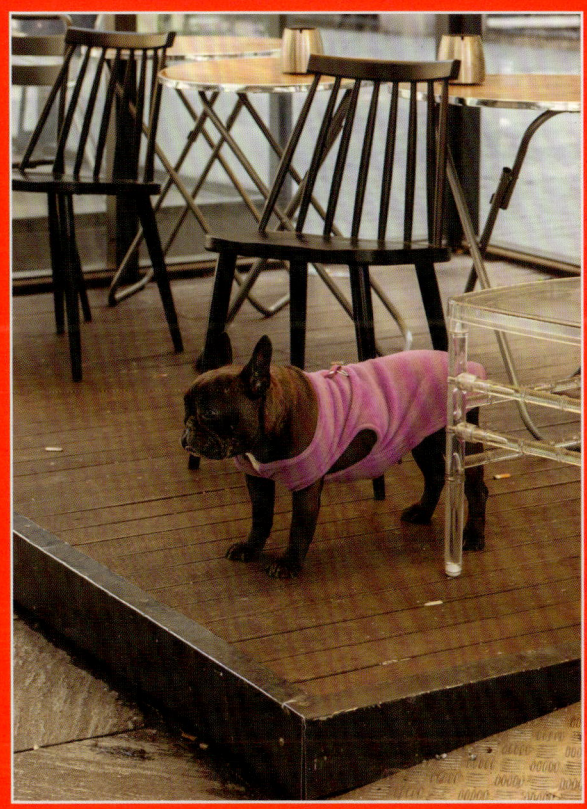

Milan, Italy

"Miu doesn't like having a sister. She would rather be an only child."

Kōichi and Yoshiko and their dogs Miu and Rin
Tokyo, Japan

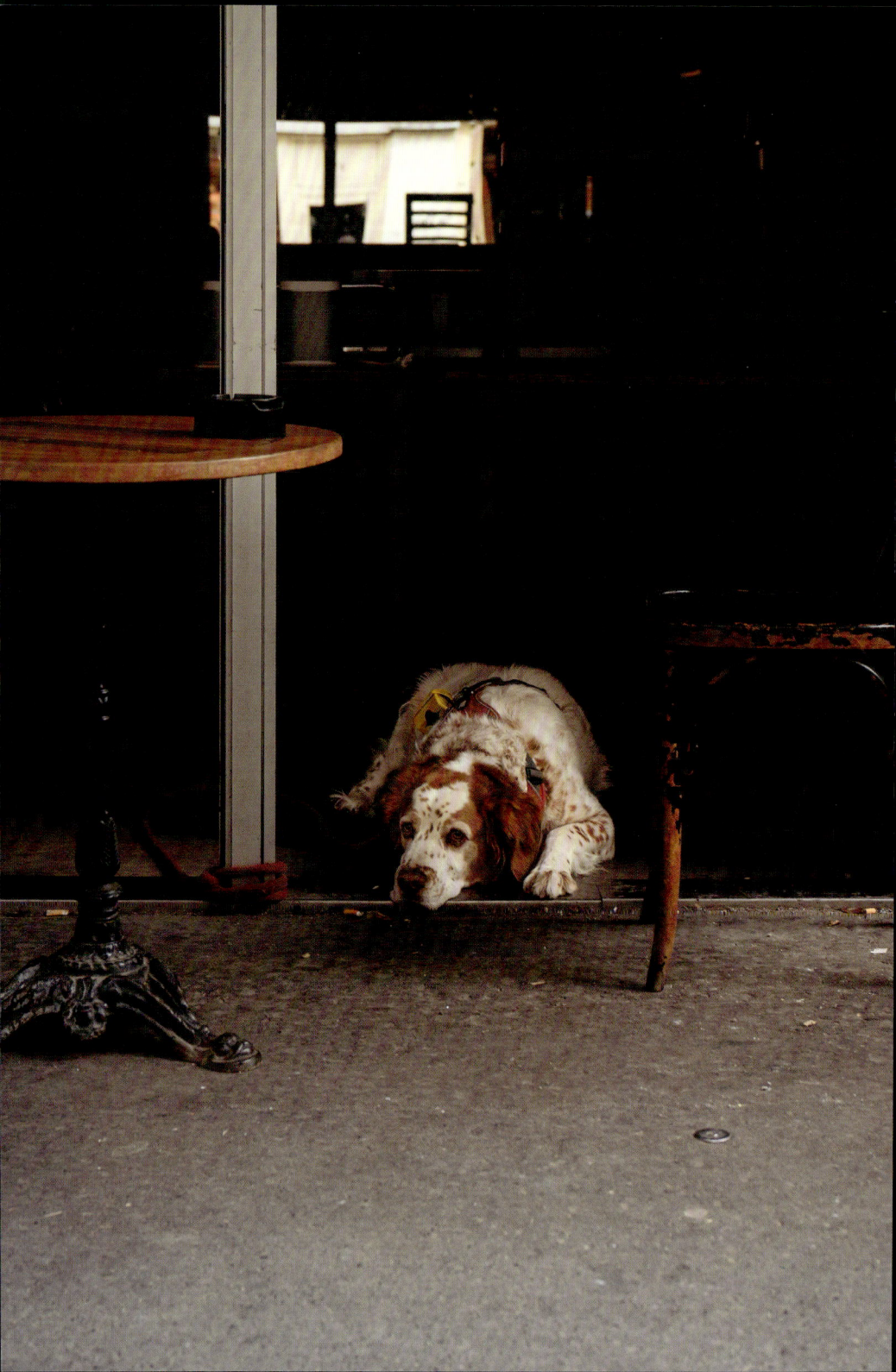

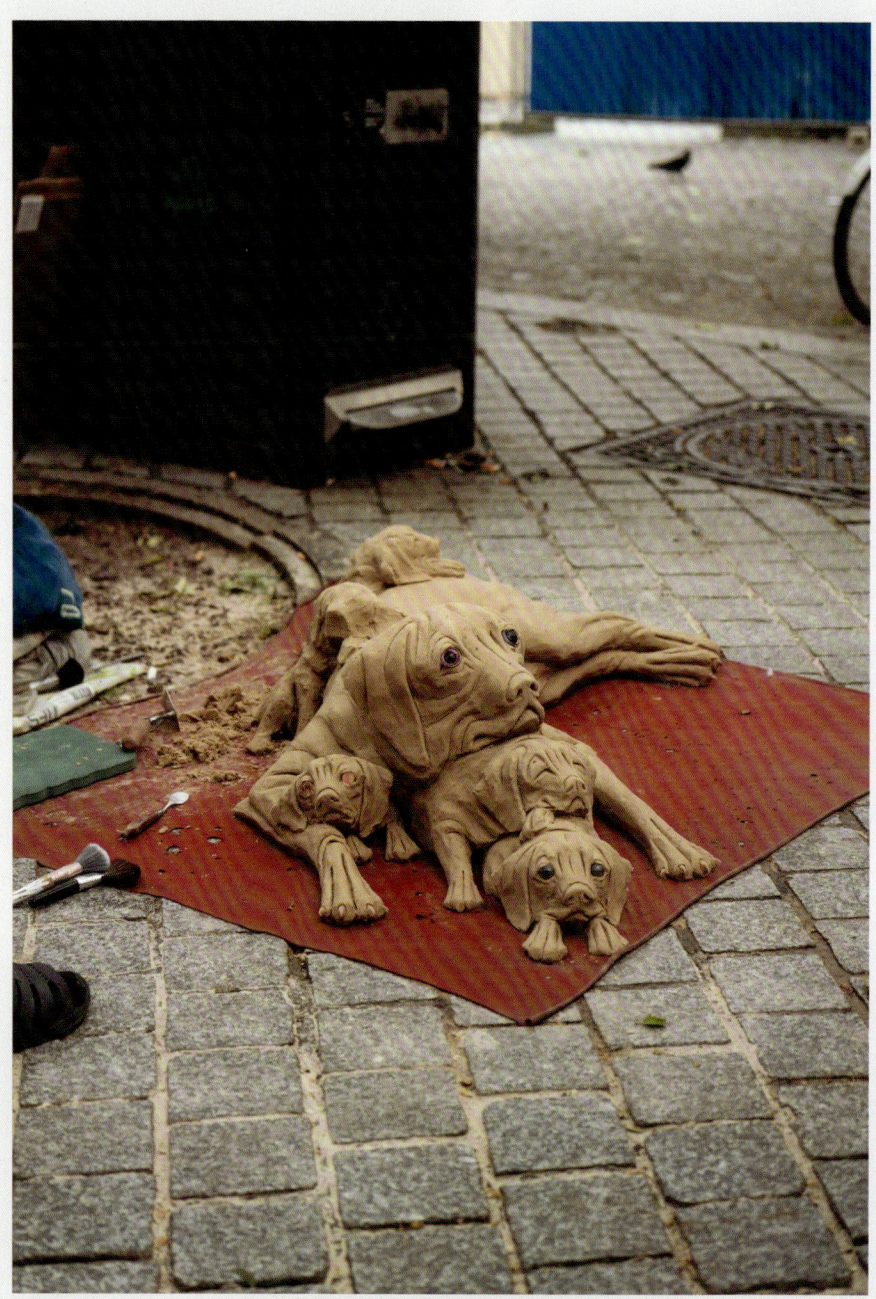

Paris, France | Paris, France

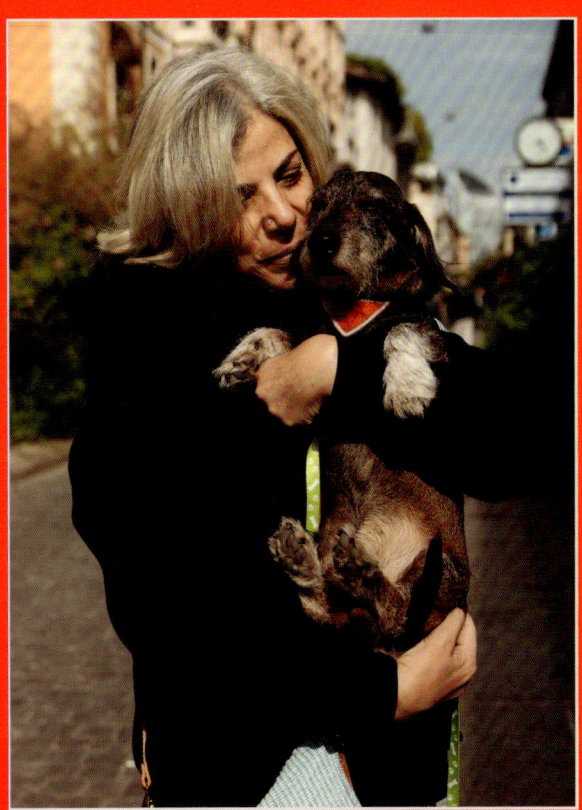

Milan, Italy

"You know what, I think he loves me to death."

Daniella and their dog Ty
London, England

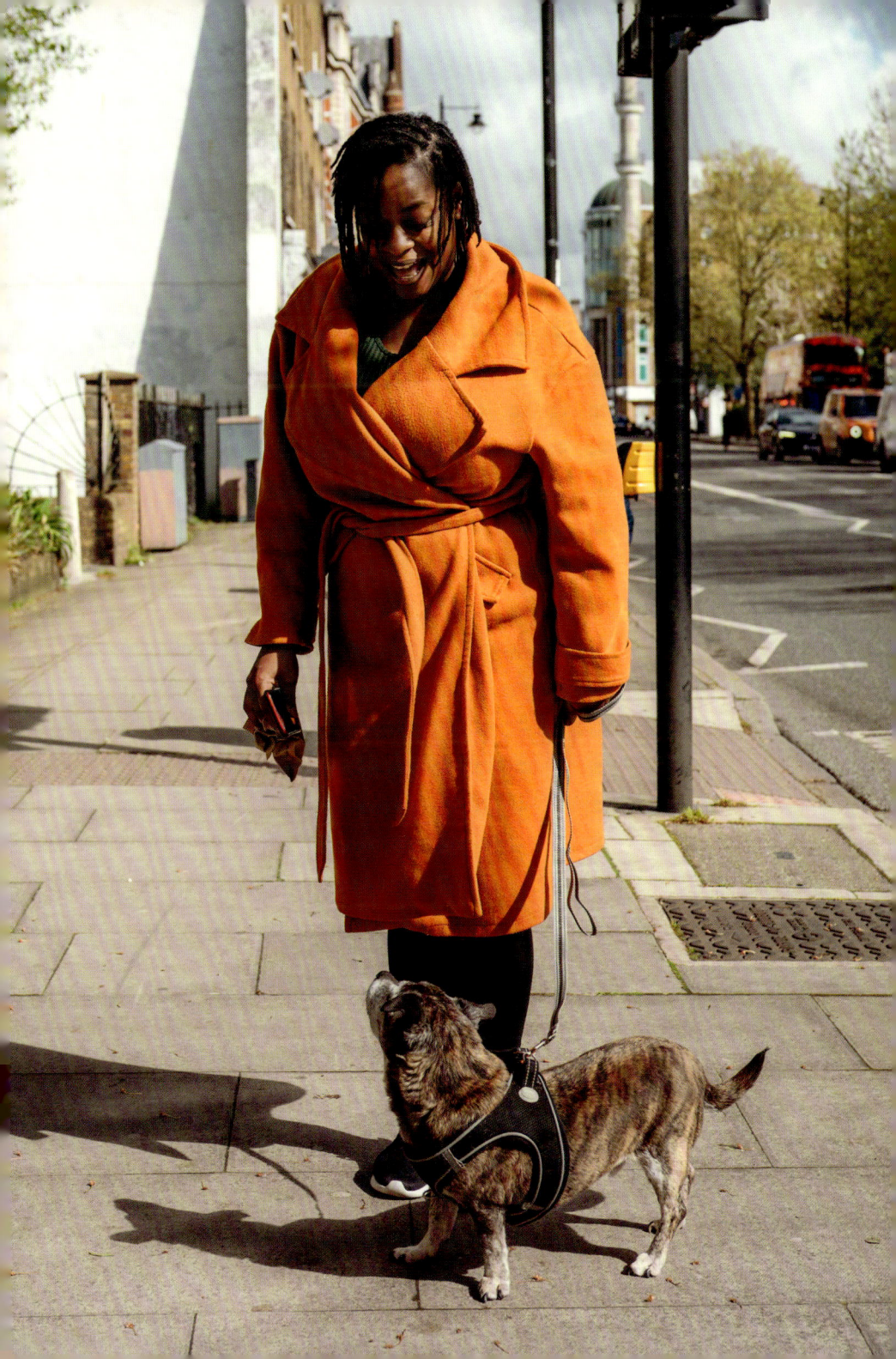

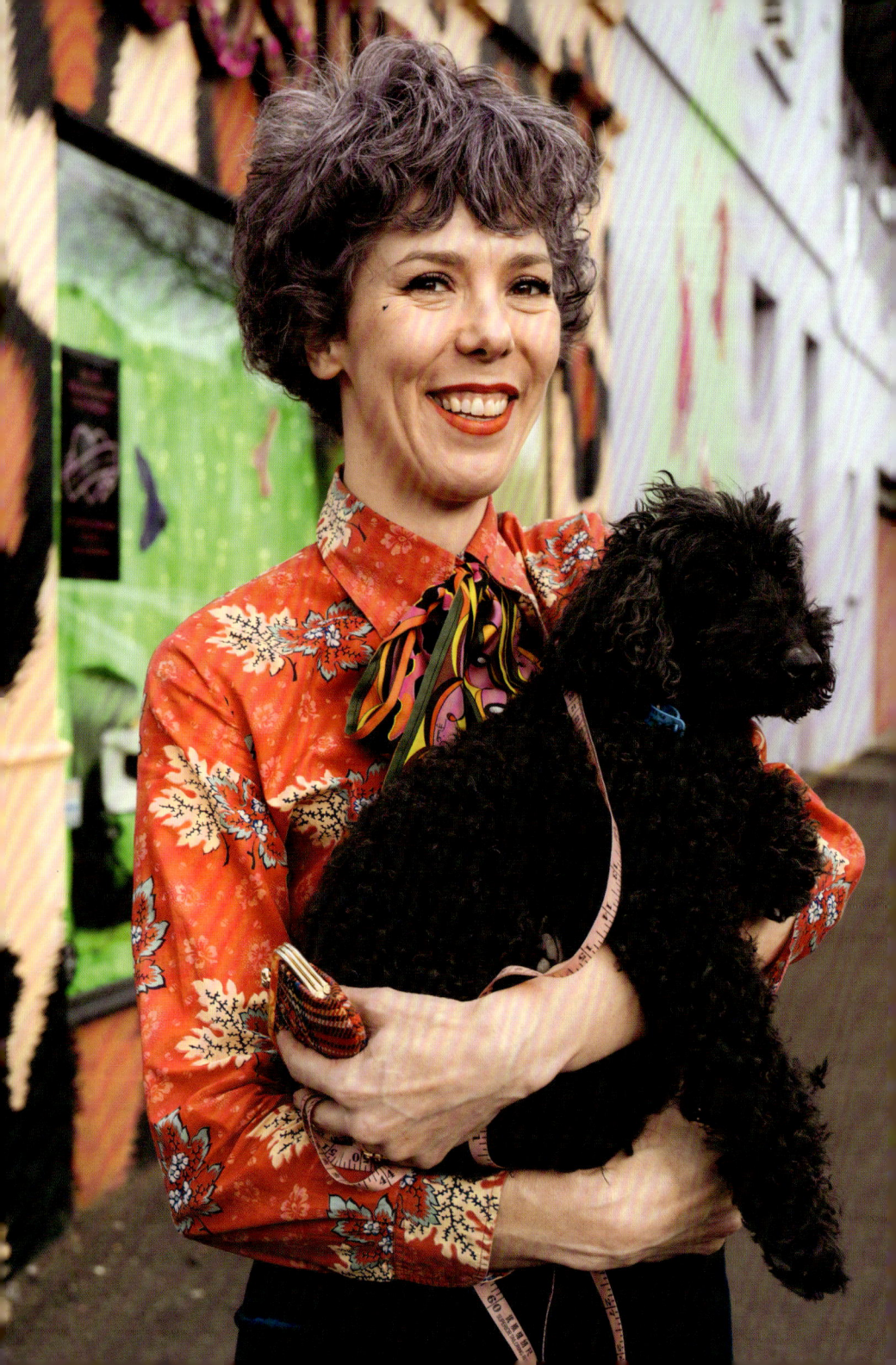

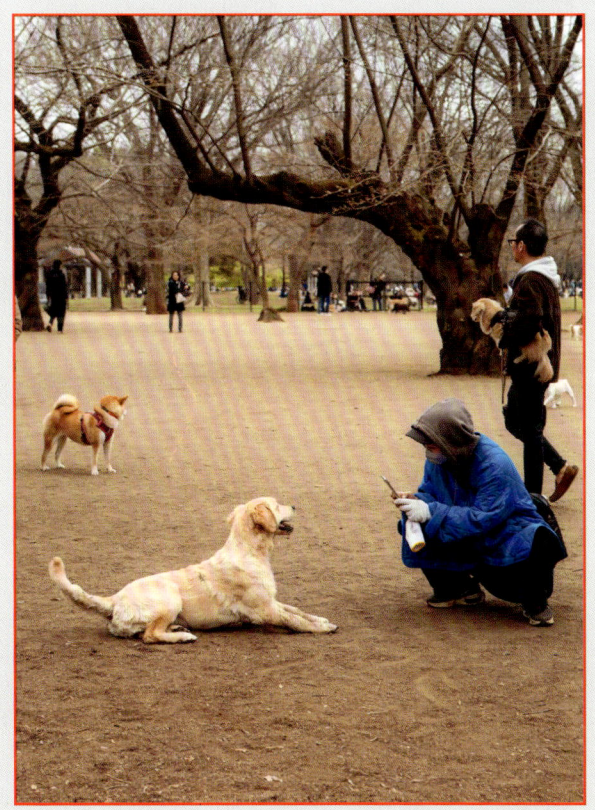

"He thinks I'm pretty compliant."

Alice and their dog Rupert
Melbourne, Australia

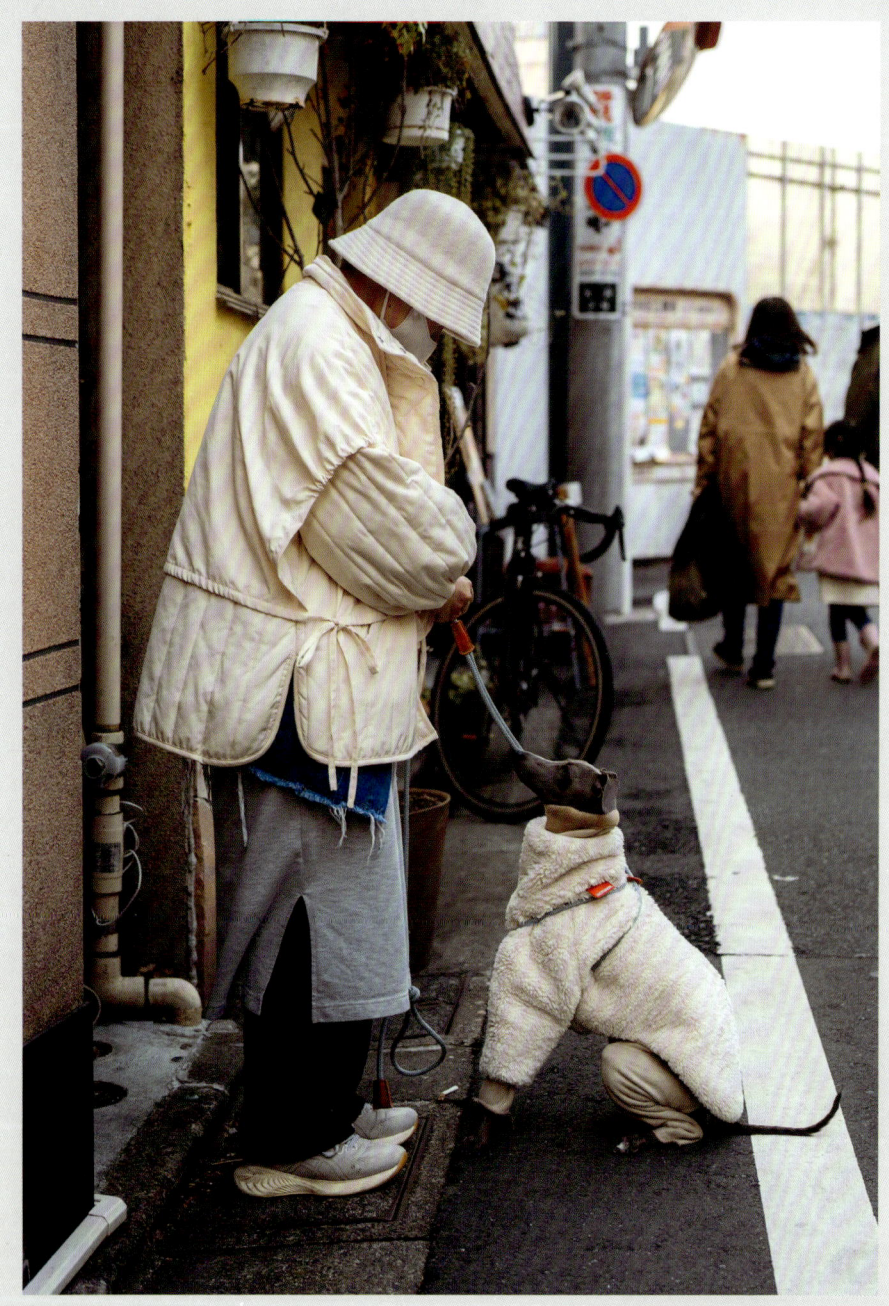

Tokyo, Japan | Milan, Italy

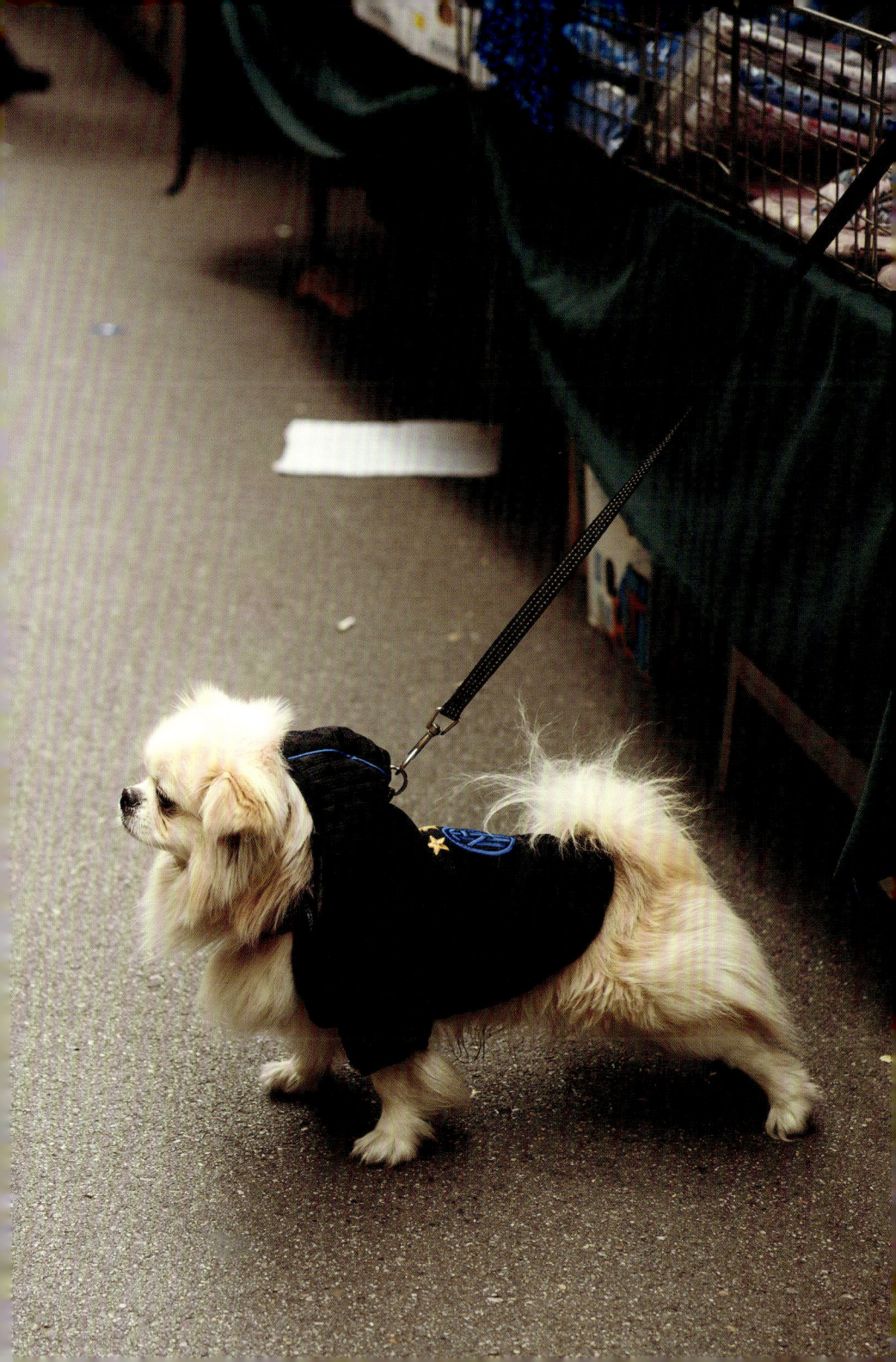

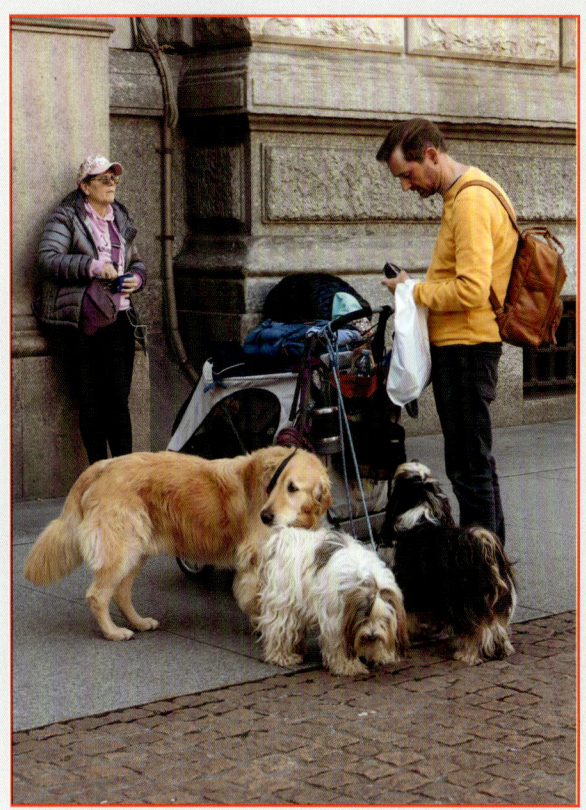

Milan, Italy

"I appreciate their company, they appreciate me bringing them out to hunt for pizza and chicken bones."

Fluffy and Salvo and their dog walker Robbie
New York City, USA

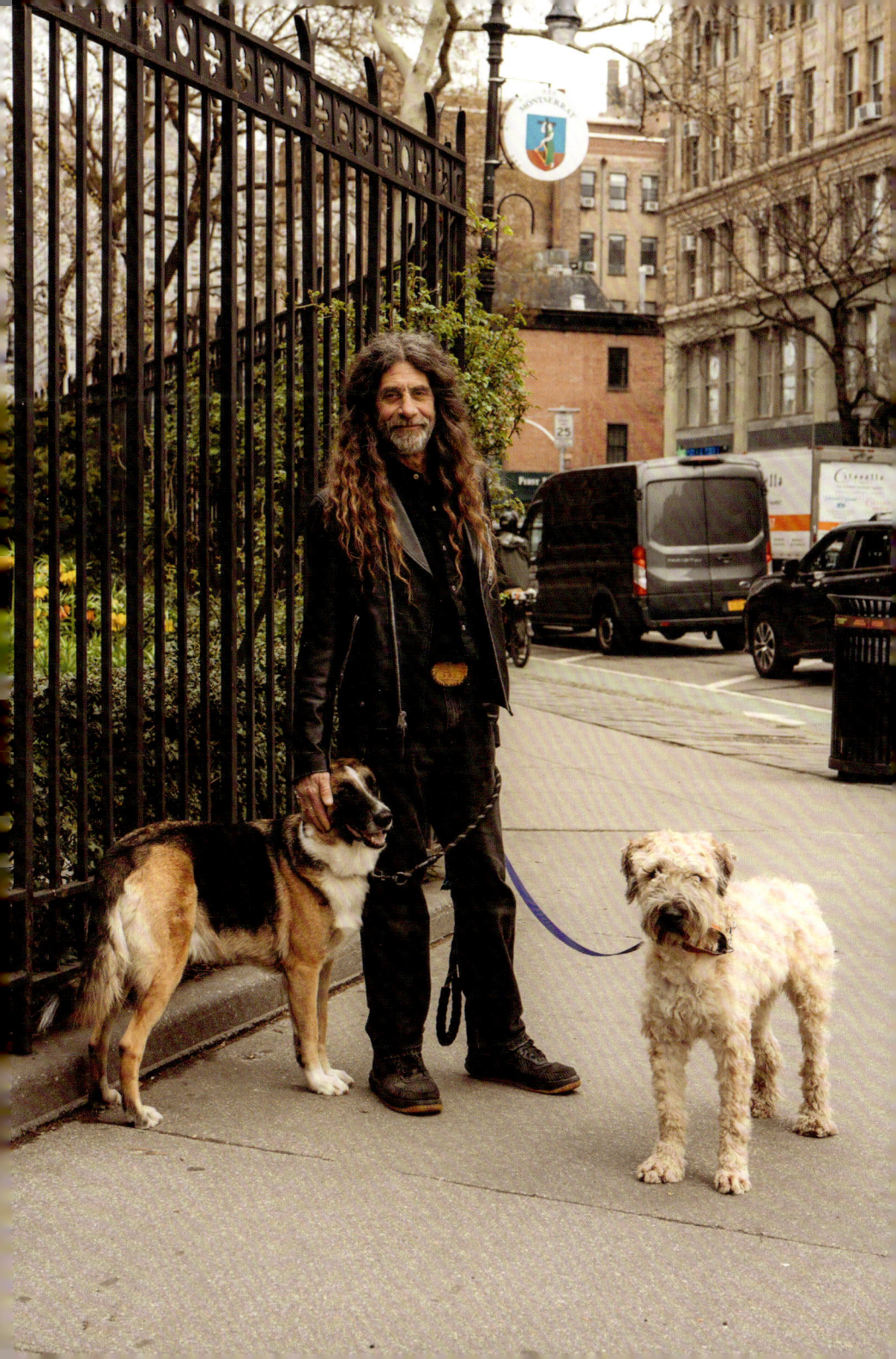

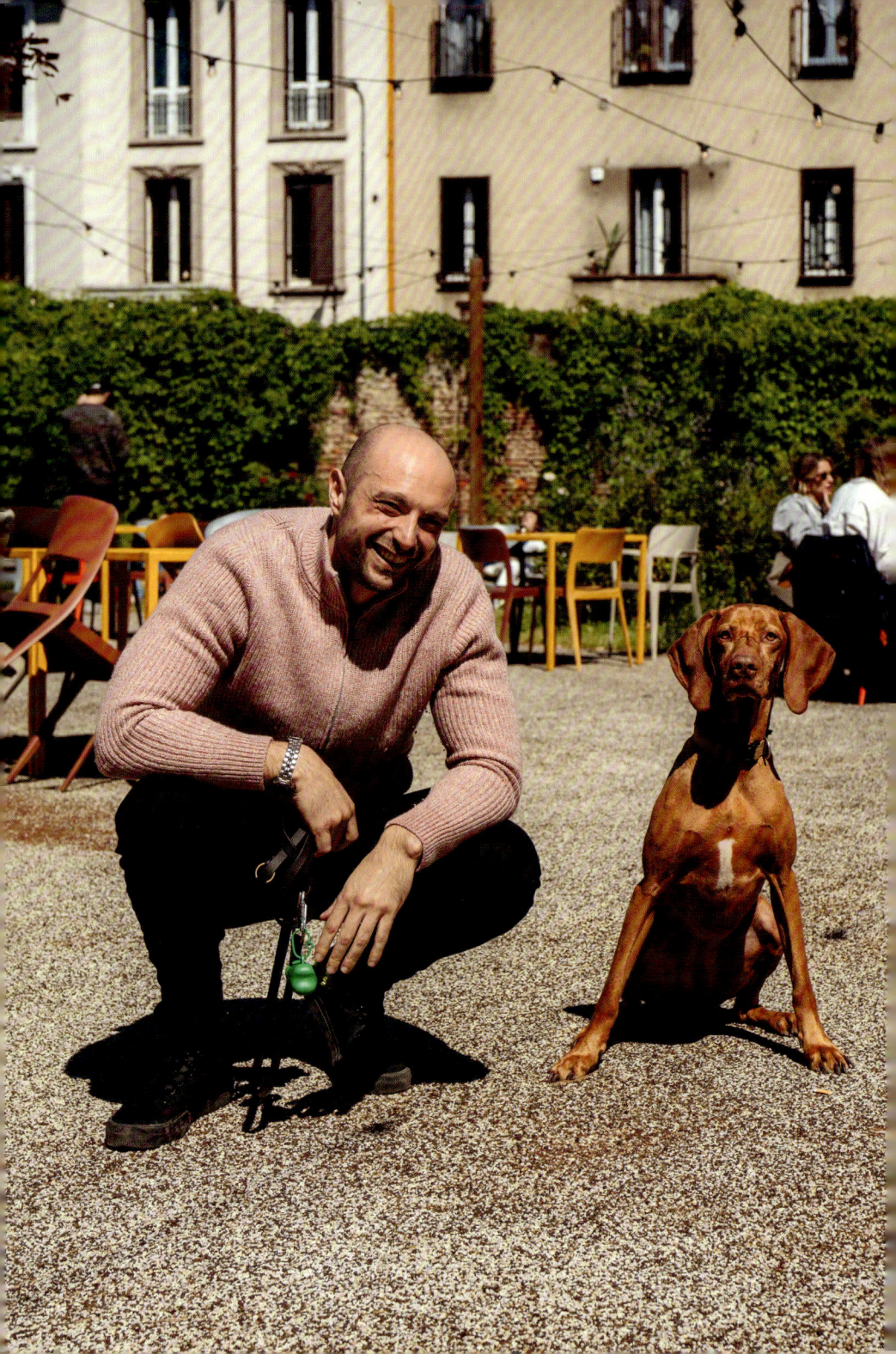

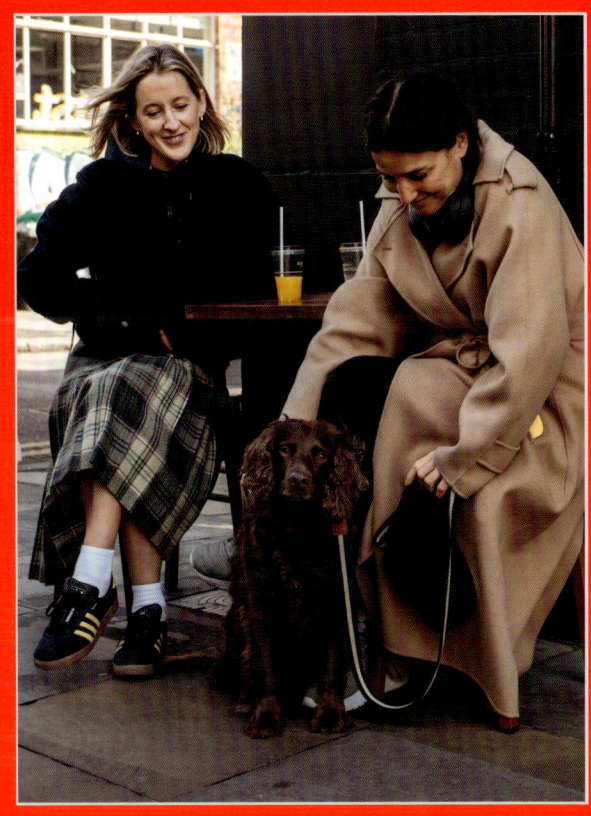

London, England

"I lost my own dogs a while ago.
So every now and then, I ask my friend
if I can take Nala for a walk around."

Marco and their friend Nala
Milan, Italy

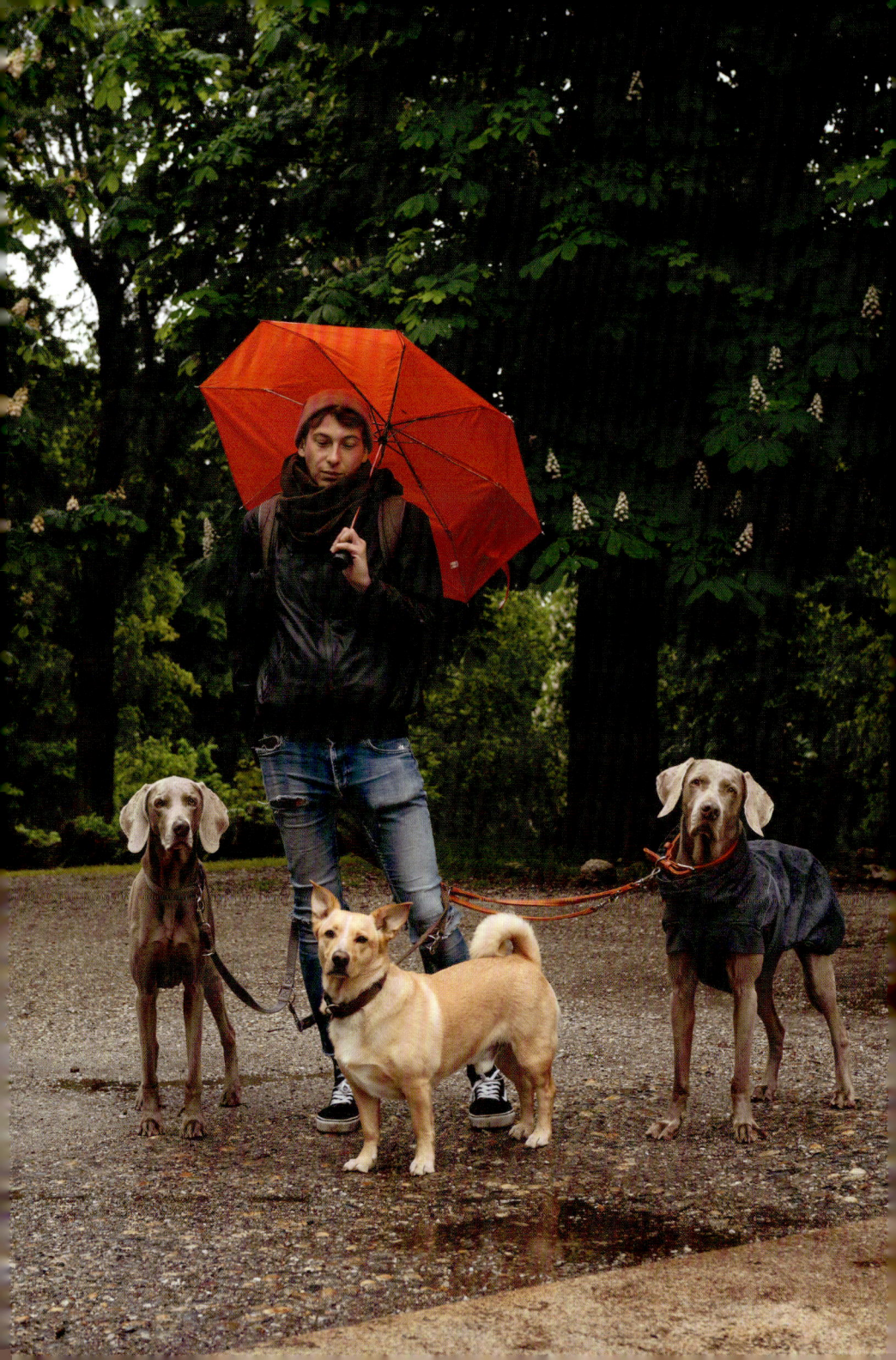

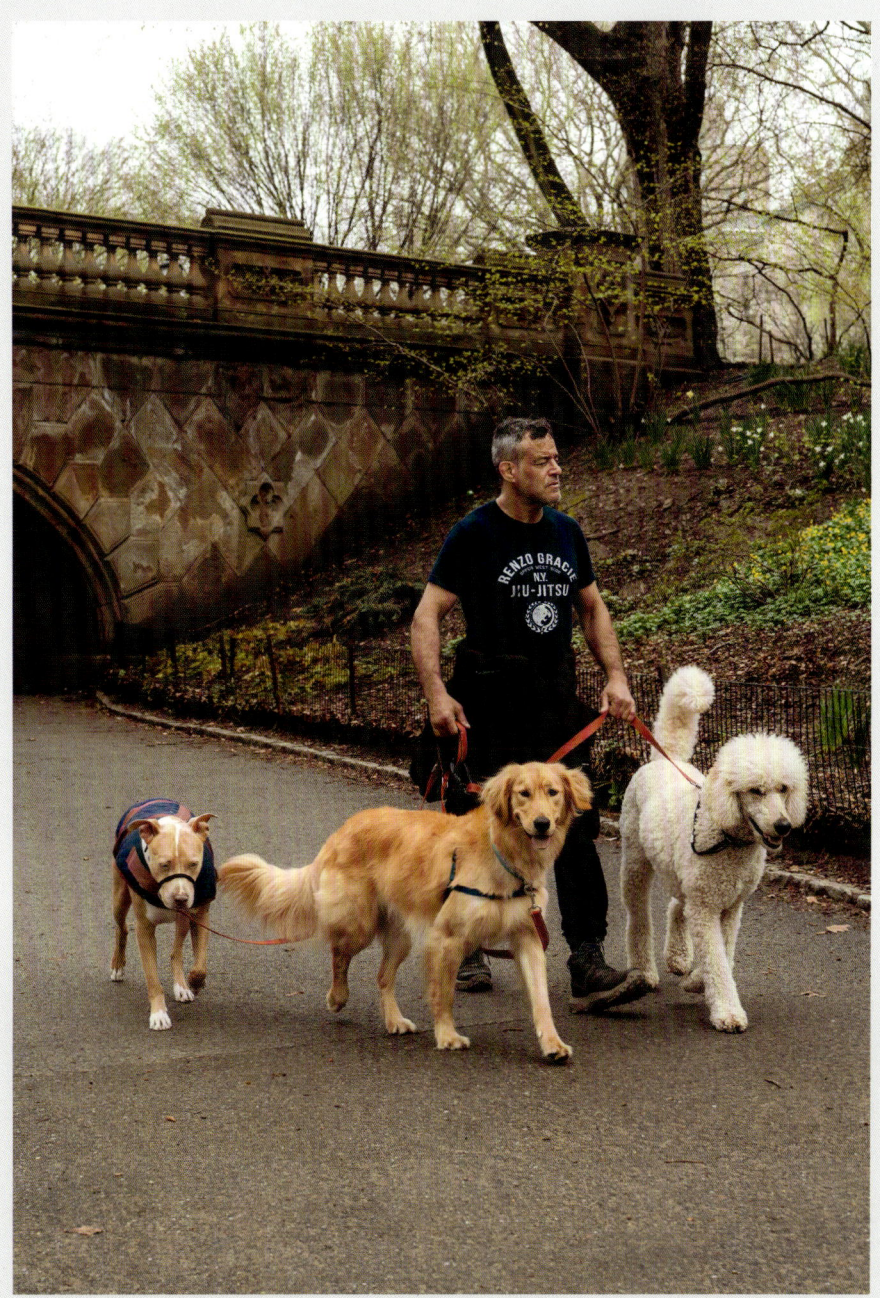

Milan, Italy | New York City, USA

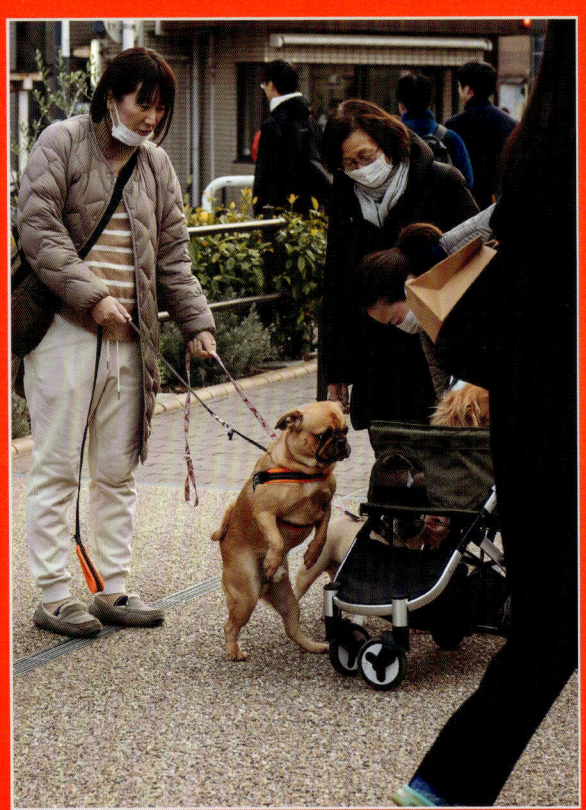

Tokyo, Japan

> "If it was up to him, we would just sleep in bed together all day."

Dan and their dog Bono
London, England

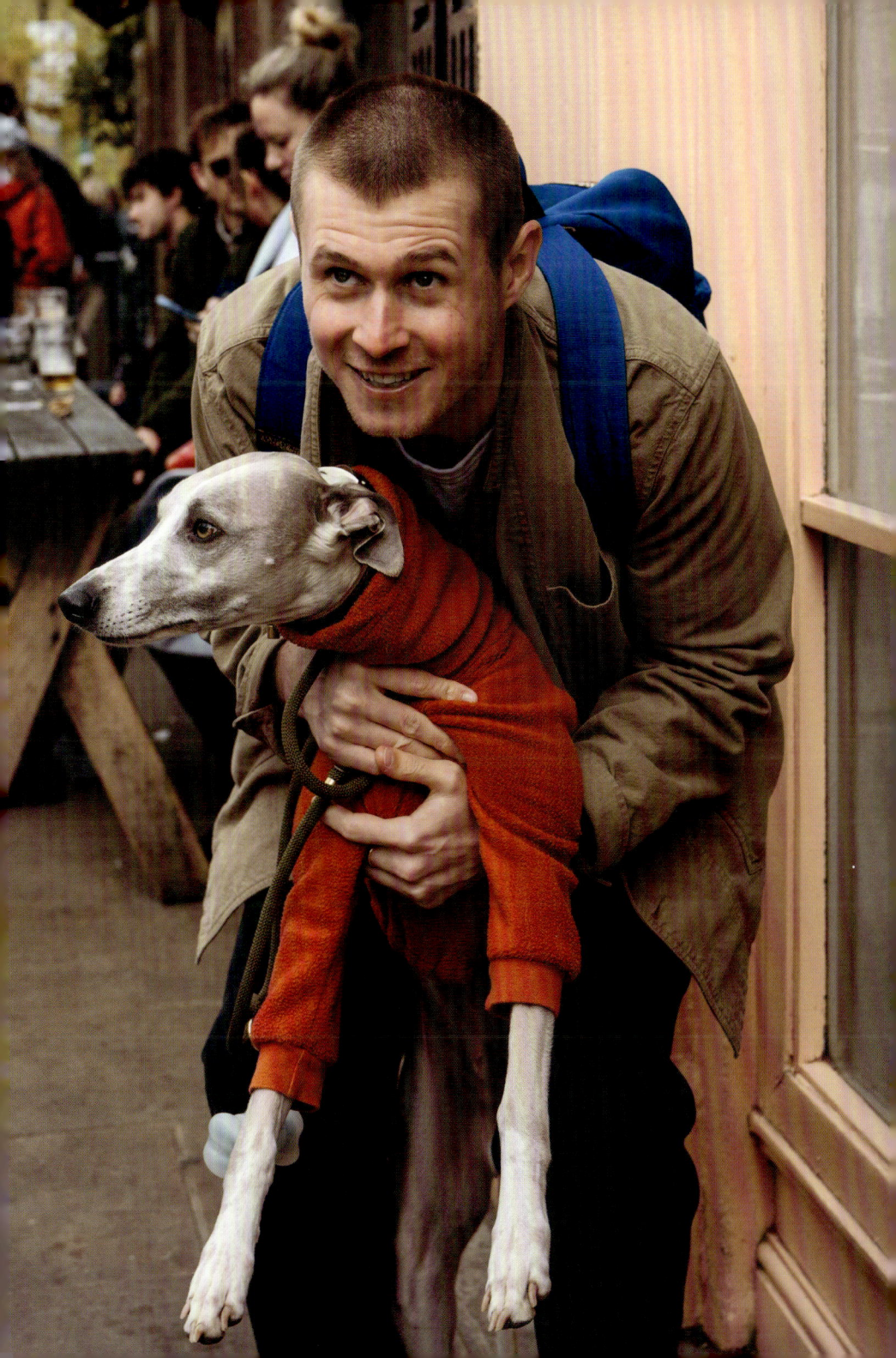

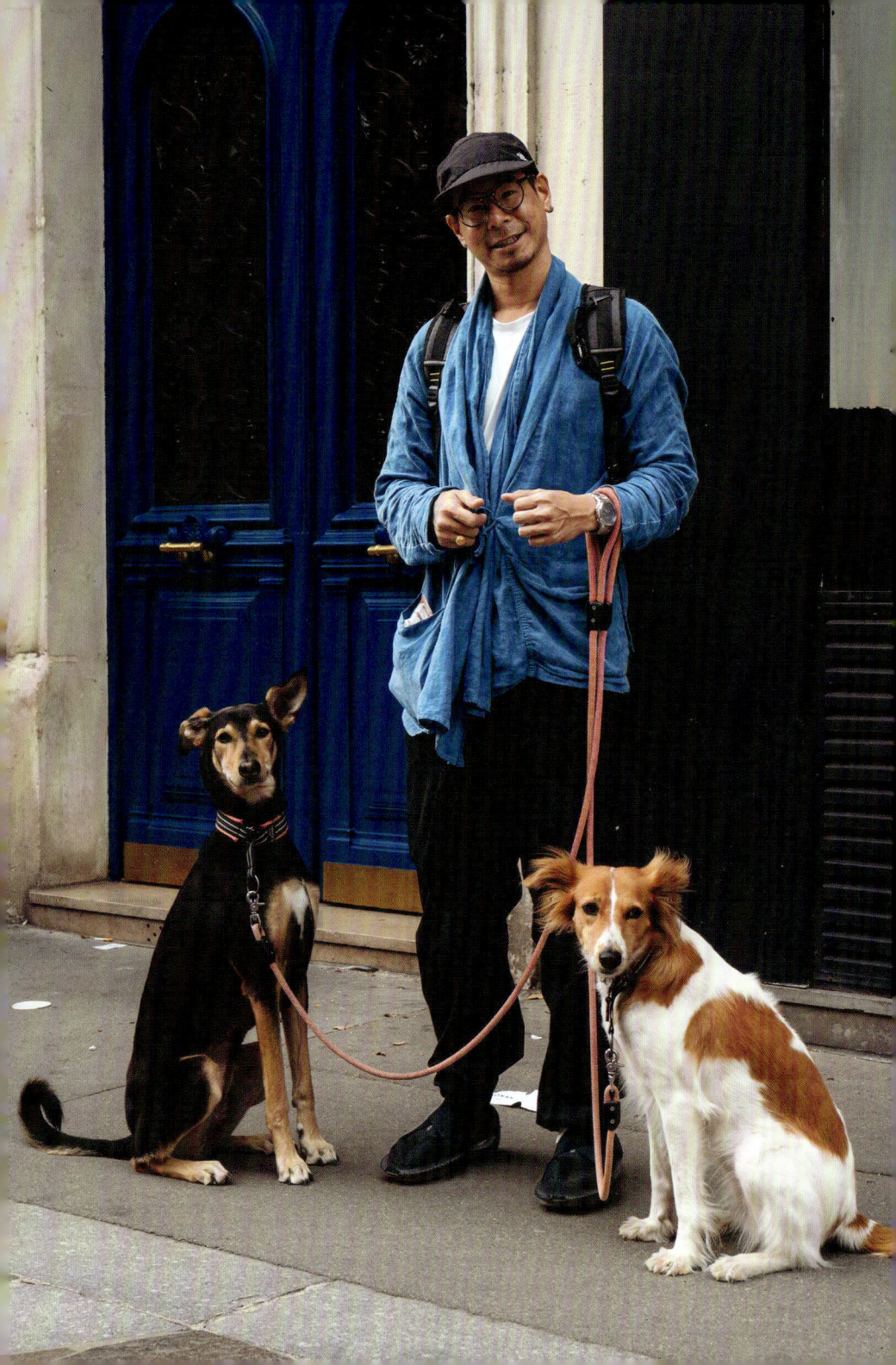

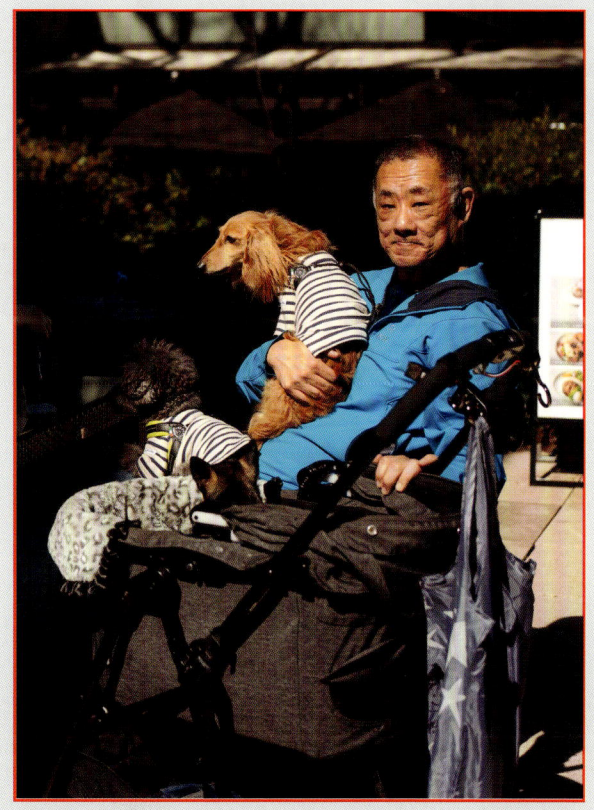

Tokyo, Japan

"It's a lot of work, but I know they're happy dogs. I'm their slave."

Albert and their dogs Puppy and Mama
Paris, France

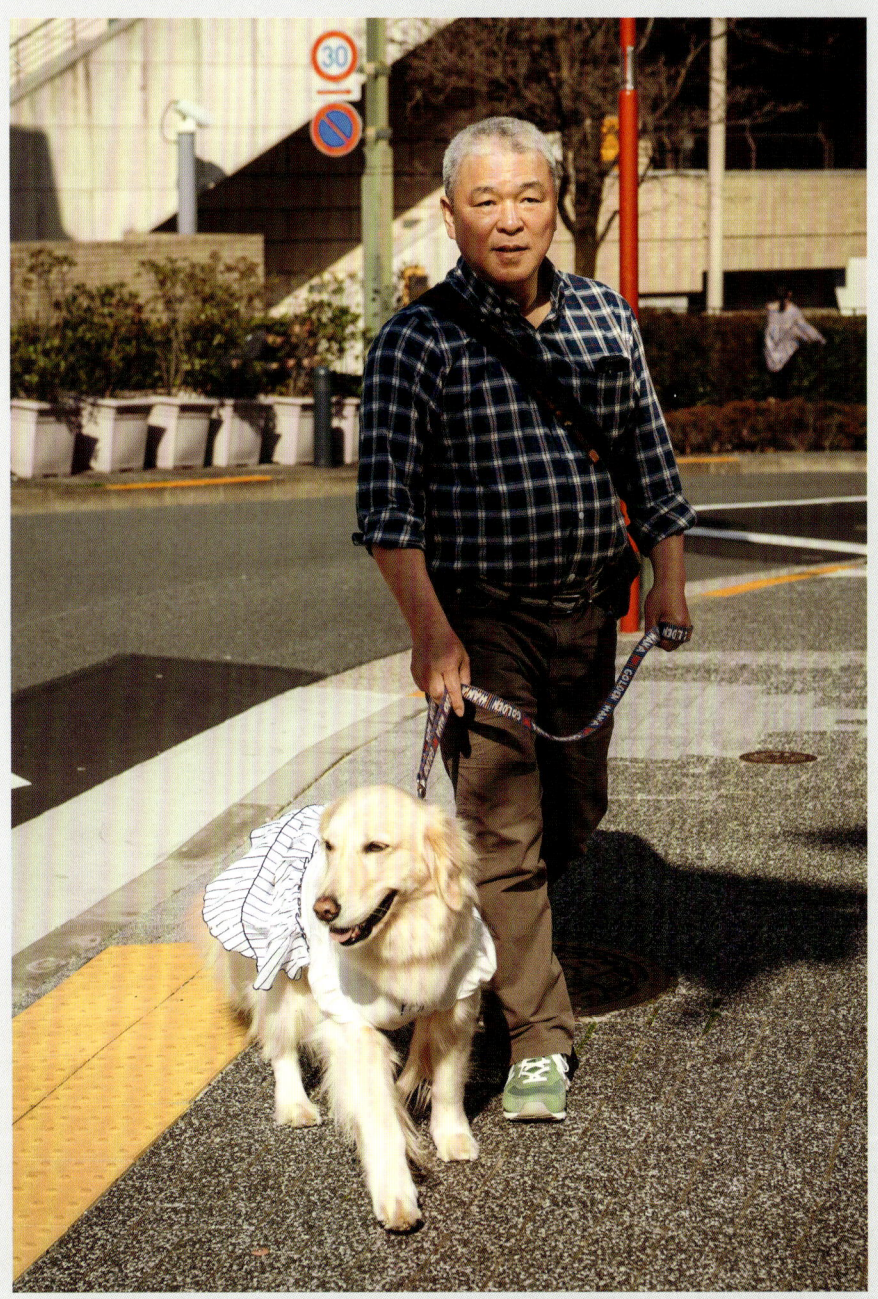

Tokyo, Japan | London, England

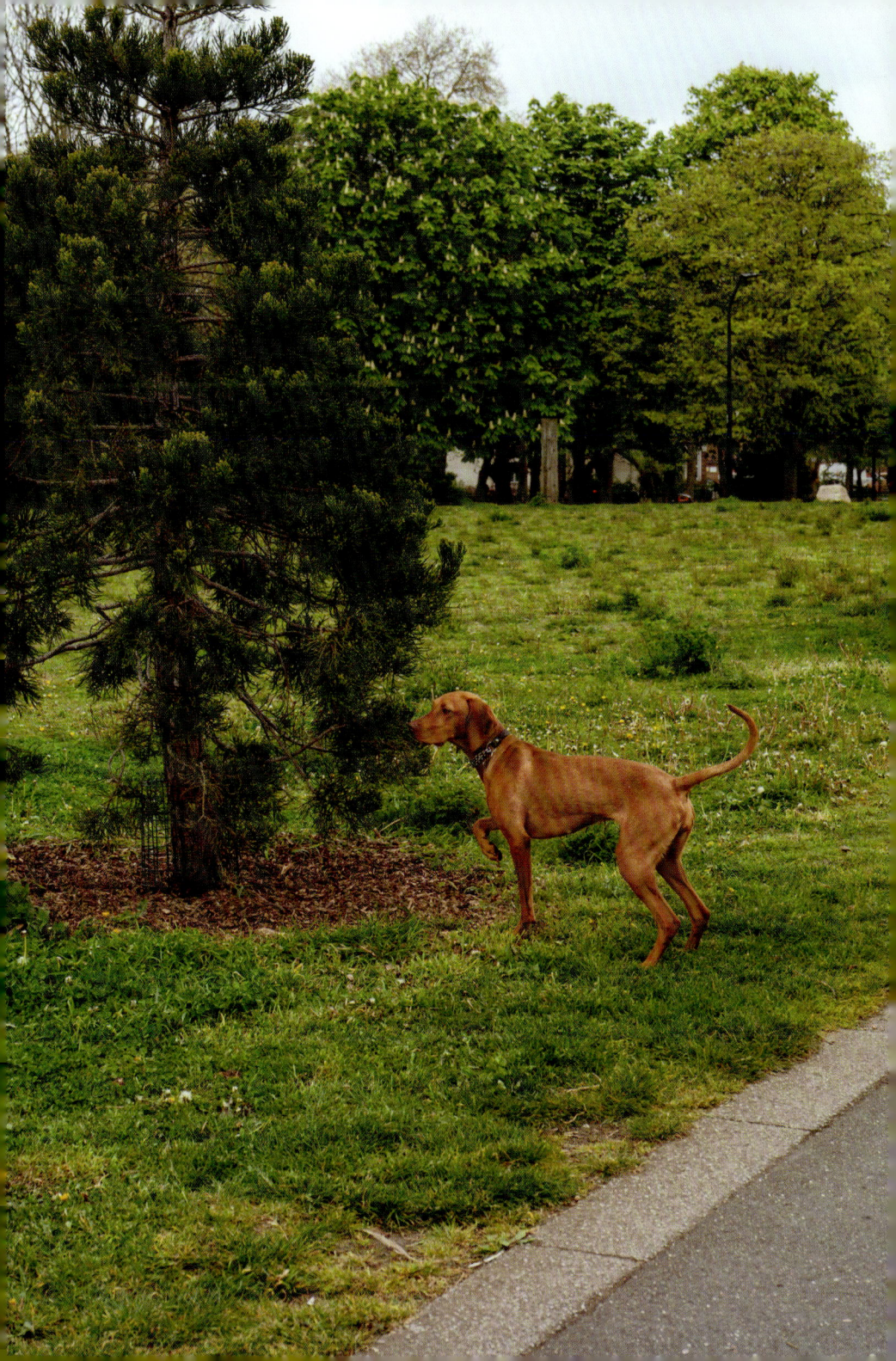

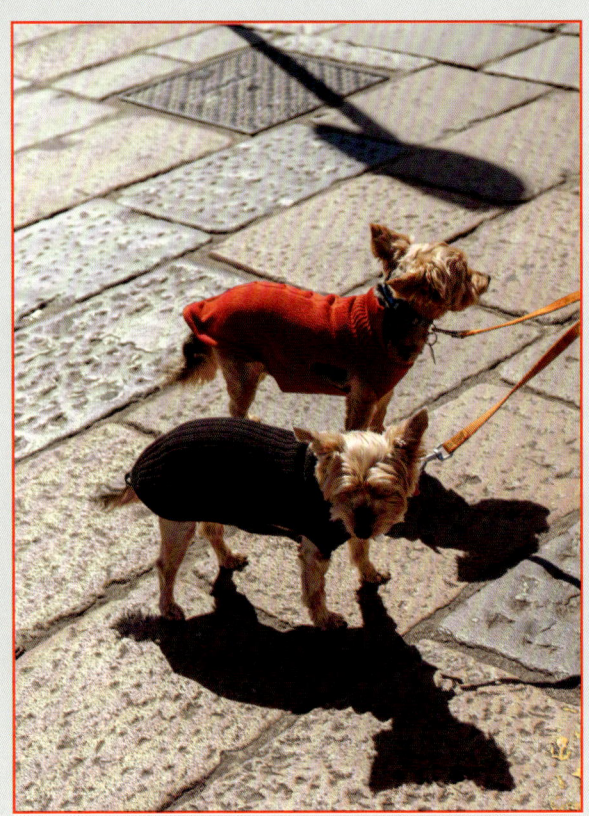

Milan, Italy

"It's a lot of pressure being two fashion dogs, but when a family is this stylish and fun, it's worth the effort."

Versace and Dior with their family
Sydney, Australia

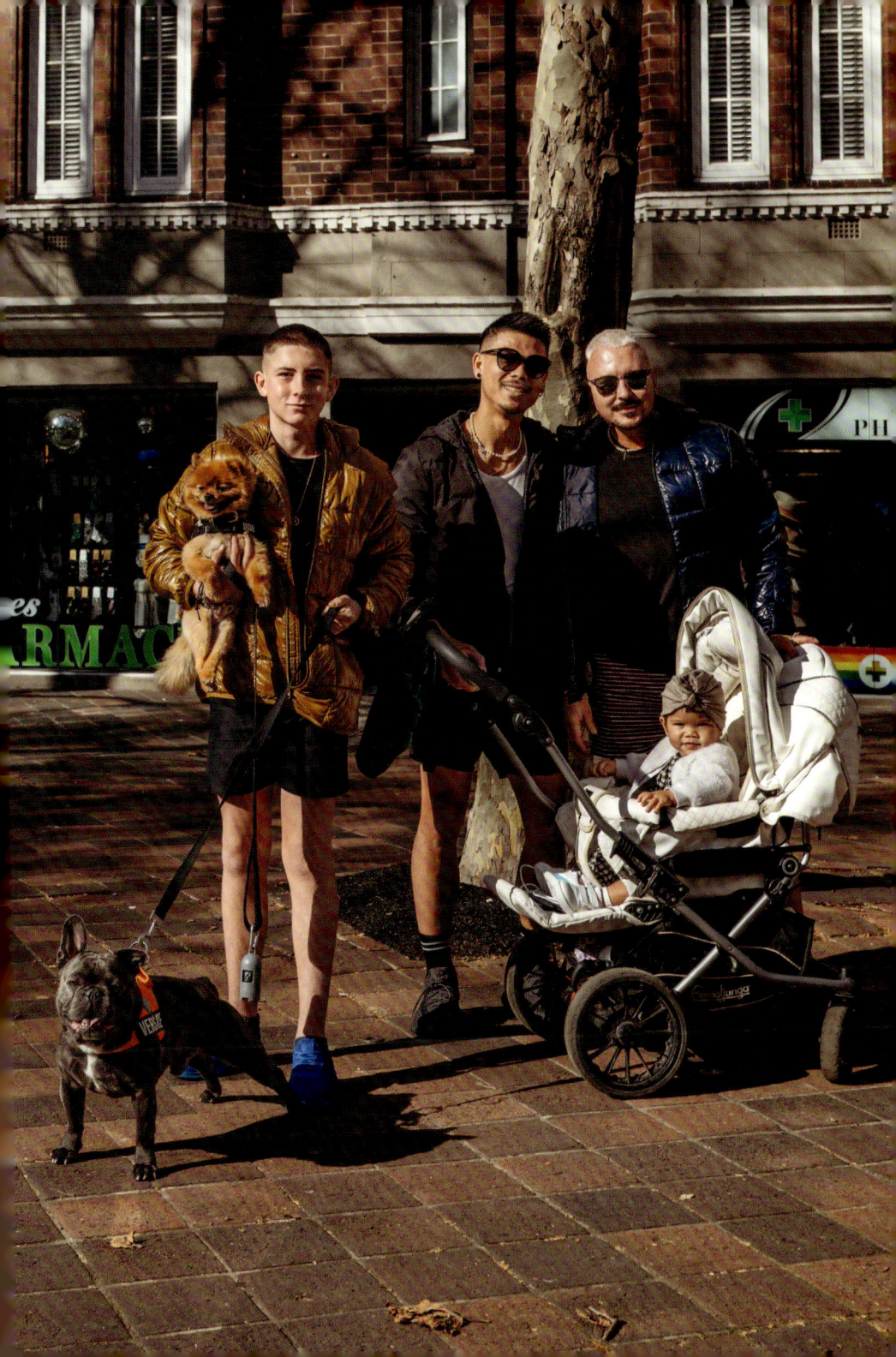

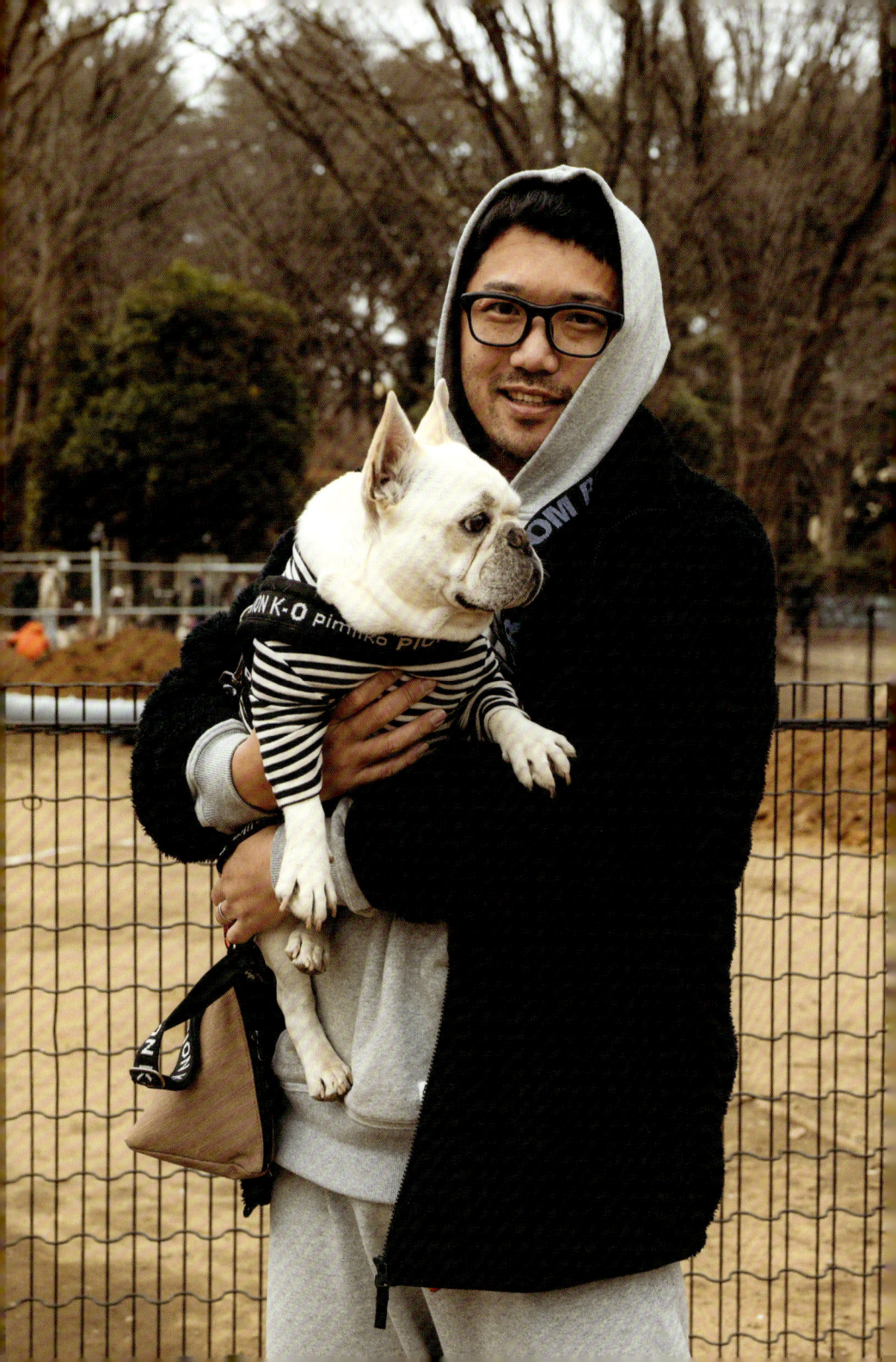

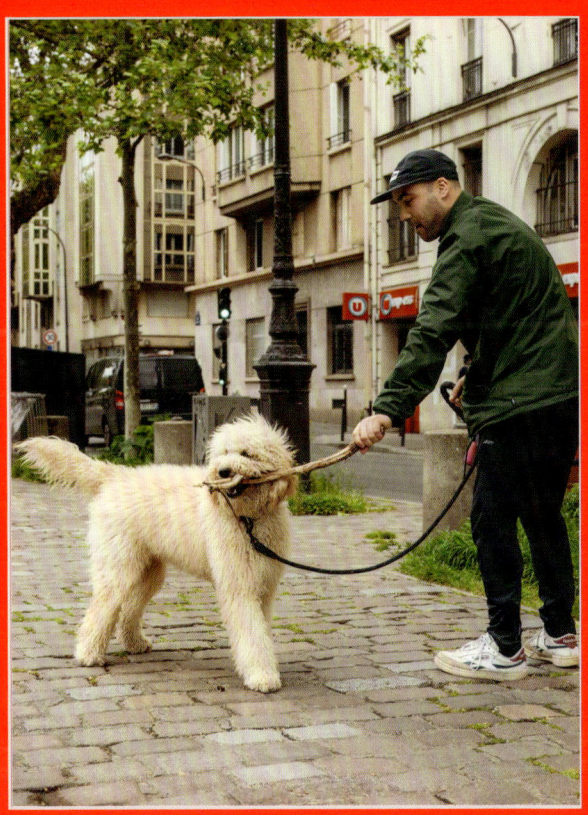

Paris, France

"I think he appreciates our friendship. I know I do."

Koki and their dog Odi
Tokyo, Japan

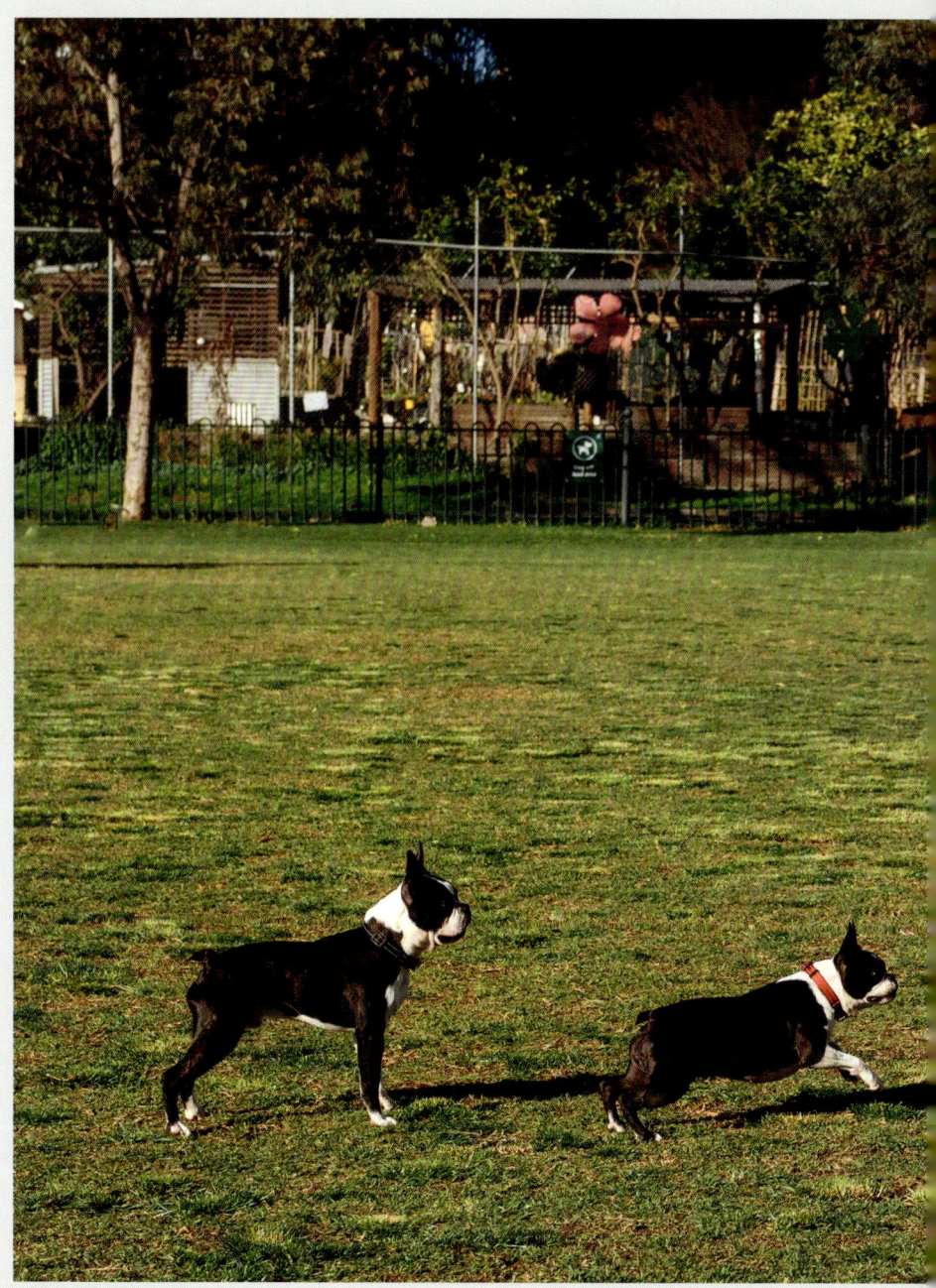

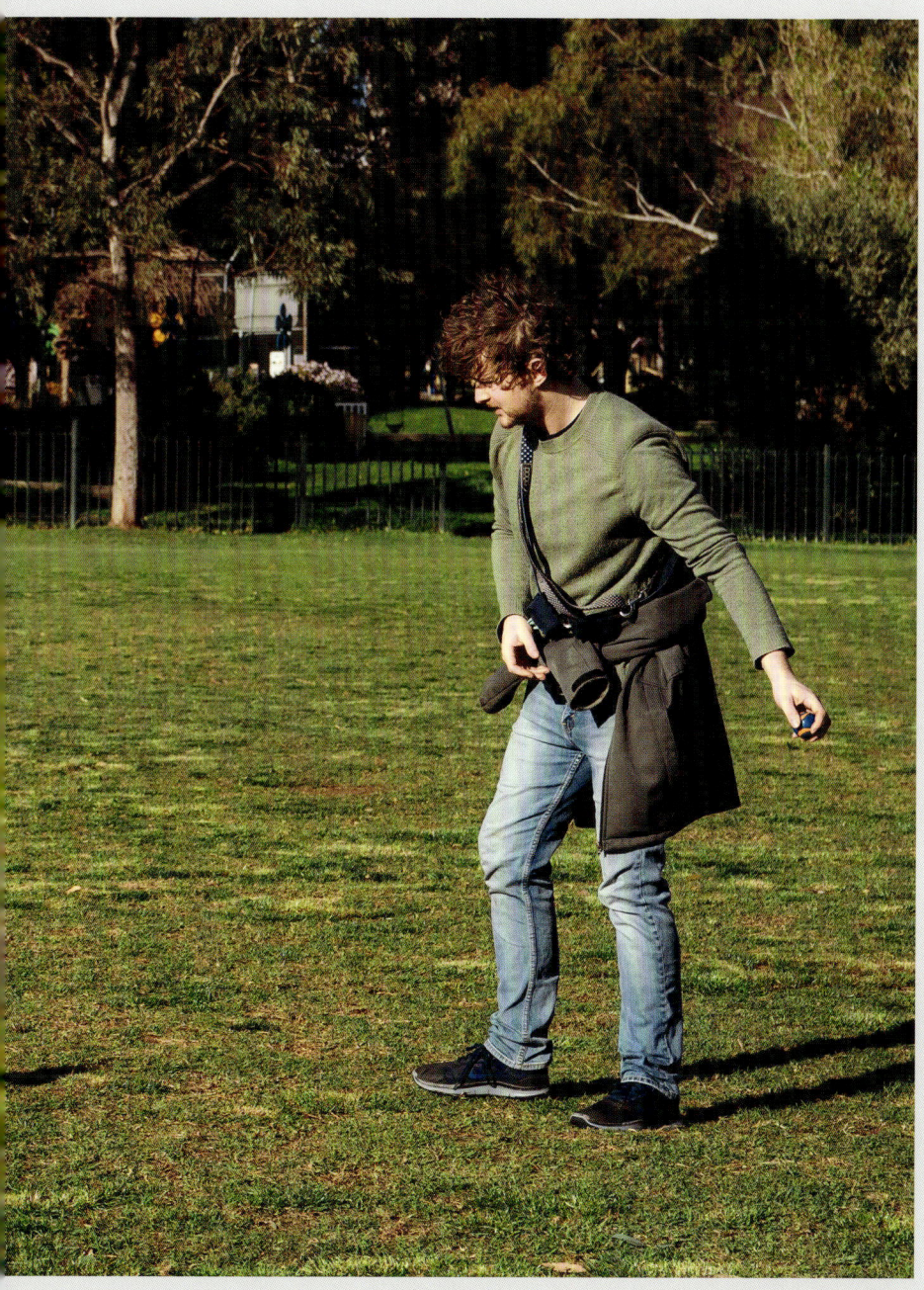

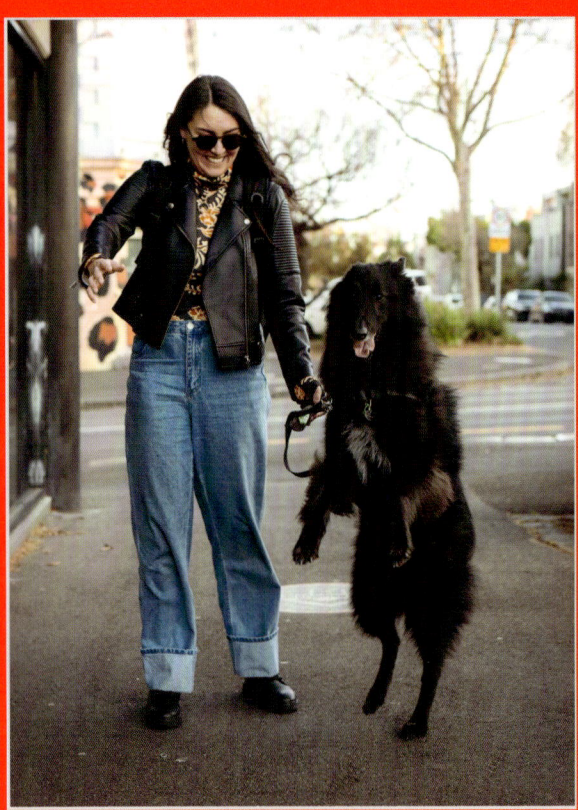

Melbourne, Australia

"He's still a puppy, so that energy is a lot. He keeps me on my toes."

Tomoya and their dog Moku
Melbourne, Australia

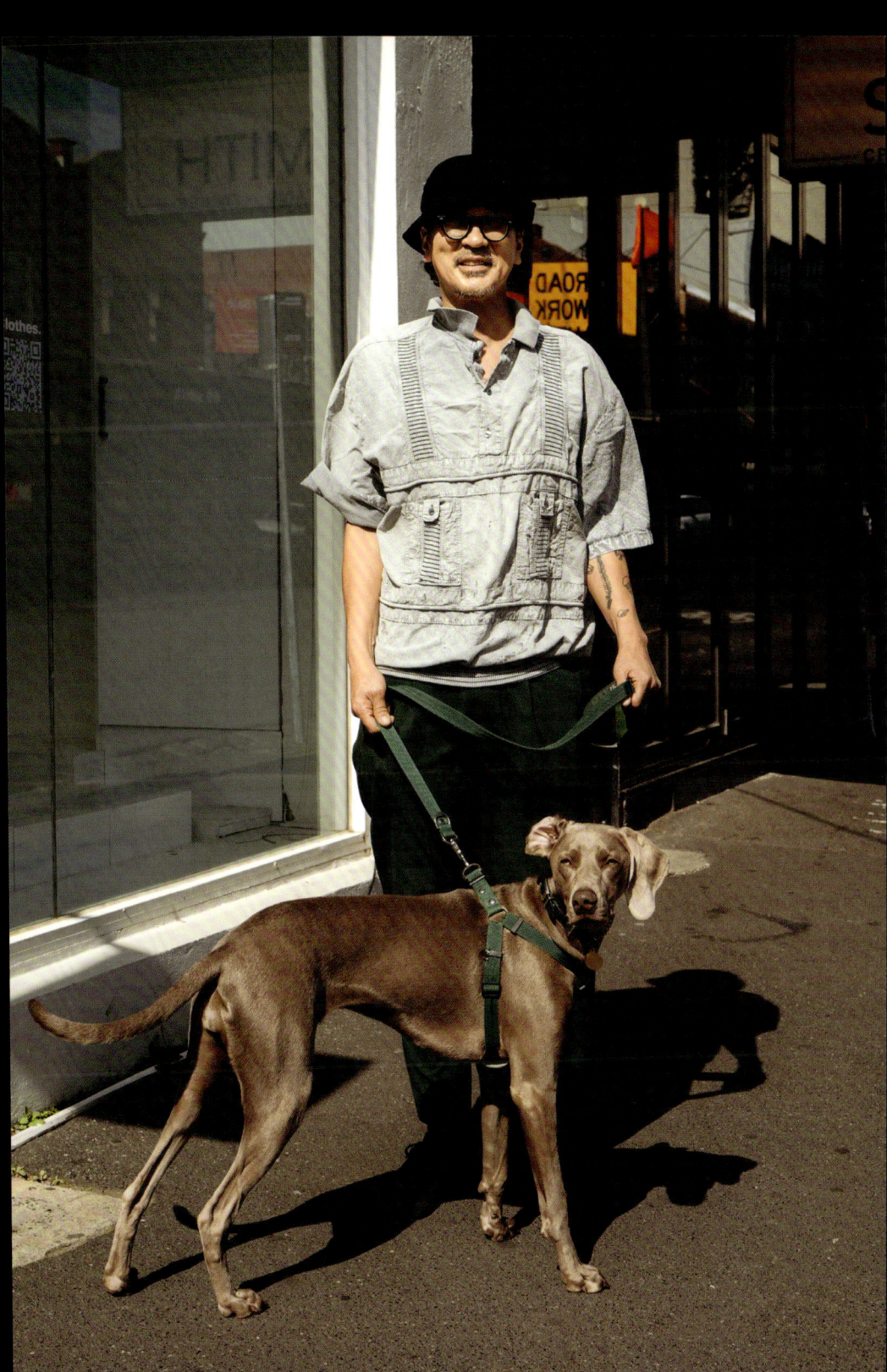

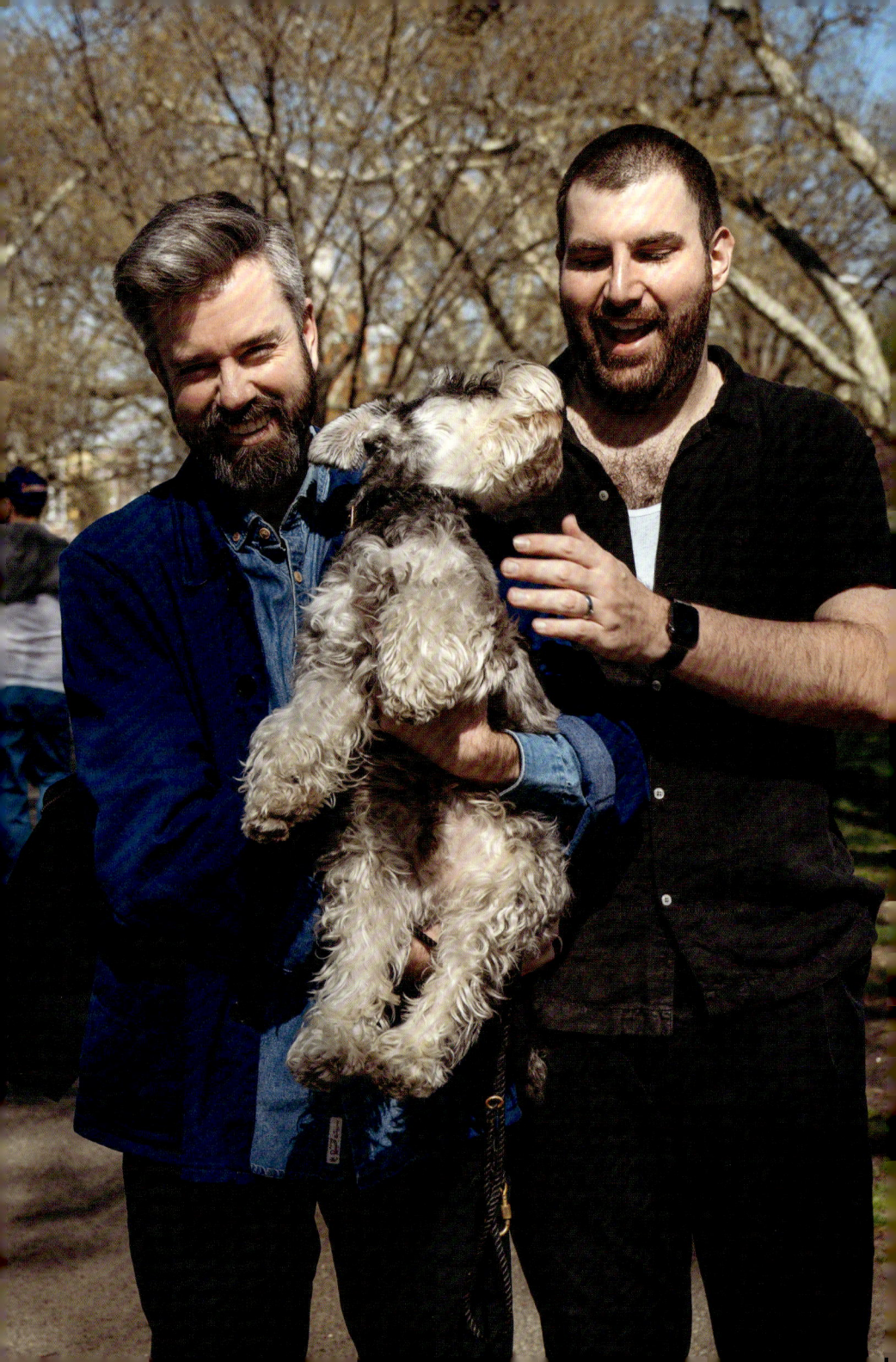

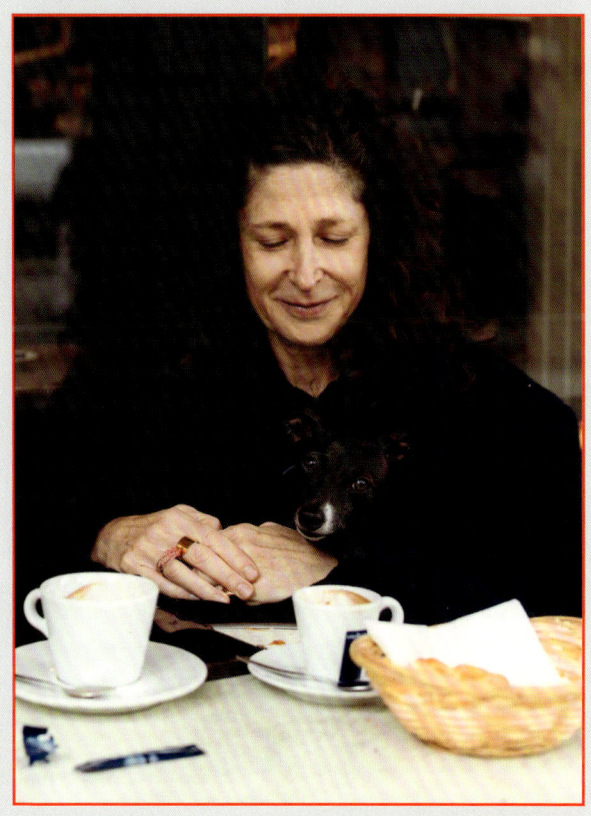

"He lets us hang out with him in his apartment, on his couch, in his bed..."

Josh and Daniel with their dog Alfie
New York City, USA

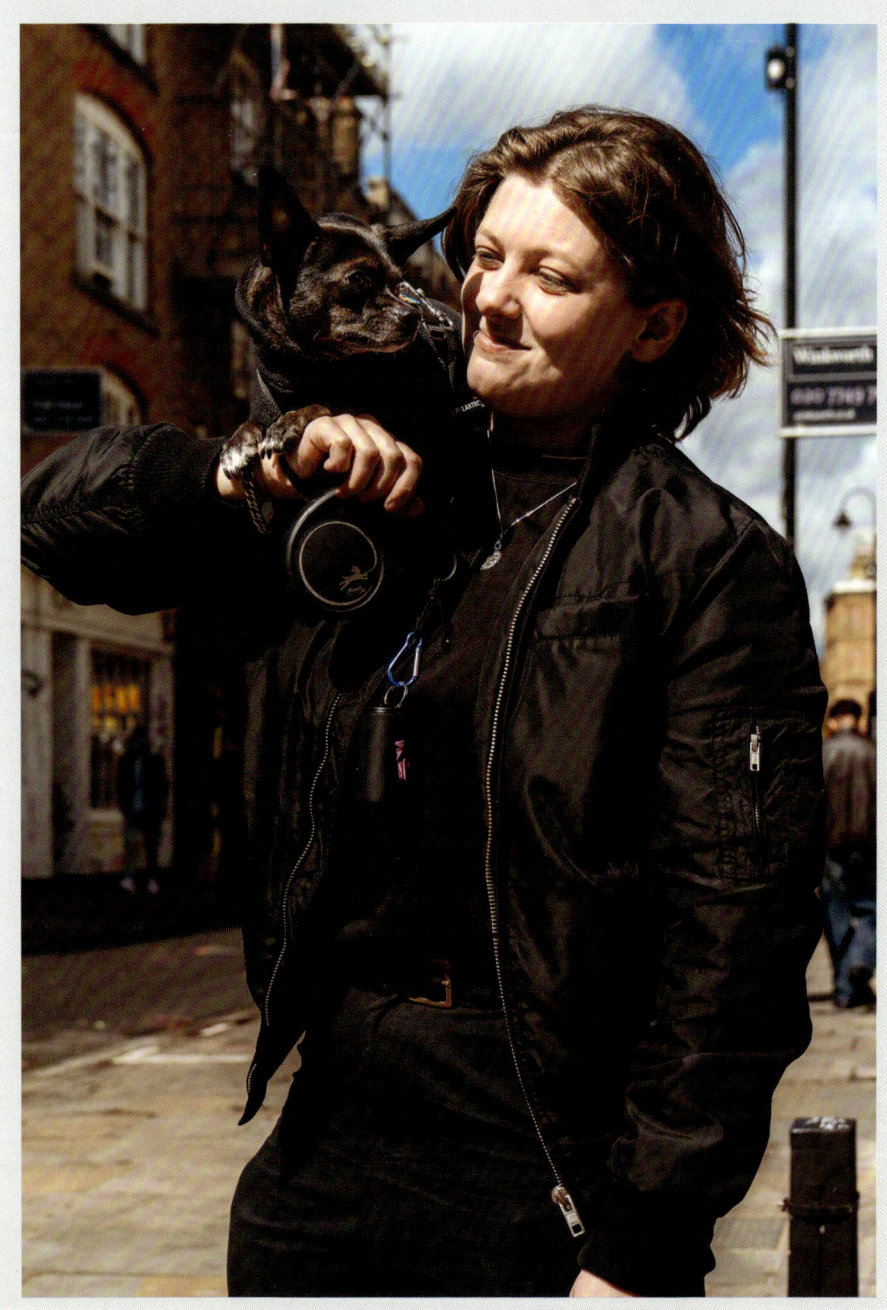

London, England | Sydney, Australia

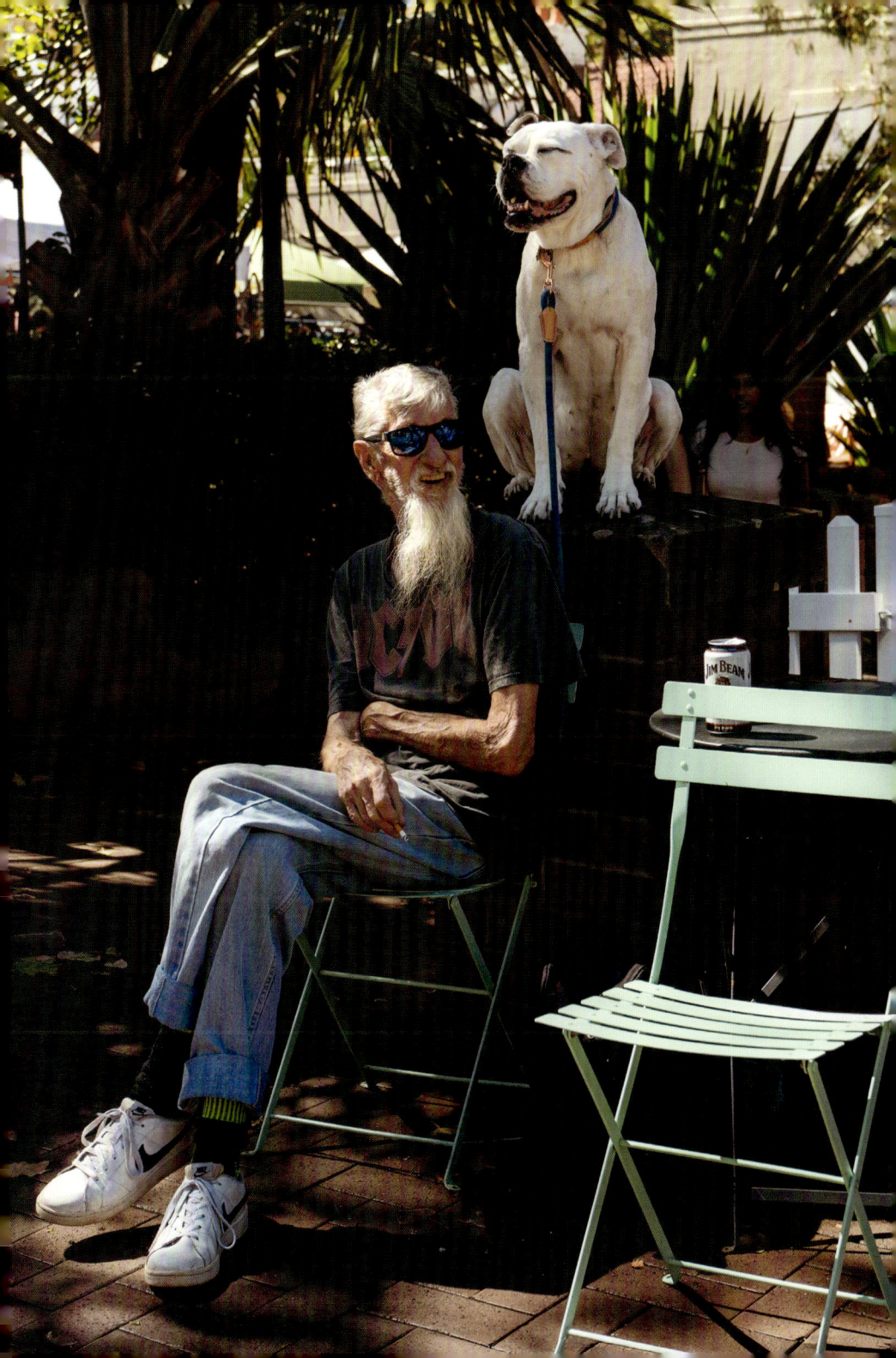

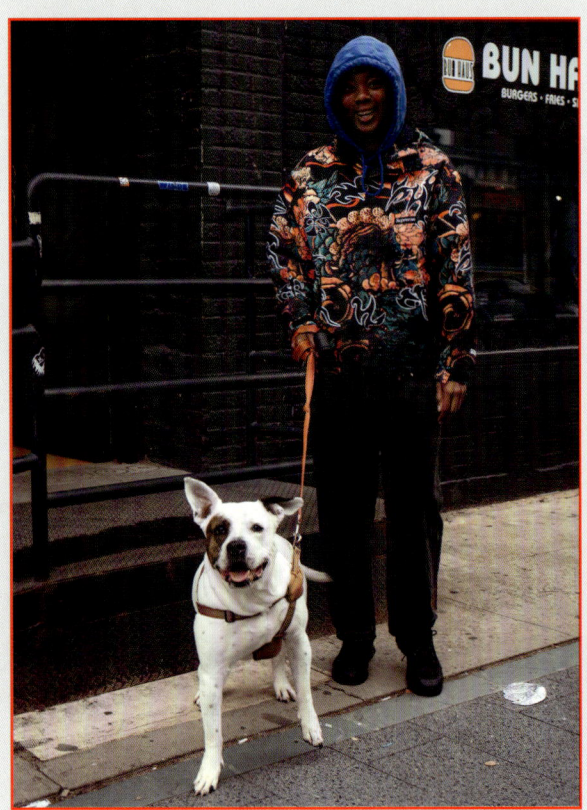

New York City, USA

"I provide the party, and she always wants to attend. It's the party of life!"

Stephonik and their dog Ruby Tuesday
New York City, USA

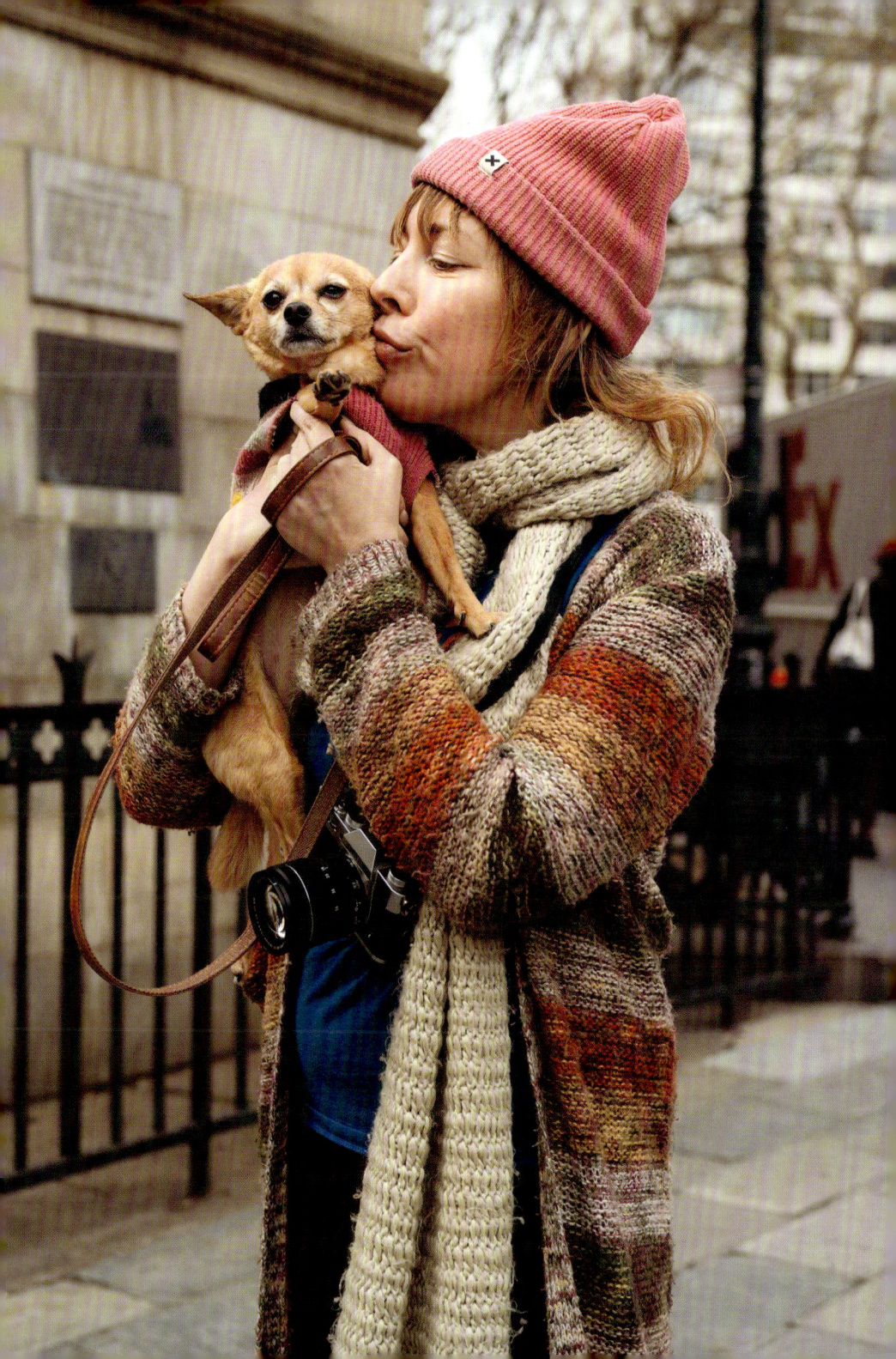

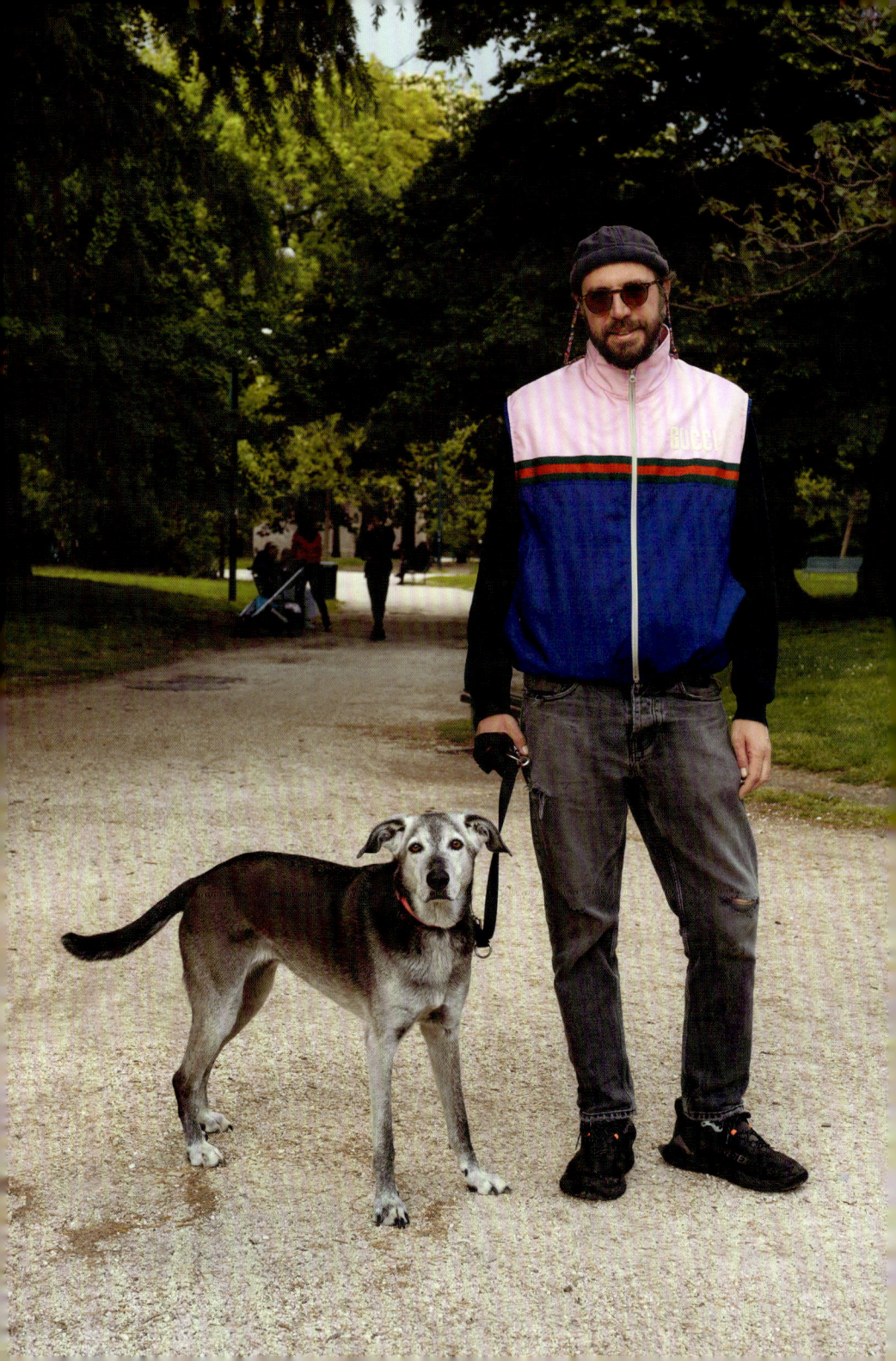

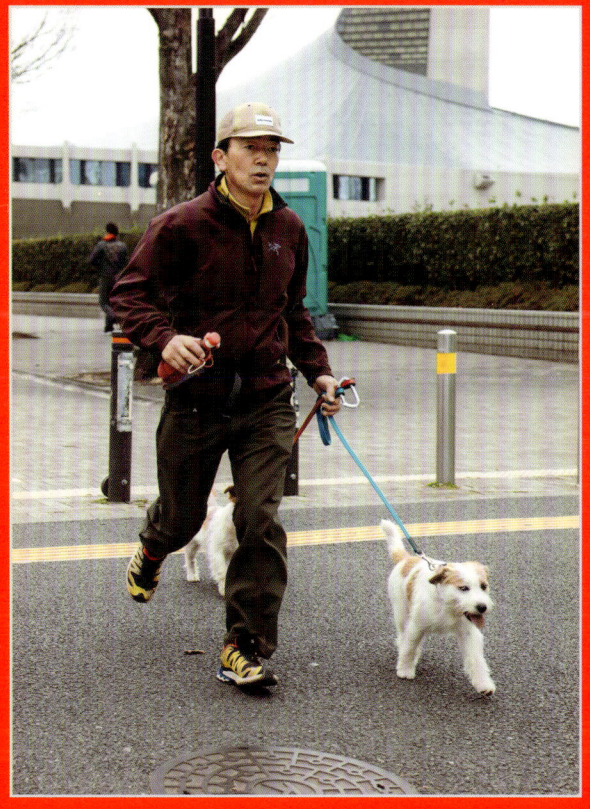

Tokyo, Japan

"She never likes to stop. Always wants to keep going!"

Andrea and their dog Nyesha
Milan, Italy

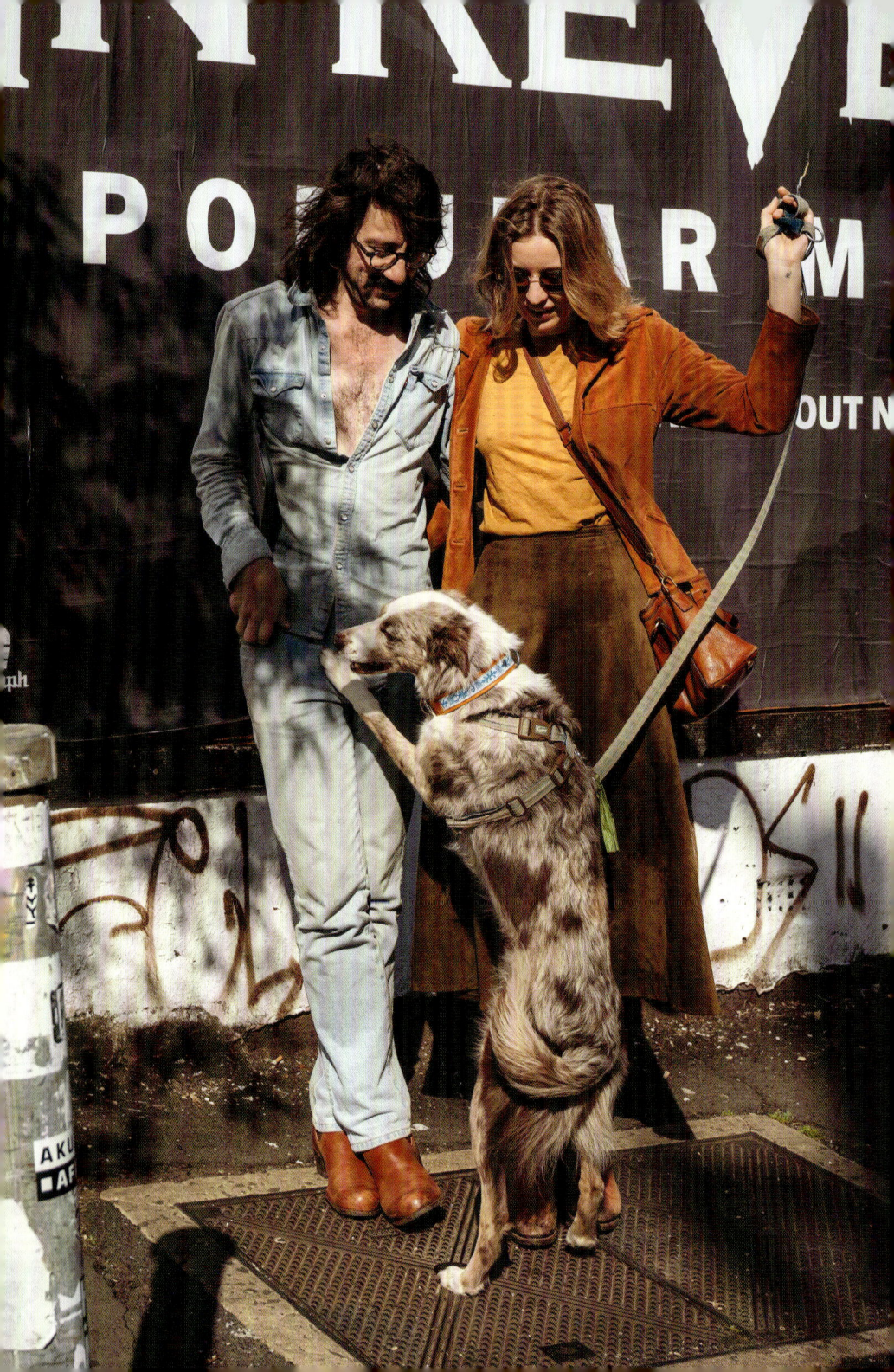

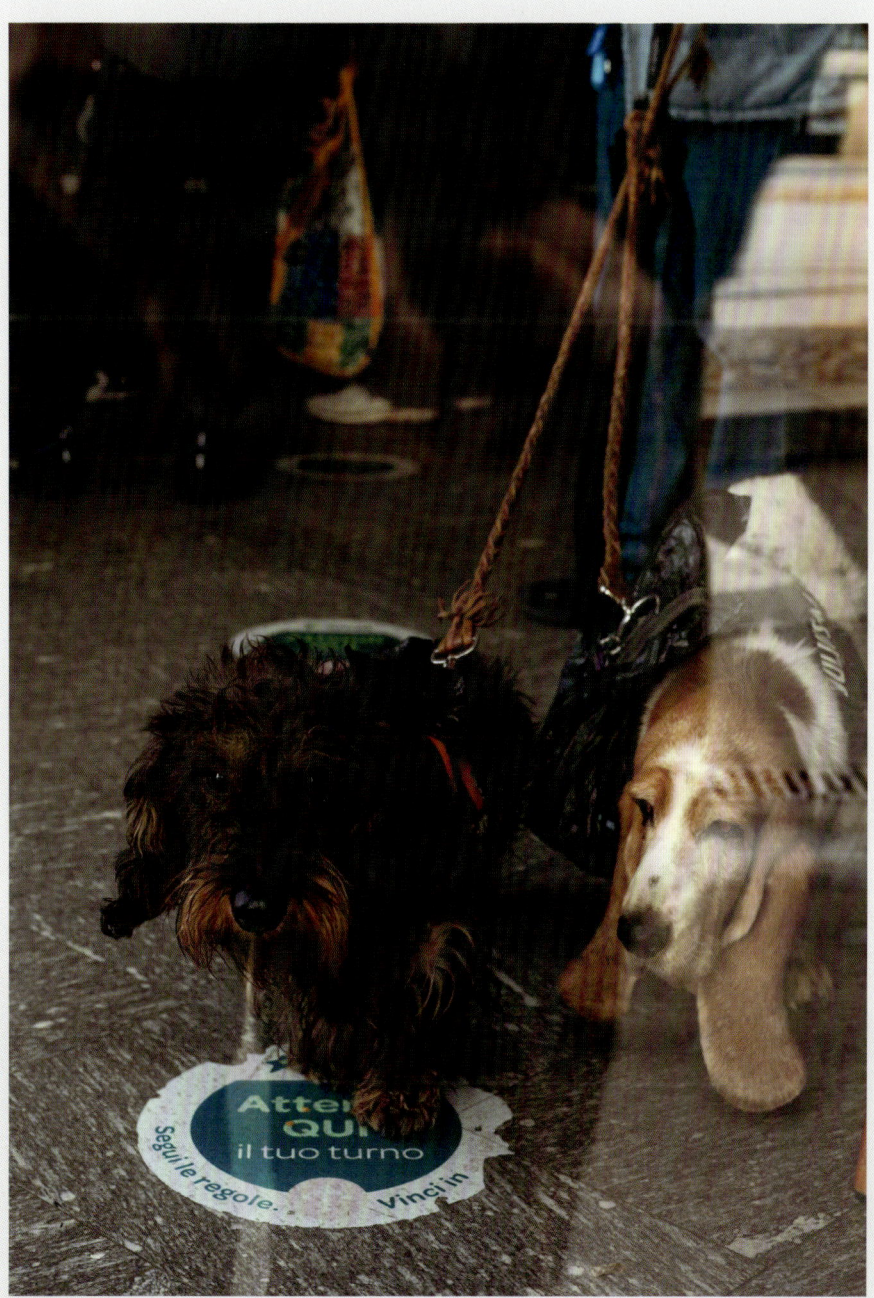

Sydney, Australia | Milan, Italy

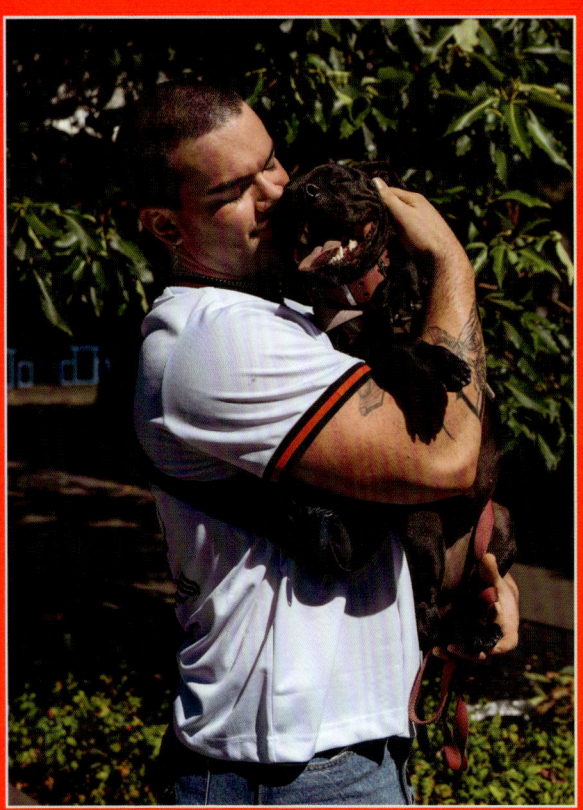

Sydney, Australia

"I'm very cuddly and very attentive."

Luna and her dog walker Ella
London, England

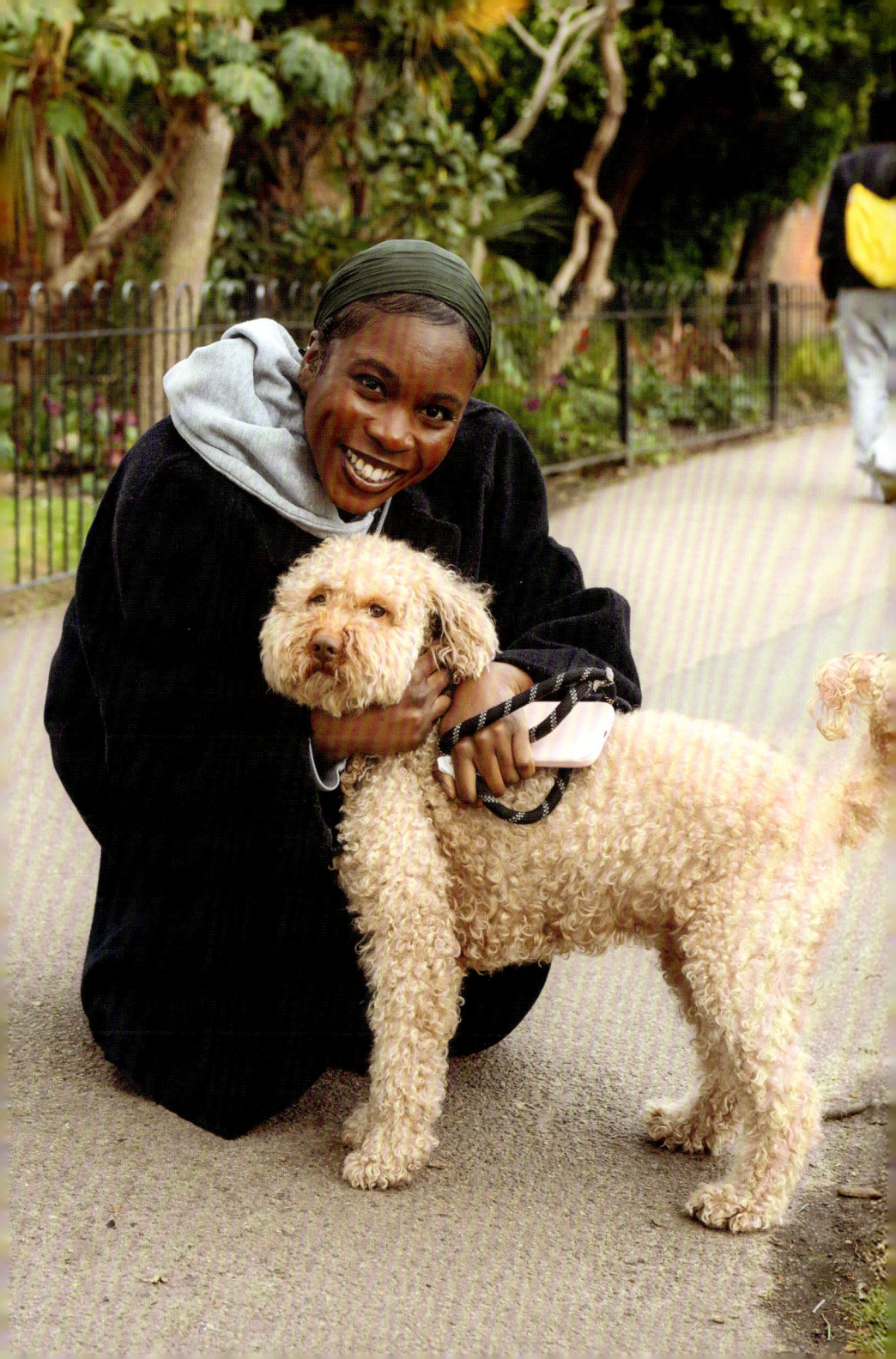

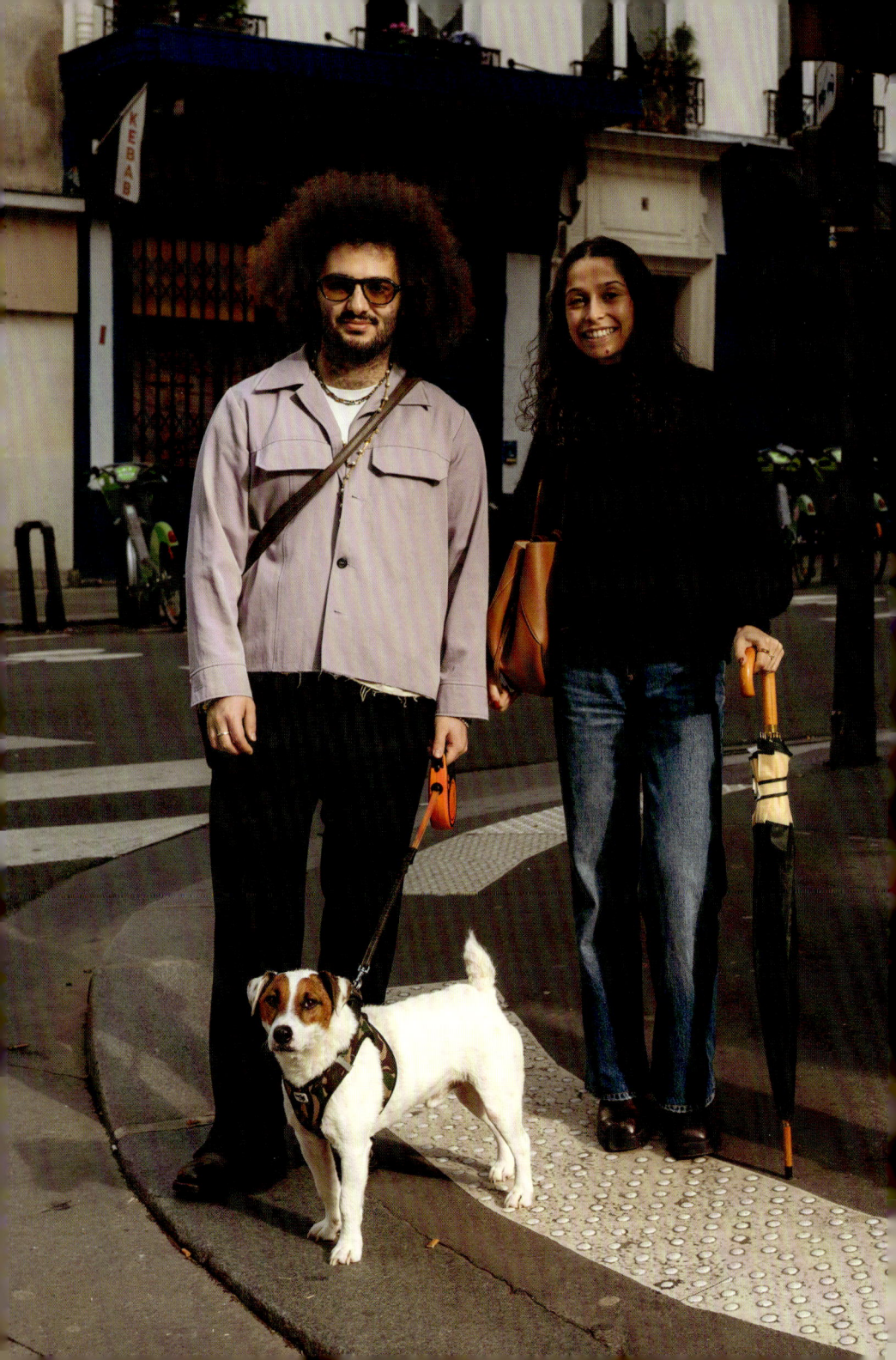

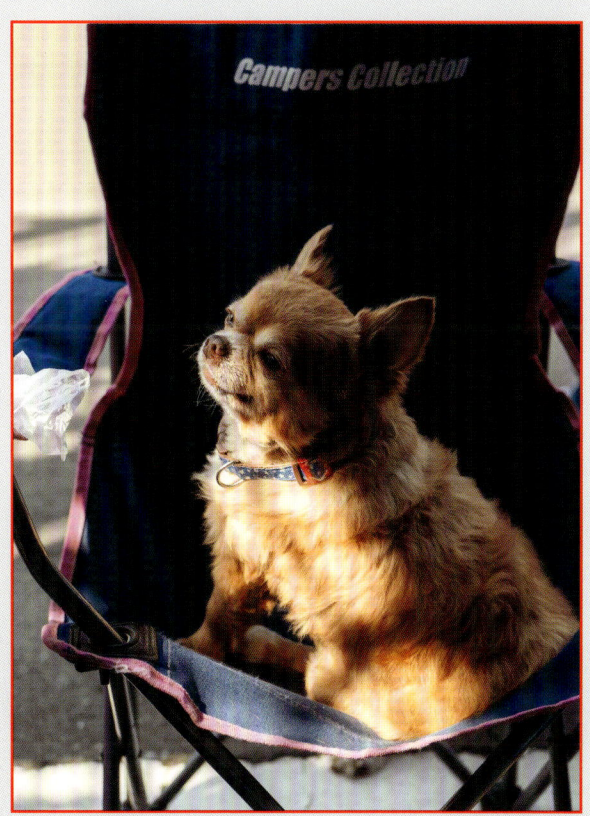

Tokyo, Japan

"Hopefully he loves us. We let him on the couch, so let's hope!"

Niko and Chloe and their dog Marley
Paris, France

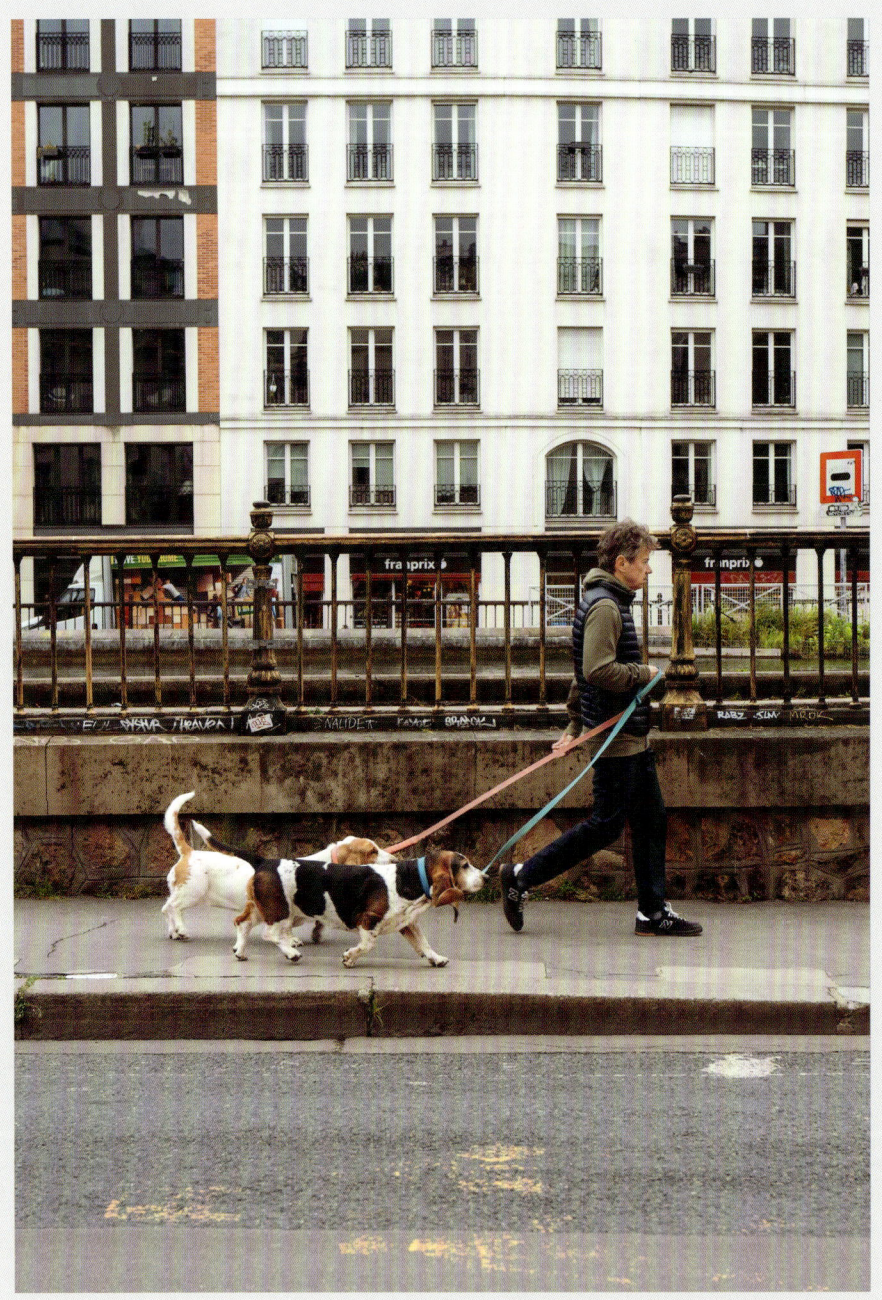

Paris, France | New York City, USA

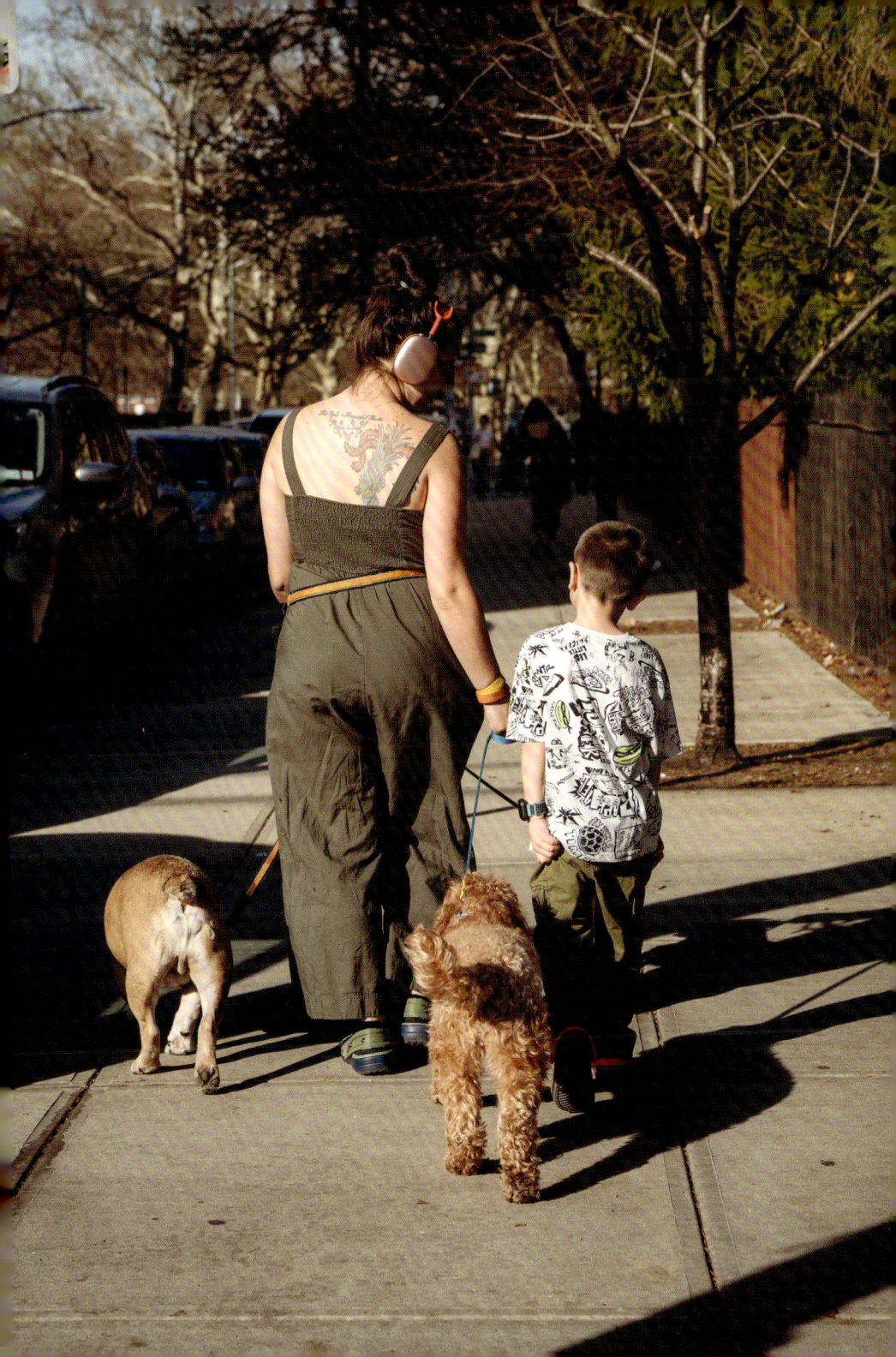

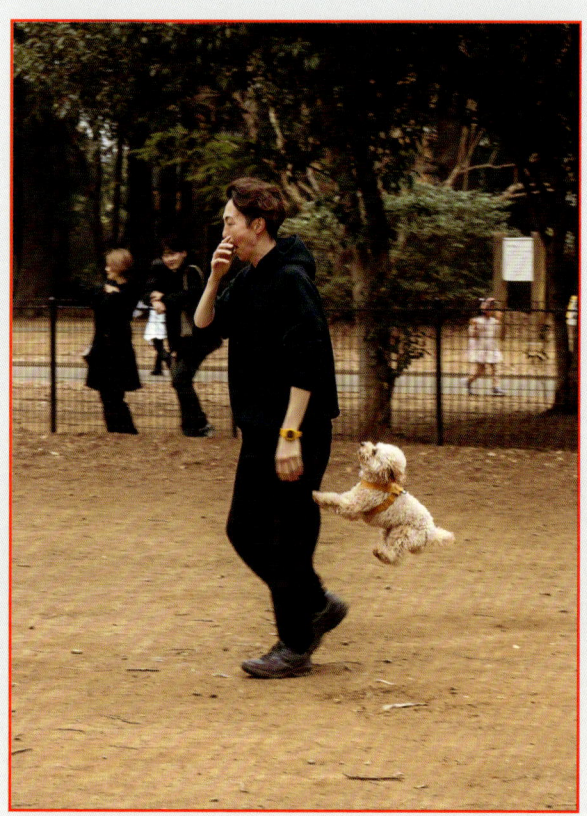

Tokyo, Japan

"I'm too sweet with him. He gets away with a lot."

Nawelle and their dog Tyrion
Paris, France

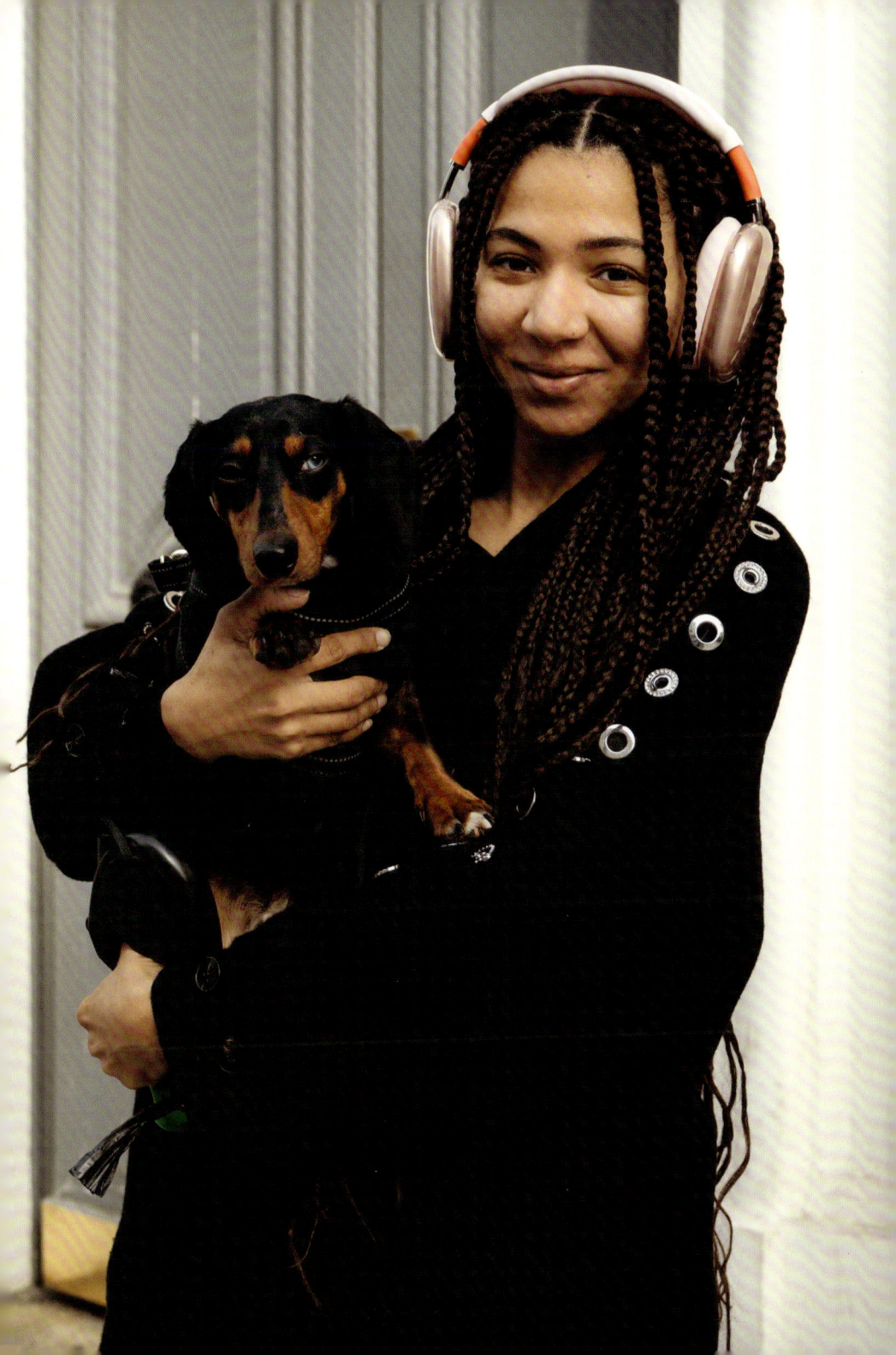

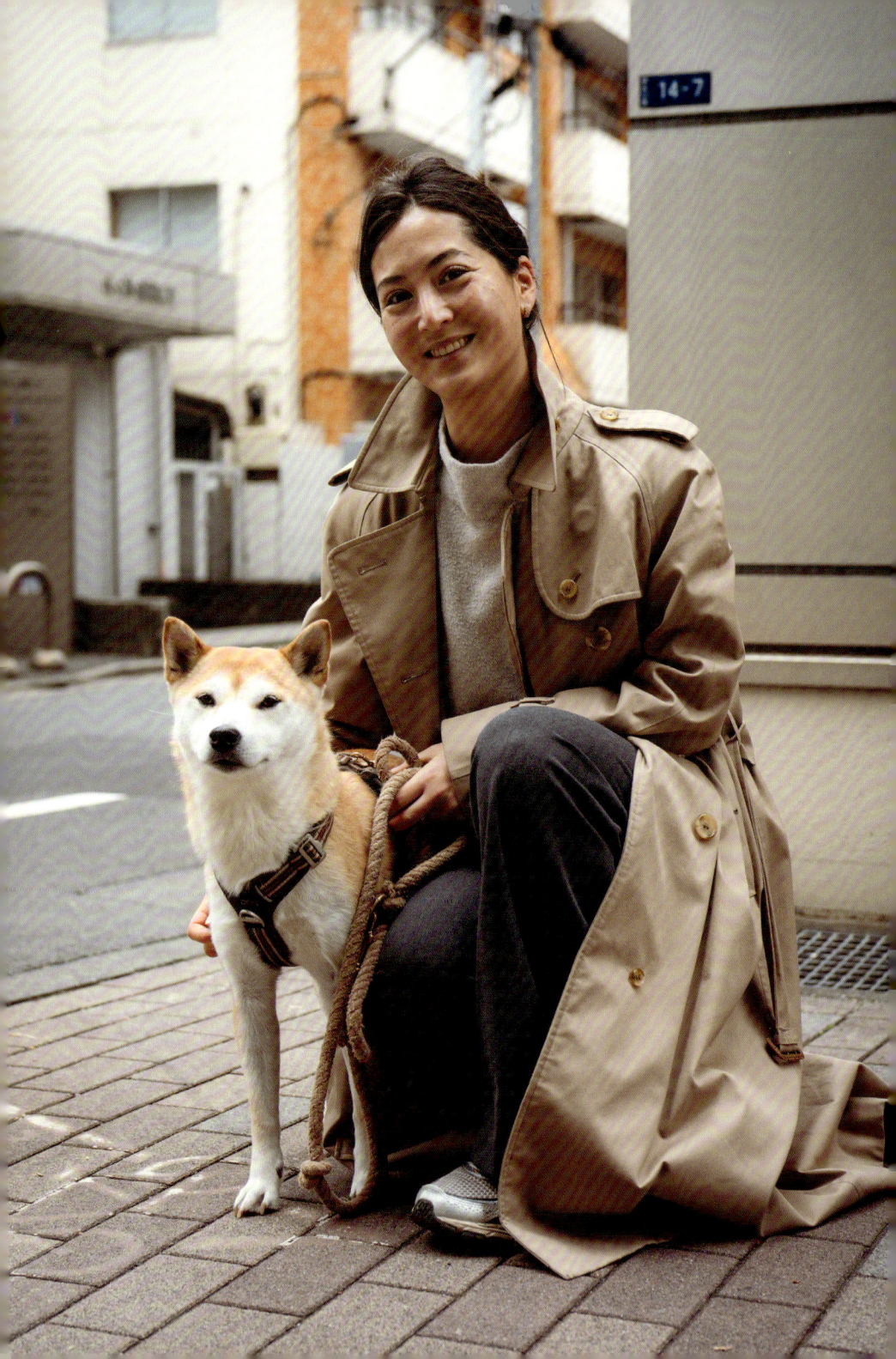

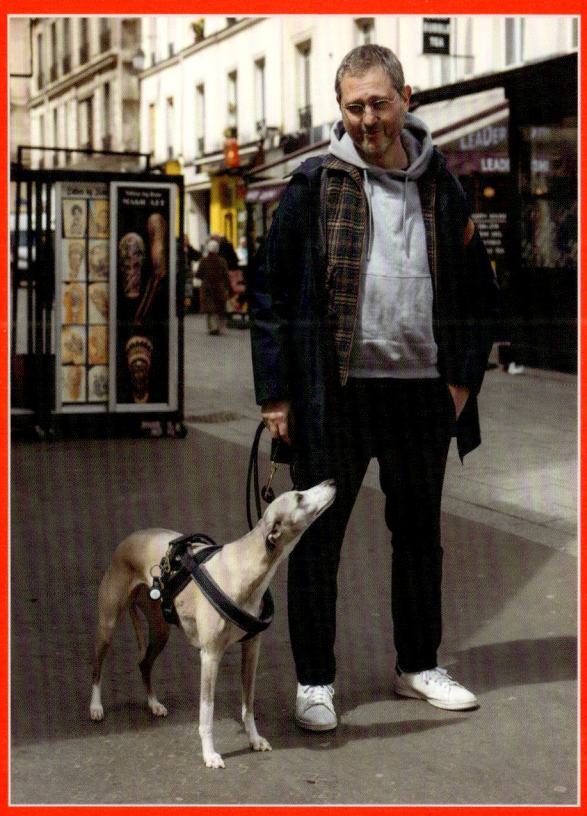

Paris, France

"We're always there for each other.
Always by my side."

Stefanie and their dog Tanuki
Tokyo, Japan

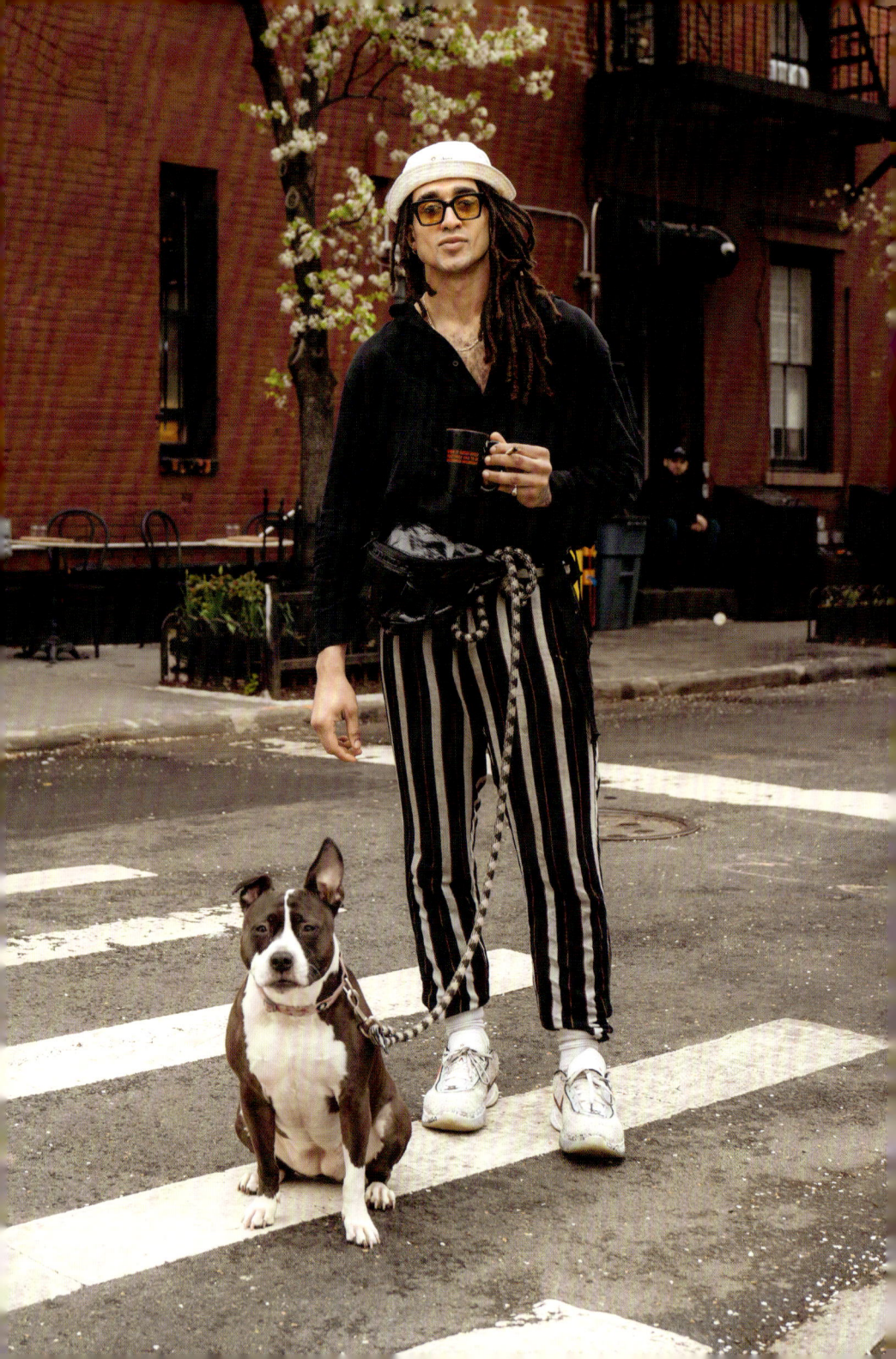

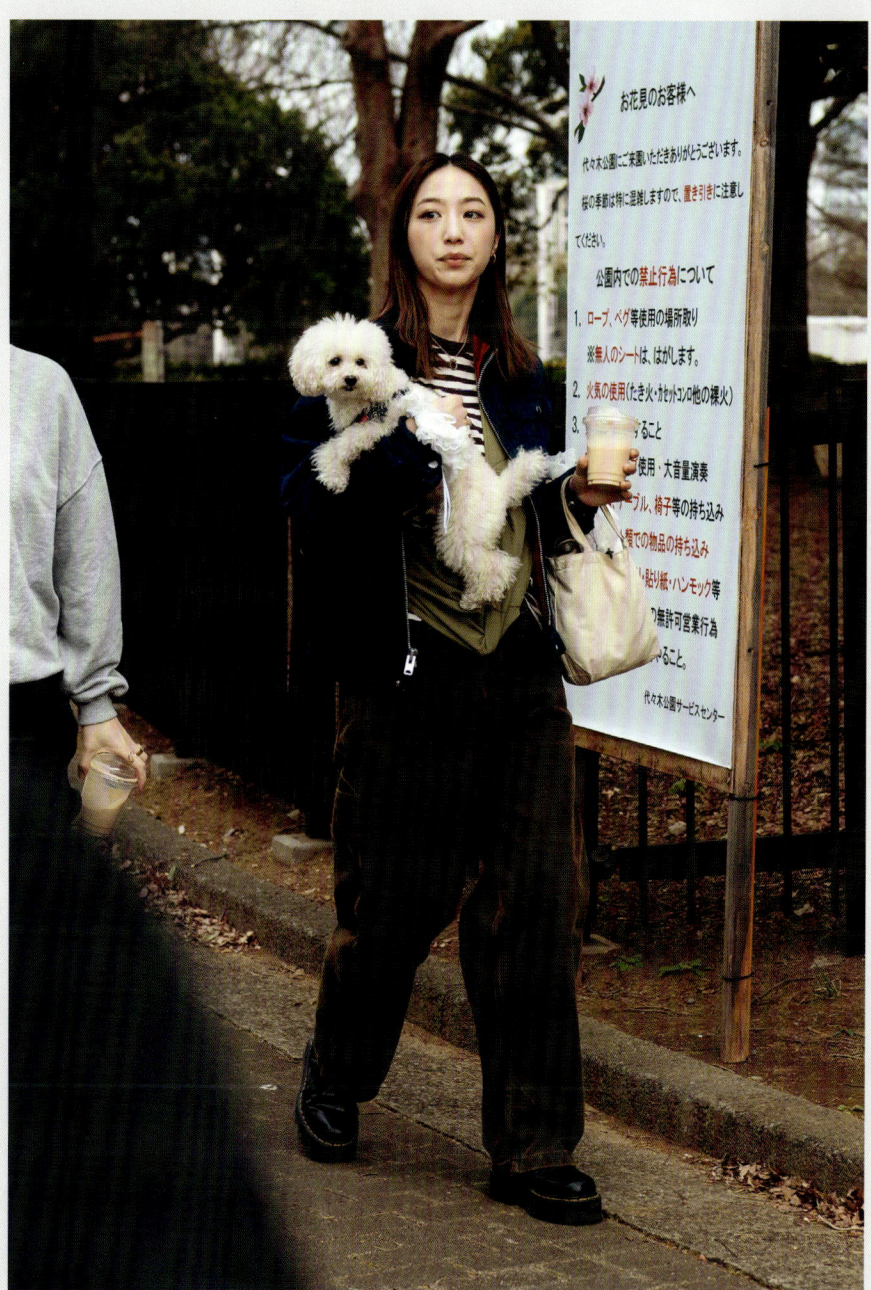

New York City, USA | Tokyo, Japan

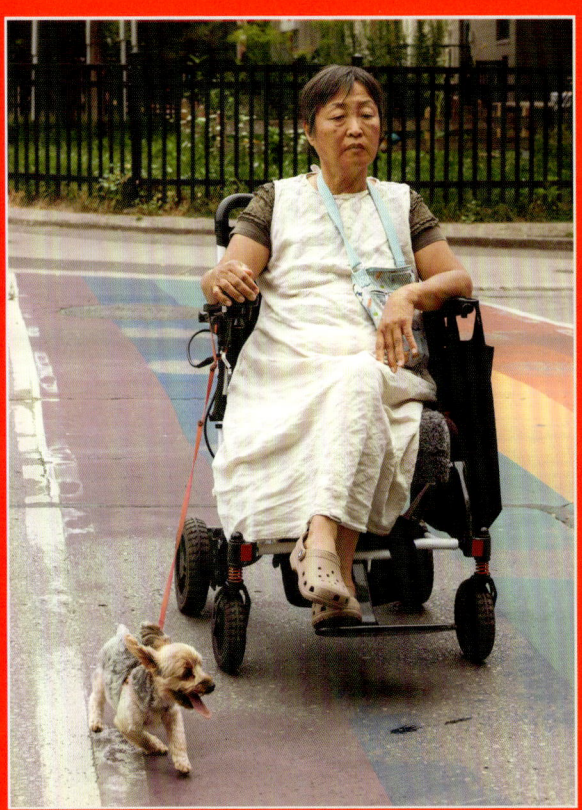

Toronto, Canada

"I think he's grateful that I found him in the dog pound when he was 2. He's 14 now, and we're growing old together."

Fraser and their dog Jimmy
Melbourne, Australia

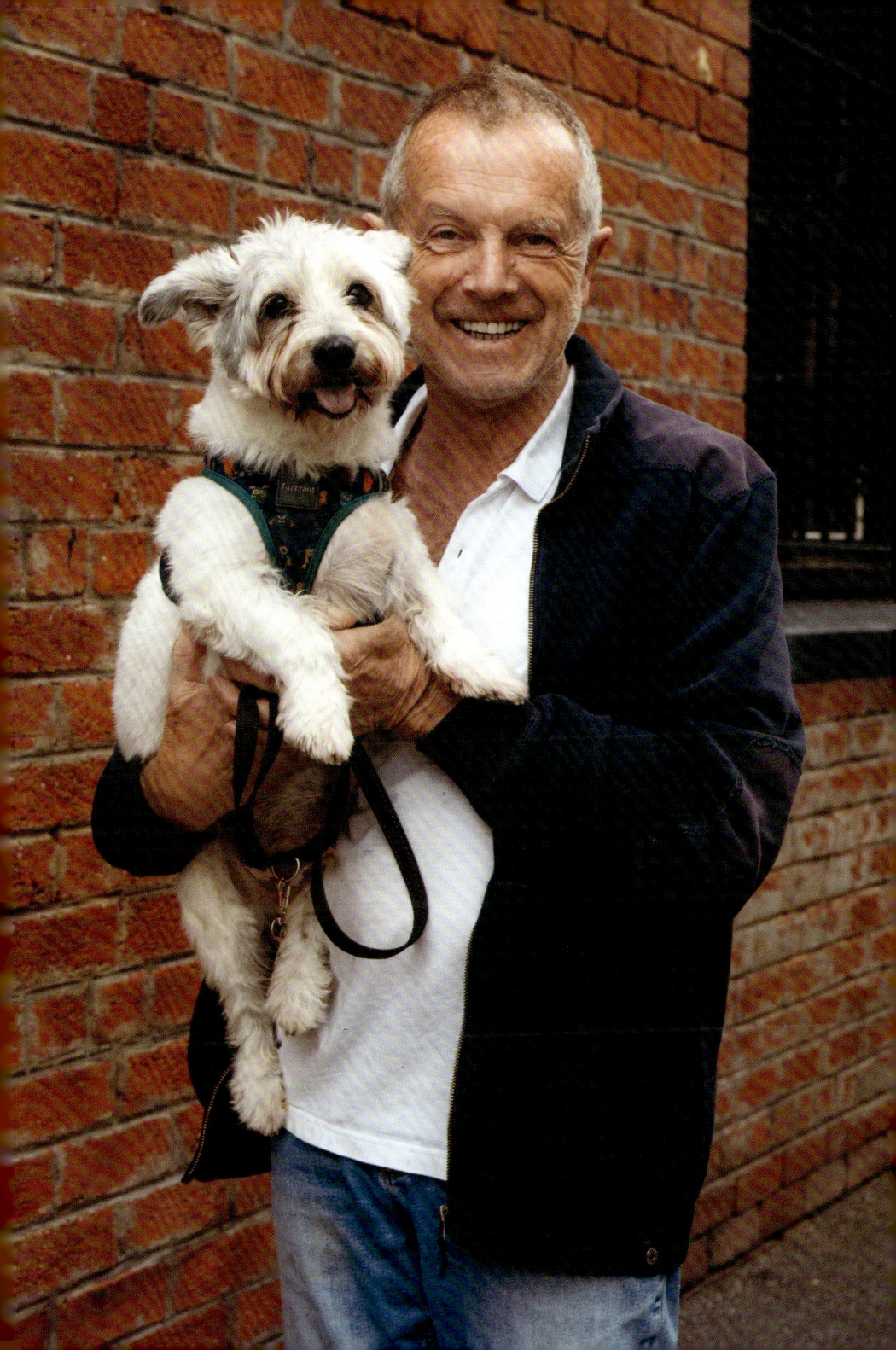

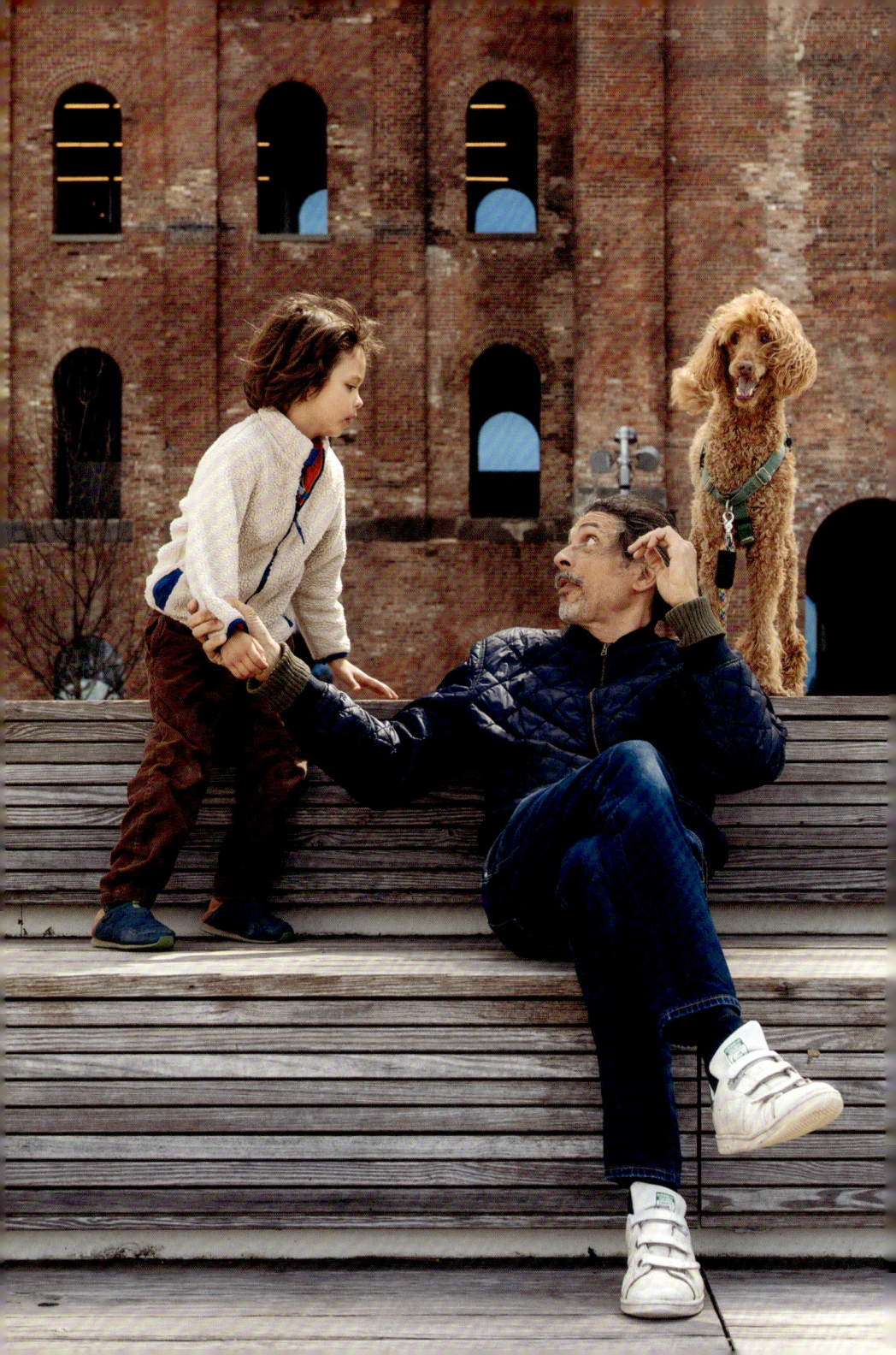

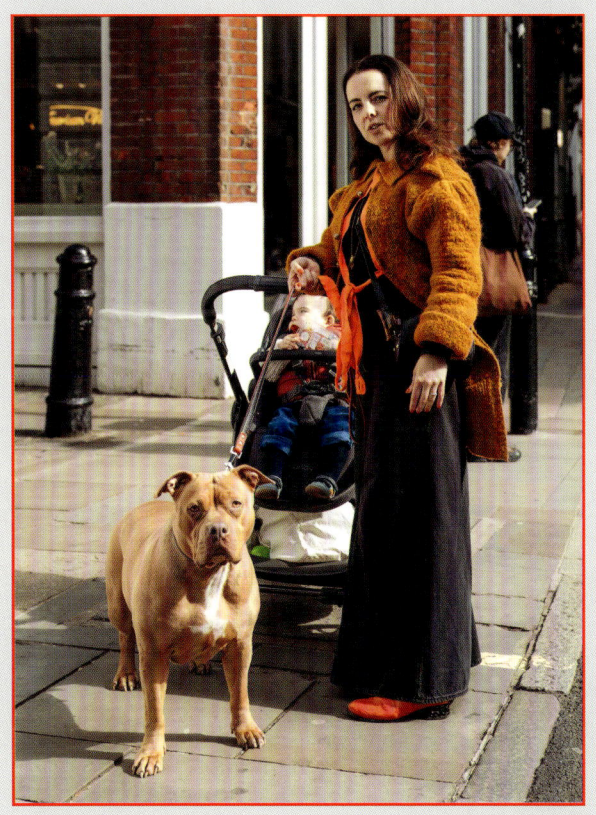

London, England

"Without her, I wouldn't be with my partner, I wouldn't have this life."

Timo and Mateo with their dog Ginger
New York City, USA

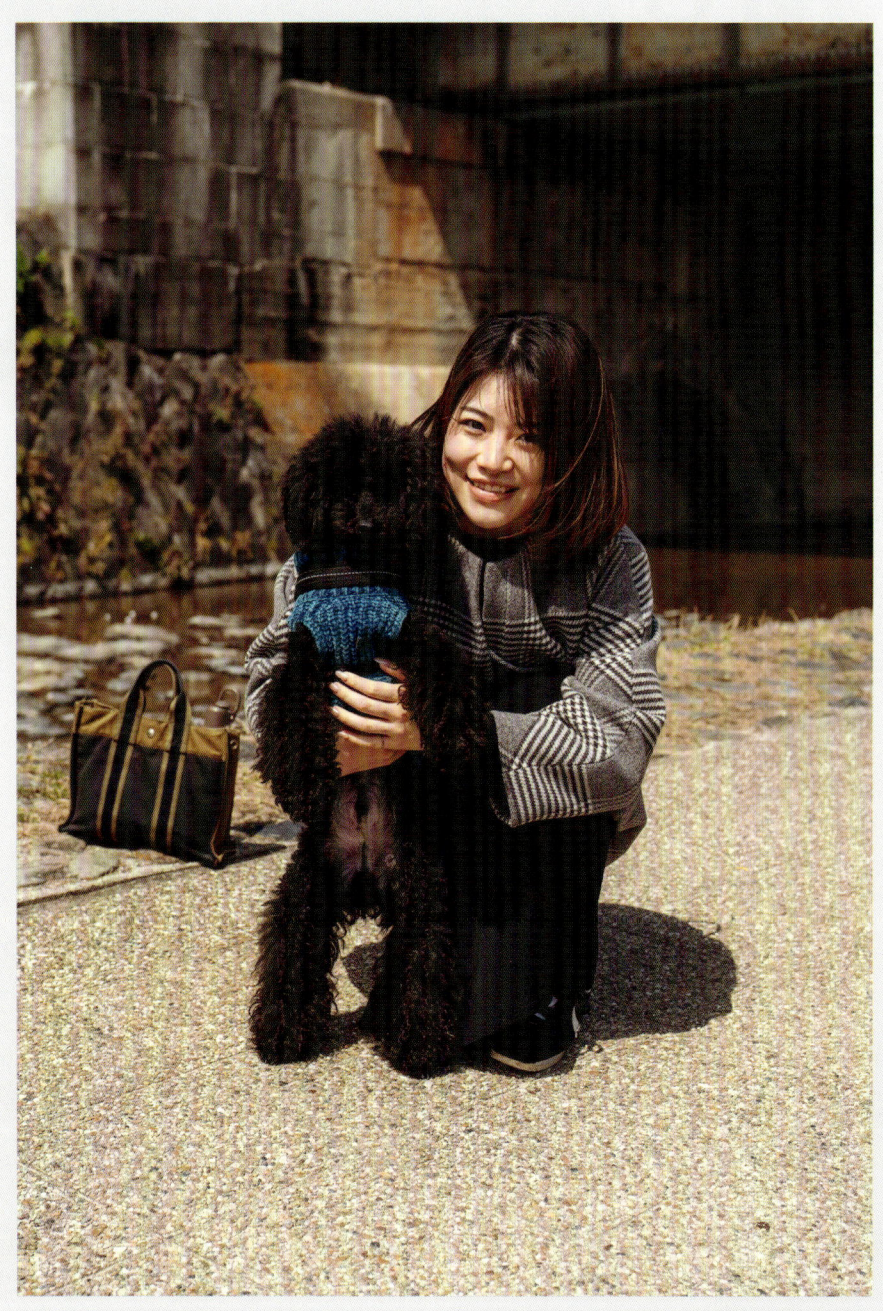

Kyoto, Japan | Tokyo, Japan

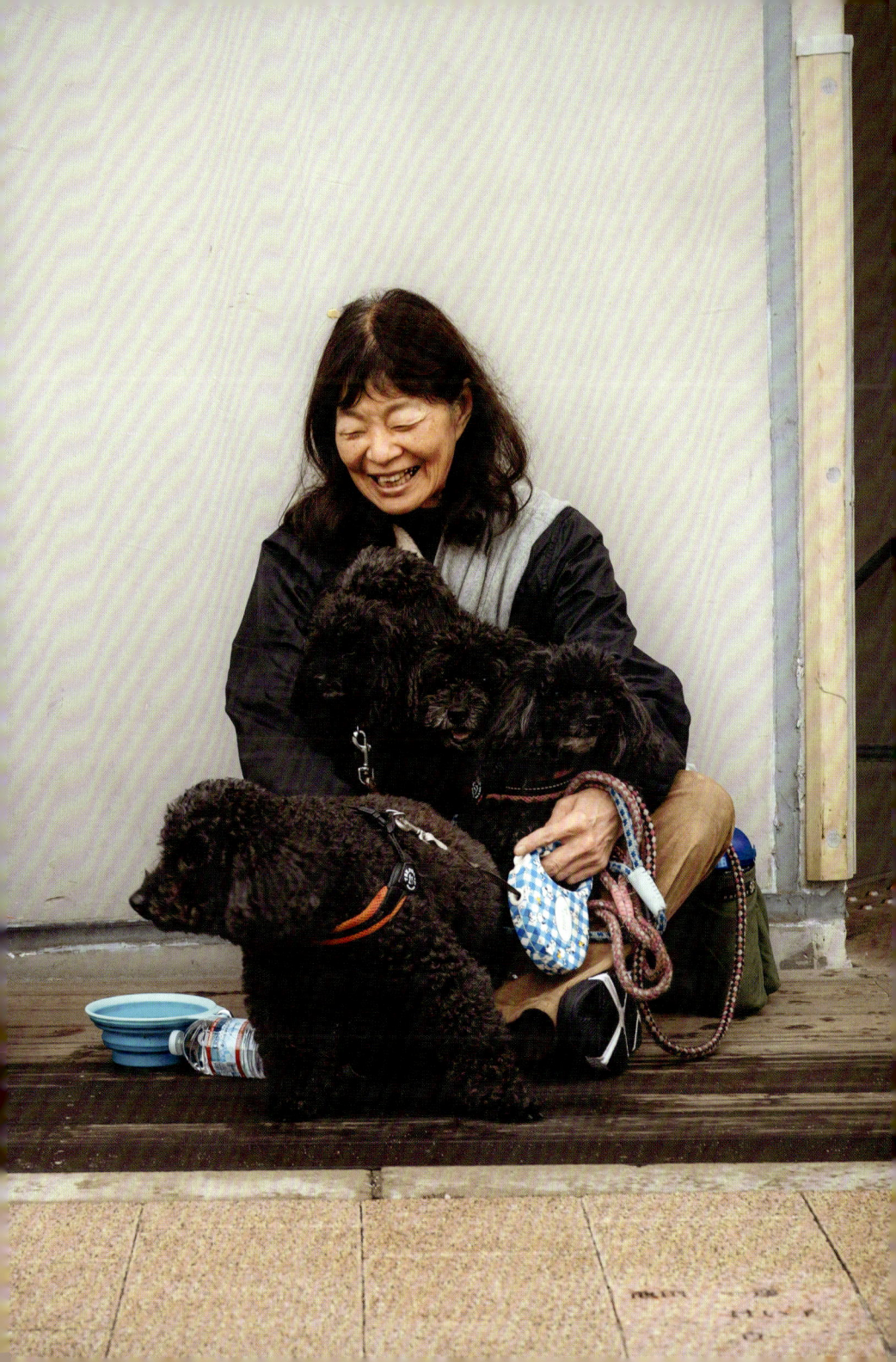

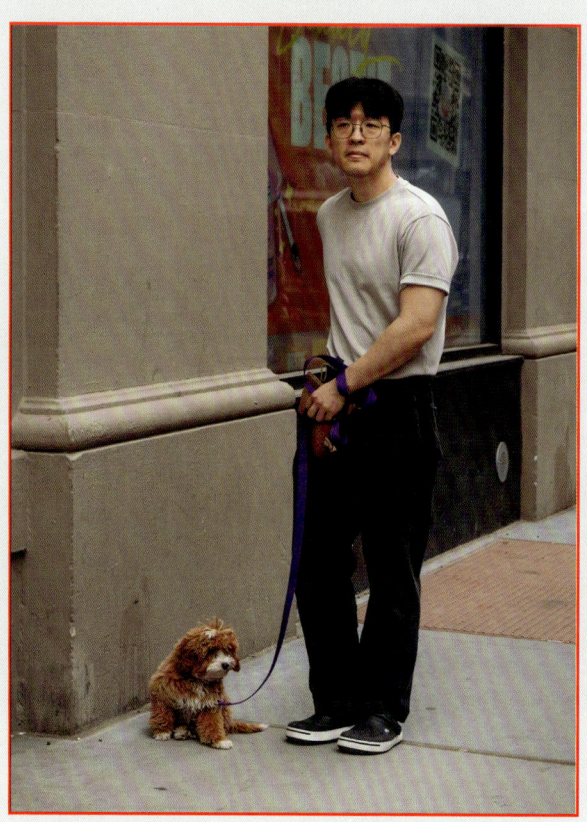

New York City, USA

"We met two weeks ago, so we're just getting to know each other."

Leão and their dog Seva
Paris, France

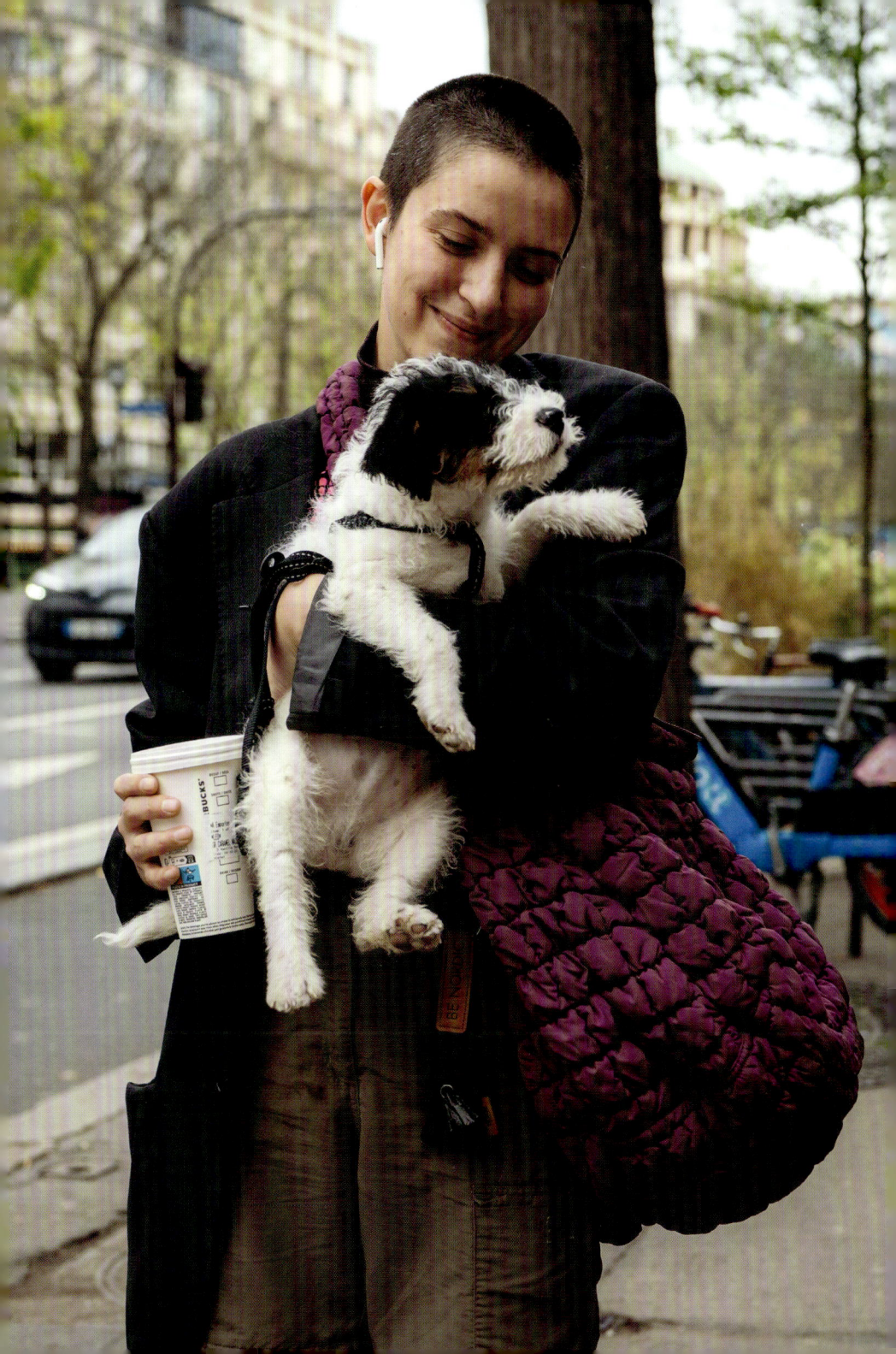

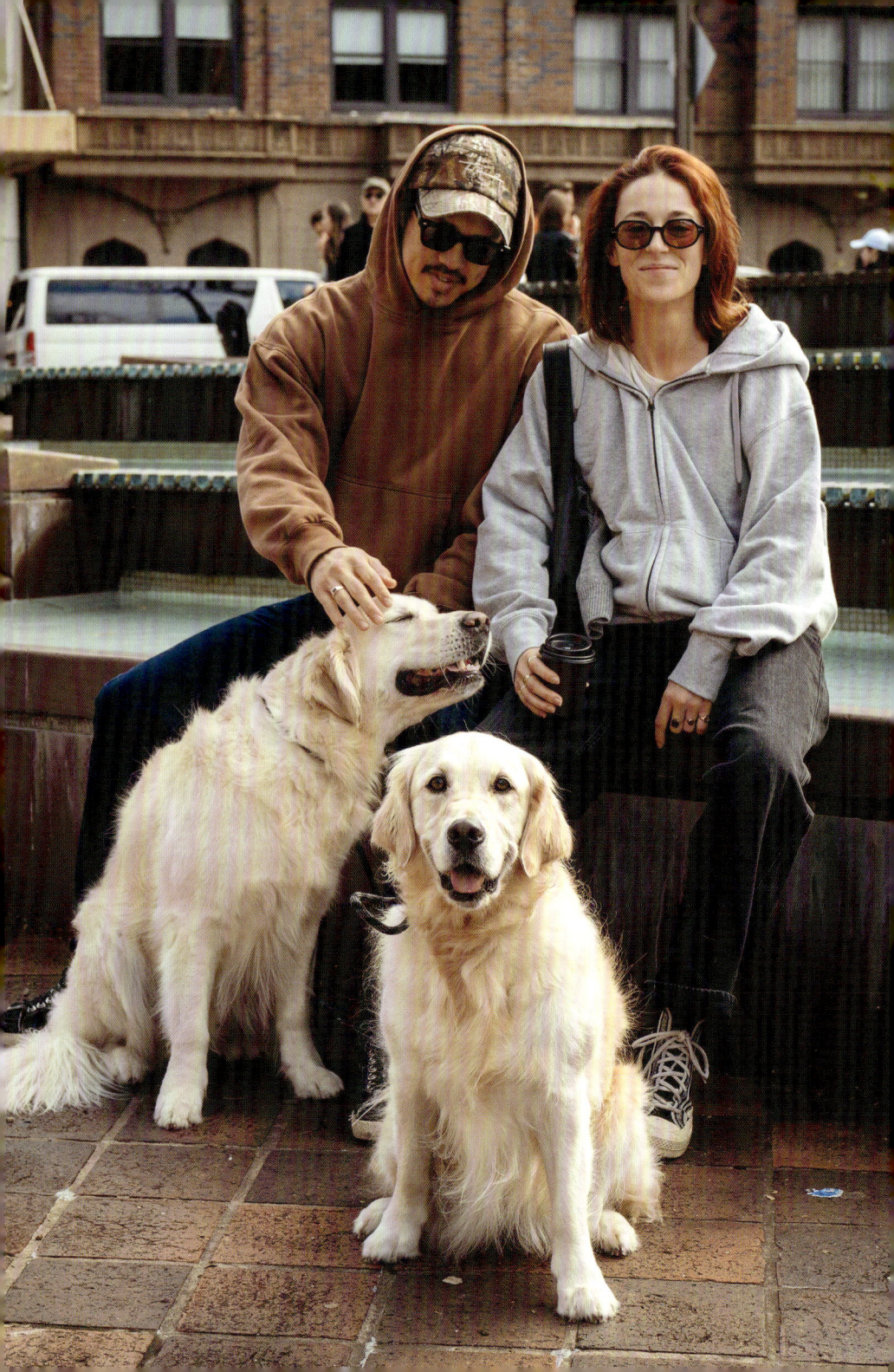

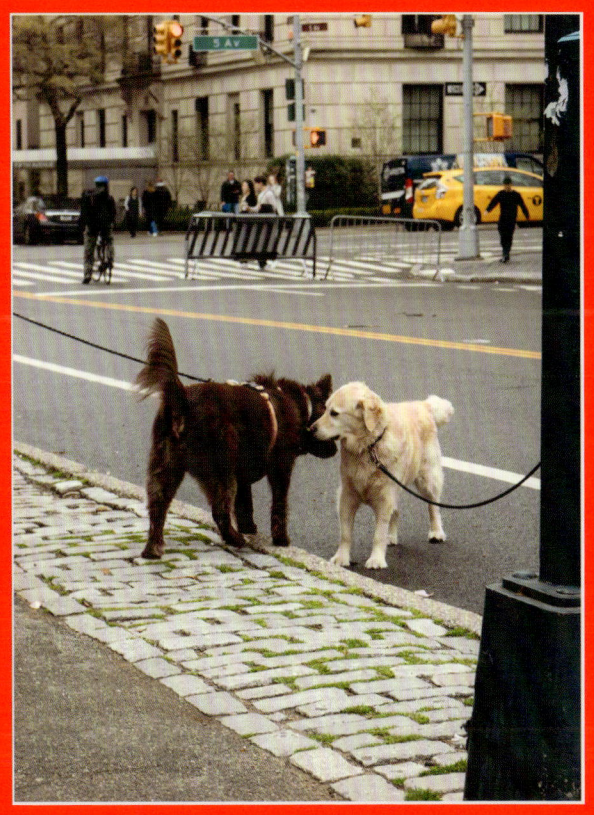

New York City, USA

"They're a great pair. Billie was inherited from a family member who passed, so Otis was a happy addition."

Alex and Nicola and their dogs Otis (left) and Billie (right)
Sydney, Australia

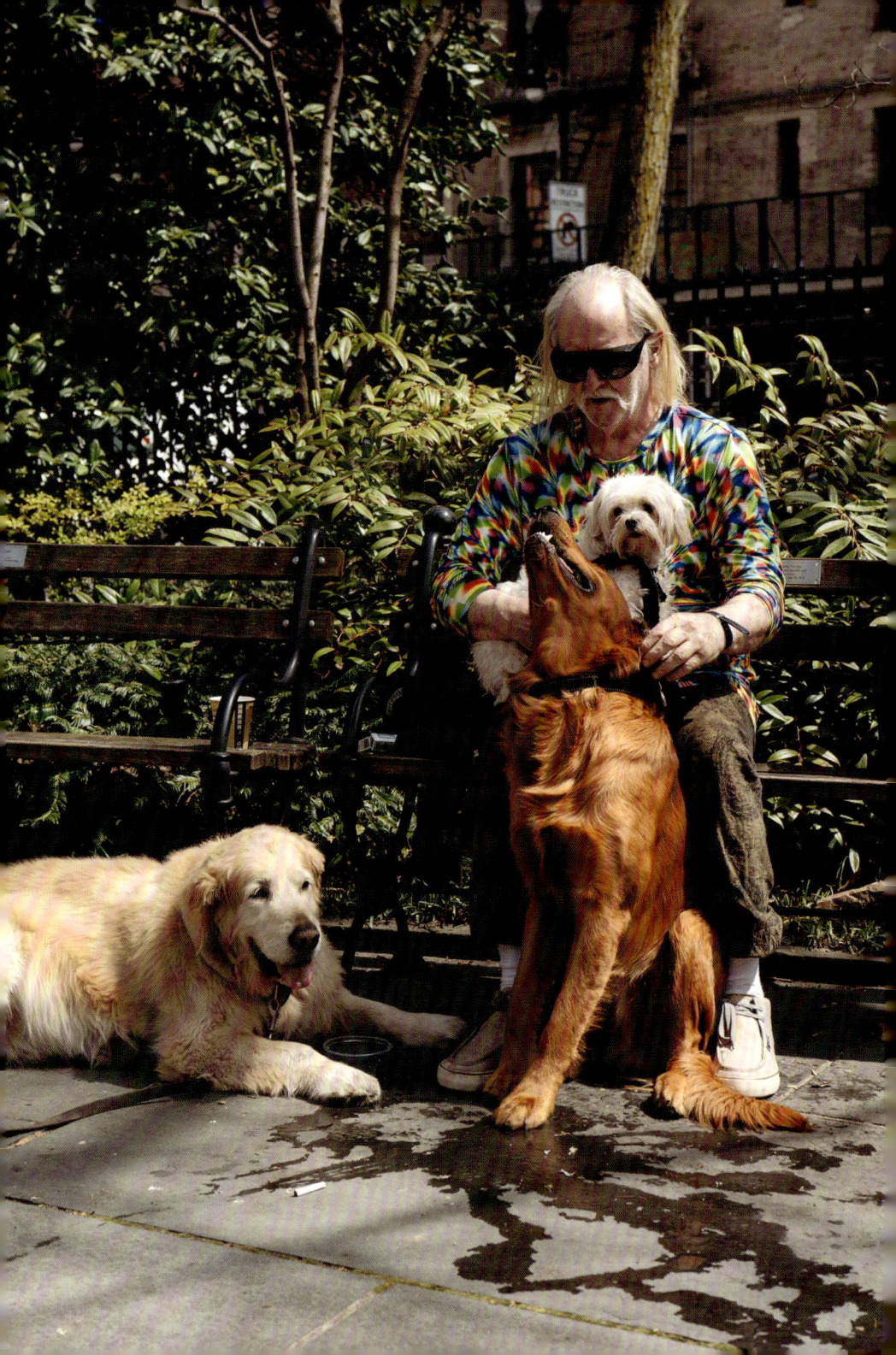

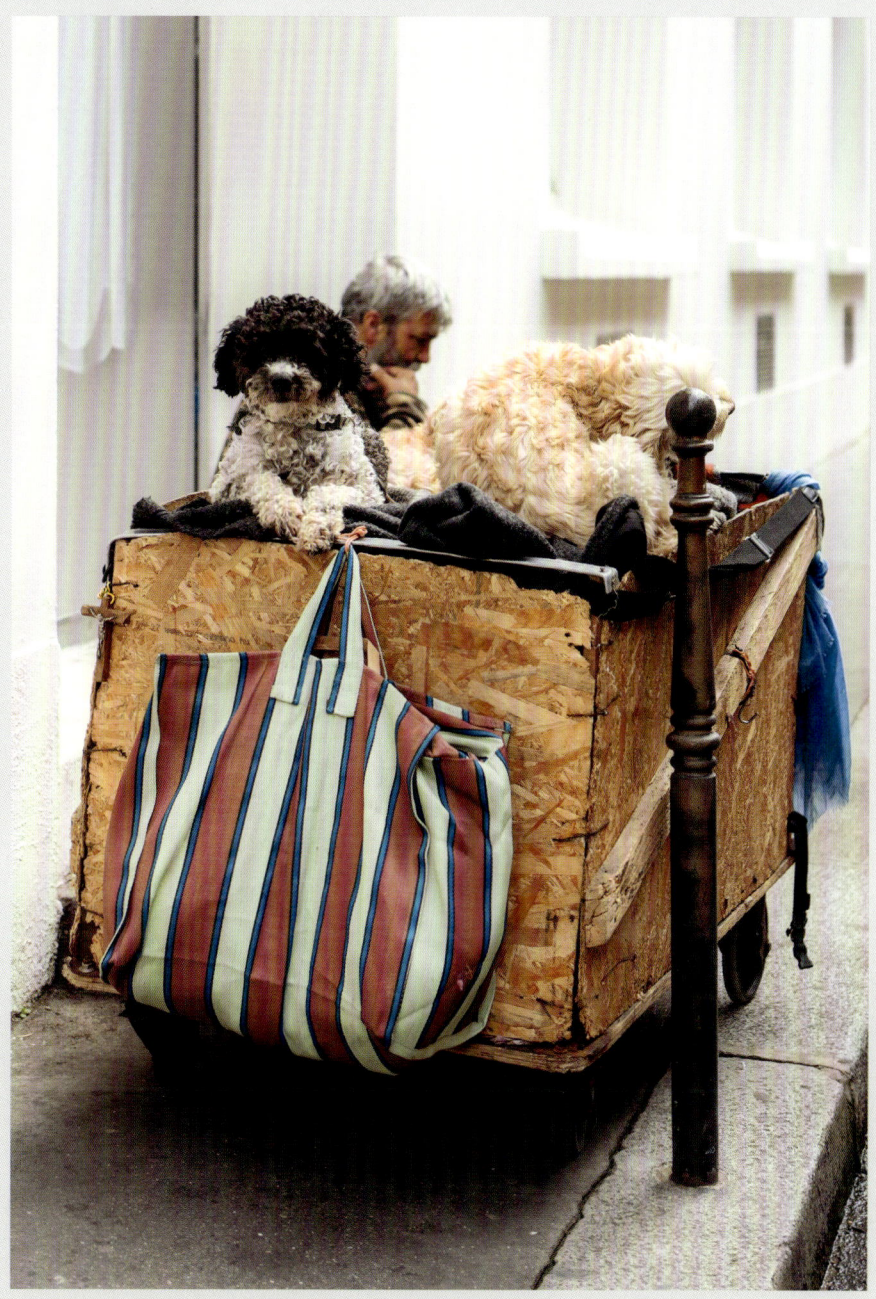

New York City, USA | Paris, France

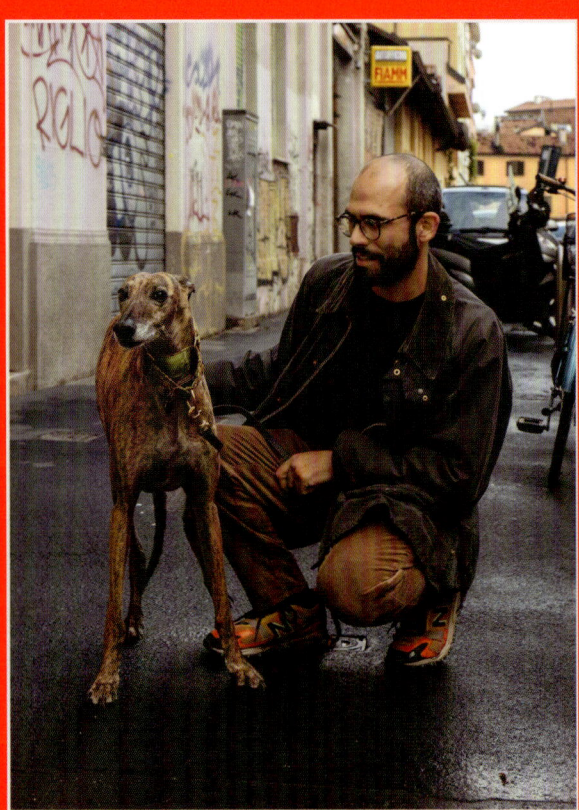

Milan, Italy

"He thinks I'm too needy.
He's a cat trapped in a dog's body."

Amol and their dog Panucci
London, England

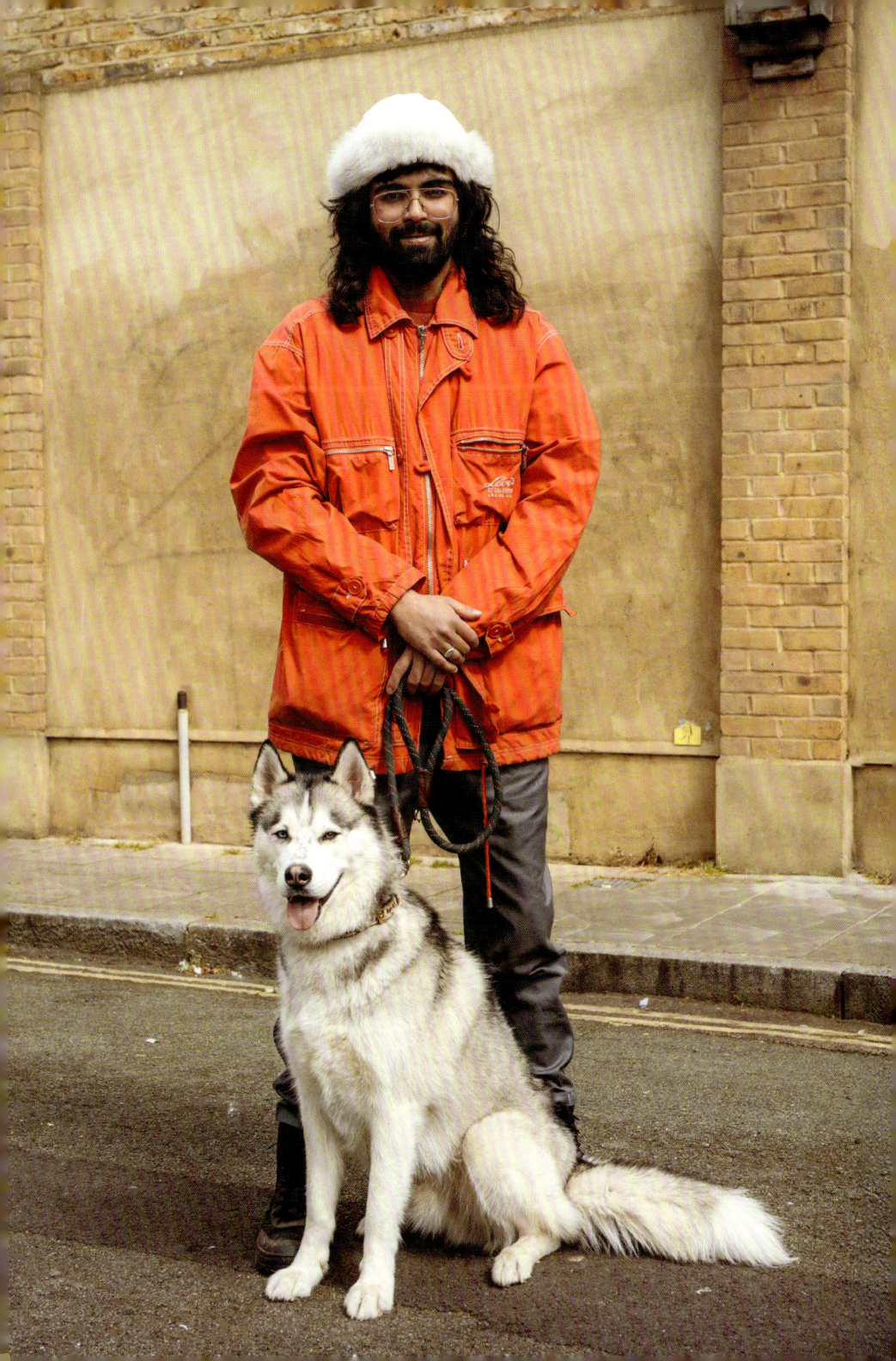

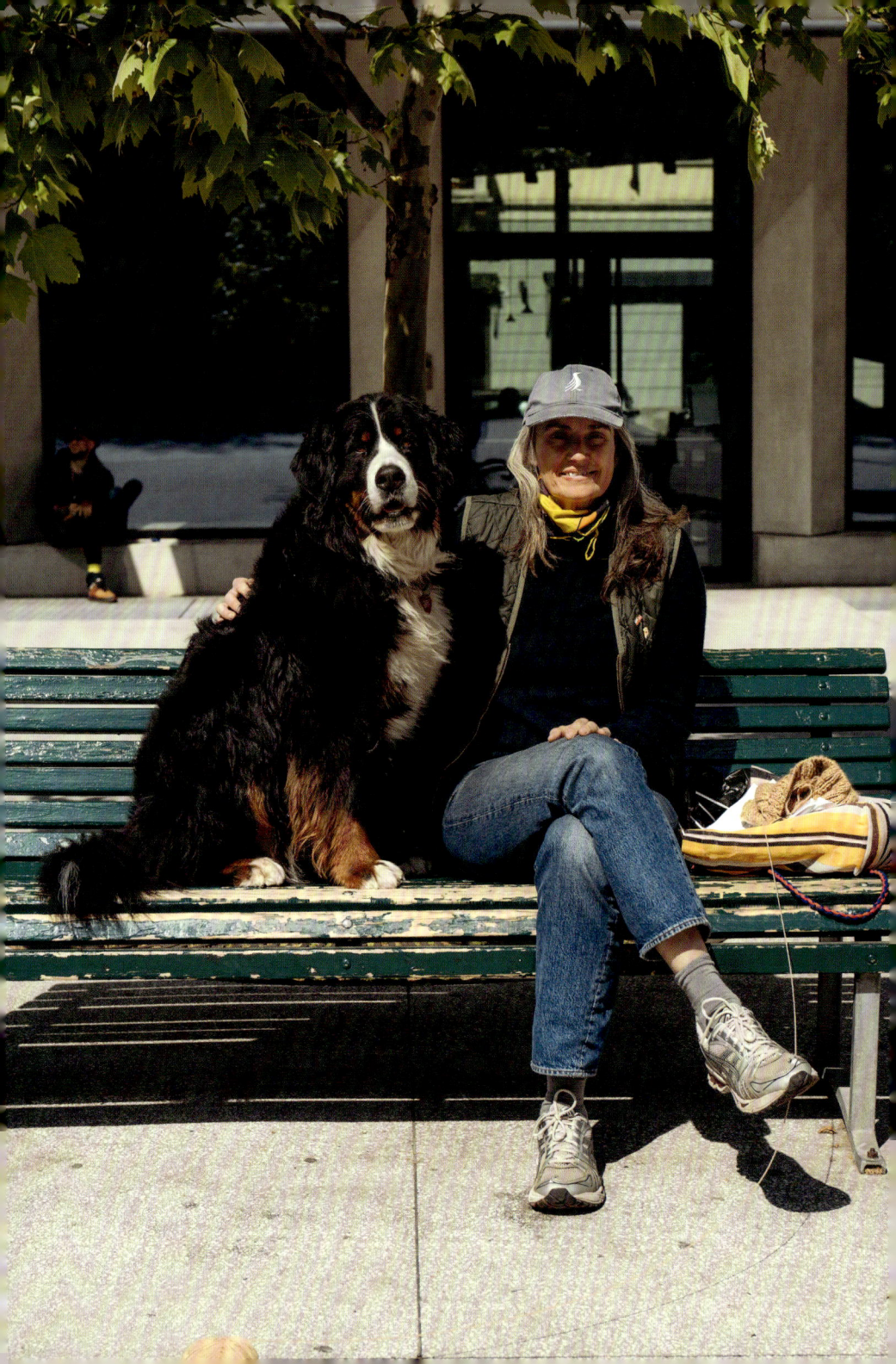

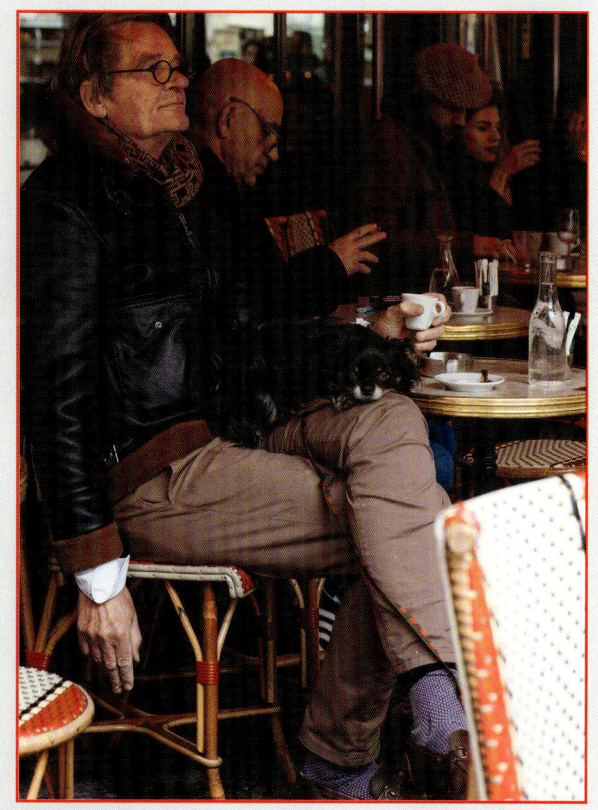

Paris, France

"I was not a dog person before him. It's my first relationship with a dog. We love spending time together."

Ellen and their dog Aslan
Milan, Italy

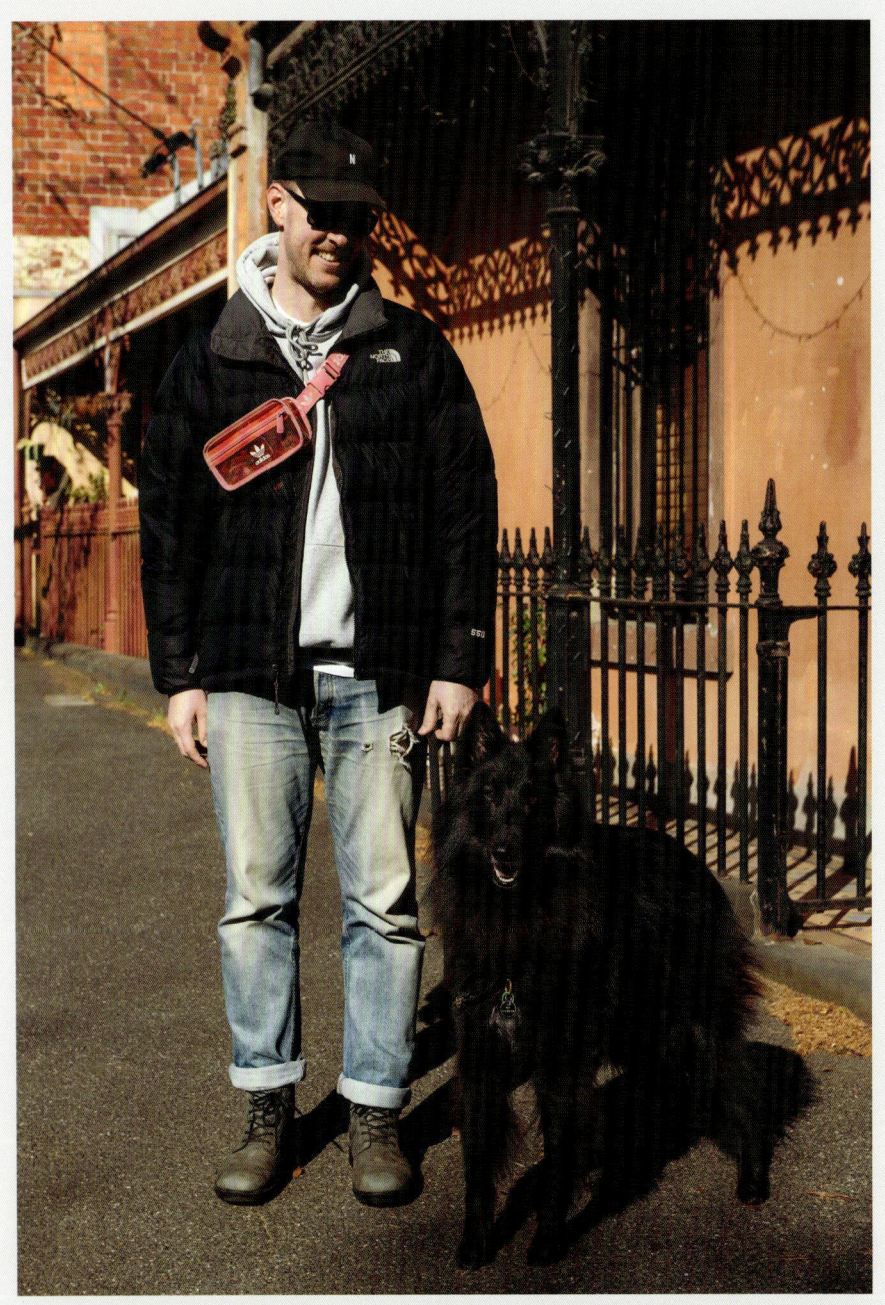

Melbourne, Australia | London, England

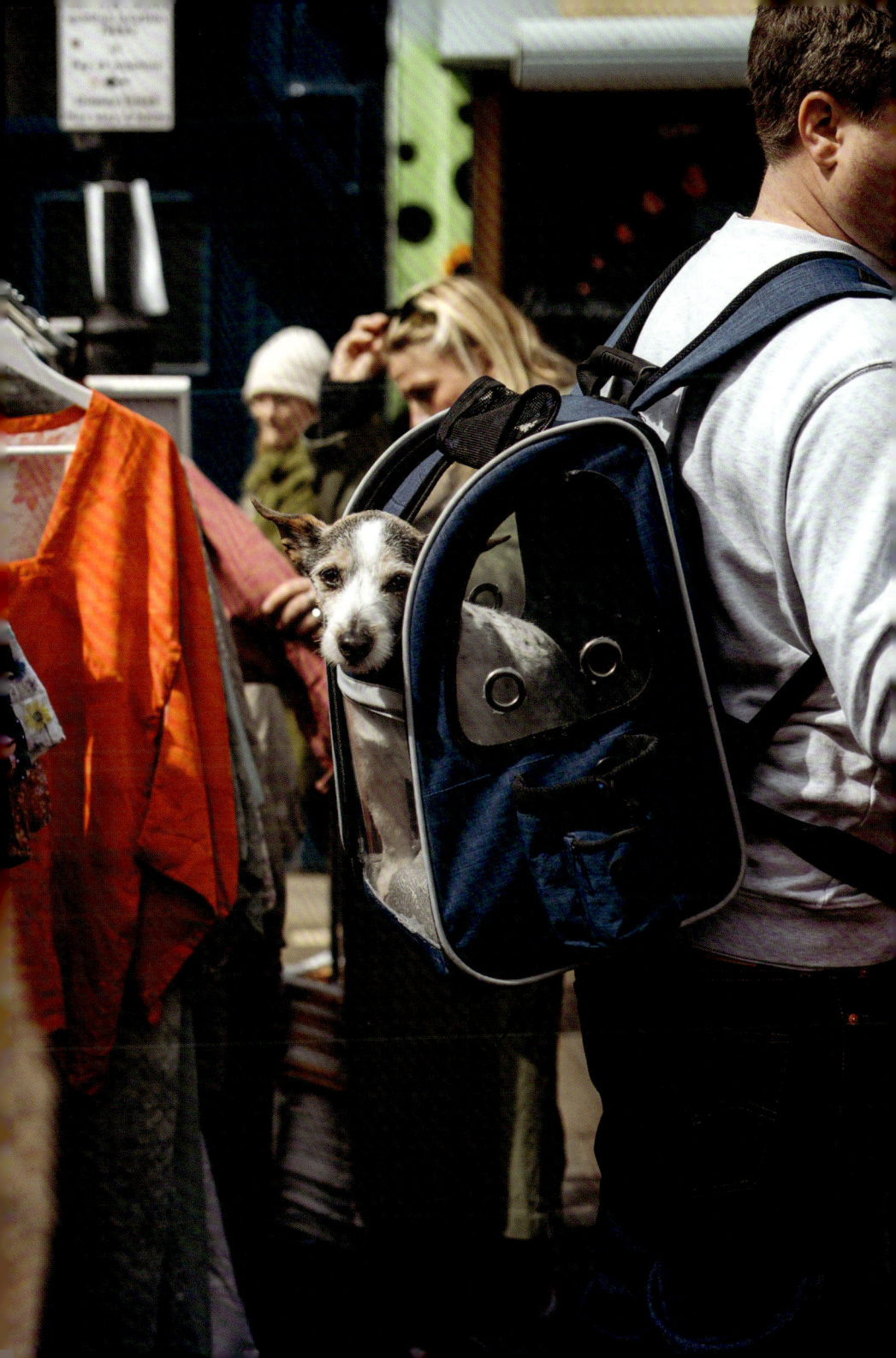

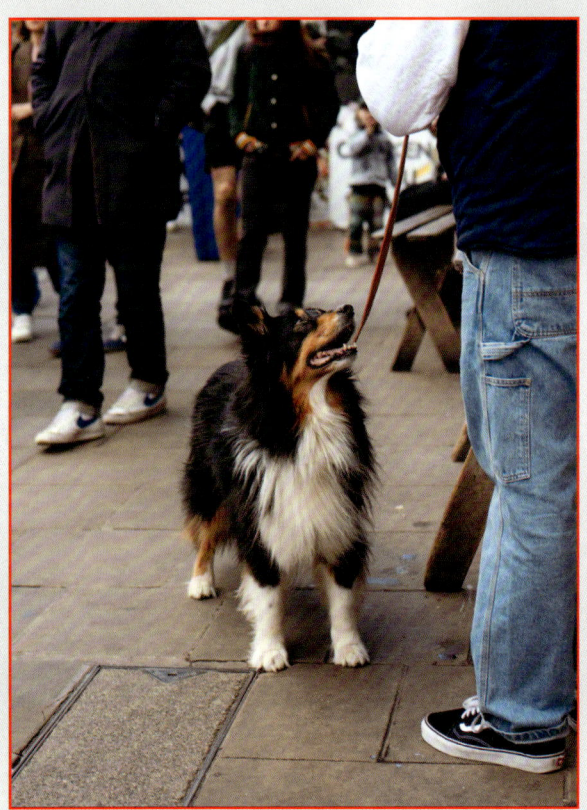

London, England

"Give me some food
you piece of shit."

Achilles and their dog Gus
Paris, France

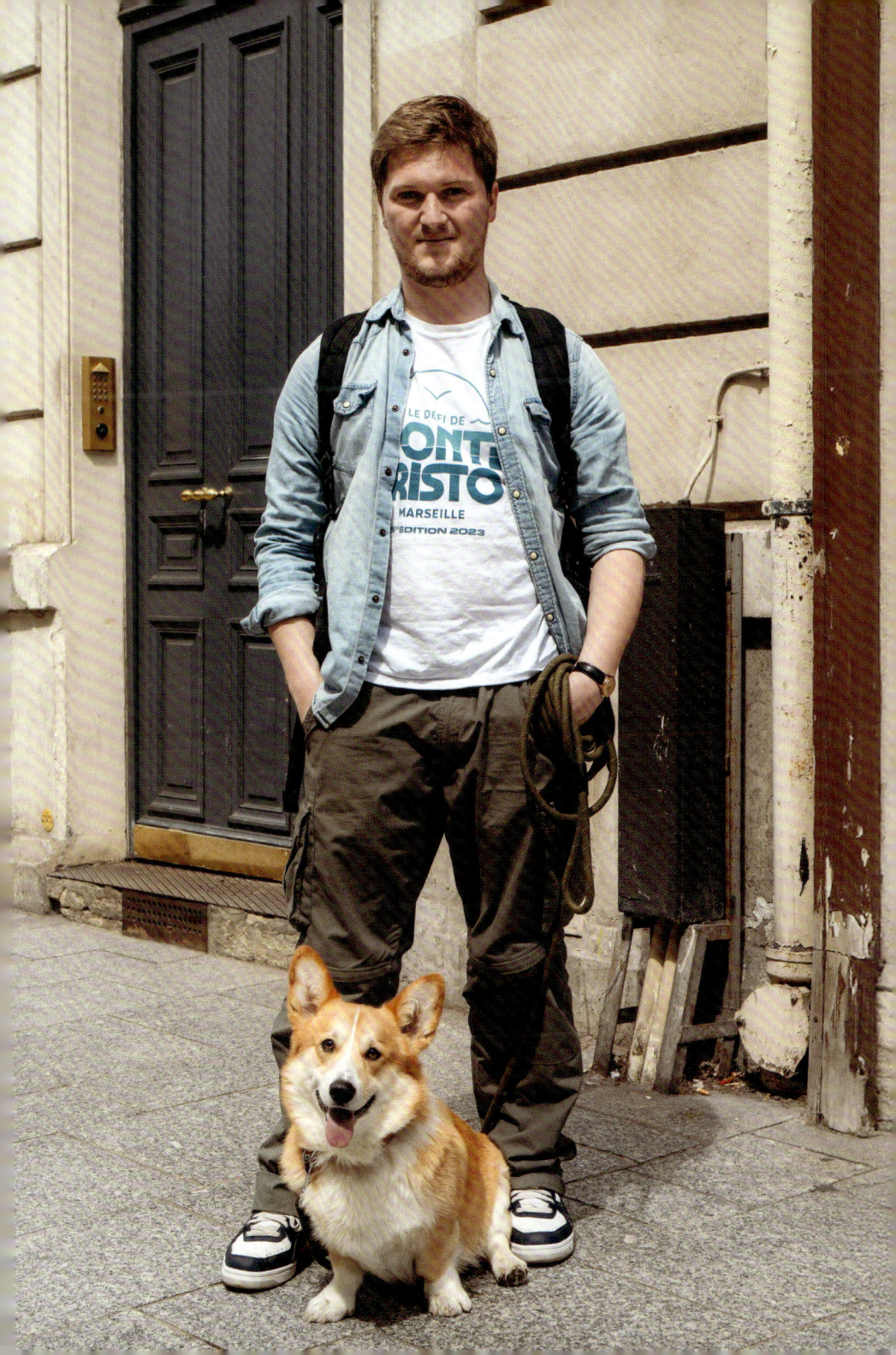

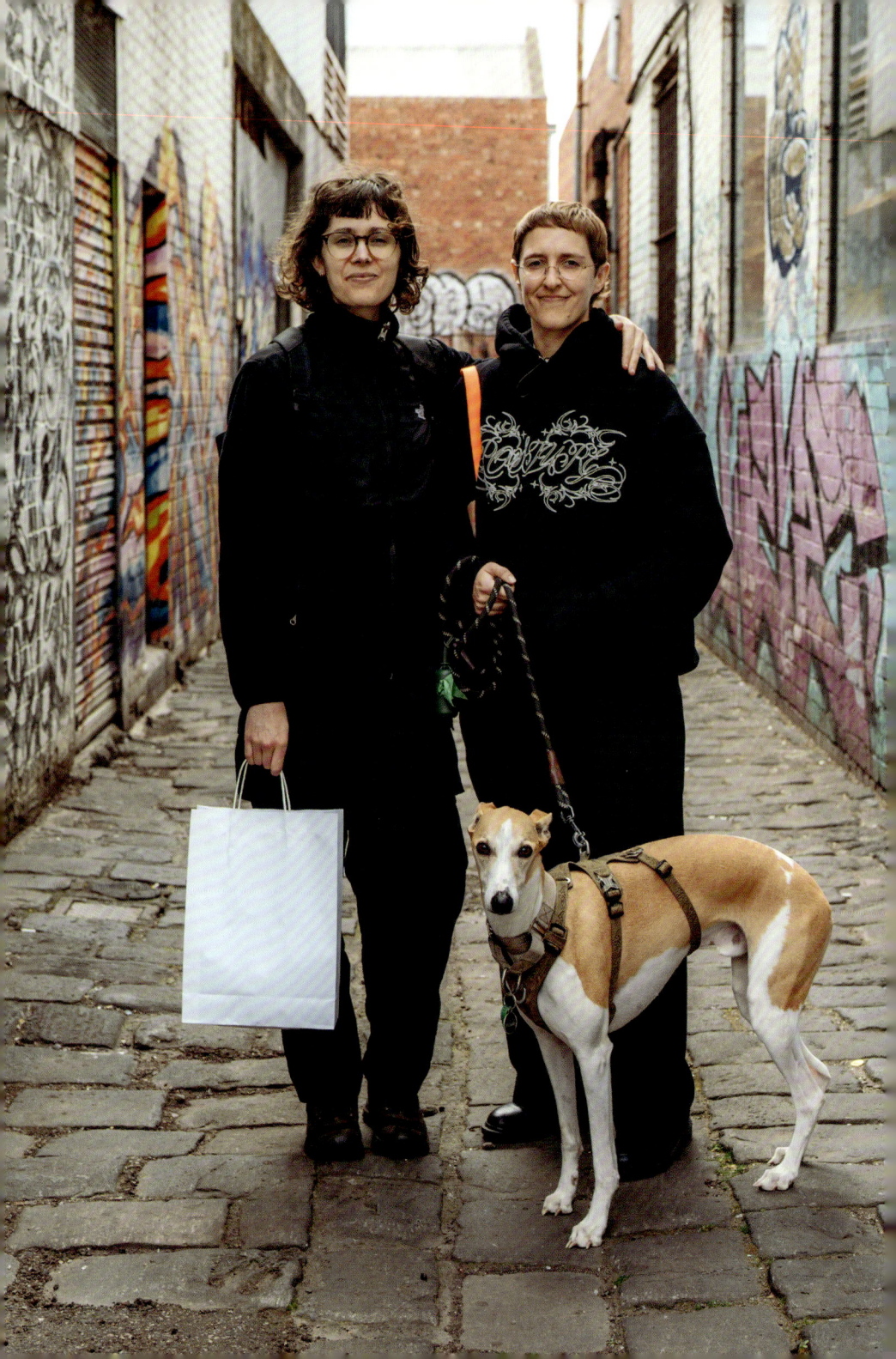

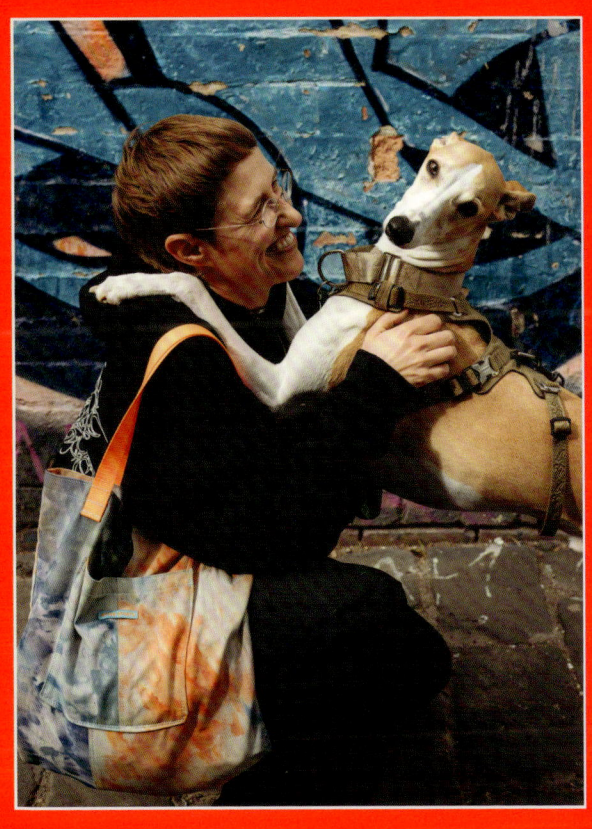

"He thinks we smother him too much."

Chloe and Tessa and their dog Theo
Melbourne, Australia

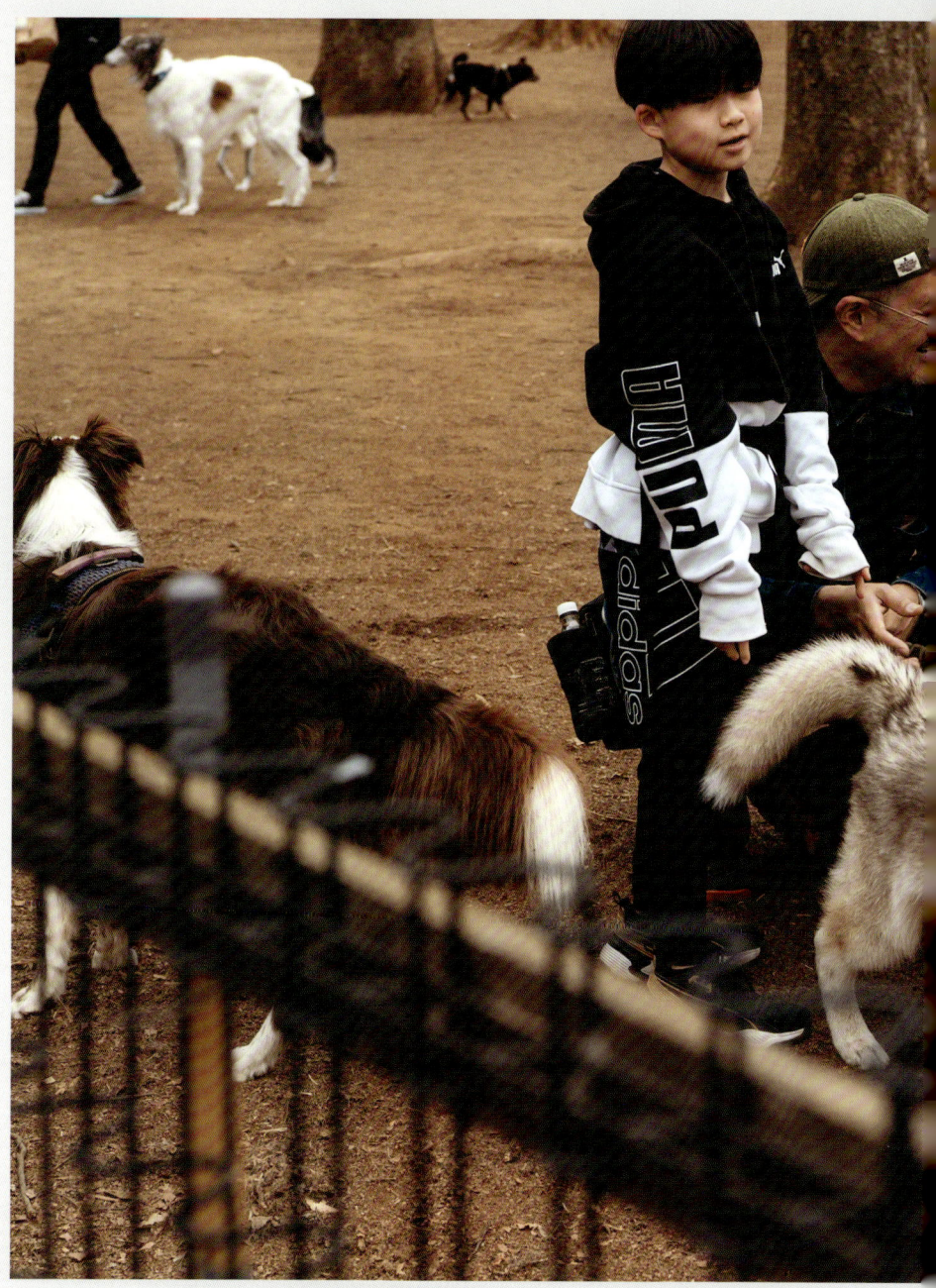

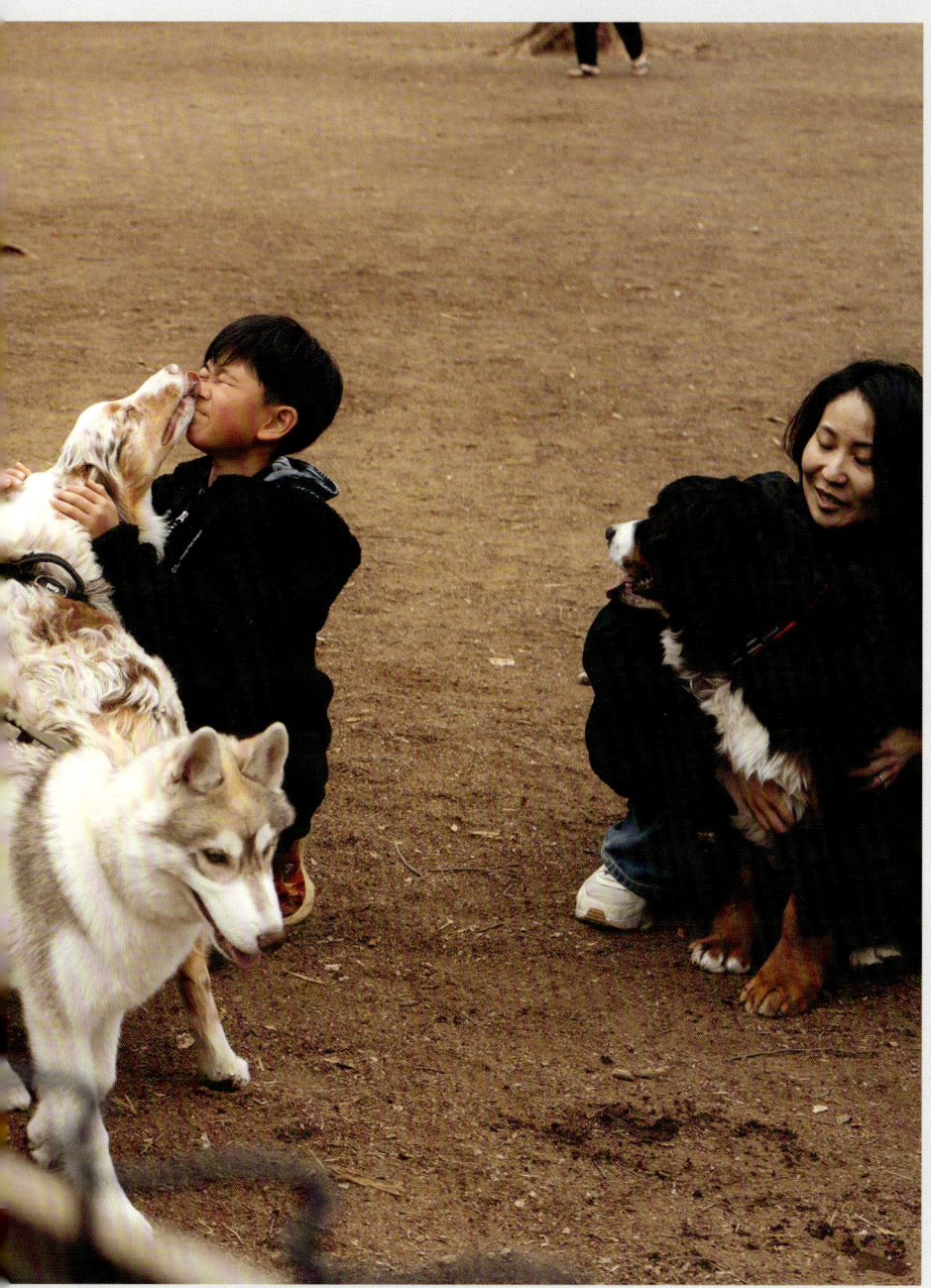

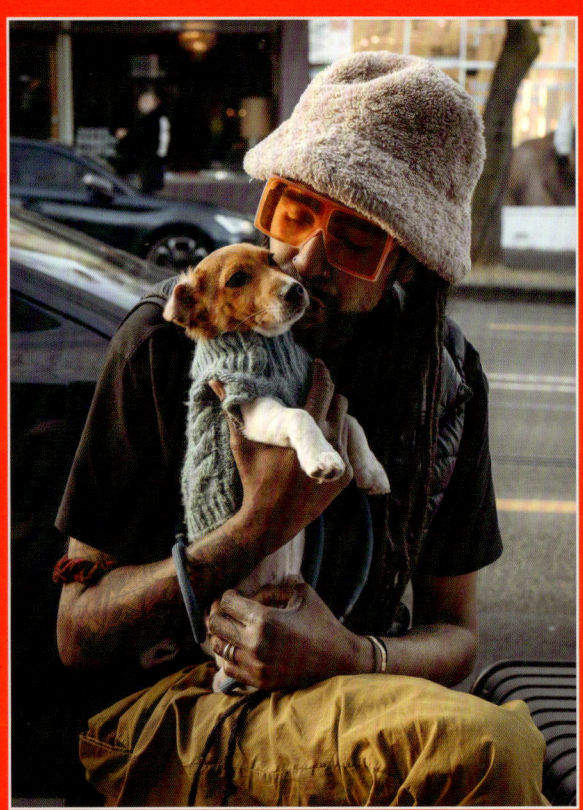

Melbourne, Australia

"I've given him a Birmingham accent, so whatever he might say, he'll sound like Mike Skinner."

Steve and their dog Banksy
London, England

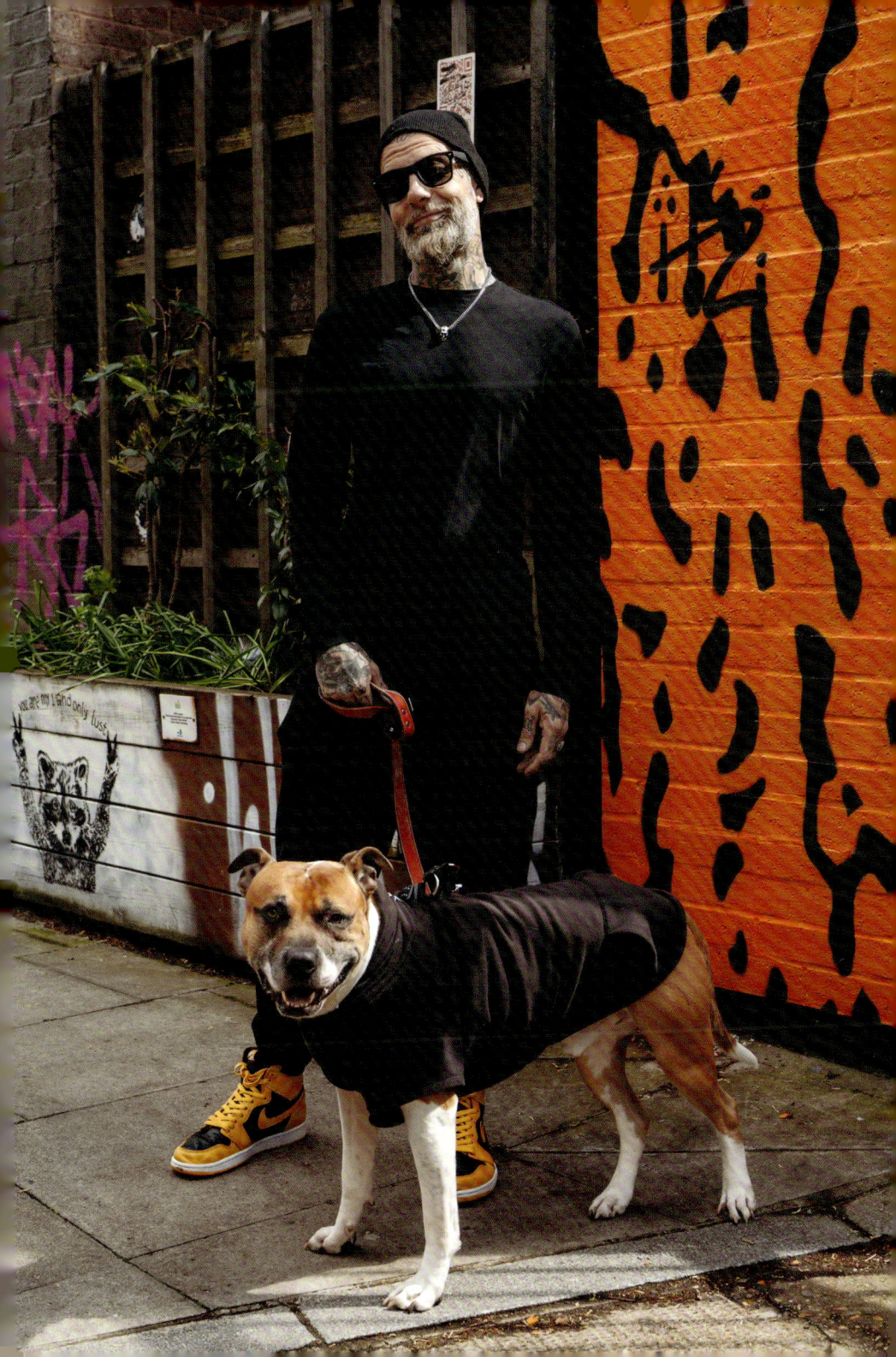

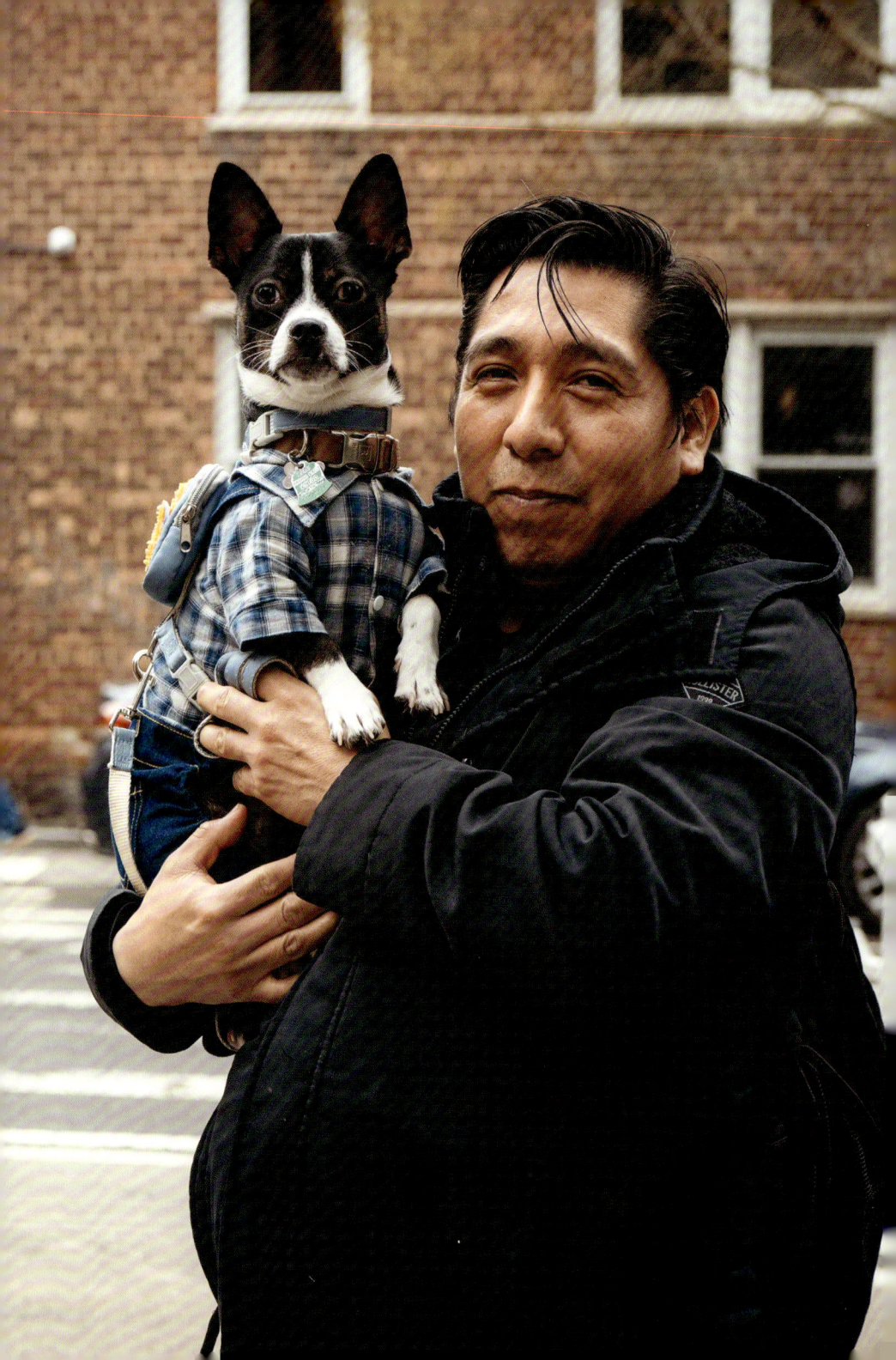

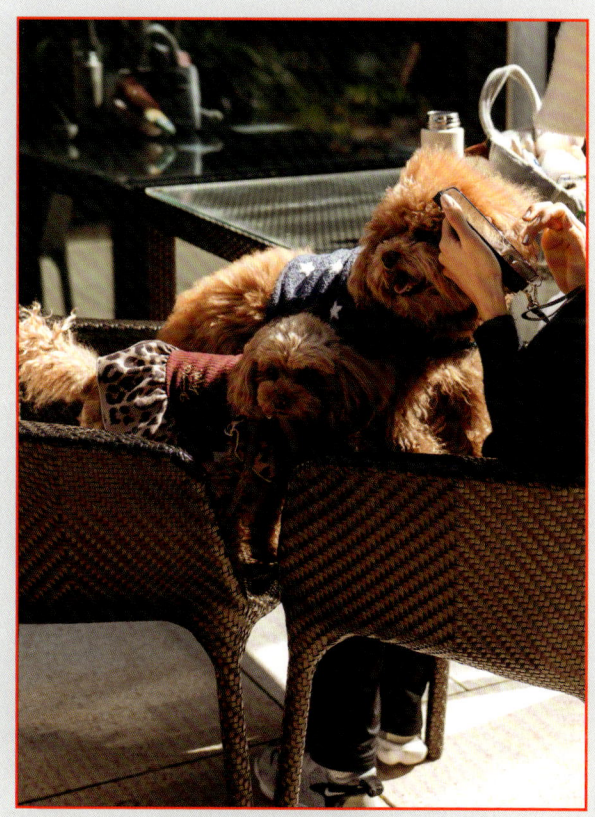

"Maybe he loves me? I don't know, but I know he likes being with me."

Arturo and their dog Paquito
New York City, USA

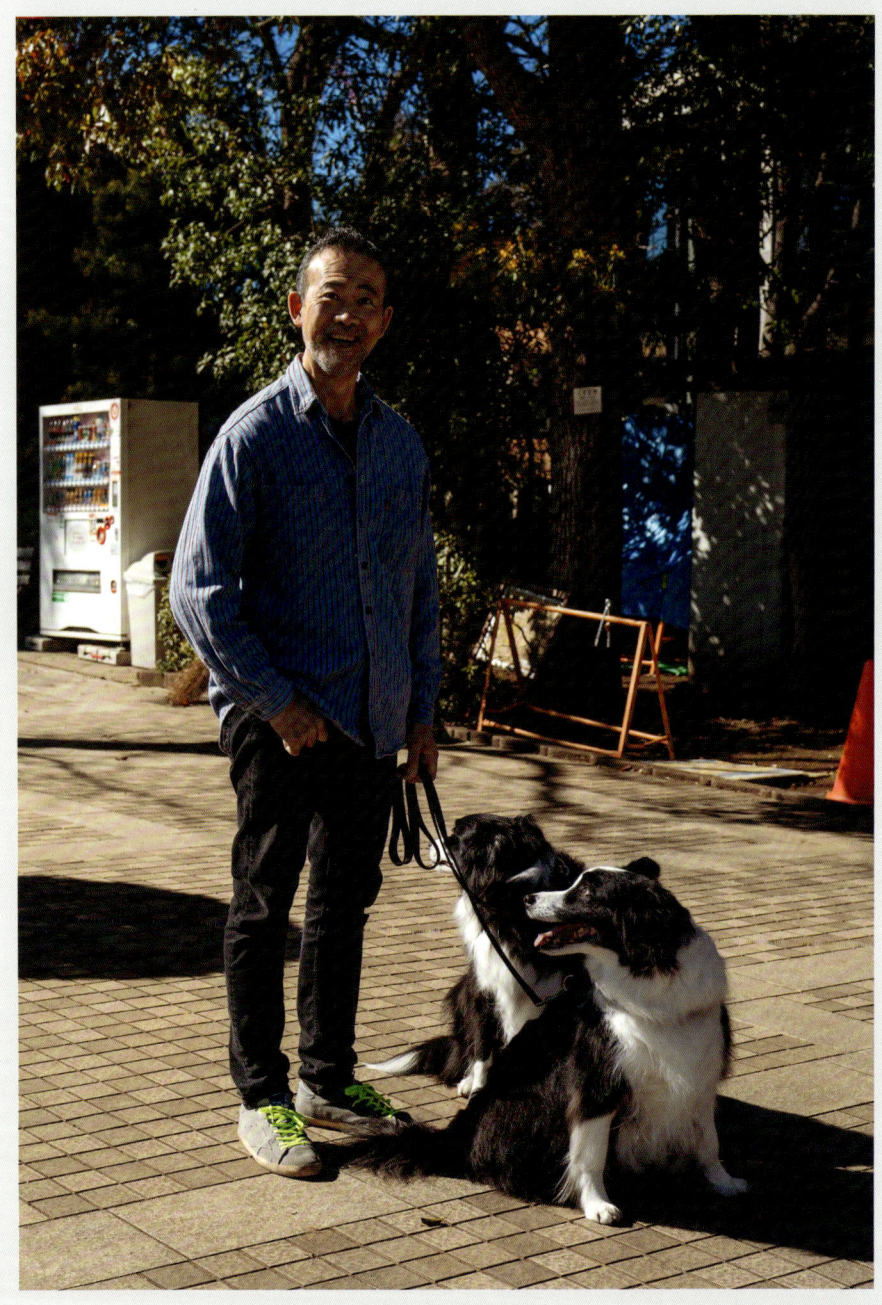

Tokyo, Japan | Paris, France

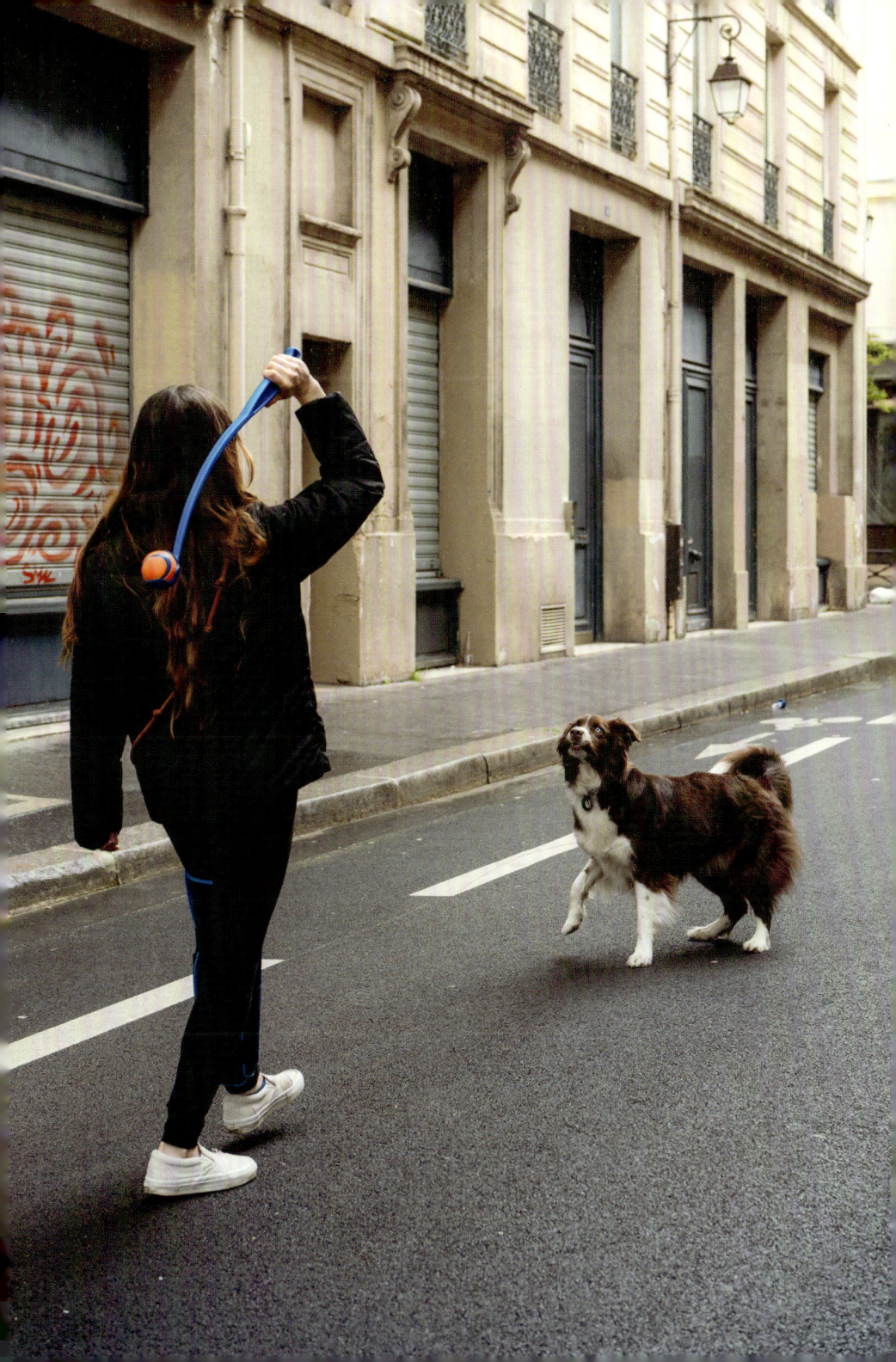

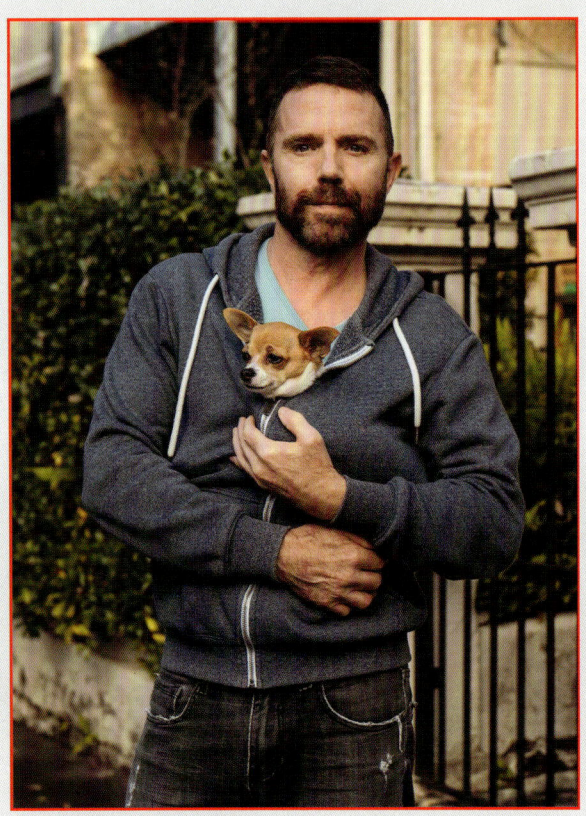

"She thinks she's taking care of us. But she doesn't actually want the responsibility."

Mayumi and Gian and their dog Ray
Milan, Italy

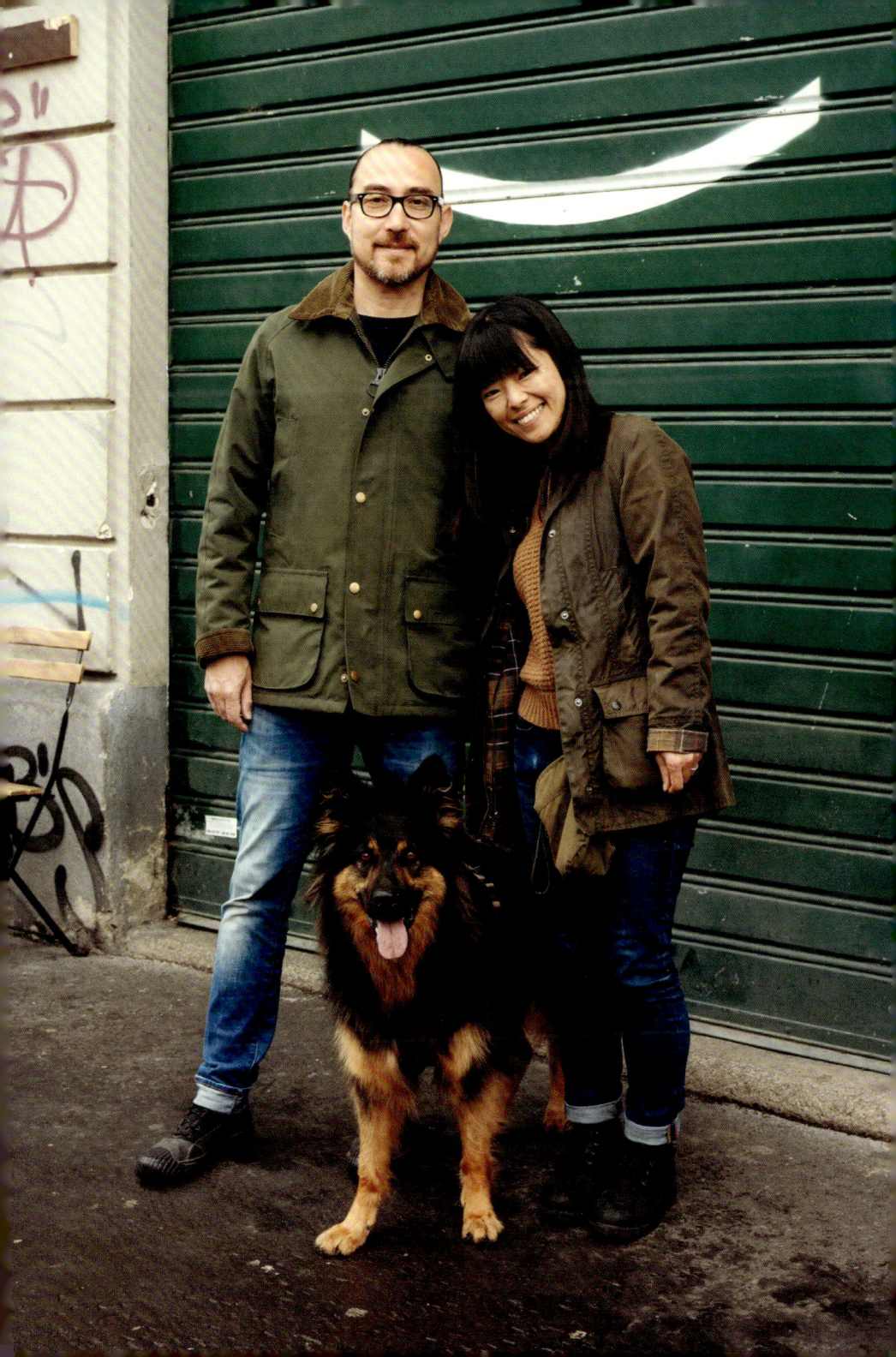

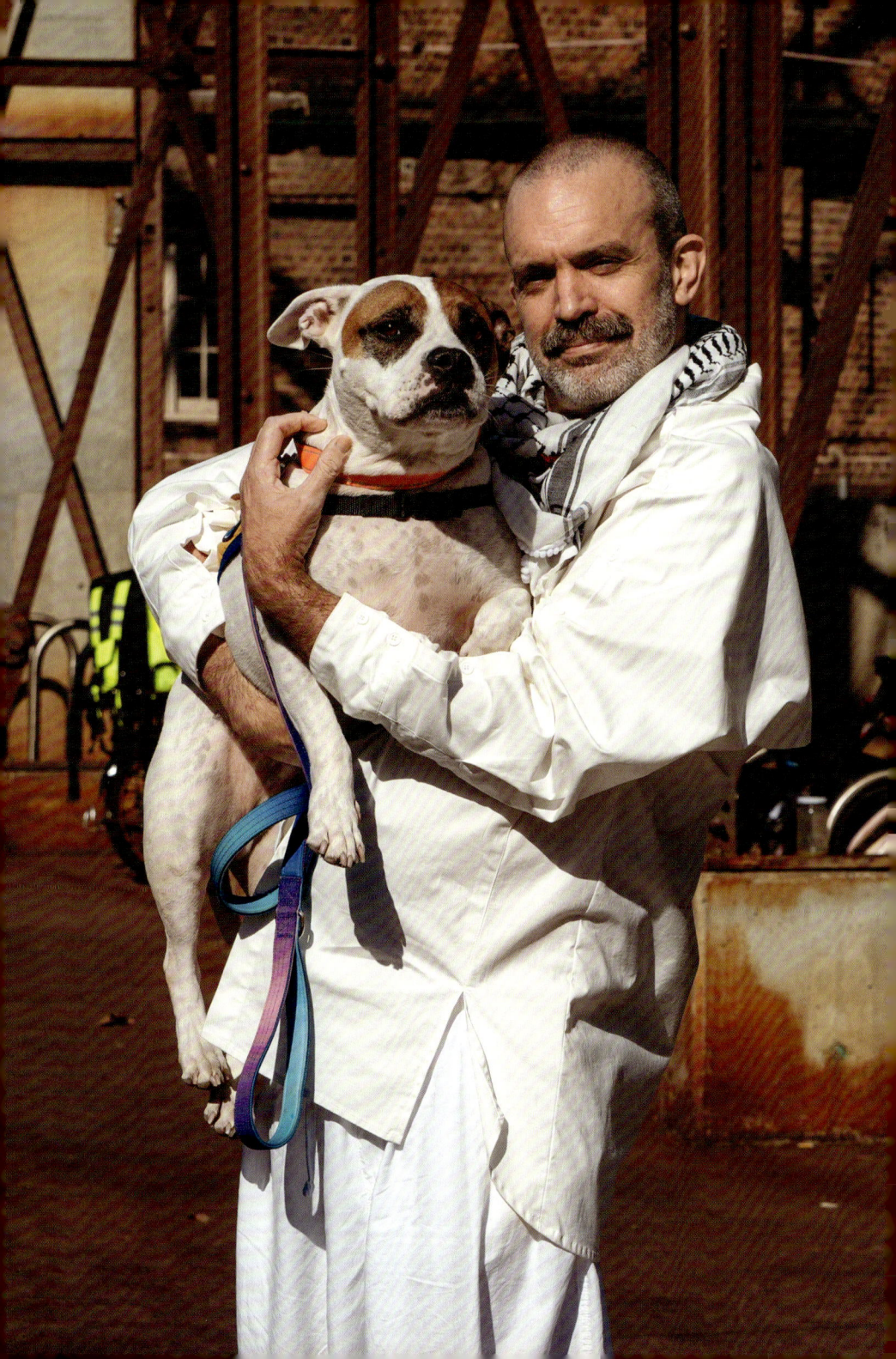

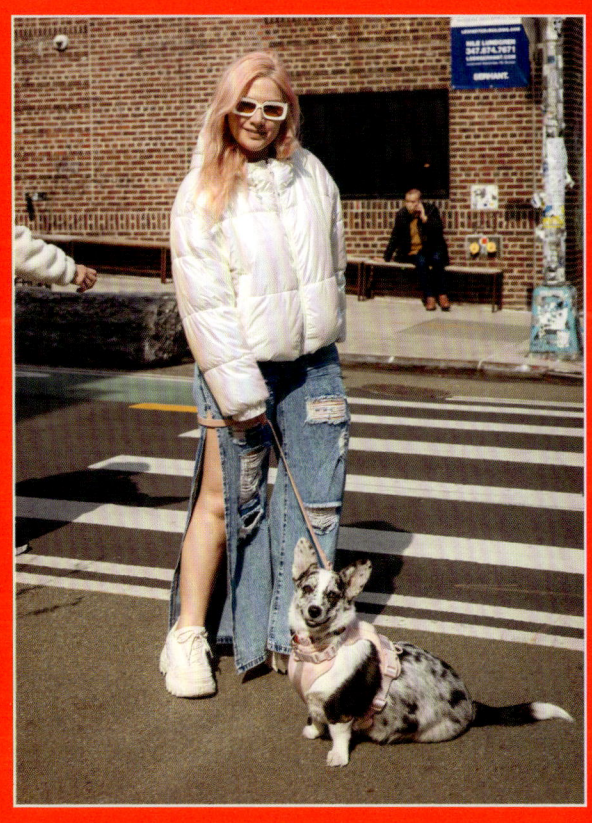

New York City, USA

"I've had a journey with depression, so he's my registered assistant dog. It's like being in a band; he's the lead singer and wherever I go, he announces my presence."

Jonny and their dog George Michael
Sydney, Australia

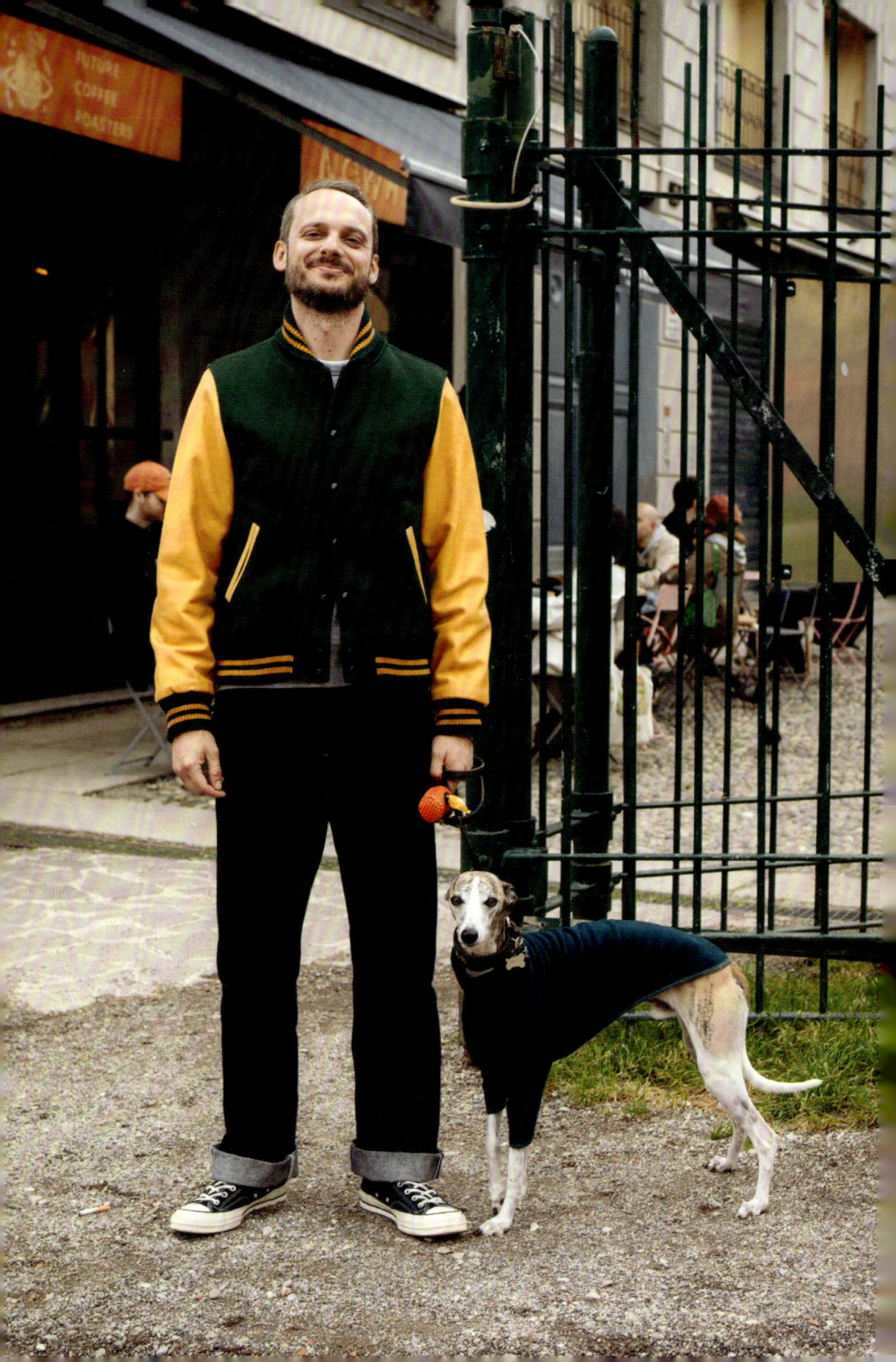

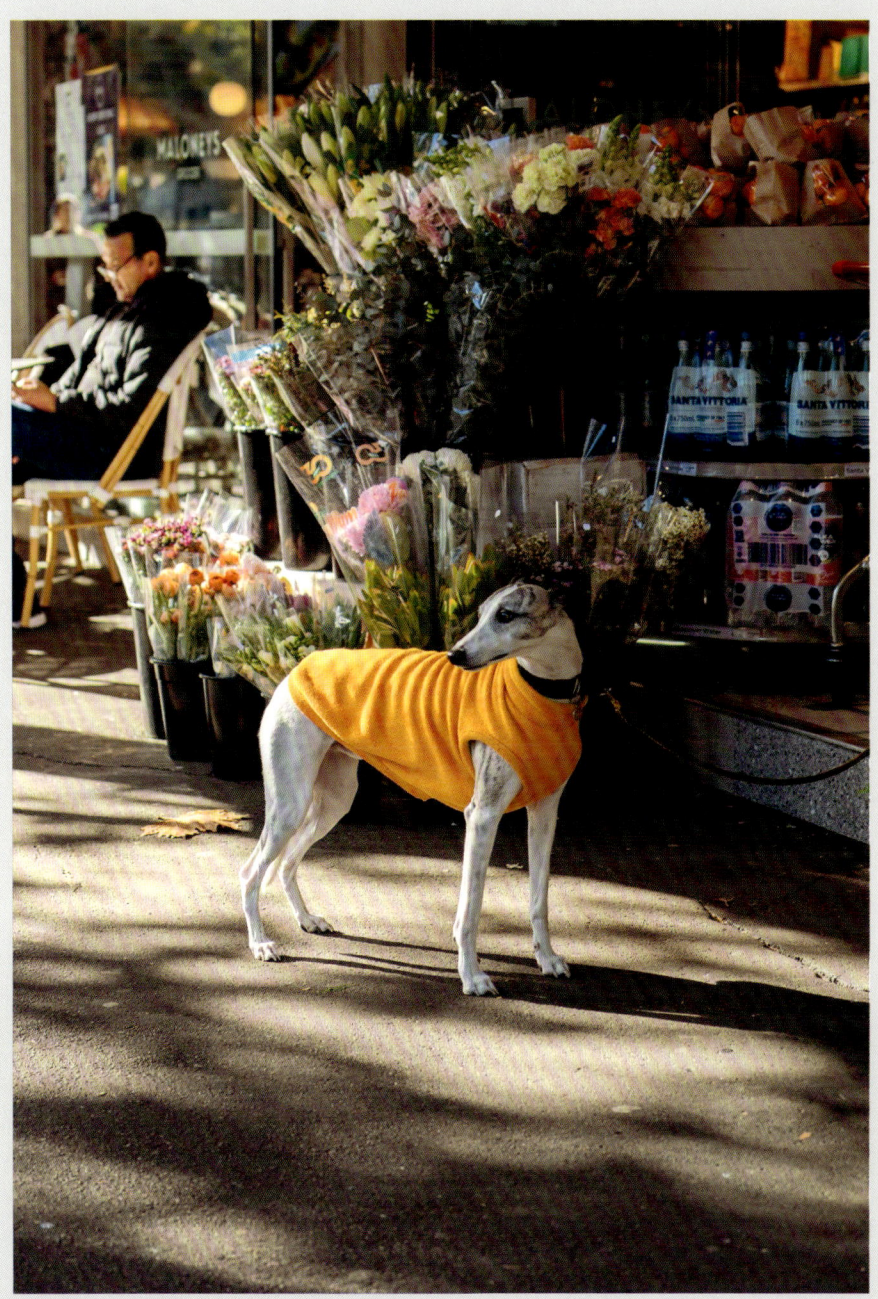

Milan, Italy | Sydney, Australia

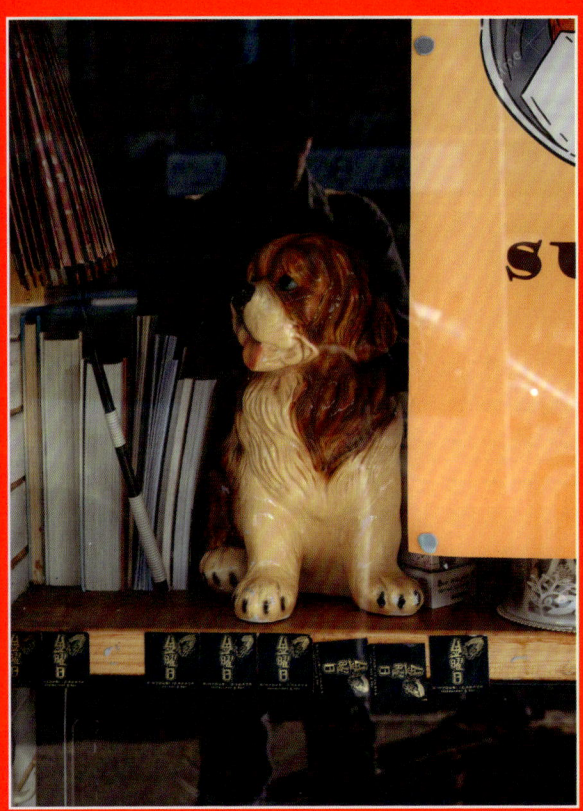

Melbourne, Australia

"He's blind and deaf, so he depends on me a lot. A psychic told us that we have a telepathic connection, so we're very in tune with each other."

Devon and their dog Scorpion
New York City, USA

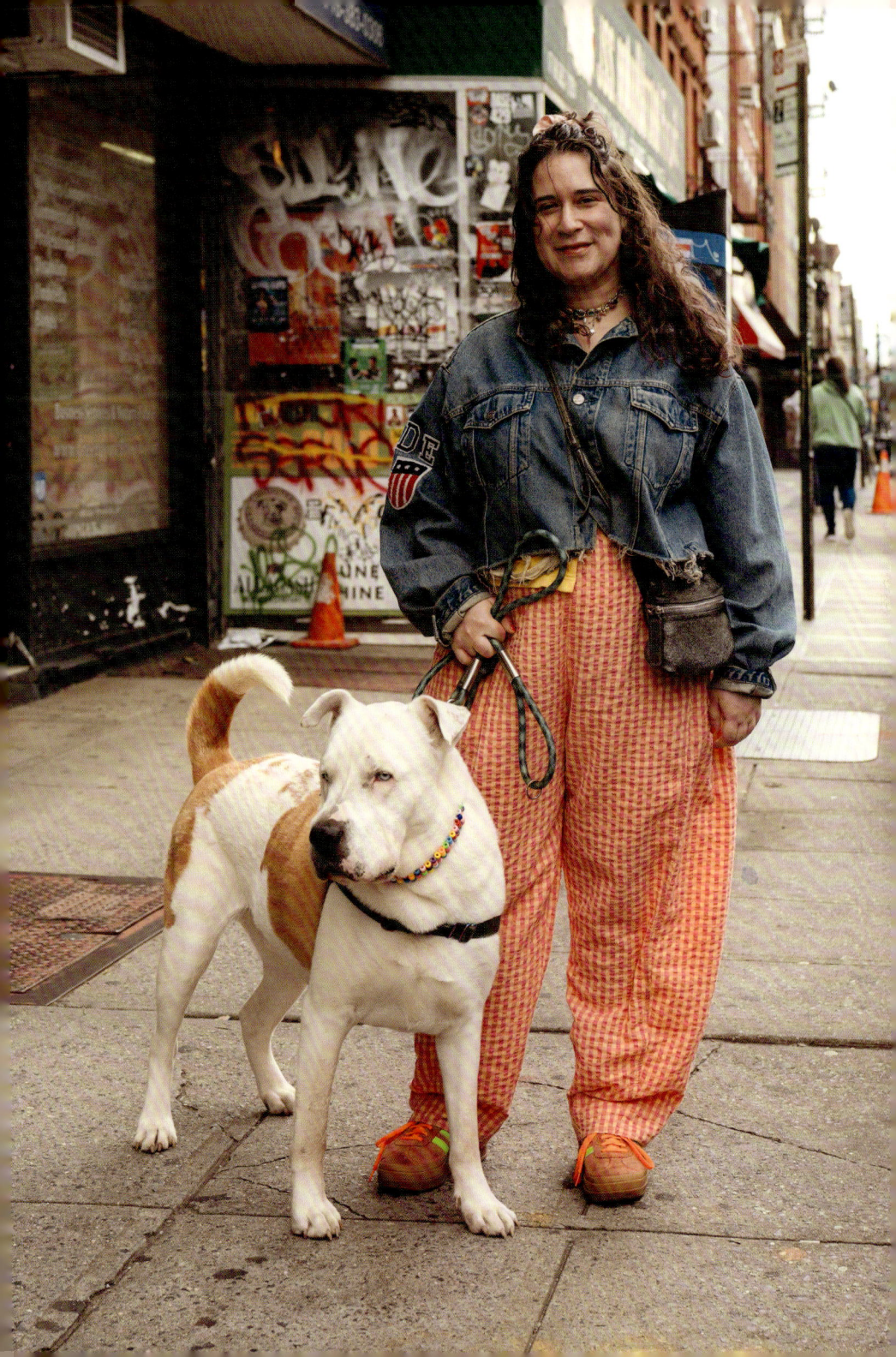

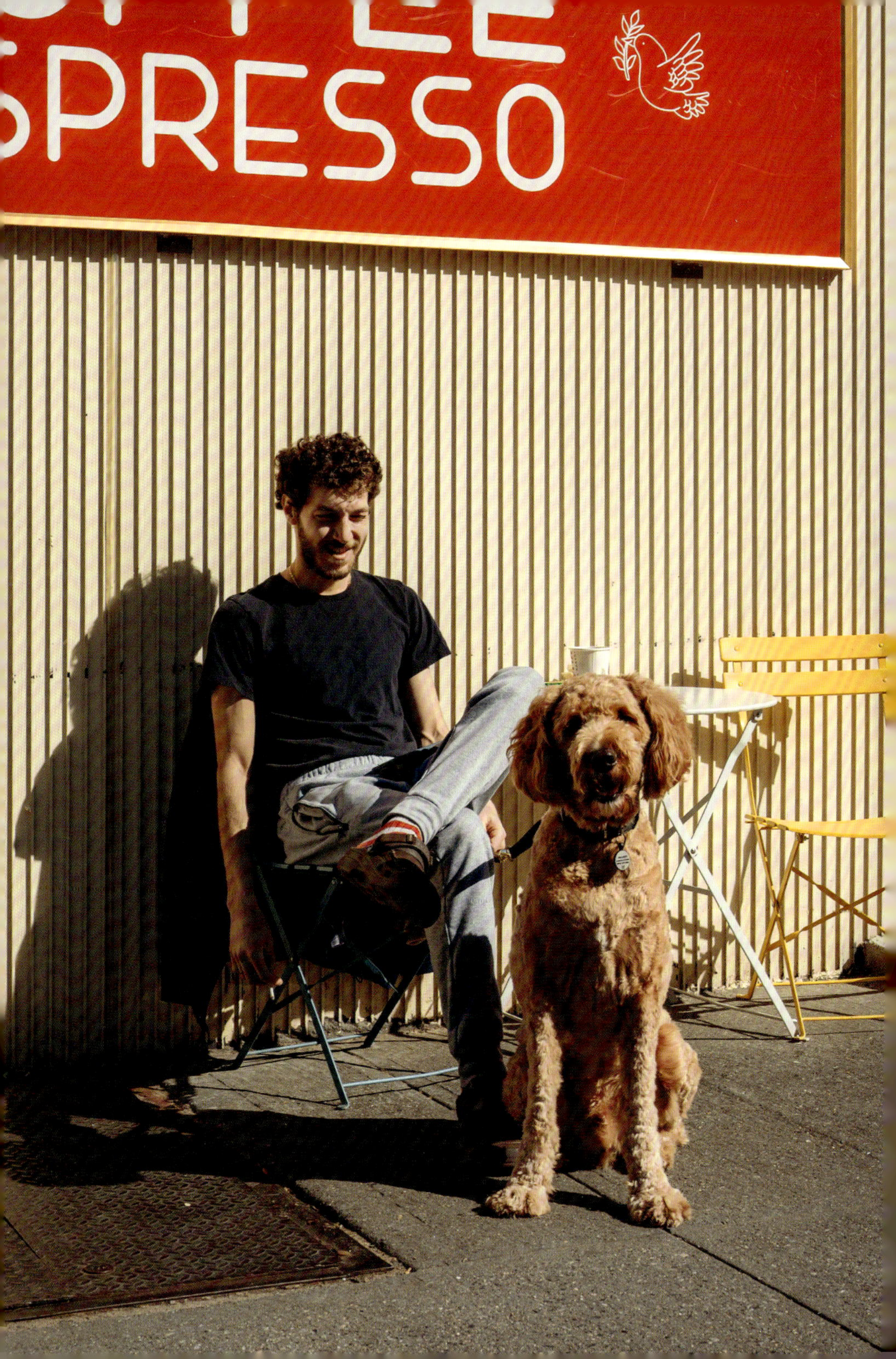
SPRESSO

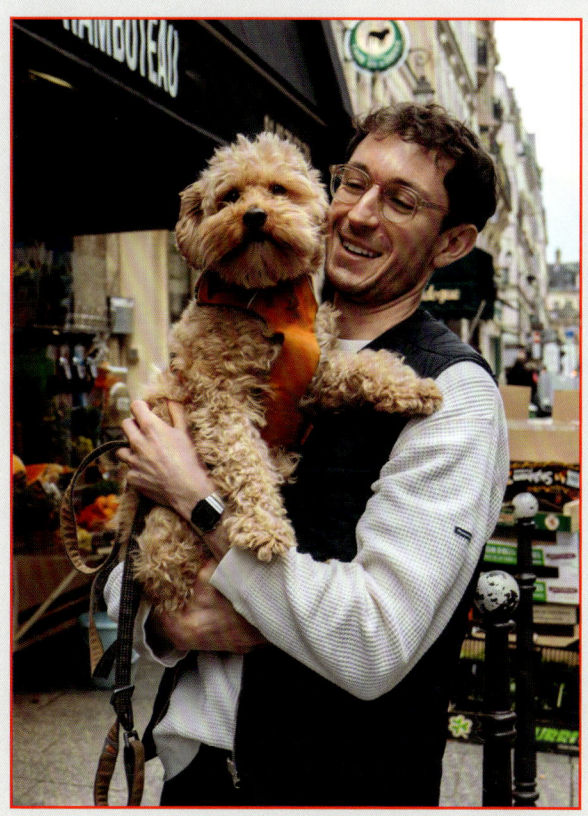

"He's like my younger brother."

Kareem and their dog Flóki
New York City, USA

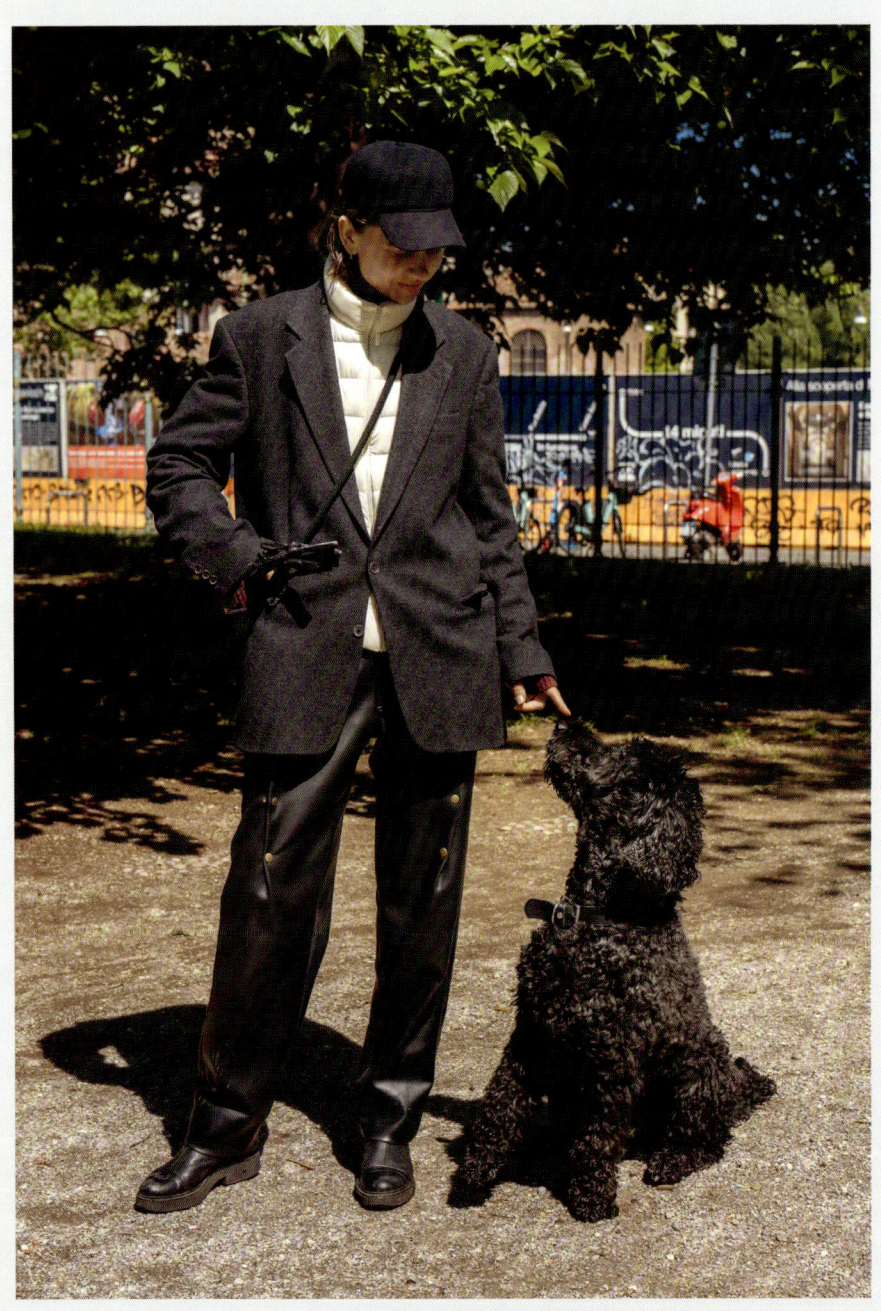

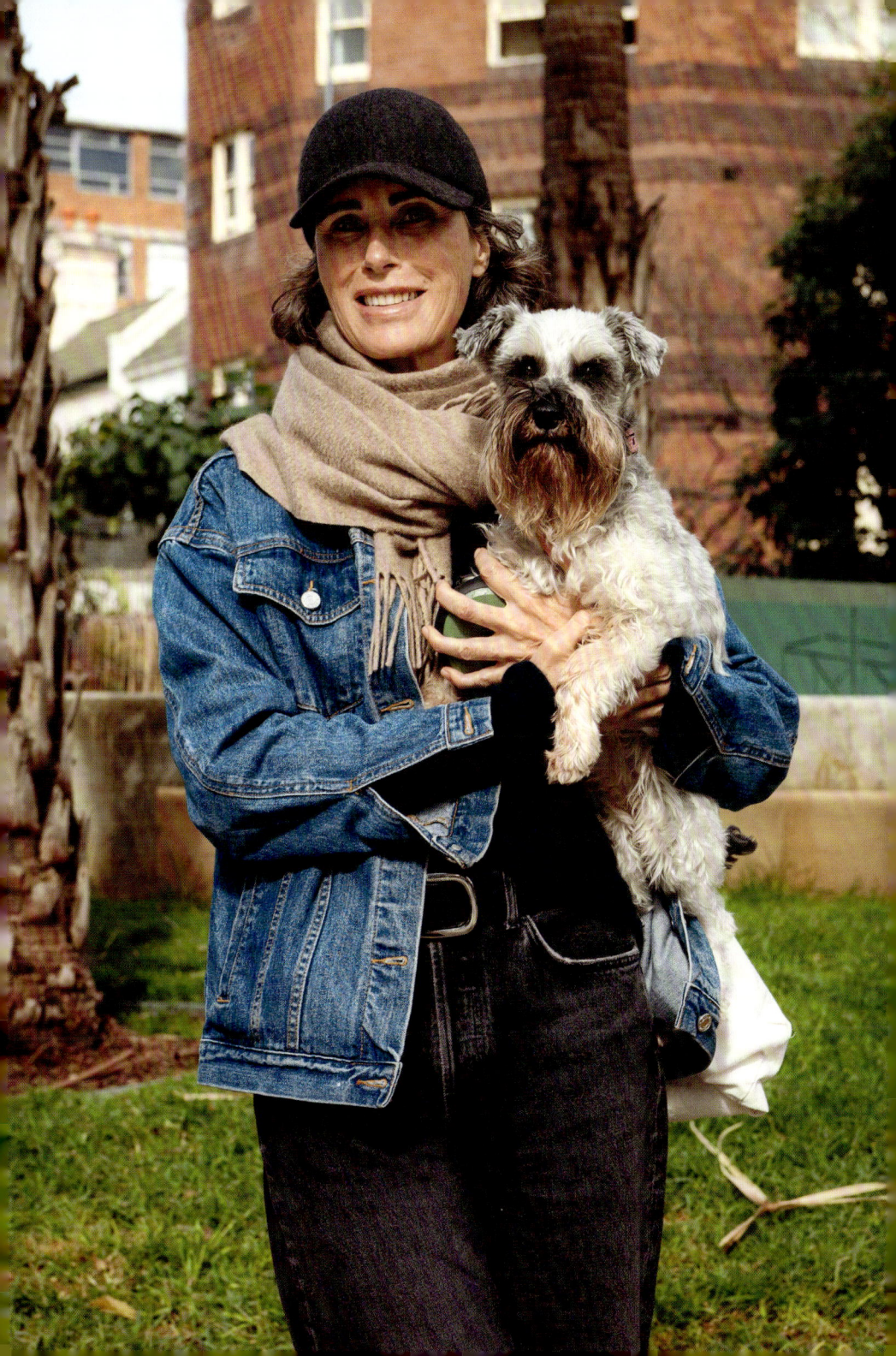

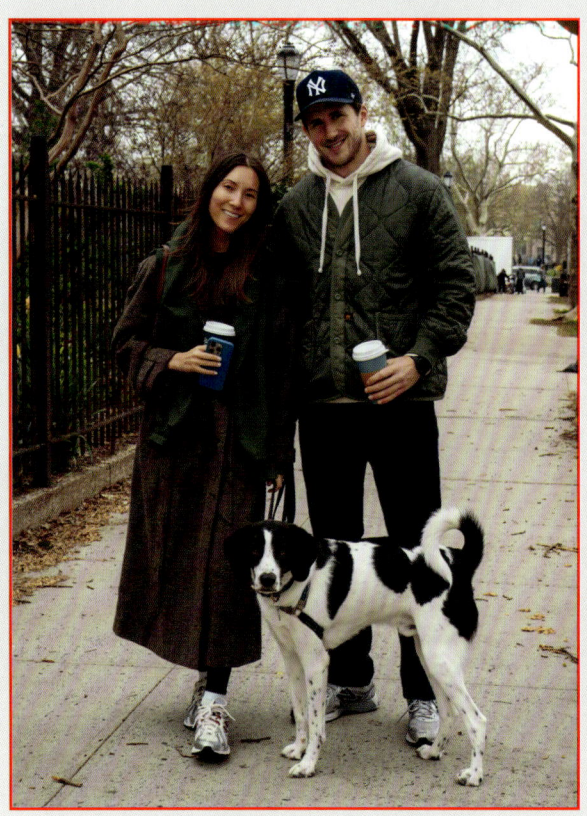

New York City, USA

"My partner and I recently split, so we share time with him. I'm definitely number two in the arrangment."

Joe and their dog Tofu
London, England

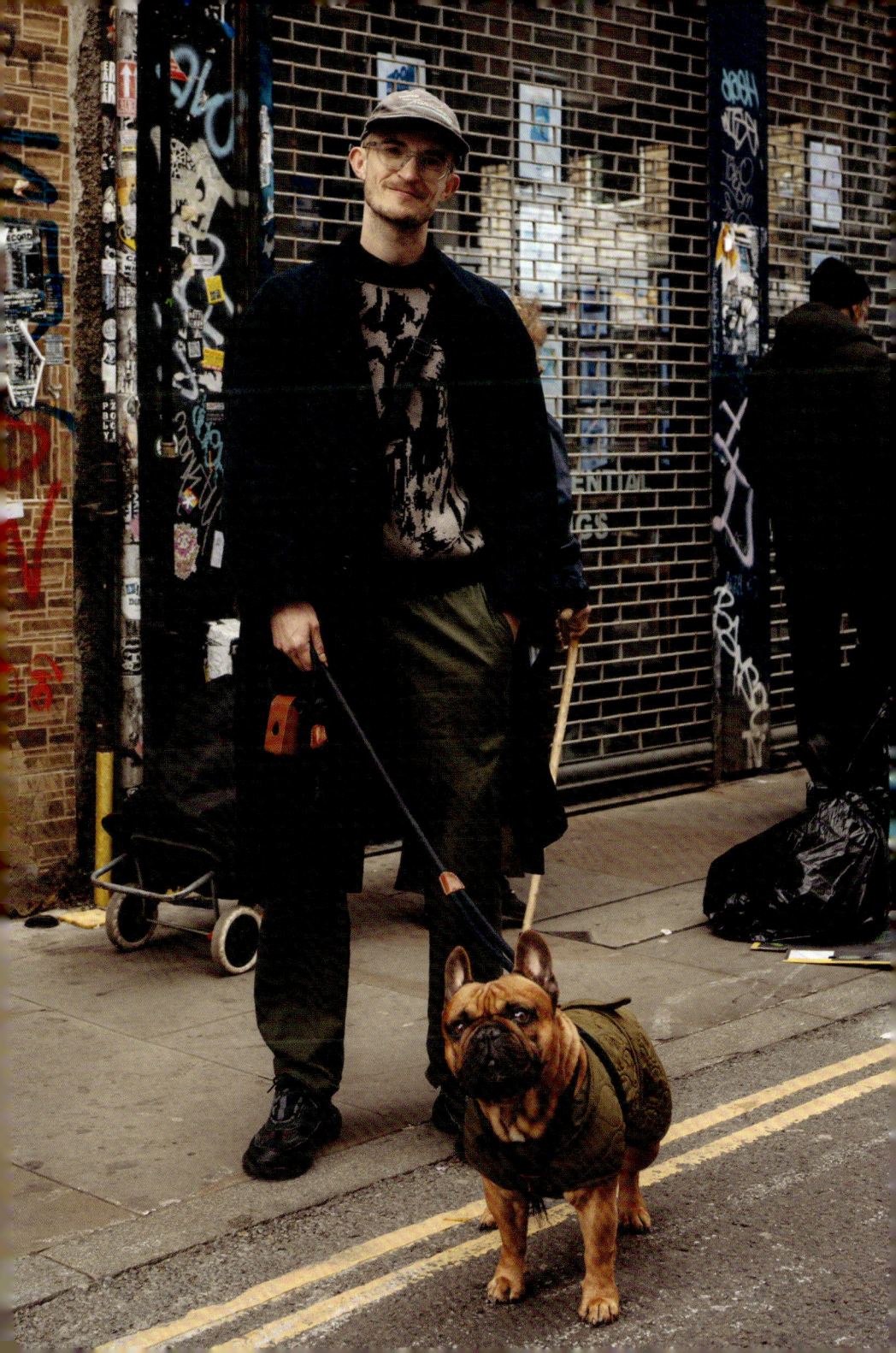

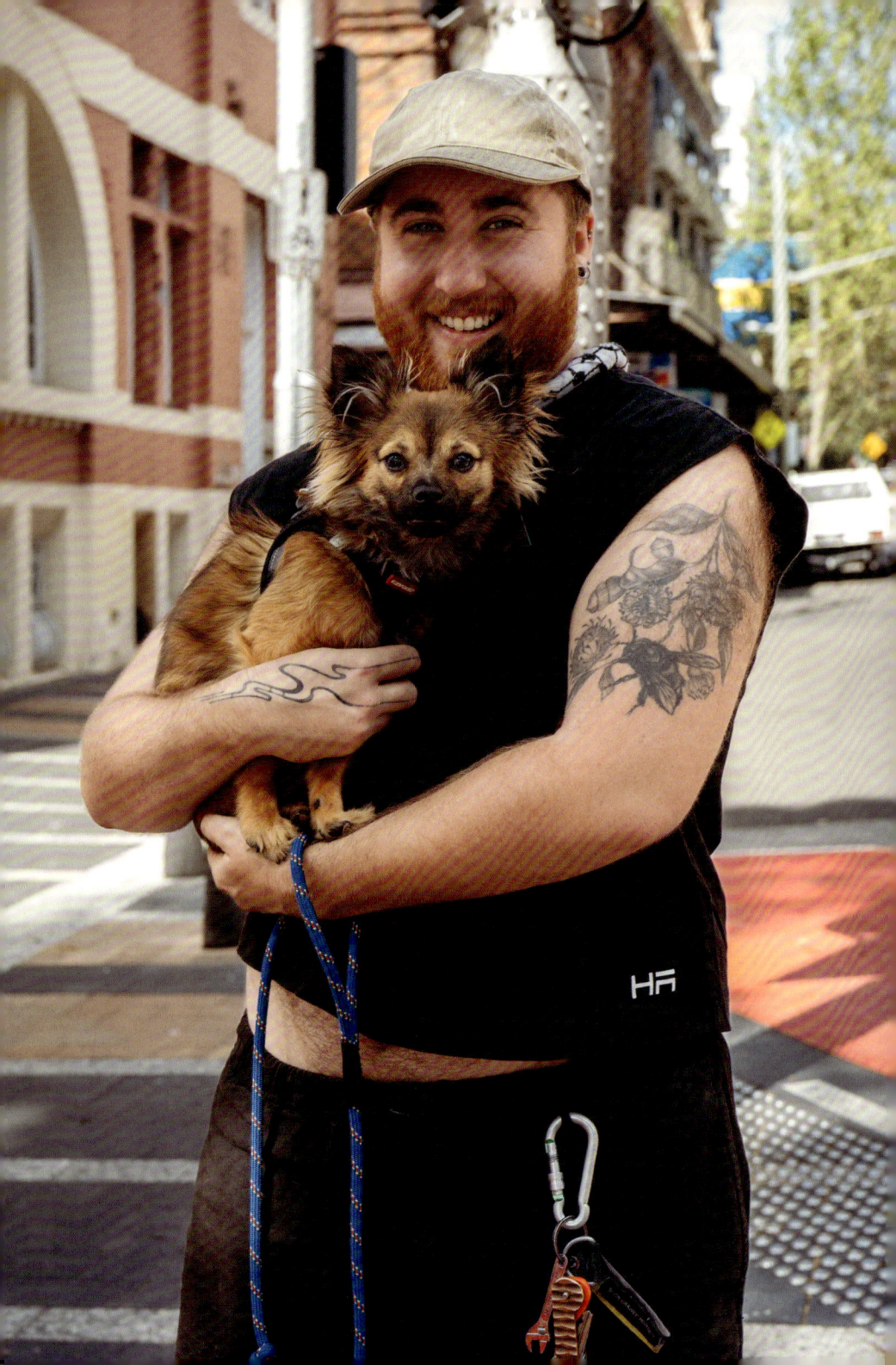

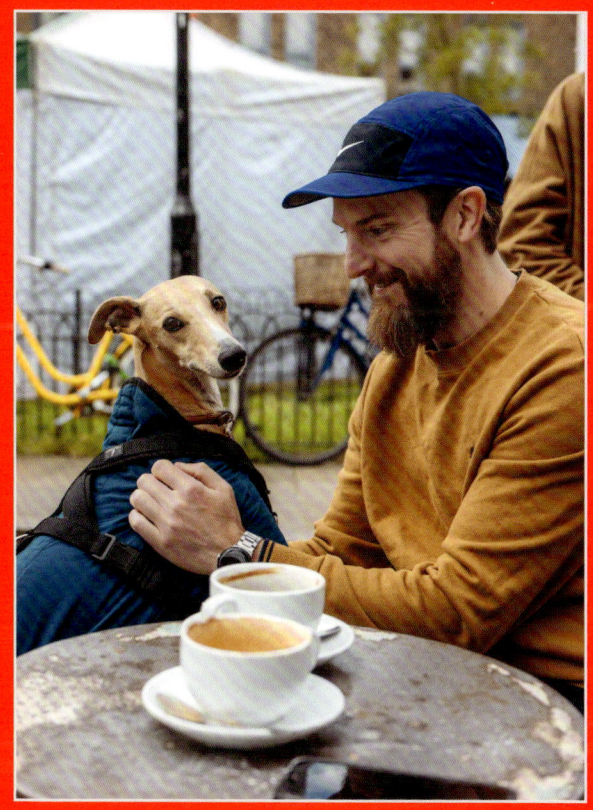

London, England

"It's a new relationship,
and I think it's going really well."

Rory and their dog Pepper
Sydney, Australia

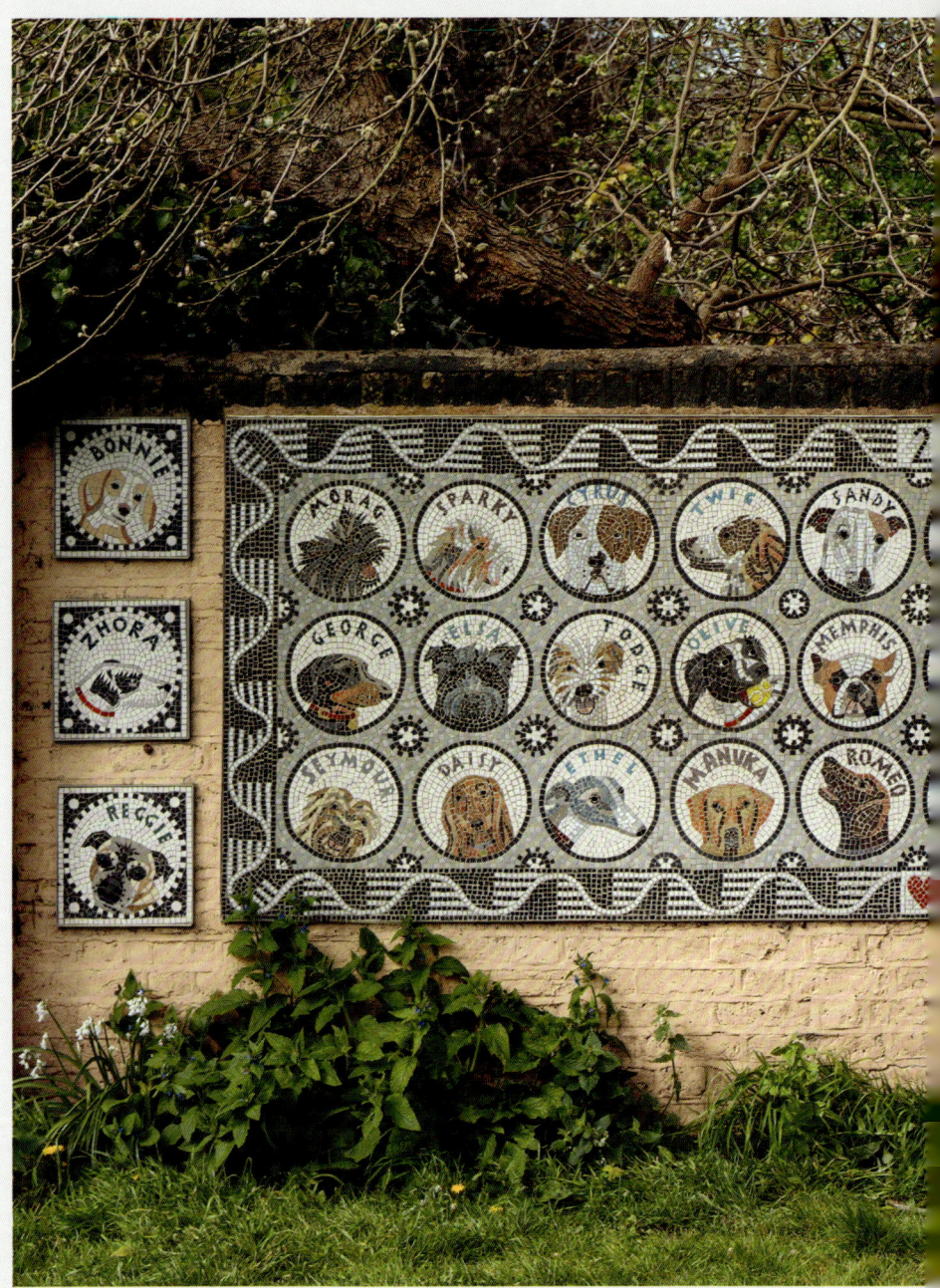

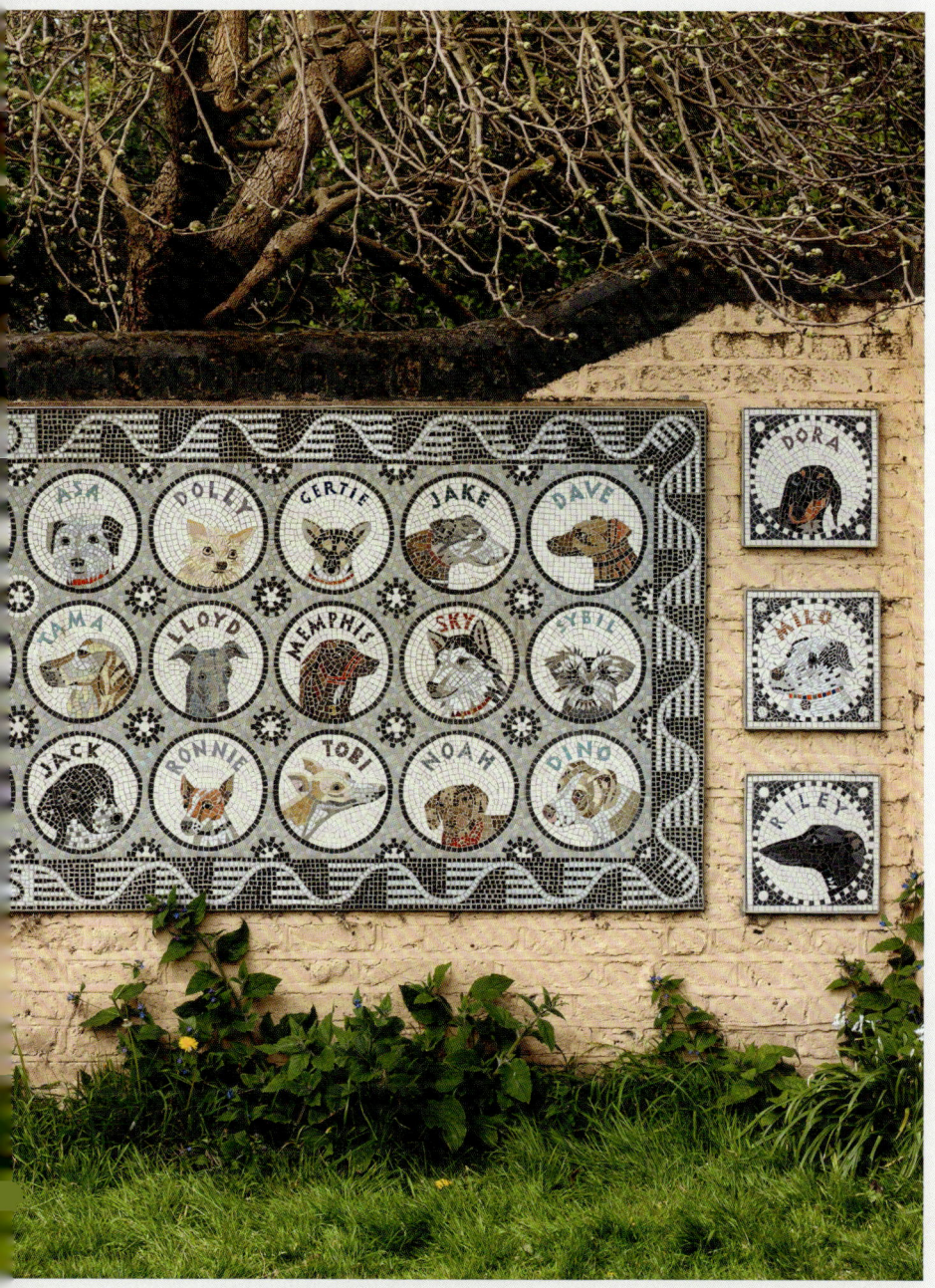

London, England

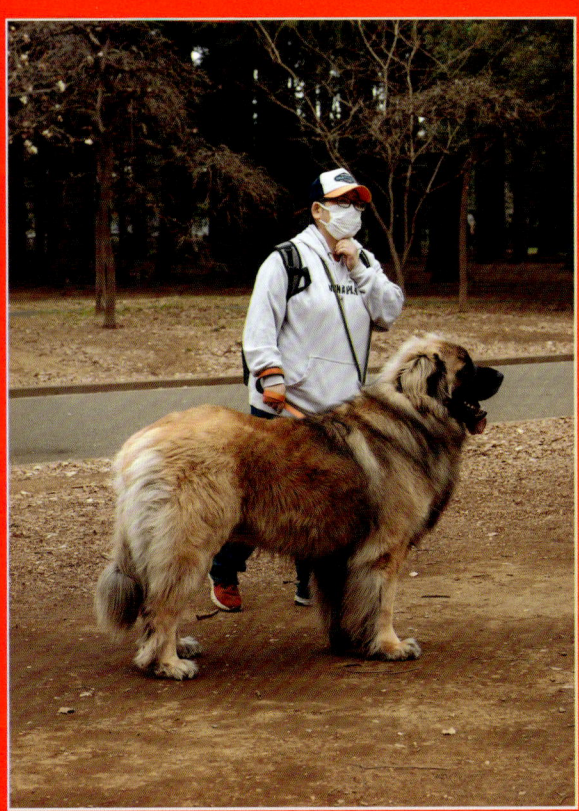

Tokyo, Japan

"She's only 6 months old. She's trying to work her way into the bed but we're trying to keep boundaries..."

Elitsa and their dog Marsha
Paris, France

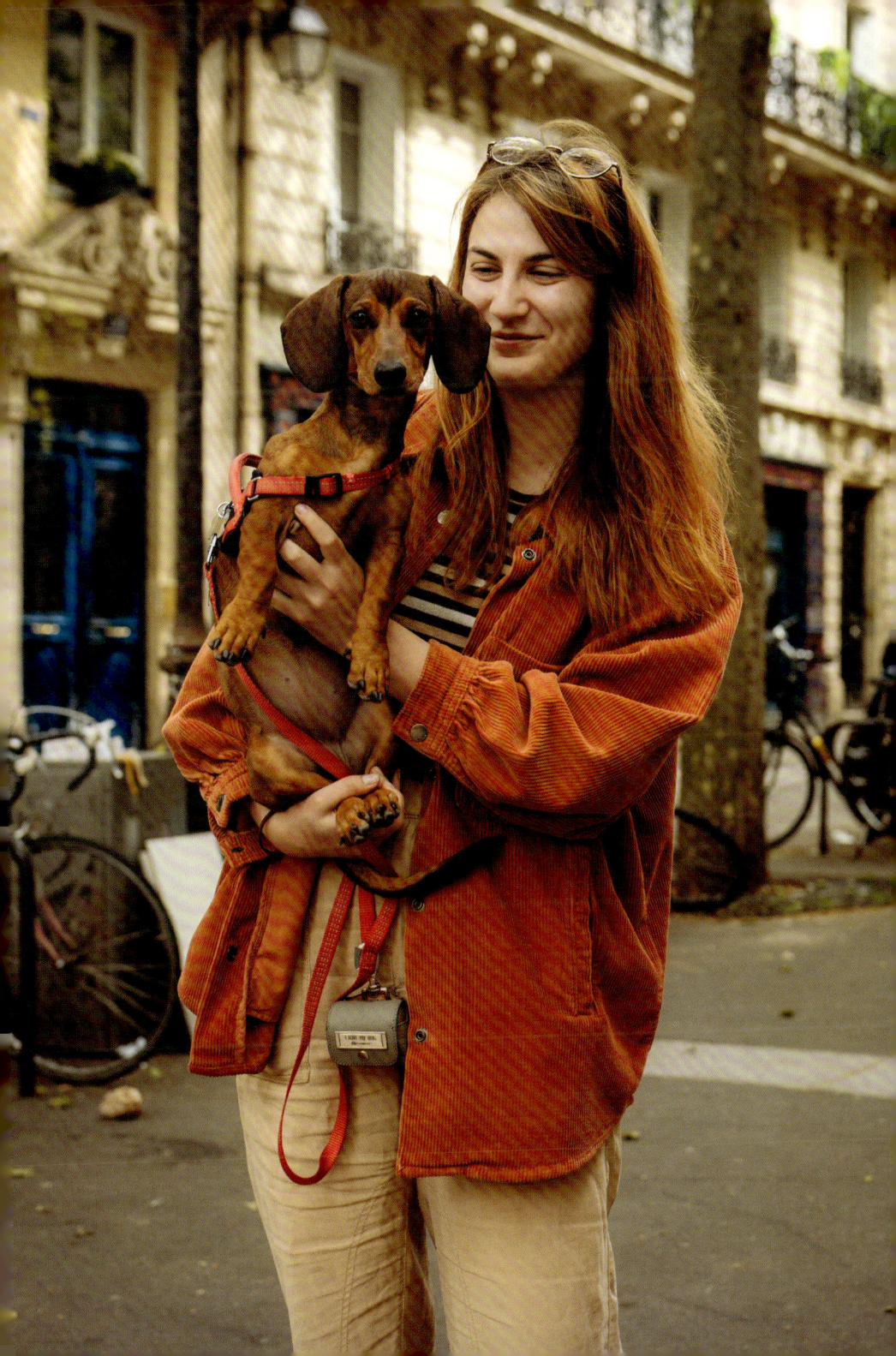

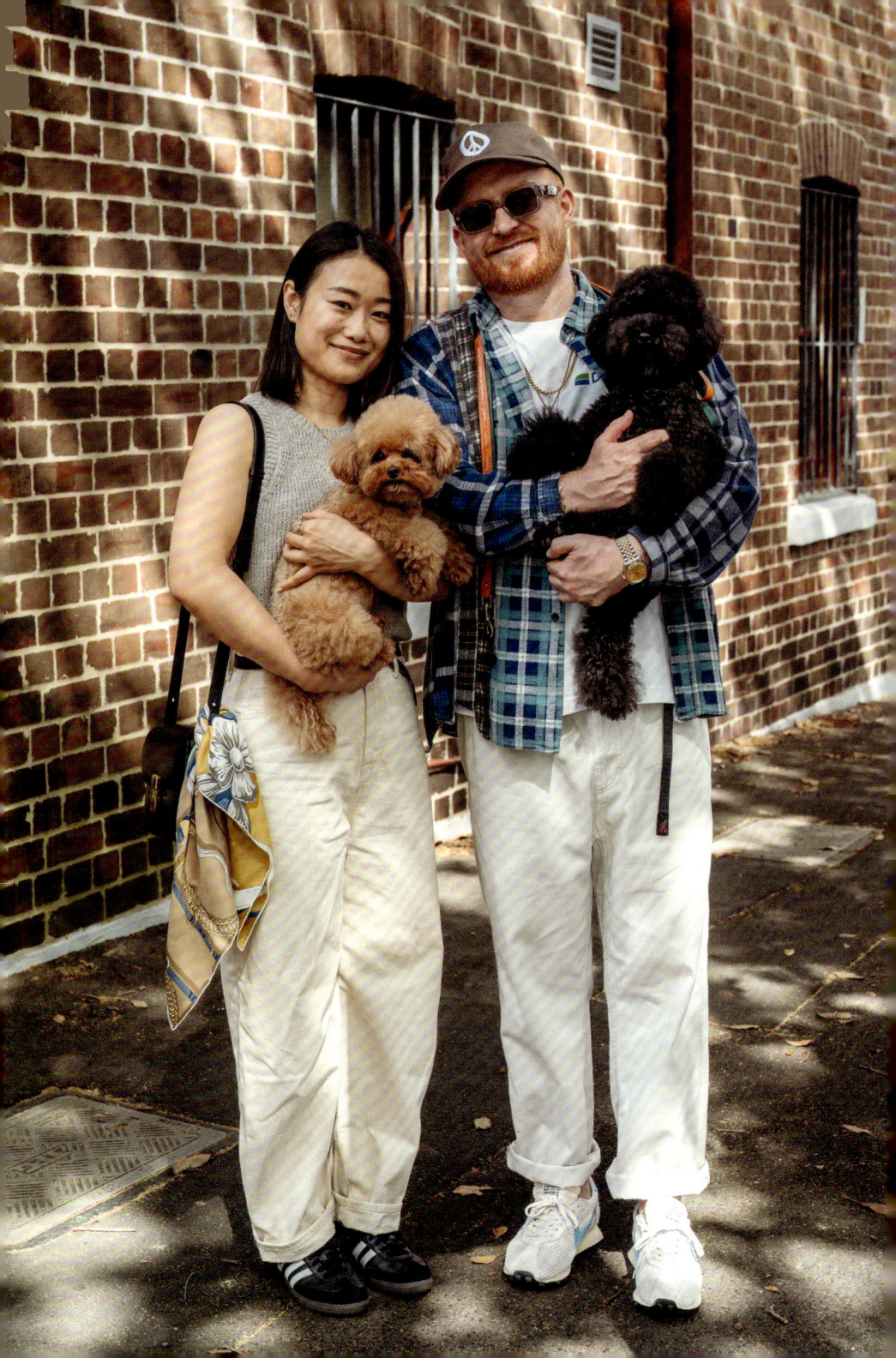

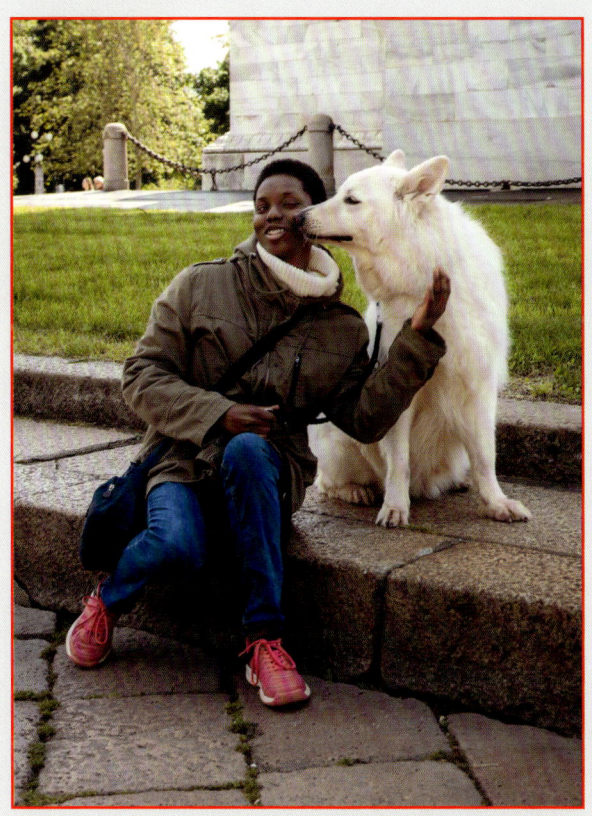

"They adore us. They love lying in our arms at night, there's no better feeling."

Noriko and Nick and their dogs Otōto and Bronson
Sydney, Australia

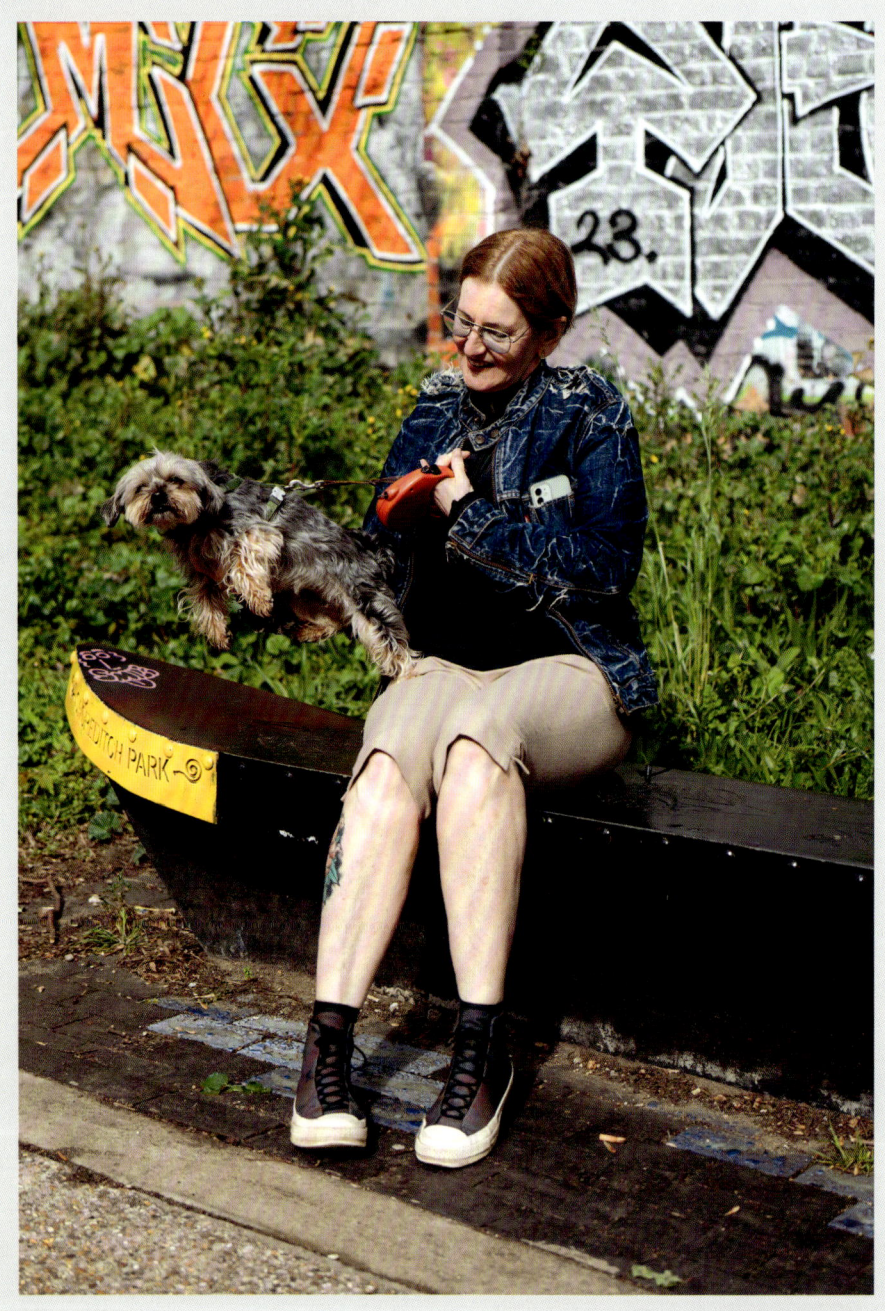

London, England | Melbourne, Australia

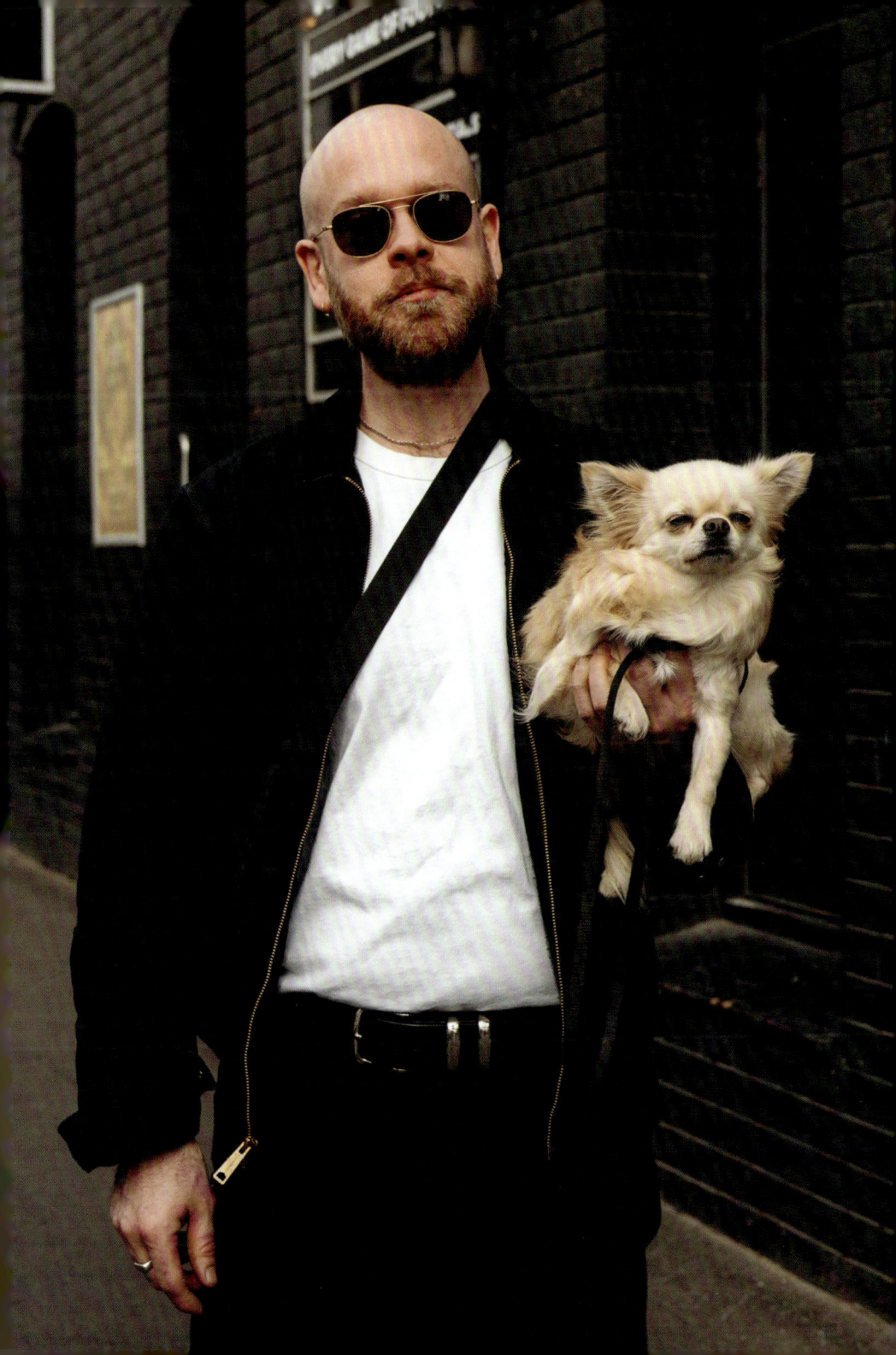

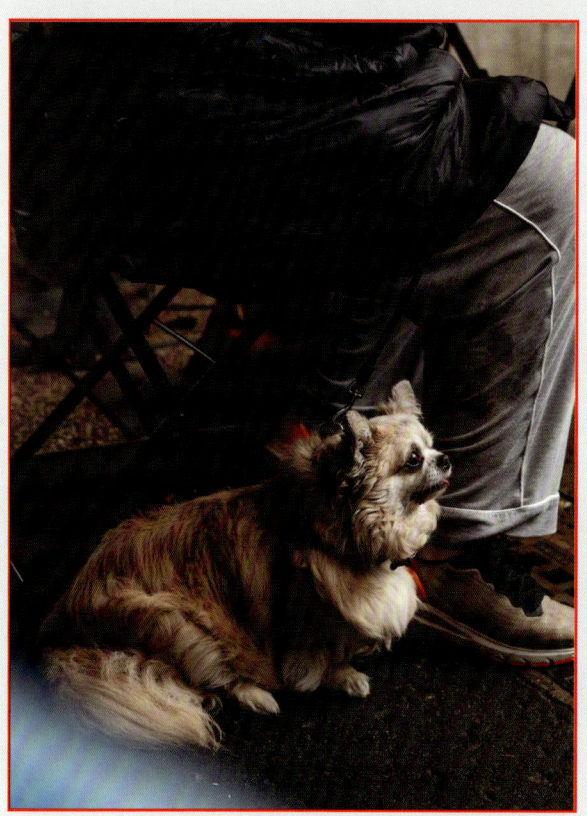

Milan, Italy

"She's currently extremely frustrated that I didn't give her half of my bagel."

Anjel and their dog Coetzee
New York City, USA

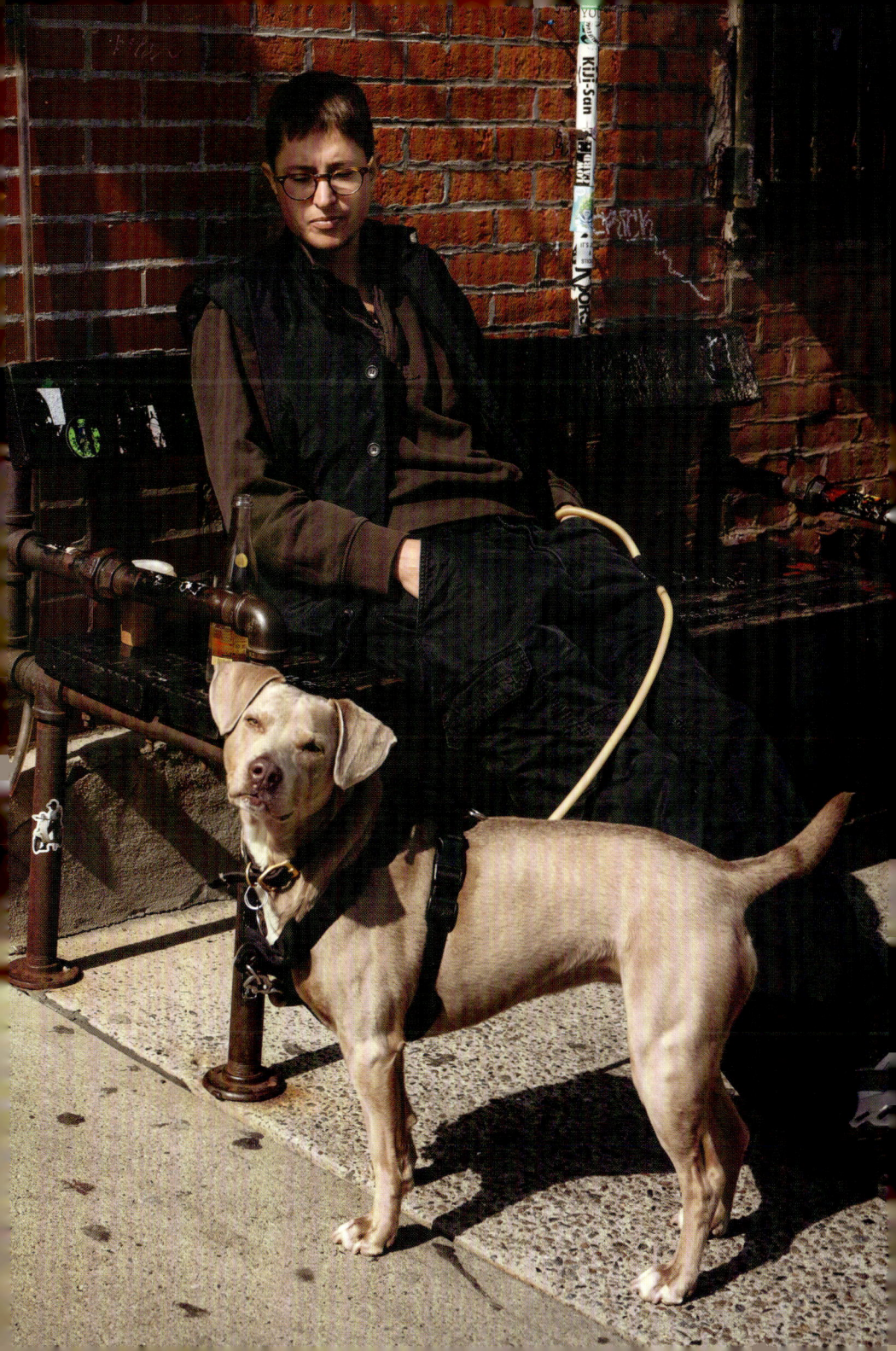

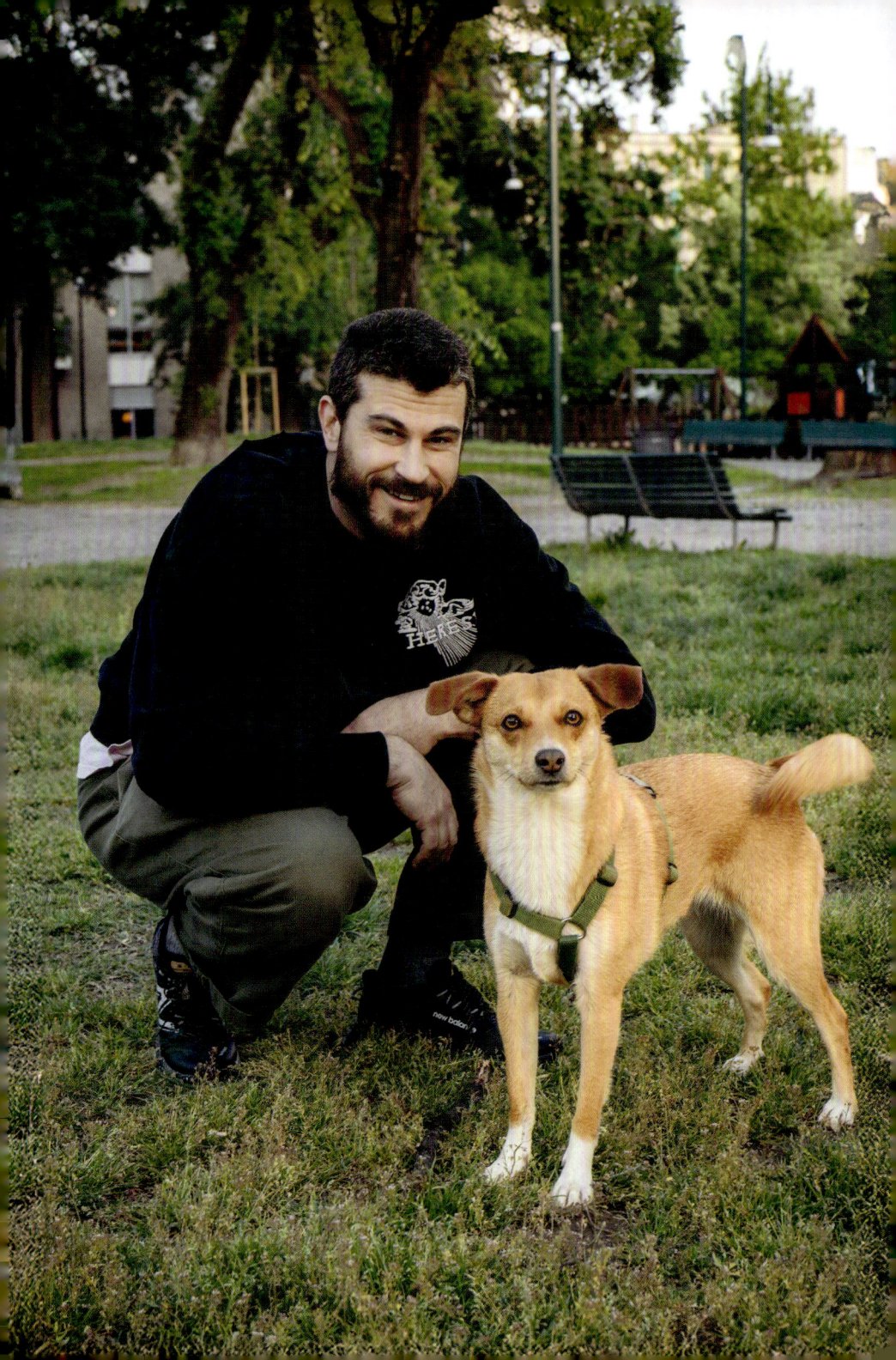

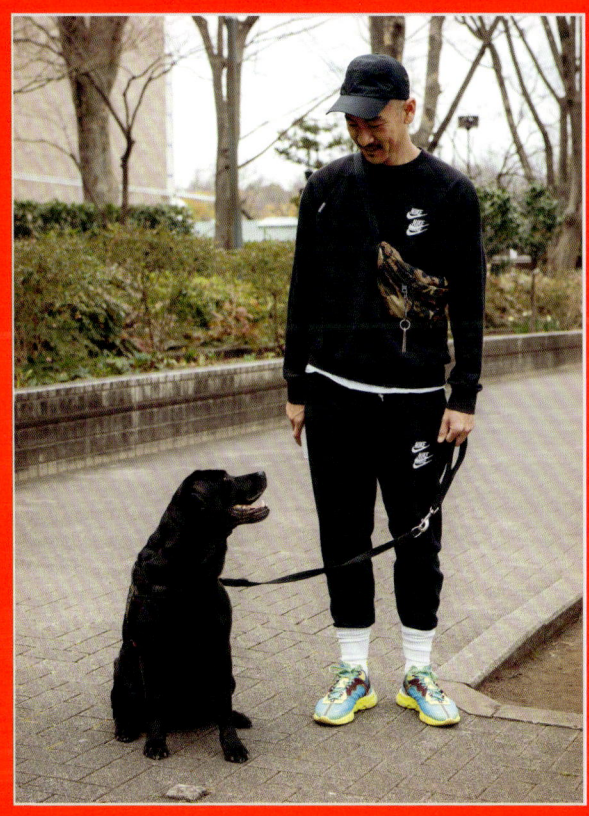

Tokyo, Japan

"All she wants is to play or eat.
So that's what I'm here for."

Andrea and their dog Blondie
Milan, Italy

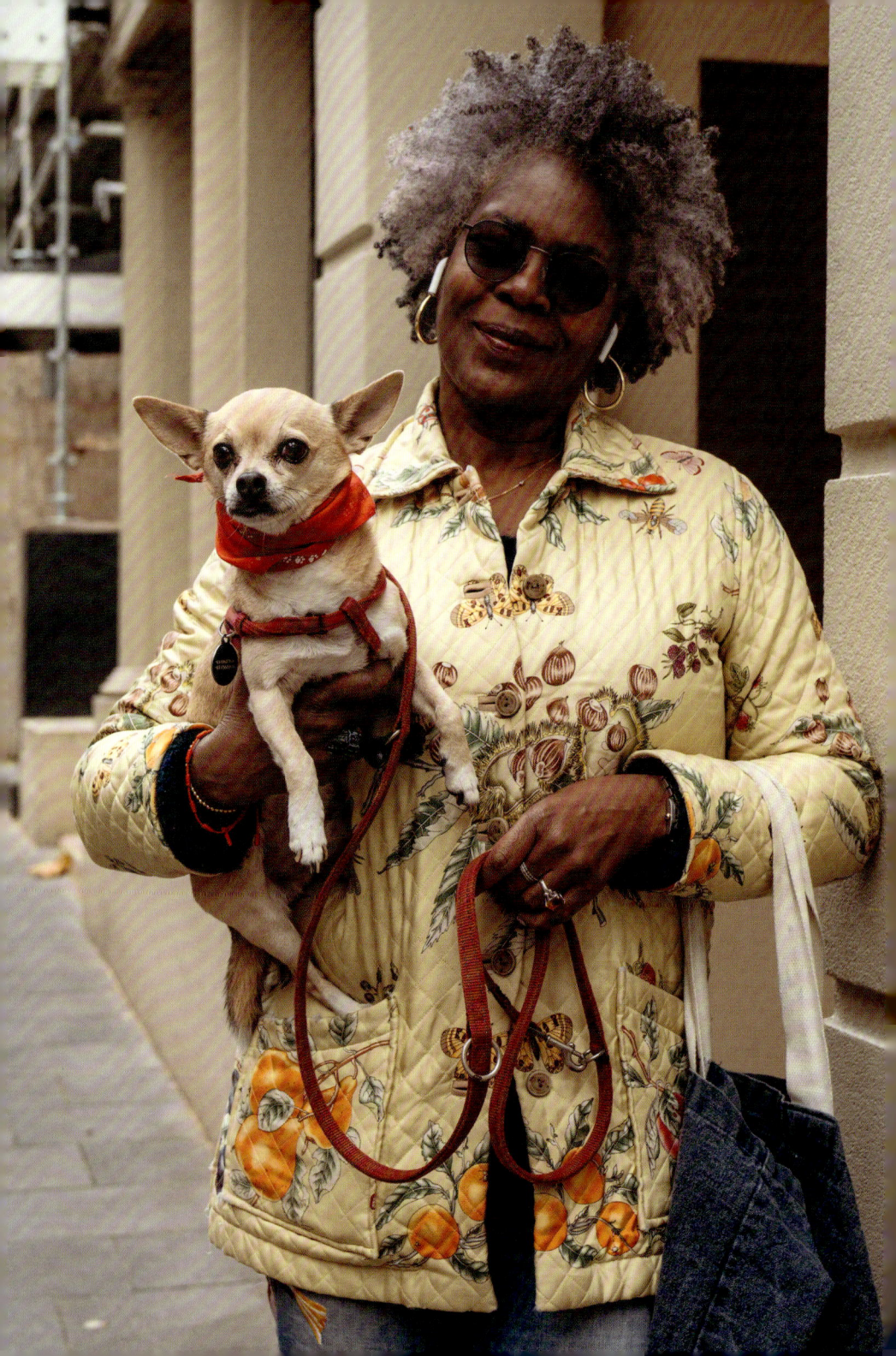

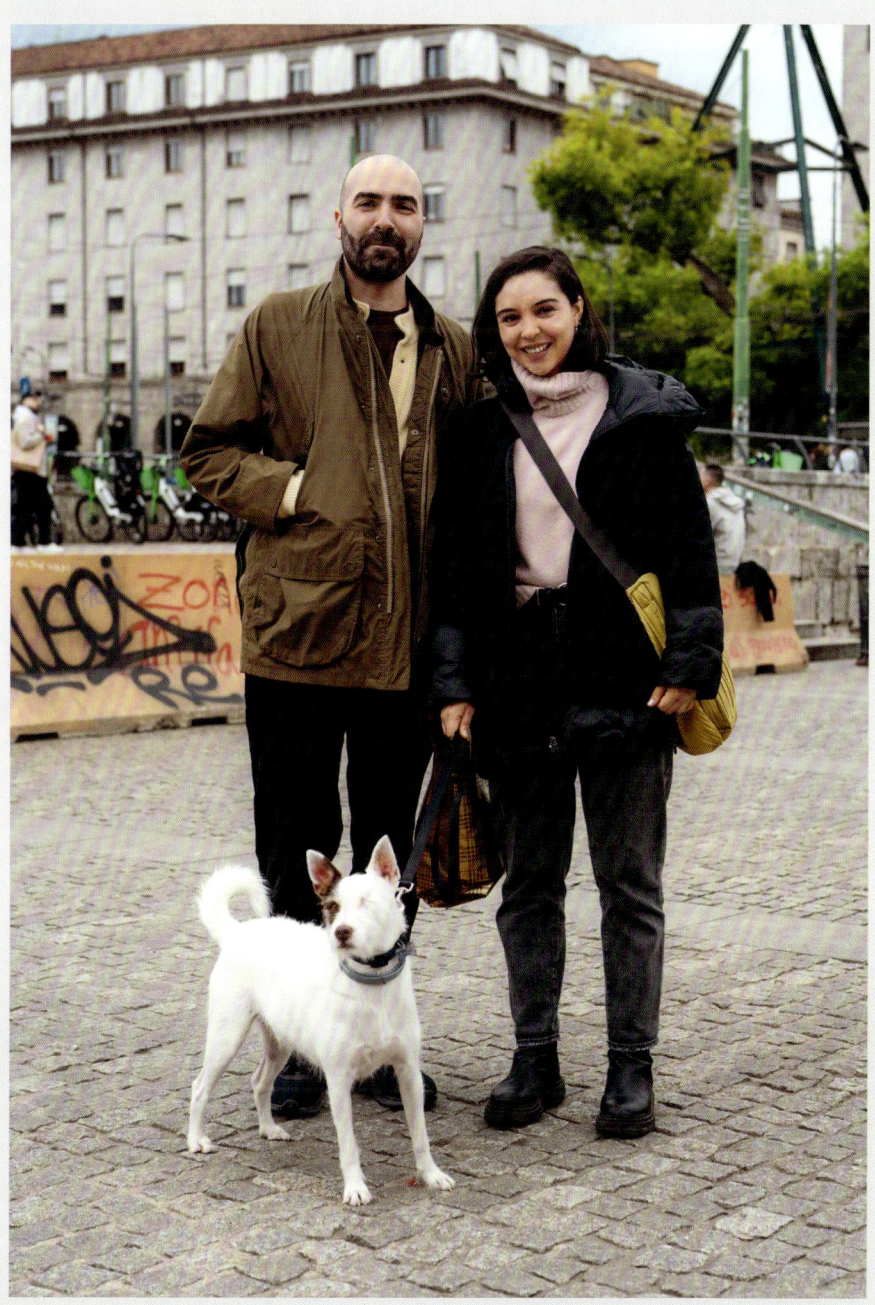

Sydney, Australia | Milan, Italy

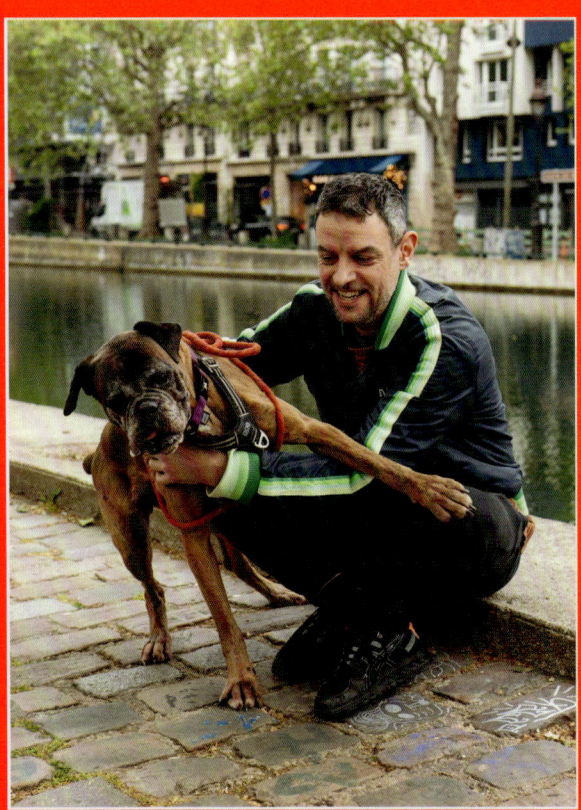

Paris, France

"I think she finds us really annoying. We never leave her alone."

Joe and Jaydam and their dog Tibbie
London, England

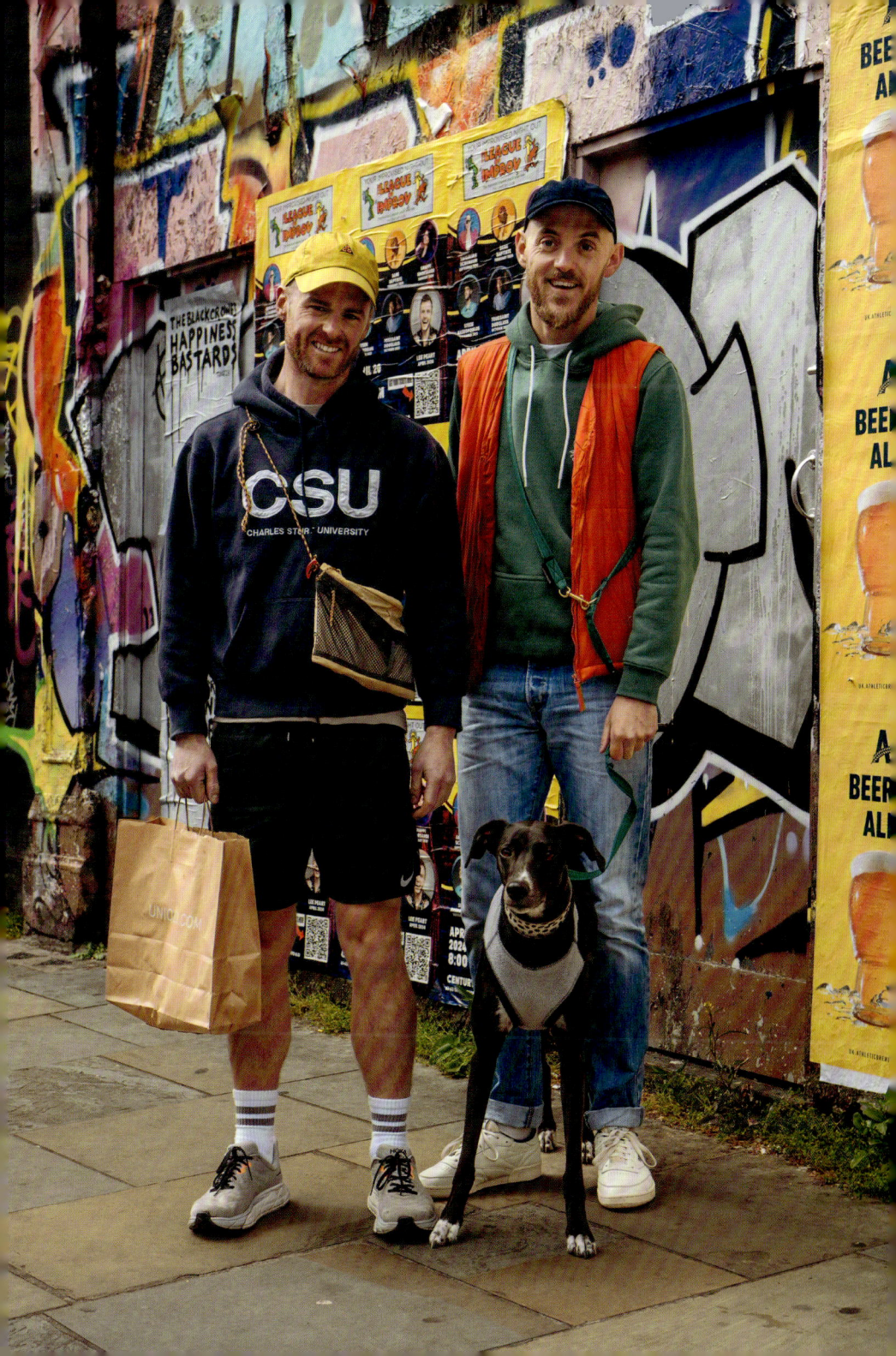

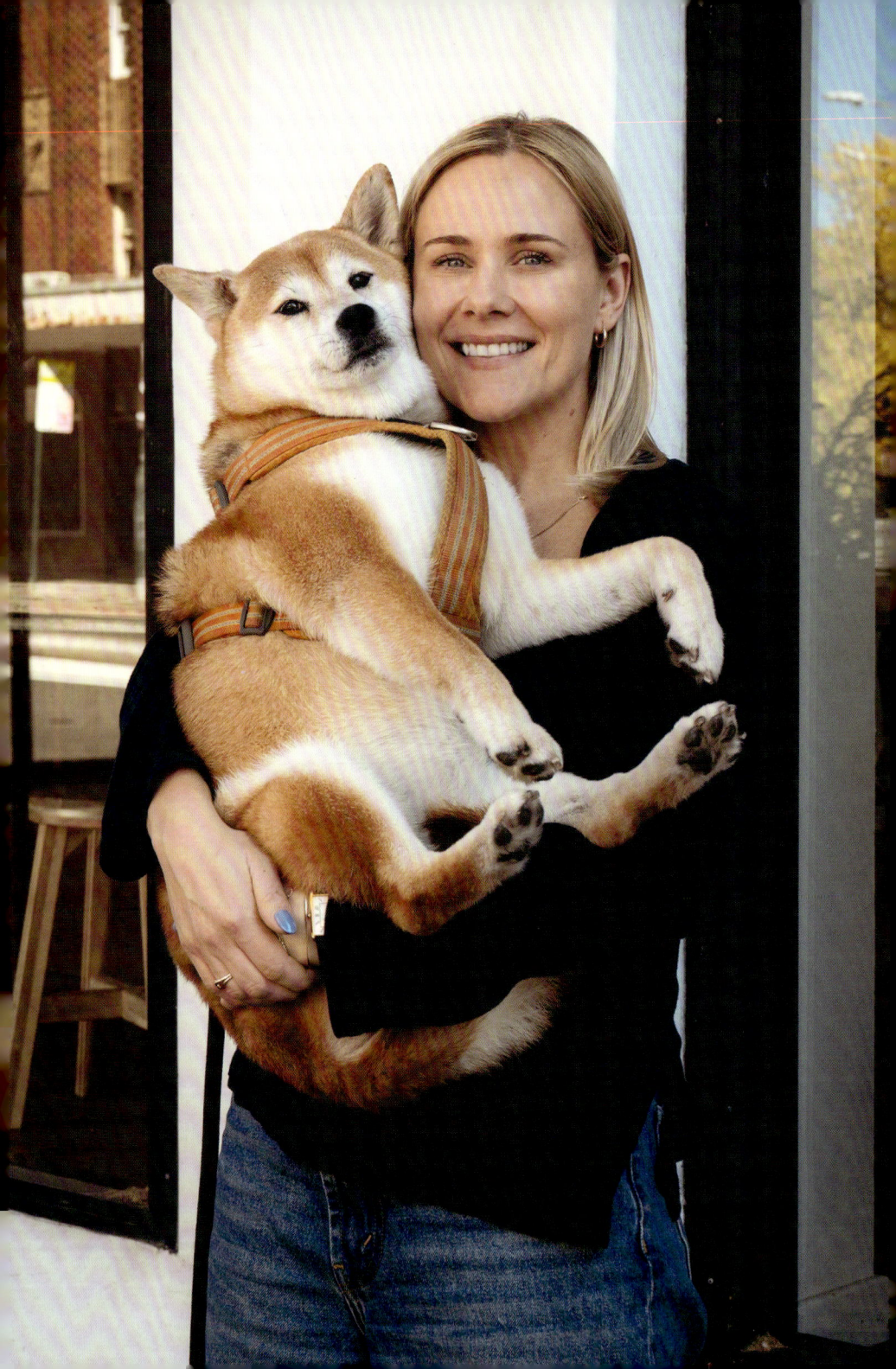

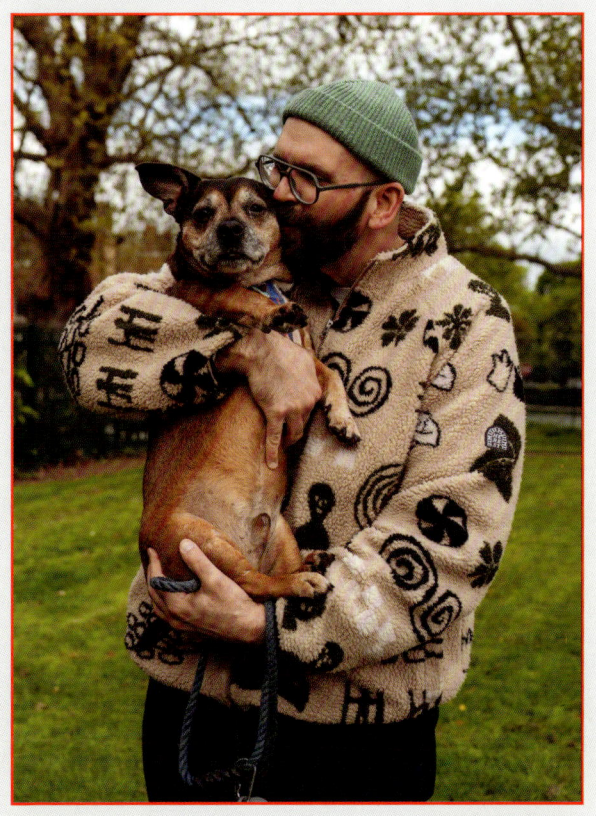

"I think she would say that I need to stop saying that she has separation anxiety and that actually I'm the one with separation anxiety."

Tara and their dog Pocari
Sydney, Australia

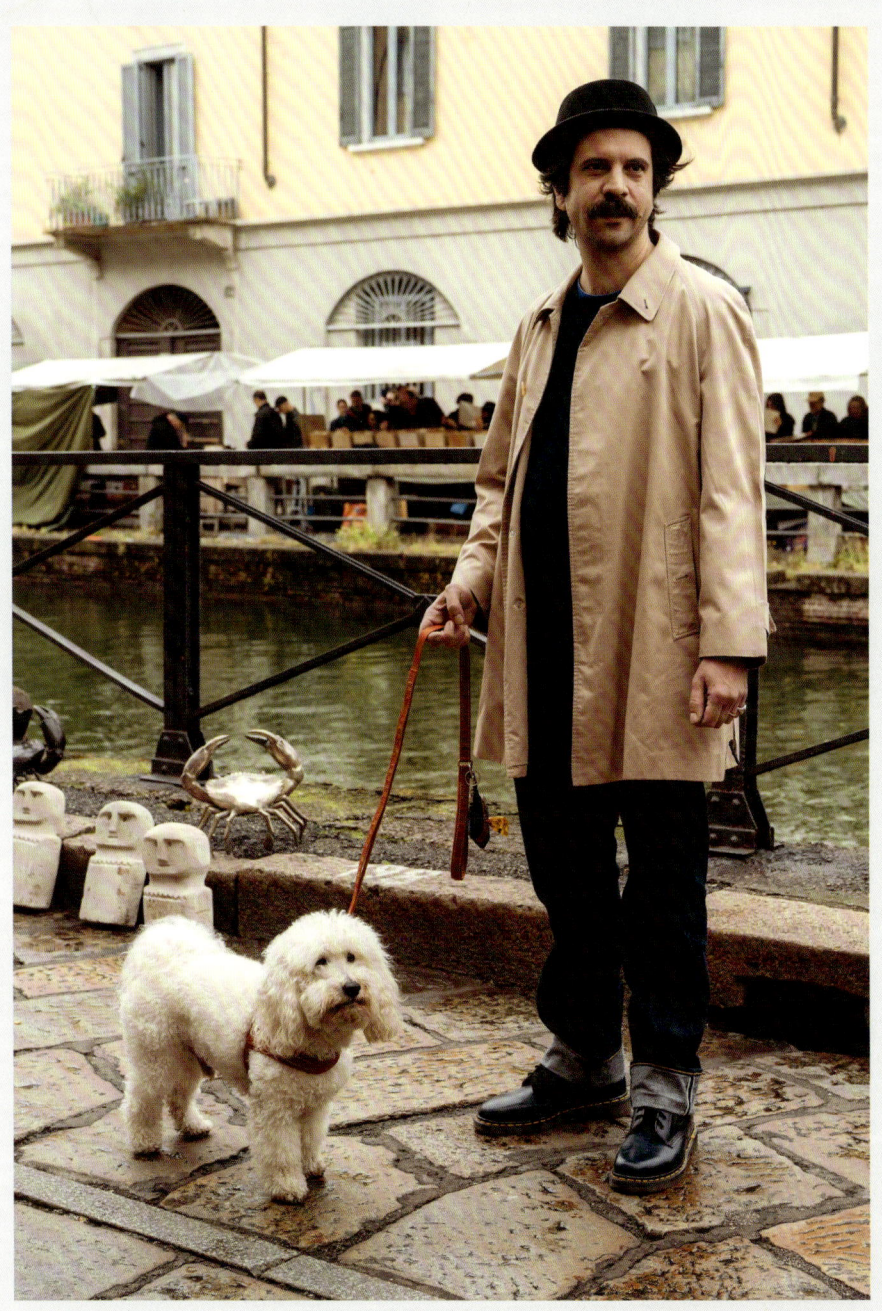

Milan, Italy | Tokyo, Japan

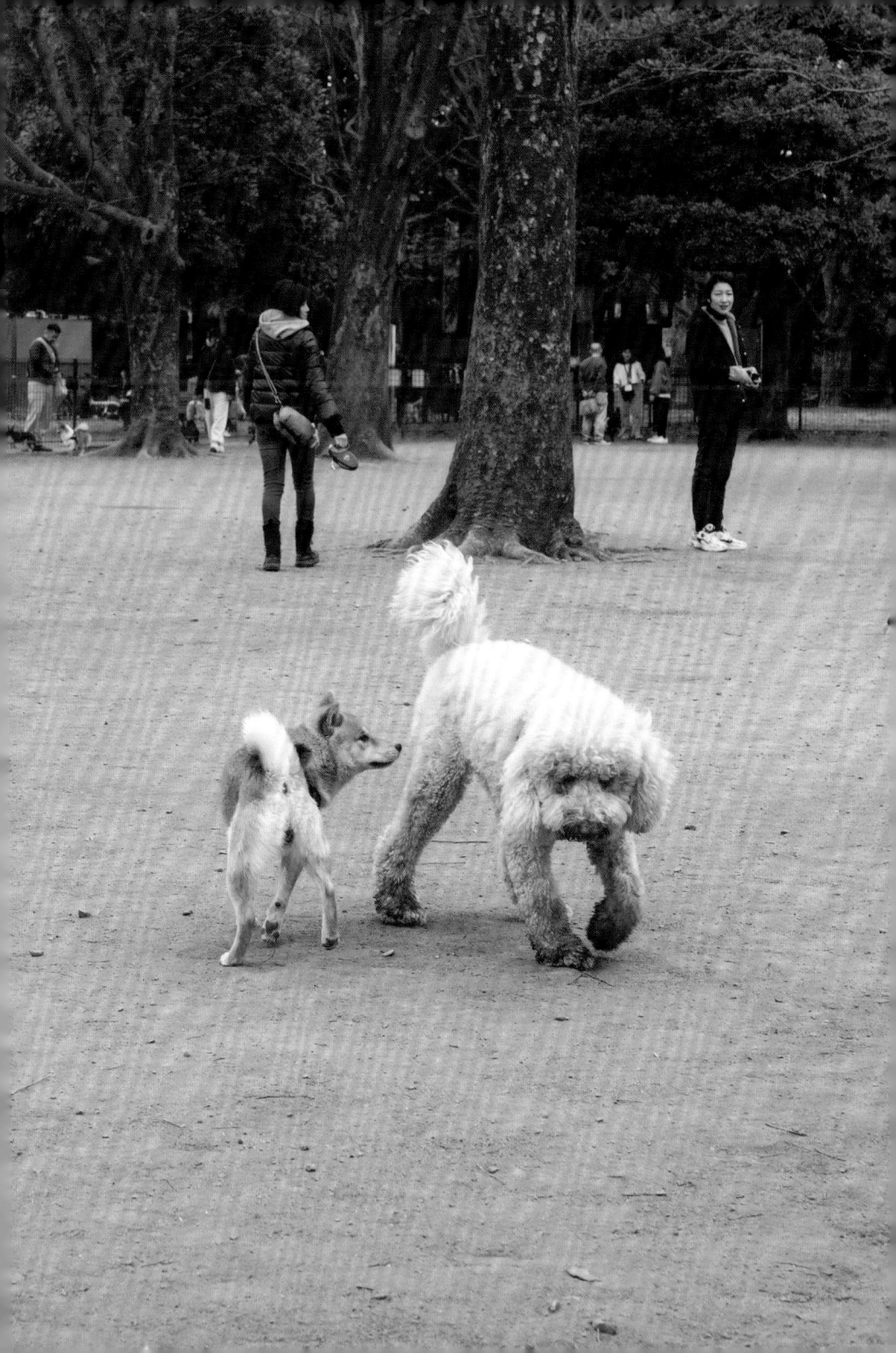

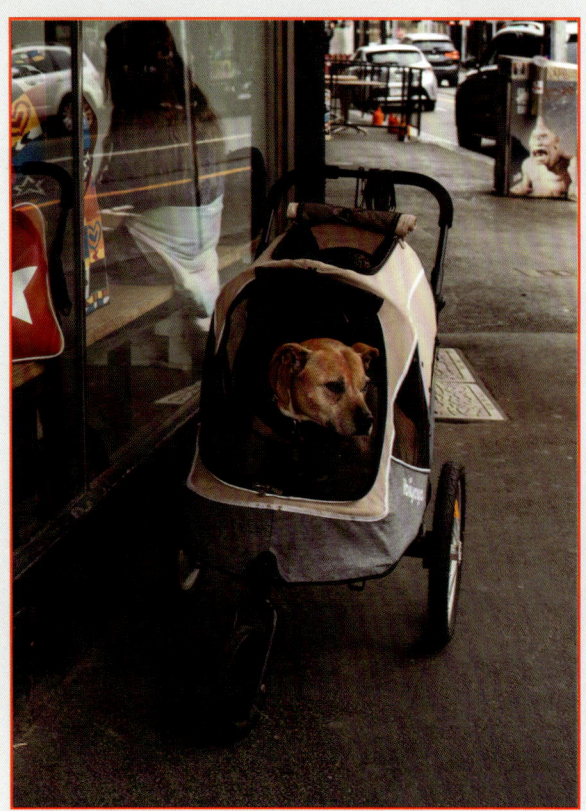

Melbourne, Australia

"They love to go for walks with us in the carriage. I think."

Melissa and Pepina and their dogs Melodie and Akile
Milan, Italy

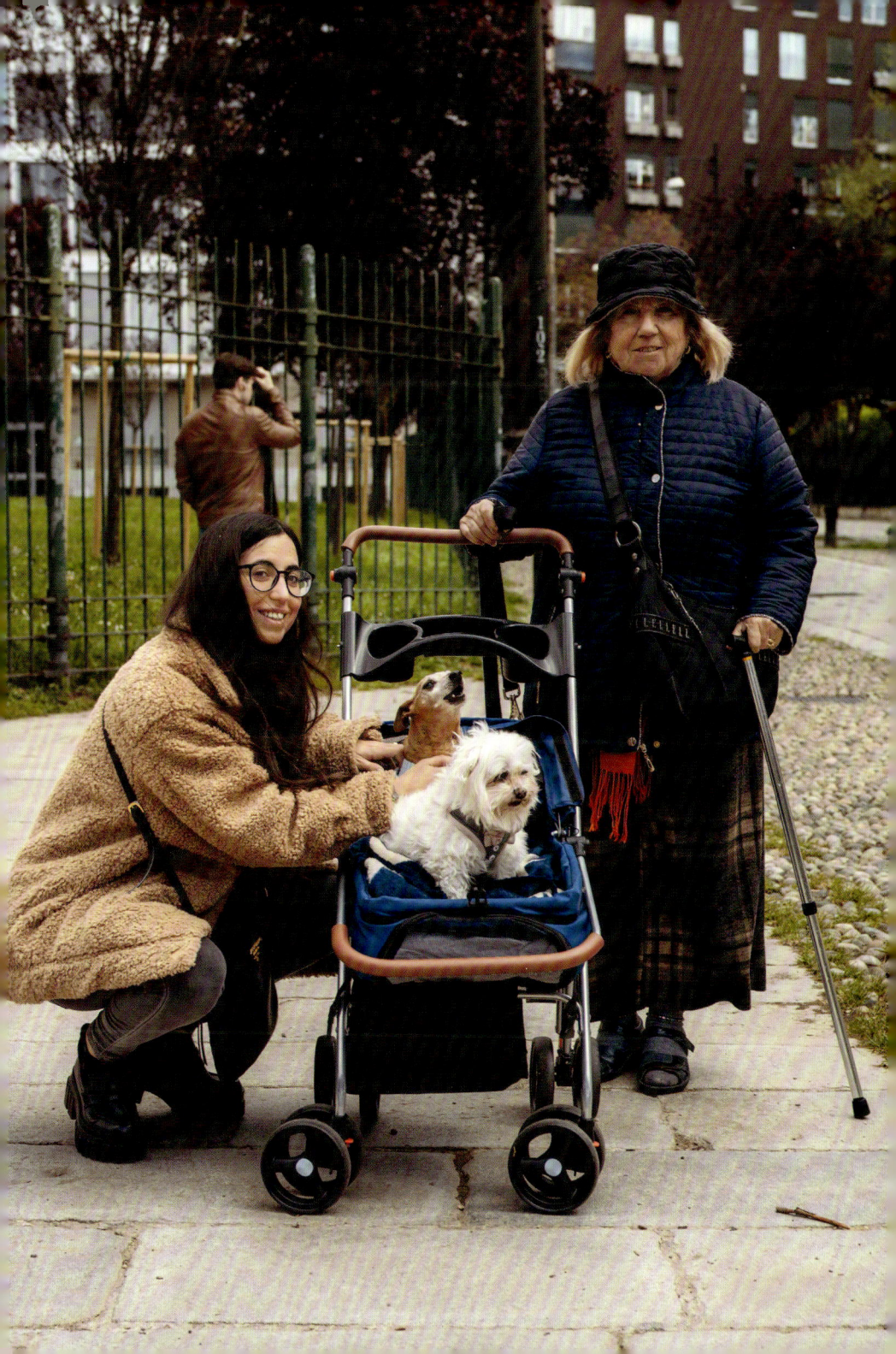

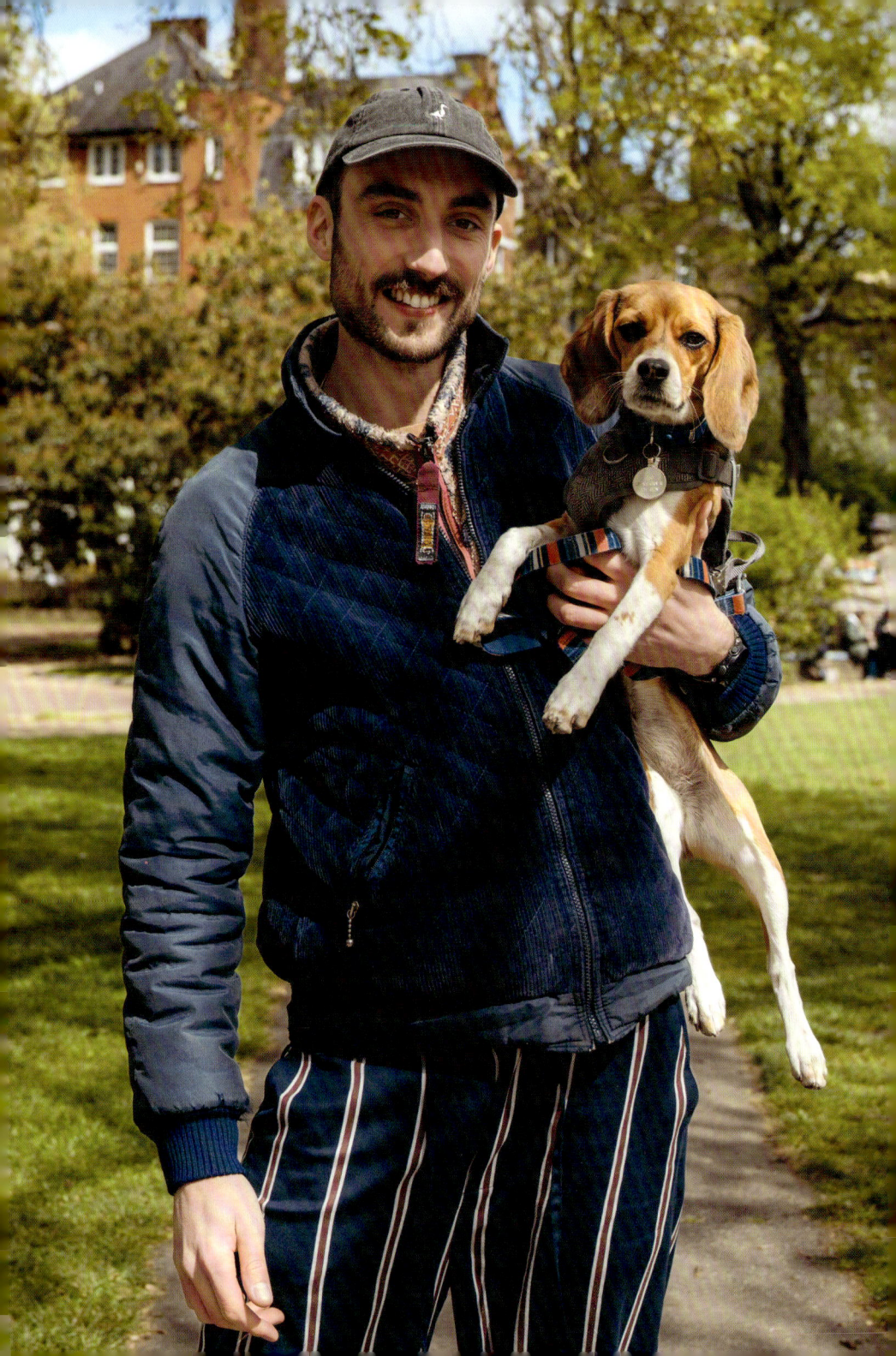

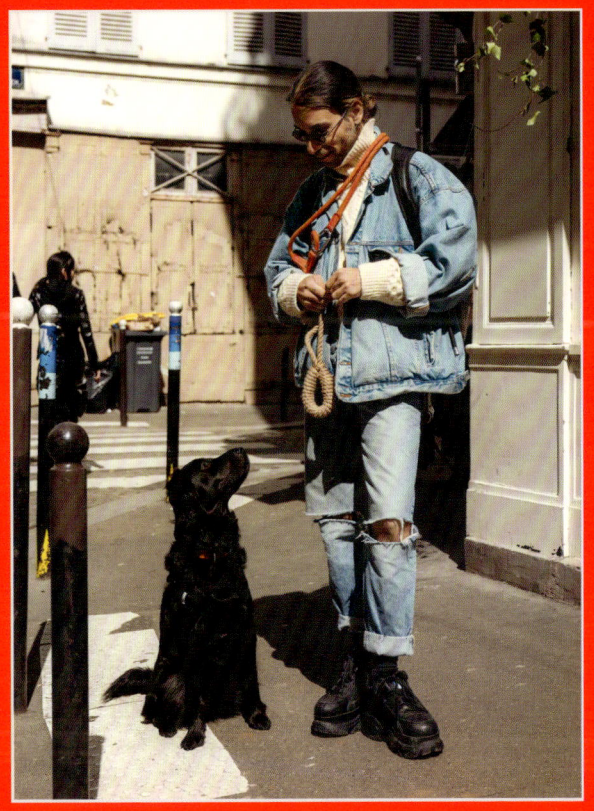

Paris, France

"She always asks why."

Stephen and their dog Nina
London, England

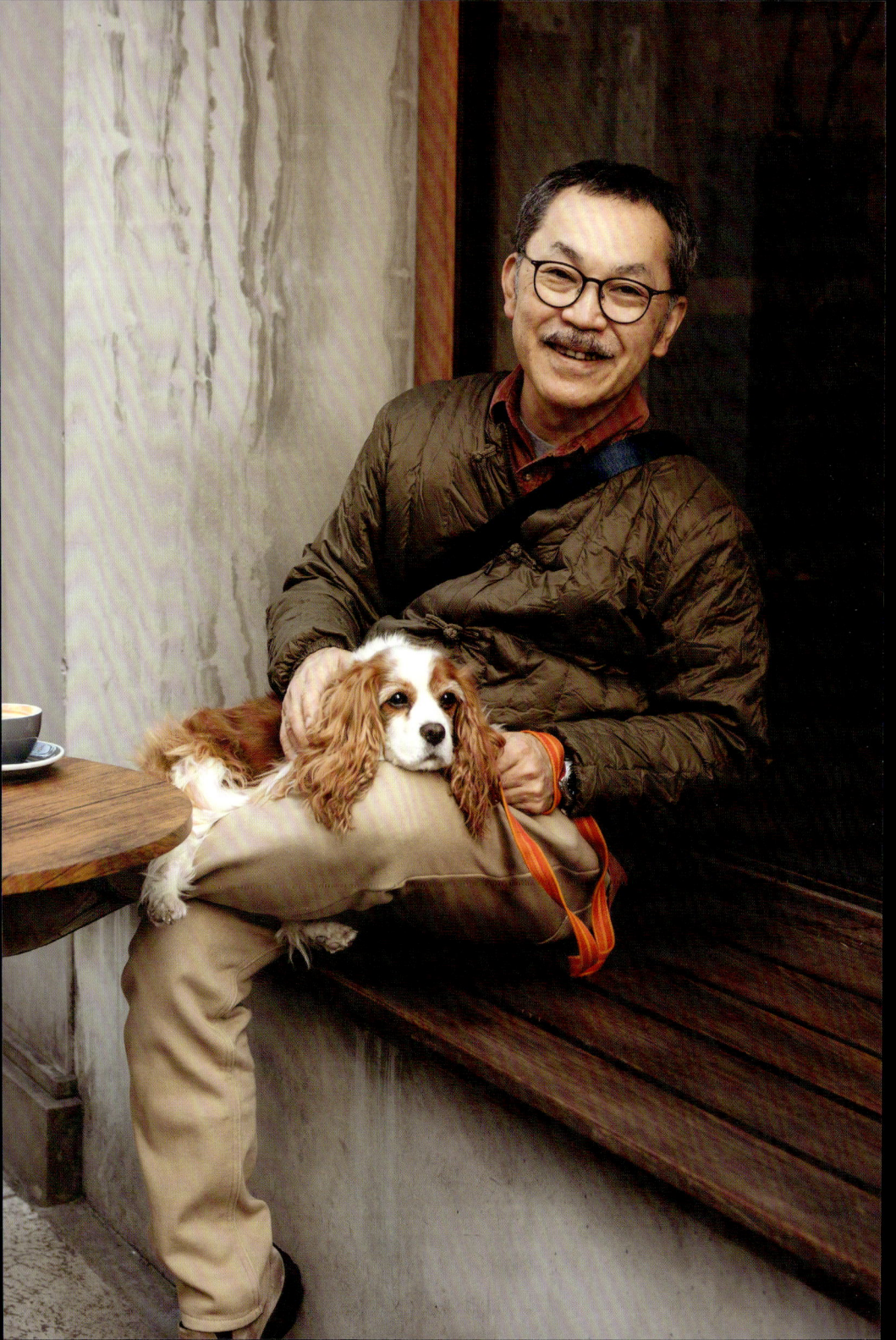

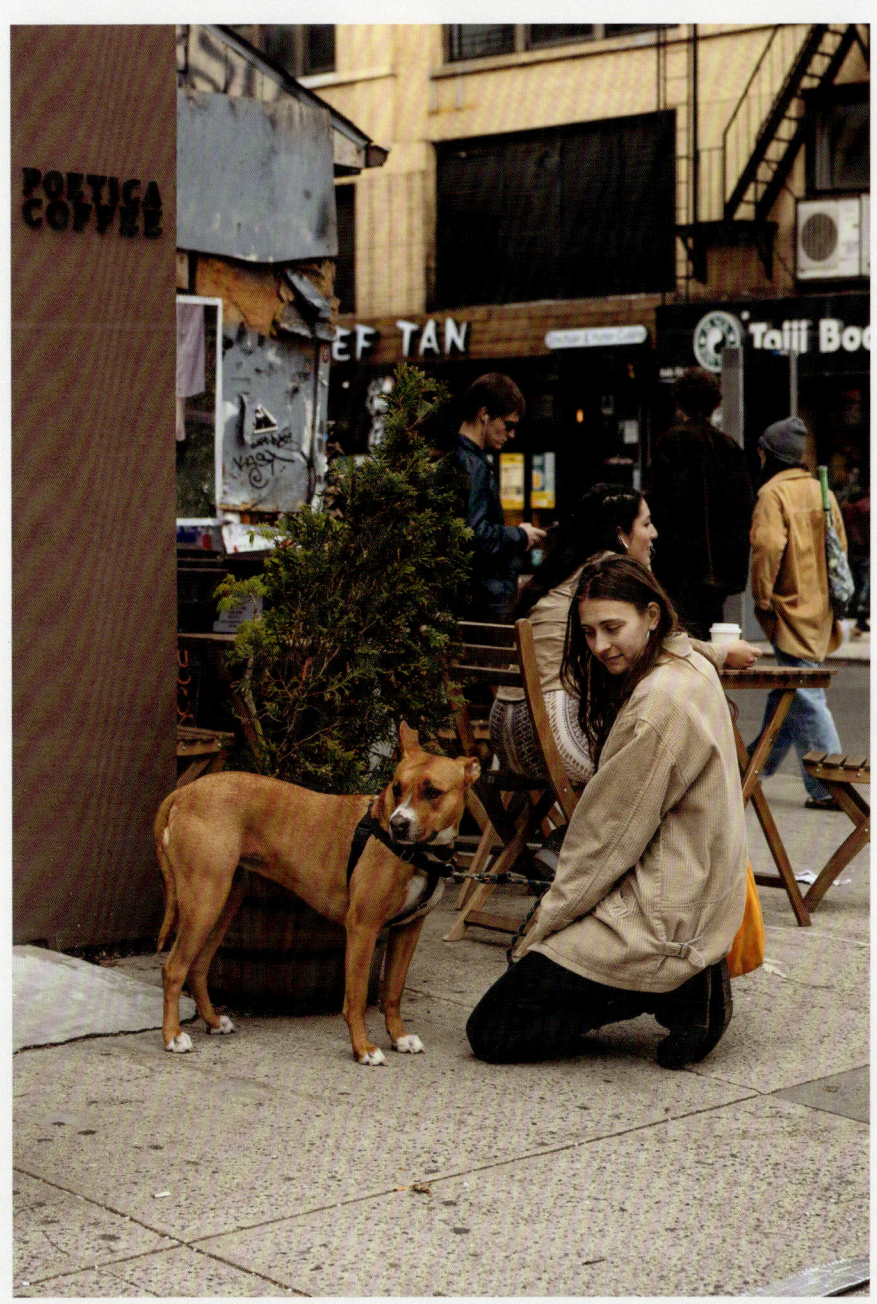

Tokyo, Japan | New York City, USA

"He lives in a fantasy land, where nothing bad ever happens, everyone loves him, the food never ends and everyone is a place to nap on. I'm pretty lucky to live in his world, even if my main role is to be his couch."

Josh and their dog Sebastian
Sydney, Australia

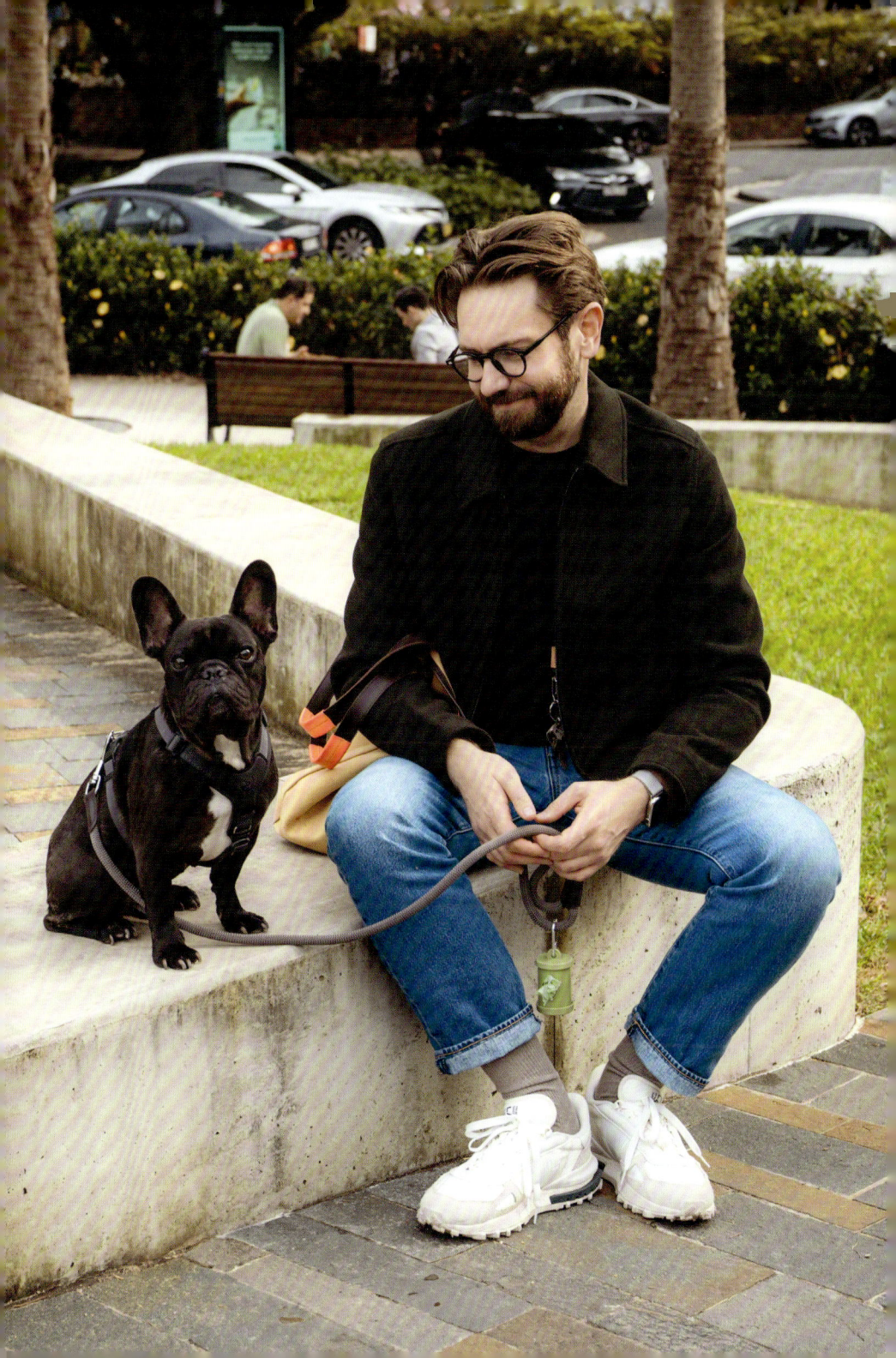

Acknowledgements

To all the wonderful people and dogs who shared a little bit
of their heart with me in this book, I am forever grateful. I had
a smile on my face during the whole process of putting this
project together.

Thank you to Paul and Smith Street Books
for inspiring this book.

And to Josh, thank you for loving our dogs so hard and so pure.
Your portrayal of love is the most beautiful I've ever seen, and it
is forever captured in my heart.

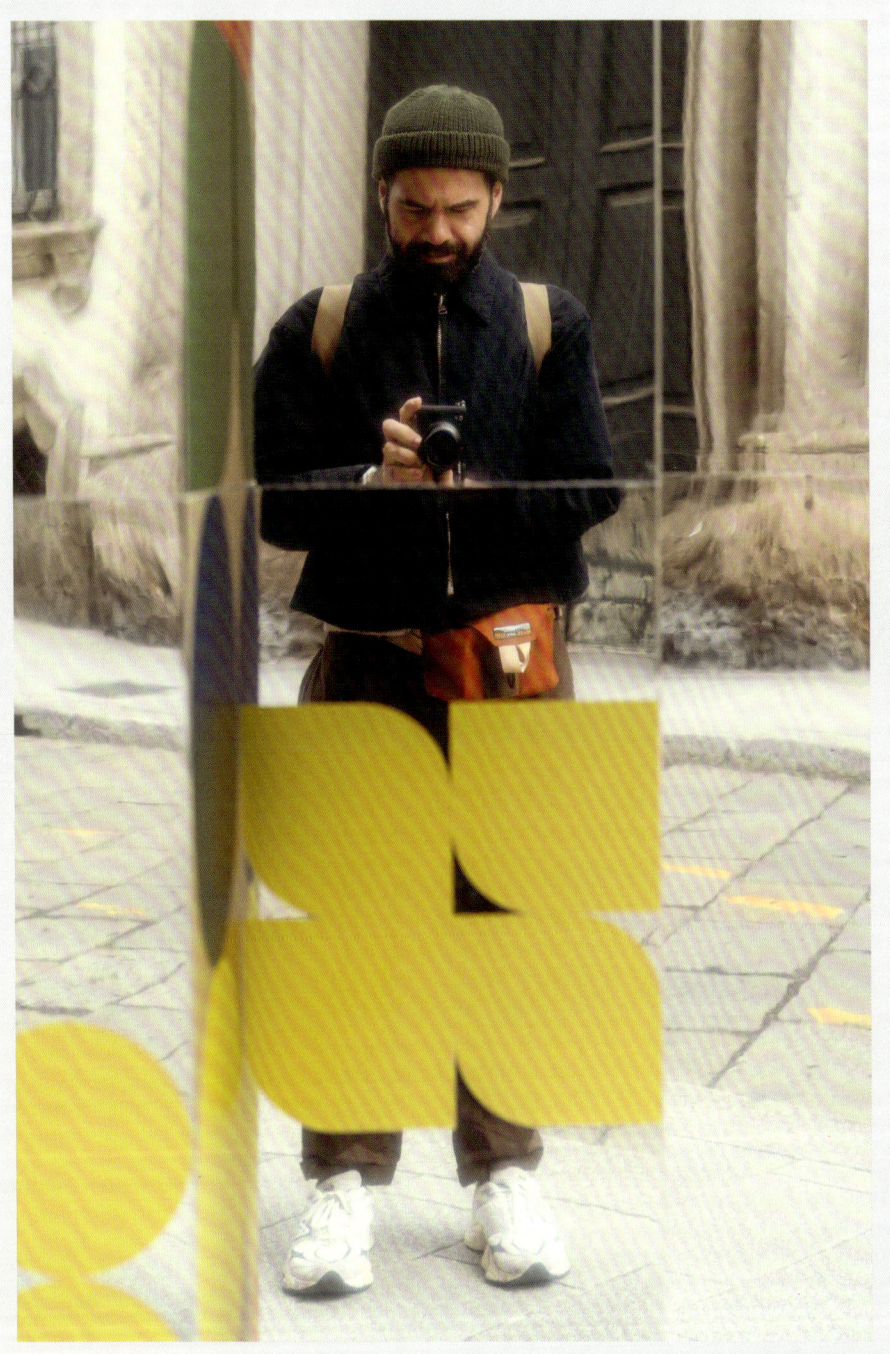

The Author

Giuseppe Santamaria is a photographer and designer originally from Toronto, Canada. He currently resides in Sydney, Australia, with his partner, Josh, and their best friend, Sebastian.

He is the author of :
Men In This Town (2014)
Women In This Town (2015)
Alone In A Crowd (2017)
A Decade of Men's Street Style (2021)
New York Style (2023)

Follow his work at giuseppesantamaria.studio
and his life in photos on Instagram @giuseppeinthistown

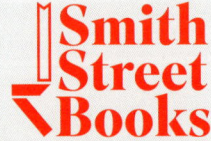

Smith Street Books

Published in 2025 by Smith Street Books
Naarm (Melbourne) | Australia
smithstreetbooks.com

Distributed outside of ANZ, North & Latin America by
Thames & Hudson Ltd., 6–24 Britannia Street, London, WC1X 9JD
thamesandhudson.com

EU Authorised Representative: Interart S.A.R.L.
19 rue Charles Auray, 93500 Pantin, Paris, France
productsafety@thameshudson.co.uk; www.interart.fr

ISBN: 978-1-9232-3917-3

Smith Street Books respectfully acknowledges the Wurundjeri People of the Kulin Nation, who are the
Traditional Owners of the land on which we work, and we pay our respects to their Elders past and present.

Publisher: Paul McNally
Art Director and Photographer: Giuseppe Santamaria

Printed & bound in China by C&C Offset Printing Co., Ltd.

Book 396
10 9 8 7 6 5 4 3 2 1